THE MYTH OF THE FREE MARKET

The Role of the State in a Capitalist Economy

Mark A. Martinez

Kumarian Press
An Imprint of Stylus Publishing

The Myth of the Free Market
Published in 2009 in the United States of America by Kumarian Press
22883 Quicksilver Drive, Sterling, VA 20166-2012 USA

The text of this book is set in 10/12.5 Sabon

Proofread by Publication Services, Inc.
Index by Publication Services, Inc.

Production and design by Publication Services, Inc.
Artwork researched and located by California State University, Bakersfield
Student Assistant, Emily Becera.

Printed in the United States of America by Thomson-Shore, Inc.
Text printed with vegetable oil-based ink.

∞ The paper used in this publication meets the minimum requirements of
the American National Standard for Information Sciences-Permanence of
Paper for printed Library Materials, ANSI Z39.48-1984

Library of Congress Cataloging-in-Publication Data

Martinez, Mark, 1961-
  The myth of the free market : the role of the state in a capitalist
economy / Mark Martinez.
      p. cm.
  Includes bibliographical references and index.
    ISBN 978-1-56549-267-7 (pbk. : alk. paper) — ISBN 978-1-56549-284-4
(cloth : alk. paper)
  1. Capitalism—Government policy.   2. Free enterprise.   I. Title.
  HB501.M33525 2009
  330.12'2—dc22
                                                              2008053510

CONTENTS

ACKNOWLEDGMENTS

I have accumulated many personal debts while writing this book. The sabbatical I secured from California State University (CSU), Bakersfield, during fall 2005 was invaluable. Although the sabbatical wasn't anywhere long enough (they never are), it allowed me to do the core research for this book and put together the basic chapter outlines by spring 2006.

My department colleagues were especially helpful. Ray Geigle took a first look at my opening chapters. His comments and encouragement were spot-on and incorporated into subsequent drafts. Gene Clark took a look at many chapters and, as is his habit, asked the most probing questions, which forced me to reevaluate some of my thoughts. Michael Ault took a look at several chapters and provided support as well.

There were other colleagues at CSU, Bakersfield, whose input I sought out during this project. David Berri, whose numerous books and articles provided a source of "competitive" inspiration, offered early comments on the first two chapters. Donovan Ropp provided encouragement and insight that counted for more than he realizes. Ken Shakoori's discussion and commentary were most helpful, especially for the final chapters where the details of collateralized debt obligations and mark-to-market valuations, among others, made my head spin.

My brother, Albert Martinez, drew on his experience as an investment banker in Silicon Valley to comment on the content of several chapters, providing insight that I would not have gotten anywhere else. My friend from Bakersfield College, Jack Brigham, offered commentary, encouragement, and kind words over breakfast (which he always treated me to). Thanks, Jack. I also want to thank Peter Loedel, my friend, former coauthor, and graduate school colleague from University of California, Santa Barbara for taking the time to look at this—even after I took my time getting him the first draft. West Chester University in Pennsylvania has a genuine gentleman and scholar in Peter Loedel.

Because one of my goals was to make this book accessible to nonexperts, I also sought the opinion of local attorney Milt Younger, a vigorous supporter of CSU, Bakersfield, and one of the best lawyers in the San Joaquin Valley. As the first nonacademic to read through the first few chapters, Mr. Younger's comments were helpful and encouraging. Thank you, Milt. In this spirit, I want to acknowledge the anonymous reviewers whose comments told me I was on the right track while, at the same time, offering criticism that proved crucial to making this work much stronger.

Over the course of the project, I tried out concepts and stories in many of my classes. I want to thank my students, especially in my International Commerce class, for pressing me with questions. To the students who had to wait two weeks to get their midterms back as I put the finishing touches on this project, I am grateful for your patience. The only other times I had done this were when my children were born. I'm sure you understand.

I also want to acknowledge the efforts of Tina Giblin, our outstanding office manager. When I was finishing this project Ms. Giblin made it possible for me to be away from the office more than a department chair should. Ms. Giblin truly deserves an award (and a raise) for her efforts, which she does every day selflessly.

My on-air radio colleagues in Bakersfield, Duane Moore and Candi Easter, deserve recognition as well. What started out as an effort to provide some balance in a market dominated by Conservative talk radio blossomed into solid friendships. I'm especially grateful to Duane Moore for bringing the International Brotherhood of Electrical Workers (IBEW) Local 428 to our radio program as sponsors (with a hat tip to Danny Kane). On many levels this book represents what the IBEW and other labor organizations stand for, and what the "laws of justice" (Chapters 1 and 2) are all about. By helping to keep us on air, the IBEW helped me sharpen many of the ideas that have made their way into this book. I also want to thank Lori Moore, whose style ensured that the staff and food at *Mimi's Restaurant* were always first rate. Thanks Lori. At the end of the day, the conversations Duane, Candi, and I have had on-air—and over a few beers—have done much to shape and make more accessible what I present in this work.

I especially want to express my deep and heartfelt gratitude to my parents. Whether it was my Dad and Connie taking Monica and Sebastian to Pismo Beach for the day, or my Mom taking care of them during my evening classes, their efforts made my life less hectic. I also want to thank Jim Lance at Kumarian Press, whose understanding, advice, and words of encouragement during this project went beyond the call of duty and helped keep this work on track.

Finally, I want to thank my kids, Monica and Sebastian. They are truly two of the best kids any parent could hope for, and they are my inspiration for finishing this book. I have always told them to work hard, be responsible, and finish what they start. For this reason their incessant and exasperating "Aren't you done yet?" commentary drove me (nuts) more than they will ever know.

In all cases, the usual caveats and qualifications regarding the contents of this book apply. I alone am responsible for any misrepresentations, errors, and omissions that may appear in this work.

Throughout the book I use the designation "Blog Commentary" to refer to my Web site, http://freemarketmyth.blogspot.com, where you'll find a collection of commentary, supplemental materials, a full bibliography, and more. I hope we can continue the discussion.

Mark A. Martinez
Bakersfield, California
October 30, 2008

ILLUSTRATIONS

Figures

Tables

Boxes

INTRODUCTION:
UNDERSTANDING MARKETS AND STATES

I can remember the first time I began to understand how the market works. Like most kids my age in the 1960s, I collected comic books and bubble gum cards. At first, our Dad would surprise us with trips to the local Stop & Go store, where he would purchase either comic books or allow us to pick up a pack of baseball or football cards. We couldn't get both comic books and cards on the same day, so we had to make choices, and we learned how to trade for what we wanted. I would trade certain "goods" with my brothers, and I would trade others with my friends and neighbors.

What I learned is that trading for the things I wanted—or felt that I needed—was a good way to satisfy me and even to make me happy. Most market economies operate on the same principle. If you trade for the things that you want, both parties tend to feel good about how things work out. But barter soon proved to be difficult because of the times when no one wanted to trade me for my *Green Lantern* comic book or my efforts to unload the baseball card of some obscure second baseman from the Kansas City Royals brought me nothing but blank stares, no matter how many I offered (why did I always end up with five of these guys?).

Whether it was because we lived thirty minutes from the Oakland Coliseum at the time or because the Kansas City second baseman never developed a bonafide career, the fact was that the second baseman as a form of "currency" was largely worthless. And the idea of giving up parts of what I believed would eventually be a full Oakland A's roster was out of the question. I was never able to get the Reggie Jackson card that I "needed" or the Superman comic that I craved.

To solve this dilemma it was necessary to introduce another "commodity" into the equation: money. Because money was scarce, for me at least, my capacity to purchase what I wanted was limited. So when my parents introduced the allowance system—in exchange for doing chores—things began to look up. Money made things easier because I didn't have to break up my unfinished Oakland A's team collection and did not have to lug my comic book and card collection around openly, which was dangerous—given that some bully always wanted to "borrow" my stuff when I brought my goods to school.

What I learned in the process is how a basic market economy works. If you want something, you need to have something that others want. This facilitates trade. Or you can work and earn money to purchase the goods that you want. It's simple enough. What I also found is that if others want the same thing that you want (like the Reggie Jackson card) and there is not enough of it to go around, the price of that good goes up. Indeed, certain cards were so valuable that friends wouldn't even bring some of their cards out for others to see.

I also learned about the role that money plays in our society. I found that money was always more fluid because it was tradable for both comic books and baseball cards. Everyone recognized its value, which meant that it was a nice medium of exchange. I didn't have to worry whether or not traders were baseball or football fans or concern myself with finding the comic books that they liked. Money's value was universally understood and helped solve a problem that economists call a *coincidence of wants:* if someone doesn't want your goods, there is no trade, period. In this manner, introducing money into my trading world, or into any size economy, enhances trade and economic activity by allowing transactions to be based on established prices and value rather than on fleeting tastes and needs.

But understanding the logic behind how markets work doesn't simply stop at understanding barter, negotiating, and the impact caused by introducing money into an economy. Our little trading economy developed because everyone had similar values (we liked sports), lived in a relatively peaceful setting (suburban America in the 1960s), and understood that playing by the rules (don't cheat or steal) was necessary if you were going to trade in the future. And none of this just happened. Market values, stability, and respect for a broad set of social and legal principles had been created by carefully planned forces and even a dash of serendipity. In simpler terms, any understanding of competitive trade and *market capitalism* is incomplete without understanding the organizing—and very political— forces that foster the conditions for market capitalism to prosper.

The challenge of modern societies is to help their citizens understand that competitive trade and the allocation of resources don't "just happen." They happen because we've made a very conscientious effort to educate citizens, protect what we have, and facilitate the conditions that enhance trade. Production and trade at the level that we see in the modern world occur because very deliberate steps have been taken to make sure that people are protected and free to pursue life objectives. The more protection and freedom that we've developed over time, the more production and trading we've been able to accomplish. And this is important for the human condition, because, as we will see in the following chapters, by learning to cooperate and protect each other, we have also learned to cooperate in other areas.

Today states and individuals understand that the more goods and resources that you have, the more powerful, attractive, and influential you become (or appear to be). The end result is that we either work more for a promised payoff, or we try to manipulate others in a manner that secures more resources for us. Even though "just do it" sounds cool and "invisible hands" is conceptually attractive, the reality in the modern world is that the conditions under which trade occurs must be cultivated, created, and carefully administered. When governments get this right, a society's ability to produce goes beyond simply turning out goods and services that can be bartered and moves toward the production of goods and services that can be bought and sold—and toward the creation of capital that can be reinvested. And this is extremely important because "capital injects life into assets."[1] But I'm getting ahead of myself.

John Jacob Astor Sees Beyond Simple Trade

Many of America's greatest creators of wealth understood the distinction between simple production and wealth creation. Kevin Phillips tells us how John Jacob Astor, who made a fortune in the American Fur Company (which he started in 1808), became the richest man in America. In spite of Astor's successes in furs on the frontier, he realized that changing demographics in a growing Manhattan meant tremendous rewards if he invested his money in real estate. A flurry of activity around farms, houses, and lots up and down the island pushed Astor to deemphasize fur and foreign shipping. When Astor passed away in 1848 he left a then-stunning $20 million estate. James Gordon Bennett, publisher of the *New York Herald*, argued that half of Astor's wealth belonged to the people of New York because Astor's fortunes "had been augmented and increased in value by the aggregate intelligence, enterprise and commerce" of the city.[2]

I tell Astor's story not to discuss appropriate tax levels but rather to illustrate that society creates the conditions under which wealth is created. Profitable trade doesn't just happen, especially if producers and traders have to grapple with the threat of invasion or expropriation. In other words, Astor could have stayed on the frontier trading in furs, but he would not have become the capitalist icon that he is today. Similarly, workers and production slow if they are burdened by an overbearing tax system. Total war and unwarranted property confiscations are also tremendous disincentives to production and trade. It is the job of government—not "invisible hands"—to make sure that the right environment is created so that production and trade occur.

The story of John Jacob Astor provides us with measures to understand several other aspects of market capitalism. For example, a house on an island with one person has a simple *use value*. No one gets greedy or self-ish unless there is a reason to horde or guard personal goods. A house on an island such as Manhattan, where others are looking for shelter and other types of exchange, develops a *market value*. Just as goods can develop a market value when exchange occurs, specific services or professions come to life and expand as society grows and becomes more complex. Adam Smith wrote,

> When the market is very small, no person can have any encouragement to dedicate himself entirely to one employment . . . There are some sorts of industry, even the lowest kind, which can be carried on nowhere but in a great town. A porter, for example, can find employment and subsistence in no other place . . . In the lone houses and very small villages which are scattered about in so desert a country as the Highlands of Scotland, every farmer must be a butcher, baker and brewer for his own family.[3]

The glue that brings and holds society together—and allows goods and services offered in the market to grow in value—is the state. Astor could have stayed in the woods and traded furs, as many did at the time. But he saw an environment that had been made ripe by a nation that helped capital come to life by guarding private property (land), glorifying entrepreneurialism (labor), and encouraging private investment (capital). Whether or not Astor owed the people of New York for half of his estate when he passed away is another matter. But there is no doubt that New York City had created the conditions that made his accumulation of wealth possible.

Conclusion: De Soto's Mystery of Capital

Bringing capital to life is important because it's what makes capitalism possible.[4] As Hernan De Soto put it, we can think of capital as similar to water in a lake. Still water has no force and reflects a resource with "dormant value." Bringing the energy potential of water to life requires looking beyond water as an asset and actively thinking about the energy that can be created by turning it into rushing water—that can be used to spin turbines and create energy. The mystery for governments is how to turn the "dead capital" of simple assets, such as a house, into productive capital. The key isn't simply to confirm the existence of assets, but rather to create a legal system that confers ownership and allows people to transfer, borrow against, and lease assets (without overextending themselves). By registering and protecting individual property rights, people are able to borrow against capital that would be dead if it were not for state activities that legally fix the economic potential of an asset.[5]

What we need to understand is that bringing capital to life is not a Frankenstein-like building process. Modern capitalist markets do not come to life simply because different parts of society are brought together and injected with money. This may just bring inflation. Rather, complex trade and investment patterns occur because capital—which is the lifeblood of capitalism—is made viable by government actions that fix and guard assets. The activities of states must go beyond national defense and building infrastructures. Even a noncapitalist state such as the former Soviet Union could do these things. Injecting capital with life also includes guarding individual liberties and creating markets that support legal infrastructures so that creativity and investments pay off. It also means making sure that others in society don't have undue advantages or wield disproportionate power in markets. This prepares the conditions for market capitalism to exist and for entrepreneurs to prosper. Getting legal rights *right* is an arduous process. There are no invisible hands here.

Forming a system of property rights that creates live capital is not simply a function of passing a few laws. People must also go beyond feeling secure in their persons. They must also be agreeable to social mores and willing to buy into other rules of the game that support the process. This occurs only when people believe that they have a stake in the system and that hard work will create a payoff at the end of the day. "Work hard and get ahead" is not simply a pithy maxim. It is also the moral justification of capitalism. If hard work brings no advances to those who contribute to the production of wealth, what's the point of capitalism?

History shows that working hard and getting ahead may be an aberration in the human experience. What created the "aberration" we call the capitalist experience was the rise of a vibrant state geared toward promoting both personal liberty and individual wealth. By looking at the factors surrounding the evolution of liberty and modern markets in America, this book examines the vital role of the state in a capitalist economy. More importantly, it illustrates that the notion that markets operate best when left to their own devices is both misleading and, quite frankly, a myth.

Notes

1. Hernan de Soto writes, "The major stumbling block that keeps the rest of the world from benefiting from capitalism is its inability to produce capital. Capital is the force that raises the productivity of labor and creates the wealth of nations. It is the lifeblood of the capitalist system": Hernan de Soto, *The Mystery of Capital: Why Capitalism Triumphs in the West and Fails Everywhere Else* (New York: Basic Books, 2000).

2. Kevin Phillips, *Wealth and Democracy: A Political History of the American Rich* (New York: Random House, 2002), 26.

3. Adam Smith, *An Inquiry into the Nature and Causes of the Wealth of Nations,* The Harvard Classics, Vol. 10, Charles Bullock, ed. (New York: PF Collier & Son Company, 1909), 24.

4. Robert Gilpin argues that the defining characteristics of capitalism are the private ownership of the means of production, the existence of free or wage labor, the existence of the profit motive, and the drive to amass capital. (This is the definition of capitalism used throughout this work.): Robert Gilpin, *The Political Economy of International Relations* (Princeton, NJ: Princeton University Press, 1987), 15.

5. De Soto, *The Mystery of Capital,* 45–47.

PART I

THINGS TO (RE)CONSIDER

CHAPTER 1

MILTON FRIEDMAN GOT IT WRONG: POLITICS IS AT THE HEART OF CAPITALISM

An ardent opponent of the estate tax, Montana rancher Lynn Cornwell went to Washington DC in 2000 to deliver the estate tax repeal bill to the White House, on a tractor no less. He wanted to dramatize the idea that small farmers would lose the family farm if the estate tax were not repealed. This was one of the key talking points pushed by the American Farm Bureau Federation and key members in Congress. With many members of the press present, it was a good show. How dare Congress force widows and grieving families to face both the Tax Man and the Grim Reaper at such a traumatic time? Theatrics aside, there were several problems with their arguments. First, when pressed, the American Farm Bureau Federation could not produce one example of a farm lost as a result of the estate tax.[1] This proved only mildly embarrassing, because the press never dug beyond the "Grim Reaper-Tax Man" storyline.

Another problem was with the large number of "Lynn Cornwells" in the movement. Ranchers and farmers who balked at the prospect of having to pay the estate tax, arguing that the grim hand of the state undermined the logic of the market, were not above receiving state handouts. In their book Wealth and Our Commonwealth: Why America Should Tax Accumulated Fortunes, *authors William H. Gates Sr. and Chuck Collins explain that, although Lynn Cornwell complained that the estate tax took "away all incentive to growing your business," Cornwell's ranch had received $415,015 in direct cash farm subsidies from the federal government between 1996 and 2001. Making Cornwell's anti-state show more bizarre is how the grim hand of the state consistently helped ensure that "the Cornwell Ranch was in the top 10 percent of subsidy recipients in Montana, the elite group that received 55 percent of Montana's $1.82 billion in farm subsidies between 1996 and 2000."[2]*

Many individuals from the private sector often complain about the state. But—as the Cornwell case illustrates—they also have a long history of asking for state favors. This raises many questions about markets. Specifically, we need to ask this question: Can market economies ever be free from government intervention, especially when the private sector is always looking for an edge? This begs the follow-up question: Is Adam Smith's self-regulating market economy little more than an aspiration, an ideal type?[3] This line of inquiry is fair, especially because a slew of subsidies, favorable legislation, and state initiatives have had a hand in creating an environment for both market success and extraordinary wealth creation. We need to keep in mind as well that greed does not simply cease as a human function just because a rancher, a farmer, or a financial analyst begins talking with a legislator. Smart market players know—and history shows—that, although hard work may be a virtue, hard work with government support can make you rich.[4]

This reality flies in the face of what we're told by politicians and representatives of market-oriented institutes who question the role of government in the economy. Getting their cue from economists—who seem to understand that the state has a role in making markets function—think tanks, pundits, politicians, and their followers downplay or ignore the *dominant role* of the state in making markets work. Like readers of the Good Book who selectively quote and cite biblical passages, they pick and choose arguments from capitalism's patron saint, Adam Smith, to make their point. But unlike economists, who argue about the degree or areas in which the state must participate, political players latch onto empty, pithy maxims such as "no new taxes," "the state is the problem," or "government is inefficient." These maxims are attractive because they're quaint and they convey conviction. They are powerful because they suggest analysis and prescription. And the aura of legitimacy that they create comes from the field of economics, a discipline that has produced Nobel laureates and is considered to be the most rigorous of the social sciences. This combination helps marginalize debate about the state's role in markets in the public square.

However, the long track record of industry bailouts, the high number of protected and subsidized groups in our economy, and the amount of industry-specific protective legislation (among other examples) tell us that "prudence" and "self-command" often take a back seat to recklessness and self-interest. Put another way, the self-interest and greed that Adam Smith embraced in the market does not magically check itself at the gates of the state. Rather, the "laws of justice" (the shifting of resources from one party to another) that Smith spoke about are broken so consistently that we cannot simply shrug and chalk it up to market aberrations.

Rather, we need to acknowledge that market players—as the Lynn Cornwell case illustrates—often view the state as another vehicle to pursue their ends. To deny that this occurs as a matter of routine is to deny reality. In addressing these and other issues, I do the following in this chapter.

First, I review the political undercurrents that helped make Milton Friedman's arguments so forceful. This allows me to question some of the basic points that Milton Friedman made about the role of the state in the market place. I then provide a brief thematic overview of issues that are presented in Chapters 2 through 6. Specifically, I discuss the inputs that are necessary for making modern markets work. I argue that the key input is a vigilant state with strong institutions that help ensure that markets work but do not degenerate into commercial vice and excess. To make my point, I argue that, because we can not eliminate human emotion, the market place requires many of the same precautions and checks that we see in the political world. To do this, I review the arguments that James Madison, Alexander Hamilton, and John Jay made in *The Federalist Papers*. Their observations are just as appropriate in a market setting. This allows me to show that, for Adam Smith's "invisible hand" to work, the guiding hand of the state must get markets right, which Adam Smith understood very well.

Atlas Shrugged and So Did Milton Friedman

In Ayn Rand's classic *Atlas Shrugged,*[5] she writes about a small segment of the workforce who decided suddenly to stop working. Because the fruits of their labor are legally confiscated and shifted to the unproductive "looters" and "moochers" of society, the workers—or "individuals of the mind"—protest by going on strike. They stop producing ideas, leadership, inventions, and new research. Unappreciated and underpaid, the *mind workers* simply disappear. The idea is to teach a free-grabbing society that the dignity and profits achieved through hard work need to be recognized and protected. The striking workers also want to illustrate that their talents and effort are the shoulders that hold the weight of their world. When society begins to falter and arrives at the point of collapse, the moral of the story becomes clear: as happened with Atlas, the Greek figure who held the world on his shoulders, the world described in Rand's book begins to crumble when workers decide to shirk their responsibilities. By dropping the weight of the world from their shoulders, the mind workers make a point: state intervention, in the form of state-authorized takings, can lead to societal collapse.

In 1971 Milton Friedman wrote an introduction to the German language edition of Friedrich Hayek's *The Road to Serfdom*. He embraces the moral of Rand's story. Friedman began by discussing the value of freedom and warned against the rising "collectivist" tide emerging in the West at the time. Friedman cited increased government spending—which grew from 25 percent of GDP in 1950 to almost 45 percent in 1993—as evidence of an emerging socialist threat to Western society.[6] He argued that society was moving toward state-led extremism, reminiscent of what Friedrich Hayek saw in the 1930s and 1940s. More specifically, he believed that the increased "coordination of men's activities through central direction" was preparing the "road to serfdom." He pointed to collectivist-tinged concepts such as "urban crisis" and "poverty in the midst of plenty" as linguistic code for—and evidence of—socialist slogans. His solution to the emerging collectivist order, or creeping socialism, was simple: reduce the role of the state in our lives and re-embrace a "framework within which individuals are free to pursue their own objectives" in the market.[7] To do less—as Rand's *Atlas Shrugged* told us—convinces entrepreneurs and our own "individuals of the mind" to disappear from Western society.

To drive home his point, after he shrugged, Friedman wrote. To underscore the importance of liberty, one of the central themes in Rand's work, Friedman proudly pointed to West Germany as a shining example of how liberty promoted prosperity. Perhaps more significantly—as was the case in Rand's novel—Friedman's writings created a sense that society's financial aristocracy and business elites should be free to do as they choose in society. He then pointed to communist East Germany as an example of collectivism run amok. The German contrast fit well with Friedman's views, which he laid out in *Free to Choose: A Personal Statement* (1990). In this work he again tied a growing state to collectivism and creeping socialism. But this time Friedman brought in the Magna Carta, Thomas Jefferson, and Adam Smith to lend weight to his arguments on the relationship between freedom and prosperity.

The problem, however, is that Friedman attributed, and exaggerated, the idea that government should do little more than act as an "umpire" in society to both Thomas Jefferson and Adam Smith.[8] He then used this forced caricature to argue that the state should do little more than create a societal framework for individuals to pursue their ends in society. Friedman's economics suddenly became very political. But, alas, according to Friedman, an interventionist state "charged with the duty of coercing some to aid others" had already been created.[9] This, in part, drove Friedman to call for rolling back the collectivist state, which became one of the hallmarks of his life's work. Although Friedman may have correctly pointed out that government in the immediate "post-World War II period was smaller and less intrusive than it is today," his commentary is riddled with holes.

He ignored, for example, how quickly opportunities grew for women and people of color in the latter half of the twentieth century as a result of state intervention. He also downplayed how the advent of industrial society and the rise of complex postindustrial societies had placed increasing demands on both state and society. And, for all of Friedman's dire warnings about collectivism and twentieth century serfdom, he also ignored how the post-World War II era—which was wrought with collectivizing states, mind you—experienced the greatest economic growth and innovative spurt in human history.[10] Friedman also ignored how growing incomes during this period (1947 to 1979) were more equitable (Figure 1.1) than growth periods before and after this period (Figure 1.2 and Figure 1.3).

Brushed aside as well was how increased incomes during this period fed and coincided with a more materialistic and detached culture in the United States. One could argue that state activities and the subsequent forces that opened opportunities for groups who had previously been excluded may have contributed to societies becoming increasingly individualistic and selfish rather than communitarian and collectivist.[11] Anyone who has ever gone "bowling alone" rather than as part of an organized team understands what this means. Given these oversights, it is hard to take Friedman's dire claims about the dangers of a growing state seriously. They also raise questions as to whether increased state activity by itself undermines both liberty and economic performance over the long-term.

Figure 1.1 The Great Compression: Income Growth and Distribution, 1947–1979

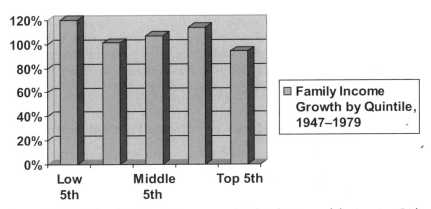

Source: Kevin Phillips, *Wealth and Democracy: A Political History of the American Rich* (New York: Random House, 2002).

Figure 1.2 Real After-Tax Income, 1979–2004

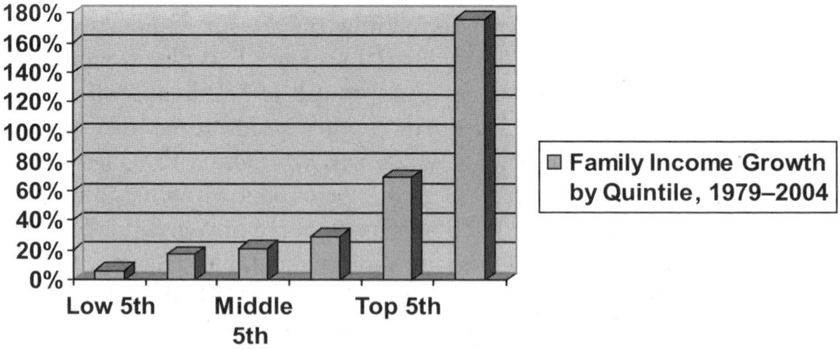

Source: Arloc Sherman and Aviva Aron-Dine, "New CBO Data Show Income Inequality Continues to Widen: After-Tax Income for Top 1 Percent Rose by $146,000 in 2004," Center on Budget and Policy Priorities, January 23, 2007, available online.

These issues and others presented throughout this work suggest that we need to take another look at Milton Friedman's arguments. Specifically, they force us to ask three questions about Friedman's umpire analogy. First, has the state ever been an impartial umpire? This question requires that we look at recent history. Second, we need to ask ourselves whether the state should be just an umpire, as Friedman suggested. This forces us to take another look at capitalism as we understand it. Finally, we need to ask this: can the state ever be just an umpire? This compels us to look at practical world developments, past and present. As I illustrate throughout this work, the answer to all three of these questions is a resounding no. The idea that the state has been, should be, or can be simply an umpire in society is supported neither by history nor by market experience. Milton Friedman's positions are both misplaced and misleading. They fly in the face of the original ideas that spurred the American Revolution[12] and subsequent historical developments, and they betray a larger political game that Friedman was playing.

Free to Choose: Milton Friedman's Political Game

Adam Smith, the intellectual godfather of capitalism, argued that greedy people in competitive environments could become good and even lead moral lives. Smith argued that, freed from abusive feudal authority and stifling traditions, greed in the pursuit of profit could be transformed into a quest to please and serve others. Simply put, customers would not return to a merchant if they were treated rudely or received a shoddy product.

Figure 1.3 Average Income Gains in America, 2002–2006 (adjusted for inflation)

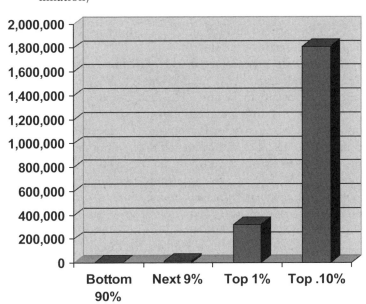

■ **Average Income Gains, 2002–2006 (adjusted for inflation)**

Source: Chye-Ching Huang and Chad Stone, "Average Income in 2006 Up $60,000 for Top 1 Percent of Households, Just $430 for Bottom 90 Percent: Income Concentration at Highest Level Since 1928, New Analysis Shows," Center on Budget and Policy Priorities, July 29, 2008, available online.

Merchants would be forced to produce quality goods and treat people well if they wanted to succeed. Hard work and moral lives would be the end result, and society would be the beneficiary. Freedom and the pursuit of profit would replace feudal customs and traditions that obligated subservience and duty. And, "like an invisible hand," the moral and material needs of society would be met.

One hundred and fifty years after Adam Smith's passing, like other classical and neoclassical economists, Milton Friedman embraced the mechanics behind Smith's observations on liberty and the invisible hand. His writings underscored their sweeping powers to fulfill societal needs. Like Smith, Friedman was not concerned about whether societal cooperation was the intended outcome of the parties involved. What was important was how greed transformed both individual talent and initiative so that people would treat one another with respect and dignity. Individuals free from the scourge of collectivism, argued Friedman, would provide others in society with the goods they need.[13] And, like Smith, he believed that markets would flourish only "so long as cooperation was strictly voluntary," if both parties benefited and if there were no "external force" or "coercion" on the part of the state.[14]

As evidence of the magic of the market, Friedman praised the economic achievements and agricultural productions of the United States in the nineteenth and twentieth century. He then asked what produced this miracle and answered his own question—clearly "not central direction by government."[15] And he's right, but only to a degree. Friedman has presented us with a false dichotomy. His writings imply that either you have markets that are free from government intervention or you have an interventionist state that is tilting toward central planning.[16] This explains, in part, why Friedman was dismayed about modern society and why he painted a picture of a growing state poised to wreak havoc on freedom and liberty. He was quite clear about this in his introduction to Hayek's *The Road to Serfdom,* in which he conflates his discussion on "collectivist orthodoxy" and "the promotion of collectivism" with the evolving practice of "socialism" in Britain and the United States.[17] Conflating state activities with collectivism is necessary for Milton Friedman for three related reasons.

First, conflating state activities—which had promoted equality of opportunity in the United States and Britain—with Soviet-style collectivism makes it easier to begin marginalizing the state. Second, marginalizing the efforts of the state makes it a lot easier to claim that the other arena for social organization, the market, is a virtuous arena of self-interested individuals. That is, of course, only if the state refrains from injecting itself into the market. It's important to note at this point that the discipline that Friedman studies is very helpful to his argument. Economics and its "presumed economic laws and principles" are embraced as being sufficiently scientific. Ergo, other "less rigorous" approaches—suggesting that the state, with all of its unpredictabilities, can make markets function more efficiently—are immediately suspect. They are even comparatively portrayed as highly "speculative philosophical discourse," which is a far cry from the rigorous methods employed in the field of economics.[18] Friedman understood this. So, on a broader level, Friedman is playing a larger political game with the academy. But this shouldn't come as a surprise. Discrediting the opposition is often as important in academia as it is in the political arena. The end result is that Friedman is able to present state activities, such as regulation and support systems, authoritatively, to imply that they are a step toward collectivism—with all its Soviet-planning subtext.

But Friedman is too clever to be trapped in the claim that the state is unimportant to the market. As previously noted, Friedman wraps the Declaration of Independence around free markets and speaks admiringly of Thomas Jefferson's position that the government's role in early American society was simply to act as an umpire.[19] With the connection to political liberty (and justice) established, Friedman proceeds to create an artificial division between the political and the economic. To do this, Friedman anchors his socialist-collectivist claims to his analysis. He uses them to claim that the road to socialism in the United States began because the country took material growth and progress in twentieth century for granted. And, like misguided do-gooders, unaware of what they were doing, policymakers assumed that they could do even better. To ensure greater equality of results, the US government began to restrict freedom arbitrarily—in the process, turning government into a market "deadening" tool.[20]

This is a difficult pill to swallow. Especially given that Friedman seems to ignore the role of technology in altering social relationships, the market excesses on the part of individuals and corporations, and the parallel increased complexities of society.[21] But instead of discussing these societally transforming and disruptive developments, Friedman argues that the collectivists and the socialists are winning the day. And, rather than focus on concrete political strategies on the part of the collectivists, Friedman steers us toward something more amorphous—the bubbly "emotionalism" that surrounds policy issues such as "eradicating poverty," for example. Making matters worse, according to Friedman, is that people like him are fighting an uphill battle, because the argument for individualism is too "subtle and sophisticated" for the general public to understand,[22] as if the choice between liberty and tyranny required nuanced contemplation.

Whether or not Friedman is talking down to the unwashed peasants among us is unimportant. What is important is how his approach has made it easier for his political followers to cast aside state-led initiatives as little more than arbitrary and value-laden decrees, regardless of their results. This has allowed Friedman's political disciples to argue that dependence on political institutions is economically inefficient and costly and that what is needed is a turn toward market-oriented solutions. His discussions on critical issues, ranging from turning military service into an all-volunteer, market-driven institution to the economic pitfalls of government-sponsored social security, have provided the intellectual weight necessary for many to question the role of the state in other areas of society.[23] This, in spite of the fact that Adam Smith offered so many qualifications to the notion of *laissez-faire* (a term that he did not coin) that, as Duncan K. Foley put it, Smith ended up "presenting a reasonably balanced view of the interaction of politics and the economy."[24]

Challenging Milton Friedman's Economic Theology

To promote the false dichotomy that you either embrace freedom or the path to collectivism, Friedman begins by disparaging state efforts to promote equality of opportunity. This is in spite of the fact that both Adam Smith and the writings of the Founding Fathers of the United States made it clear that creating opportunities was at the core of the political and economic systems stamped by the ideas of the Enlightenment. For Friedman, however, the quest for equality of opportunity has been reduced to an attempt "to achieve equality of results,"[25] which allows him to mischaracterize the central role of the state in making markets work for everyone. For my part, Friedman's argument is a bit too casual and dismissive to be taken at face value.

How can we ignore the role that Manifest Destiny and land giveaways played in creating opportunities? How do we downplay the role that land-grant colleges played in helping spread information and technology? How do we marginalize the government-financed extension services that were critical for making informed decisions? He mentions these initiatives but then dispenses with them because they played a "negligible" role.[26] Other state-led schemes that played a "negligible" role in growing opportunities in the United States include canal building, railroad subsidies, relocation of Native American populations, public education, child labor laws, civil rights, and other progressive campaigns designed to protect and create opportunities throughout society. To claim that one or two of these programs had a negligible effect might stand up to scrutiny. But to maintain that the cumulative effect of these and other state-led efforts had a negligible effect on opportunity, competition, and economic growth is a stretch. At this point we see some space between economists, the politicians, and the pundits who follow them.

Most economists acknowledge the crucial role of the state in making markets work.[27] They discuss, in varying degrees, the role of security, stability, education, infrastructure, and other public goods provided by the state. By the middle of the twentieth century, with the Keynesian Synthesis in vogue (see Chapter 9), economists were quite clear about the crucial role that monetary and fiscal policy played in the economy in the postwar period. For the most conservative politicians, conservative pundits, and their followers, the rhetoric began to take a different tone. Led first by US Senator Robert A. Taft (R-Ohio) in the 1940s and early 1950s and spurred by Barry Goldwater's presidential defeat in 1964, conservatives once again embraced the idea that economic freedom is at the heart of political freedom.[28] They—like the characters in Ayn Rand's book—saw the private sector as the dominant and most efficient sector in society. This was in spite of the fact that the Founding Fathers had made it clear that the public and private sectors were coequals among many countervailing ambitious pressure centers that would help keep tyranny and monopoly power at bay.[29]

At the same time, with Milton Friedman (and others, such as Friedrich Hayek) providing the intellectual validation, political conservatives moved beyond simple complaints about New Deal statism. By the 1970s conservative complaints that "the government is the problem" to all of society's ills began to resonate; "getting the state off of my back" and "no new taxes" became political clarion calls for conservatives and anti-state groups alike. We need look no further than the rise of Margaret Thatcher and Ronald Reagan to understand the political potency of these one-sided rhetorical claims. Milton Friedman understood these dynamics well. But the real power of the Friedman-inspired view is how it turned the mix of *economic freedom, laissez-faire* economics, and the *invisible hand* into a Market Trinity that Duncan K. Foley called an "economic theology."[30]

By elevating the economic over the political, the rhetoric helped many lose sight of the fact that modern markets rest upon very political agreements. These political agreements are our modern liberal constitutions, and they are the essence of what John Locke was speaking about when he discussed the social contract. Constitutions, or our social contracts, are like breathing organisms: their strength comes from social tensions that manifest themselves in the form of political movements. These movements end in proposed legislation, new laws, and even constitutional changes that validate our economic arrangements.[31] To dismiss these political dynamics, or to elevate the economic over the political, is to ignore the forces that shape markets in ways that Adam Smith never imagined, especially today.

Democracy Is for People Who Are Not Sure They Are Right

At this point, some professional economists might argue, "I know the state has a role; what we're saying is that the farther it stays away from the market, the better off we all are." For this reason, I want to be clear: I'm not suggesting that the logic behind the invisible hand does not exist. Decentralized decision making in the market place is a good thing. Instead, I am arguing that the logic of the invisible hand is made possible because the state has gone beyond Friedman's "umpiring" model to get the politics right. There are times when the state gets it right, and there are times when it gets it wrong. For example, we know that market players seek and get favorable legislation.[32] We can't assume this away or refer to these developments as market aberrations.

Democracy is what it is—a political system in which people compete over policy, legal power, and political favor. Subsidies and unwarranted protections are the result of very legitimate (however skewed) political processes. That the end result often leads to violations of Adam Smith's "laws of justice" should come as no surprise. Good legislators can be sold a bill of goods by lobbyists; responsible people don't always do the right thing. But in a vibrant democracy, responsible actors and states also admit mistakes and do things over.[33] As E. E. Schattschneider put it, "Democracy is a political system for people who are not sure they are right,"[34] and we have slavery, segregation, and a history of denying women the right to vote as evidence of this. Then there are the subsidies, protections, and market favors. Democracy allows us to try again.

If we follow Friedman's umpire logic, however, we are inclined to dismiss these political dynamics as a violation of *laissez-faire* principles. Or we downplay them as market aberrations that are driven by special interests that alter political processes. For example, taking steps to correct discriminatory policies is often viewed as interventionist or might be characterized by Friedman's disciples as part of the collectivist movement. Or, in the case of the latter, those with the means can either buy their way into the system[35] or invest in think tanks and research institutes that help shift public debate.[36] Both have a way of legitimizing or whitewashing favoritism via congressional stamps of approval (which makes favoritism "legal") or through vigorous media campaigns that distort issues.

If we want the state to get it right, we need to acknowledge that the greed Adam Smith embraced for the market has many faces and many tactics, and does not magically check itself at the gate of the state. We cannot downplay these dynamics simply because they're viewed as aberrations that distort the model or because influential economists believe that they lend themselves to collectivist trends. Yet, many of us do this on a regular basis. This is interesting, because trying to gain market advantage through the state or attempting to improve our lot in life by securing legally sanctioned favors is—as *The Federalist Papers* point out—part of the human condition.

Favorable legislation and state efforts to open up opportunities might also be viewed as aberrations because many economists put too much faith in the automaticity of good behavior. Milton Friedman, for example, wrote that a decentralized market "reduces the area over which political power is exercised."[37] This may be true. Then he claims that decentralized markets occur only if people are "free to choose." And this is probably true as well. But he fails to discuss, as did Adam Smith, how this was supposed to happen—as if we're supposed to believe that freedom alone is sufficient to induce individuals to cooperate. This reasoning ignores why human beings ever left the state of nature. It also ignores the rationale behind Locke's social contract. Finally, it ignores the freedom-granting economic and political disaster that was the Articles of Confederation.[38] This is not to suggest that Friedman is confused—or Pollyannaish—about human behavior. Rather, it suggests that we need to understand better how the state—in conjunction with the market—has been able to transform our emotional faculties into "rational" ones (see Chapter 3).

At the end of the day, the United States has an economic system that embraces Adam Smith's invisible hand and even turns it into a religious science for many.[39] But the same system ignores that our economic arrangements often compromise the "laws of justice" that Adam Smith made clear were crucial for society and markets to function.[40] Because the laws of justice are violated on a regular basis, the state has had to remedy the situation by exercising its authority. This is not interference. It is democracy in action. On a broader level, by guarding opportunities, it is market enhancing. By taming arbitrary authority and removing obstacles to participation, the omnipresent authority of the state enables society and the invisible hand to function. This is something that the Founding Fathers understood very well.

Adam Smith's "Laws of Justice" and *The Federalist Papers*

As discussed in Chapter 2, market opportunities are difficult for everyone to achieve (even in liberal societies) and are not something that "just happens." Opportunities grow when government removes the stagnant blood of political privilege. Opportunities are created when we seek to eliminate stifling social practices that prohibit certain groups from participating. Opportunities multiply when policymakers seek out and defeat market conspiracies. Opportunities grow when the state moves against favorable legislation that lowers competition. Finally, opportunities emerge when the quest for advantage and power in markets—which is very similar to the search for power and advantage in politics—is tamed by both constitutions and the law. To fend off the tendency to take our hard-fought opportunities "for granted" (as Friedman might argue), it is imperative that society sign off on the oversight and regulations that are necessary to help markets function smoothly. The reasons for this are simple and twofold.

First, if there was anything that Adam Smith believed would undermine the market and the logic of the invisible hand, it was the unearned acquisition of resources (and he wasn't talking about assistance to the poor). We can understand this by looking at the state's historic role in transferring funds, granting subsidies, and protecting specific industries. While prefacing his discussion on the importance of the "laws of justice," Adam Smith argued that deliberately shifting a "greater share" of resources to an industry "than would naturally go to it" would retard "the progress of society toward real wealth and greatness."[41] Specifically, Smith wrote,

> Every man, as long as he does not violate the laws of justice, is left perfectly free to pursue his own interest his own way, and to bring both his industry and capital into competition with those of any other man, or order of men.[42]

But, as we know, there are undue subsidies, protected industries, and tax obligations that are not absorbed equally across society. There's also the prospect that private players will not provide the goods and services that they say they will. It's one of the reasons Adam Smith believed that proprietors of private roads (who charge tolls) should be placed "under the management of commissioners or trustees."[43] These are the dynamics that Adam Smith worried about. He understood that the quest for advantage and power in politics has a parallel world in markets. To ensure that the laws of justice were not violated, it was the duty of the state (i.e., "the sovereign") to protect the "system of natural liberty." This would occur only if the state made an effort "to protect every member of the society"—to the extent possible—"from the injustice or oppression of every other member" in it.[44] Smith was arguing that, even though it is good to believe in natural liberty, the state has to confirm the conditions that make it work. Put another way, when it comes to the forces of the market that create harmony, it is good to "trust, but verify." This is where the warnings and caveats on human nature from *The Federalist Papers* become important for us.

As many might recall, *The Federalist Papers* was a series of articles prepared by John Jay, Alexander Hamilton, and James Madison to convince the states to ratify the new Constitution (although James Madison evidently did most of the writing). They are also considered philosophical masterpieces. Among the many observations made, the articles warned about the dangers of allowing small groups, or factions, to run roughshod over a weak central government. The real danger for the new nation was that small, powerful groups might be able to capture the levers of a weak government and place their narrow interests above those of the nation. The significance of the subtext here is equal in voltage to that of the larger argument. Specifically, *The Federalist Papers* warned a young nation of human frailties and about the dangers inherent in the individual quest for power.

In *Federalist #10*, for example, Madison bluntly tells us that "If men were angels, no government would be necessary." For our purposes this means that we would not need government if those pursuing wealth and profit were angels. But they are not. In spite of Milton Friedman's optimism, there is little to indicate that markets are immune from the emotions and biases that dominate the human condition. The seeking of advantage, jealousy, ego, poor judgment, and the search for power all get the best of us. This is why the concerns that Adam Smith had with reference to the laws of justice and natural liberty are warranted. Simply stated, although the pursuit of wealth may drive people to work hard, the prospect of wealth and power also drive us to violate the laws of justice.

It is not a stretch to argue that the individual search for power through commerce and wealth—like the search for power through government and authority—pushes people to conduct themselves in a manner that is not commensurate with the actions of angels. This is why our political and economic world requires institutional checks and balances. This helps explain why Adam Smith believed that among the duties of the state was the need to "verify" that the laws of justice in markets were not violated. These concerns were not lost on James Madison.

James Madison Explains the Role of the State (in the Market)

One of the primary points addressed in *The Federalist Papers* was the seeking of advantage as it applies to the quest for property. In *Federalist #10* Madison made it clear that the situation in postrevolutionary America had deteriorated to such a degree that even "virtuous citizens" were concerned that greedy factions could threaten and undermine the proposed Union. The reasons were clear: the public good had been "disregarded in the conflicts of rival parties" whose "factious spirit" worked against as well as "tainted our public administrations." Madison argued that these factions—what we call "interest groups"—cannot be eliminated. The sources of faction are too diverse to control: religion, private interests, government business, community standards, and others all work to inspire "human passions" that have "divided mankind into parties" and "inflamed them with mutual animosity." Simply put, the causes of faction reflect our most basic beliefs, needs, and desires.

Madison believed that any attempt to eliminate factions would be destructive to the freedoms that the country fought so hard to win by revolution. They would also be foolhardy, because the "latent causes of faction are thus sown in the nature of man." The need to create an arena for competing centers of power was driven by the realization that even petty disputes have the capacity to "excite the most violent conflicts." And, although religion is often tagged as a primary source of disagreement by many, Madison was clear that "the most common and durable source of factions has been the various and unequal distribution of property."

> Those who hold and those who are without property have ever formed distinct interests in society. Those who are creditors, and those who are debtors, fall under a like discrimination. A landed interest, a manufacturing interest, a mercantile interest, a moneyed interest, with many lesser interests, grow up of necessity in civilized nations, and divide them into different classes, actuated by different sentiments and views.[45]

How did Madison propose that we deal with these potentially disruptive competing economic interests? He embraced Adam Smith's notion that the laws of justice needed vigilance, but he was much more explicit:

> The regulation of these various and interfering interests forms the principal task of modern Legislation, and involves the spirit of party and faction in the necessary and ordinary operations of Government.[46]

When it comes to protecting natural liberty and freedom, the perspectives of Adam Smith and James Madison converge. But it is left to Madison to discuss the specific role of the state. Part of the reason that Adam Smith "had argued for minimal government intervention" was because he focused on the reality that "government usually intervened on behalf of monopoly and privilege."[47] The state's role shaped by Madison was based on his view of human nature. Specifically, Madison believed that, as long as "the reason of man is fallible, and he is at liberty to exercise it," the state would be challenged by people who were "disposed to vex and oppress each other." This is why, according to Madison, the new country needed a political system with viable political institutions and a very public arena: ambition had to "be made to counteract ambition" out in the open.[48]

The solution for dealing with societal disputes and commercial challenges was to vest oversight in a Republic form of government, with an institutional body made up of representatives of diverse interests, who would negotiate, cajole, and fight with each other in the public square. There they would discuss and inject their views on "private debts," "domestic manufacturers," the "landed" classes, the "apportionment of taxes," and other issues of the day. Each issue would be exposed, and each position taken by elected representatives would be open to scrutiny. To do otherwise would allow specific groups to overrun societal interests. This would lead to the manufacturing sector, for example, drawing tax policy so that "every shilling with which they [manufacturers] overburden the inferior number, is a shilling saved to their own pockets."[49] To avoid these situations, according to Paul Starr, we create constitutions, pass laws, and actively pursue public policies that are designed to guard what our social contracts (the US Constitution) promise.[50]

The federalist principle and the three branches of government were supposed to guard freedom through a multilevel system of public and private "checks." Specifically, the private sector would act as "a sentinel over public rights" while the "republic" would guard "the society against the oppression of its rulers," in the process defending "one part of the society against the injustice of the other part." Nowhere do the Framers say that this framework and logic are to be jettisoned because the logic of free markets is more sacred than maintaining political balance.[51] A stable society depends on competing power centers, on many levels, to provide checks and balance. The key point to understand here is that when the competing power centers of the state are involved, the solutions arrived at are not "aberrations." They are the law of the land. Madison, Jay, and Hamilton believed so strongly in letting people slug it out over commercial and other interests that they wrote eighty-five articles explaining how and why the state had to do more than "umpire" the game.

Conclusion

So, what are we to make of the writings of James Madison, John Jay, and Alexander Hamilton? All were guardians and supporters of individual freedoms. All agreed that controlling commercial interests was not a good idea.[52] But all three were also clear that what Adam Smith referred to as the "laws of justice" could, and would, be violated in a market setting because of "the various and unequal distribution of property." Human failings and inequalities always exist. Their solution lay not in controlling the causes of faction. What they were after was controlling their effects. This would be done by pitting groups against one another and making issues more visible.[53] Both required the protection of individual liberties. More people in life's arena, with protected rights, would intensify and expand the scope of conflict. As more people were attracted to the debate, the hand of government would be forced, especially where injustice and gross inequities became clear.[54]

In this way political freedom facilitates—or is supposed to facilitate—commercial integrity. On this score, the results suggest that Western governments have gotten many things right. Still, the scope and complexity of modern markets have helped muzzle the democratic impulse. Offered the prospect of fabulous wealth and cheaper goods, the average citizen is not only increasingly loathe to question wealth-creating activities[55] but is also increasingly incapable of doing so. Because we have bought into the mantra "We're making money, you will benefit, so leave us alone," poor transparency, weak regulations, and misguided incentive schemes have been allowed to both emerge and camouflage certain market activities (see Chapter 10). The integrity of commerce suffers as a result. The practice of *vendor financing* helps illustrate these points.[56]

To boost sales, firms often extend credit or lend their consumers money to make purchases. But things can get out of control, as they did for Motorola. In February 2000 Motorola announced that it had sold $1.5 billion worth of equipment to Turkey's wireless carrier, Telsim. Motorola's investors waited more than a year to learn that the company had actually lent Telsim $2 billion for the sale. Was this a sale that generated profits, or should the books reflect something else? A sale is good for executives because it helps boost profits and, not coincidentally, bonuses. And besides, there was nothing to worry about according to Motorola because, as it reported in its financial statements, Telsim pledged 66 percent of its stock to Motorola in case of default.[57] However, almost immediately after announcing the deal, Telsim found itself in financial trouble. Telsim couldn't pay its bills and would soon find itself in default. Telsim did not panic. To generate cash Telsim would simply sell more stock in Turkey. The problem was that Telsim sold so much stock that it flooded the market. The value of Motorola's collateral fell from 66 percent of Telsim's total stock holdings to just 22 percent. At the end of the day Telsim's collateral was little more than a financial façade. Motorola was forced to write off $2 billion as bad debt.

Motorola's experience in Turkey is significant because it bolsters former Securities and Exchange Commission (SEC) Chairman Arthur Levitt's claim that you "can't take the attitude that investing in high-quality companies protects you from financial trickery."[58] For my purposes it demonstrates that, if allowed, many market players do what's in their best interests (their quarterly bottom line) and will go to great lengths to camouflage certain transactions. And if it's not illegal, all the better. These types of deals occur because, ultimately, citizens and consumers have bought into the notion that the market should be left alone. In the process, consumers and citizens essentially waive away their democratic rights — that is, their oversight responsibilities—to individuals who don't always play by Adam Smith's rules. If nothing else, Adam Smith was adamant about transparency. In this case, a company spokesman for Motorola made it clear that, because vendor financing is a competitive tool, "it was not in Motorola's interest to reveal how much it had lent to finance its customer equipment." Not considered, by Motorola, was the financial cost to shareholders and, no doubt, to US tax payers when companies like Motorola write off billions against their earnings. Also not considered is how these tactics allow certain market players to claim earnings and bonuses on sales that, ultimately, are the product of creative bookkeeping. Finally, what is not considered by firms that engage in these practices is that, apart from being less than honorable, they also undermine the integrity of the market.

In spite of the number of cases that follow the example of Motorola (and Turkey's Telsim), market players consistently fight suggestions of government oversight, as if their immediate financial interests supersede the long-term societal interests that come with market integrity. What they lose sight of is that less than honorable market tactics—and not some scheming bureaucrat "who doesn't understand the market"—are what make the presence of the state necessary in the economy. And falling back on the argument that "it was legal" doesn't make it right by the market. If nothing else, the Motorola example illustrates that today's market players don't always practice, and often don't seem to care about, what Adam Smith was speaking to when he wrote about market capitalism (as addressed in the following chapter).

Notes

1. William H. Gates Sr. and Chuck Collins, *Wealth and Our Commonwealth: Why America Should Tax Accumulated Fortunes* (Boston: Beacon Press, 2003), 68.

2. Gates and Collins, *Wealth*, 73. Blog Commentary.

3. Blog Commentary.

4. Vernon W. Ruttan, *Is War Necessary for Economic Growth? Military Procurement and Technology Development* (New York: Oxford University Press, 2006). Blog Commentary.

5. Ayn Rand, *Atlas Shrugged* (New York: Plume, 1999).

6. Friedrich A. Hayek, *The Road to Serfdom,* Introduction by Milton Friedman (Chicago: University of Chicago Press, 1994), xvi.

7. Hayek, *The Road*, xi.

8. Milton and Rose Friedman, *Free to Choose: A Personal Statement* (New York: Harcourt, Brace, Jovanovich, 1990), 4.

9. Friedman, *Free*, 5.

10. Susan Strange, *States and Markets*, 2nd edition (London, UK: Pinter Publishers, 1994); Ethan Kapstein, *Sharing the Wealth: Workers*

and the World Economy (New York: Norton, 1999); John D. Nagle, *Introduction to Comparative Politics: Challenges of Conflict and Change in a New Era,* 4th edition (Chicago: Nelson-Hall Publishers, 1996).

11. Robert Putnam, *Bowling Alone: The Collapse and Revival of American Community* (New York: Simon & Schuster, 2001); Dan G. Blazer, *The Age of Melancholy: Major Depression and Its Social Origins* (Sussex, UK: Routledge, 2005).

12. Paul Starr, *Freedom's Power: The True Force of Liberalism* (New York: Basic Books, 1997), 53.

13. Friedman, *Free,* 2.

14. Friedman, *Free,* 1–3. Blog Commentary.

15. Friedman, *Free,* 3.

16. Writings and policy papers that advocate this approach can be found on the Web site of the Ludwig von Mises Institute.

17. Friedman, *Free,* ix, xi, xvii.

18. Duncan K. Foley, *Adam's Fallacy: A Guide to Economic Theology* (Cambridge, MA: Belknap Press, 2006), xiv–xv; Robert Gilpin, *Global Political Economy: Understanding the International Economic Order* (Princeton, NJ: Princeton University Press, 2001), f.13, 311; George Soros, *Open Society: Reforming Global Capitalism* (New York: Public Affairs, 2000), 41–53. Blog Commentary.

19. Friedman, *Free,* 4.

20. Friedman, *Free,* 4–5, 6.

21. Robert E. McGinn, *Science, Technology, and Society* (Englewood Cliffs, NJ: Prentice-Hall, 1991). Blog Commentary.

22. Friedman, *Free,* xii.

23. Blog Commentary.

24. Foley, *Adam's,* xiv.

25. Friedman, *Free,* 2.

26. Friedman, *Free,* 3.

27. Foley, *Adam's,* 220.

28. Friedman, *Free,* 2.

29. Starr, *Freedom's,* 53.

30. Foley, *Adam's, xv,* 215–216.

31. Starr, *Freedom's.*

32. Blog Commentary.

33. Starr, *Freedom's,* Chapter 6.

34. E. E. Schattschneider, *The Semisovereign People: A Realist's View of Democracy in America,* with an Introduction by David Adamany (Hinsdale, IL: The Dryden Press, 1975), xiv.

35. Schattschneider, *The Semisovereign,* xix. Blog Commentary.

36. See Gates and Collins, Chapter 3, *Wealth*; Thomas Dye, *Top Down Policy Making* (New York: Catham House Publishers, 2001); David Sirota, *Hostile Takeover: How Big Money and Corruption Conquered Our Government—and How We Take It Back* (New York: Crown Publishers, 2006).

37. Friedman, *Free*, 3.

38. Hayek, *The Road*, xii. Blog Commentary.

39. Foley, *Adam's*.

40. Adam Smith, *An Inquiry into the Nature and Causes of the Wealth of Nations*, The Harvard Classics, Vol. 10, Charles Bullock, ed. (New York: PF Collier & Son Company, 1909), 466.

41. Smith, *The Wealth*, 466.

42. Smith, *The Wealth*, 466.

43. Smith, *The Wealth*, 477.

44. Smith, *The Wealth*, 466–467.

45. *The Federalist Papers*, #10, in Karen O'Connor and Larry J. Sabato, *American Government: Continuity and Change*, 2004 edition (New York: Pearson-Longman, 2004), 536–540.

46. *The Federalist Papers*, #10.

47. Starr, *Freedom's*, 80.

48. *The Federalist Papers*, #51, in Karen O'Connor and Larry J. Sabato, *American Government: Continuity and Change*, 2004 edition (New York: Pearson-Longman, 2004), 541–543.

49. *The Federalist Papers*, #10.

50. Starr, *Freedom's*.

51. Lawrence Herson, *Politics of Ideas: Political Theory and American Public Policy* (Chicago: Dorsey Press, 1984), 56, 63. Blog Commentary.

52. Blog Commentary.

53. Starr, *Freedom's*, 52.

54. Schattschneider, *The Semisovereign*, xxii–xxiii.

55. Robert B. Reich, *Supercapitalism: The Transformation of Business, Democracy, and Everyday Life* (New York: Knopf, 2007).

56. This story is drawn from Arthur Levitt (with Paula Dwyer), *Take on the Street: What Wall Street and Corporate America Don't Want You to Know* (New York: Pantheon Books, 2002), 165–167.

57. Levitt, *Take*, 167.

58. Levitt, *Take*, 167.

CHAPTER 2

FREE MARKETS AND WEALTH (RE)CONSIDERED

After leaving his position as chairman of the SEC, former brokerage and financial industry heavy weight Arthur Levitt wrote a book about the challenges of operating in financial markets. But Levitt wasn't interested in discussing how to make individual investors rich per se. He was more concerned about educating small investors about the tricks of the trade and how the underlying logic of free markets can turn otherwise decent people into unscrupulous financial sharks. Arthur Levitt also showed how industry tricks—and greed run amok—undermined the integrity of the market, which worked to chip away at the confidence that we have in our capitalist system.

In his book Take on the Street: What Wall Street and Corporate America Don't Want You to Know, *Levitt described one case that he saw as chairman of the SEC. A married couple with five children fell into some money and opened a trading account at a brokerage firm. They were, one assumes, planning for their children's future. What they didn't count on was that their broker, who was paid a commission for every trade executed, was making more than two hundred trades on their behalf in just a few months. The fees that he racked up padded his monthly compensation package. But this wasn't all. The broker borrowed money from the firm on the couple's behalf to help cover losses and expenses. Borrowing money on the couple's behalf—a practice known as "margin purchases"—didn't matter to the broker because he wasn't on the hook to repay the loans. In a little more than four months the couple's settlement money "had all but disappeared."[1]*

Financial tricks like this pale when compared to what Bernard Madoff did with his client's money. With an investor pool that included Wall Street heavyweights and renowned socialites, Madoff used their money for a Ponzi-like investment scheme that lost billions of dollars. Madoff's "rob Peter to pay Paul" scam was exposed when several of his investment

"Pauls" became jittery during the 2008 market collapse and asked for some of their money back. But there were no more "Peters" to siphon from in a collapsing market. The details of Madoff's Ponzi scheme aren't as important as the fact that the SEC had advance notice of Madoff's activities but—after receiving information voluntarily produced by Madoff—refused to act. Arthur Levitt's larger points on the need for market regulation and transparency couldn't be any clearer after the Madoff affair.

The lessons from Arthur Levitt's book alert us to one very simple reality: although freedom to operate in markets is necessary for enhancing personal wealth, it is not sufficient for protecting assets or ensuring that the conditions that create level playing fields are respected. More specifically, the "laws of justice," which Adam Smith argued were critical for efficient markets to function, are not automatic.[2] Respect for uniform rules, the protection of private property, and the protection of civil liberties crucial for human dignity and creativity exist because states make the effort to get laws right.[3] This explains why the founders of the United States made a conscientious effort to outline a level of state intervention in the market. The goals of the US Constitution were largely twofold. First, to reject the rigid mercantile system imposed on them by the British.[4] Second, to address specific issues related to commerce and law, the new nation jettisoned the Articles of Confederation and replaced it with the US Constitution. This brought symmetry to commercial rules, weights and measures, currency use, taxes, tariffs, and justice.

To safeguard individual opportunities and to shape the commercial environment necessary for transactions to prosper, the Founding Fathers created a US Constitution that protected civil liberties via the Bill of Rights and brought a semblance of stability to the commercial environment through Article I, Section 8 of the US Constitution. Together, the Bill of Rights and Article I, Section 8 are the taproot of civil law and commercial regulation in American society. British philosopher Jeremy Bentham understood the relationship between laws and markets well. One of the earliest advocates of economic freedom and free trade, Bentham was so convinced that "property and law" were "born together and die together" that he wrote, "[b]efore the laws, there was no property; take away all laws all property ceases."[5] By distinguishing between civil society and the state of nature, Bentham helped us understand that the state not only creates civil society but also gives life to capital.

The logic behind Bentham's observation, however, has been undermined by a political culture in America that goes to extremes to embrace the "Great Man" myth as the primary propellant of economic progress.

This attitude was chiseled into America's political culture by the stories of early pioneers, the "robber barons" in the nineteenth century, and, later, was aided by some of the excesses and failures of government programs in the twentieth century. What is ignored is how government's role, as President Lincoln put it, is to "clear the path" so that, when individuals work hard, they might prosper. In this manner, a "government of the people" was expected to work "for the people."[6] In spite of what Lincoln and the facts tell us about the role of the state in creating wealth, we get a sea of state-denigrating rhetoric that is largely empty grandstanding.

To demonstrate that many of these remarks lack historical substance and to put ideology above results, I begin by looking at the anti-state commentary from the contemporary period. Next, in addition to a much larger discussion of this topic throughout this work, to help illustrate why the anti-state commentary is out of line, I provide a brief overview of the state's role in creating and guarding wealth. To underscore the role of the state in the market, I show how the market does not always correct for social inequities and even deepens some (as when it creates markets for slaves). I argue that, although "working hard to get ahead" may provide the moral justification of capitalism, the promises of this maxim have not always been available for certain groups. This helps us understand why the state is absolutely critical for removing obstacles that create opportunities.

After presenting a brief review of politically driven anti-state rhetoric, I take a look at the role of the state in guiding and creating wealth. This is followed with an evaluation of the inability of markets to remove social inequities that deny opportunity, which leads me to ask this question: Why is the version of capitalism put forth by Milton Friedman and others at odds with reality? To address this question and other issues, I argue that the bucolic visions that we have of capitalism are quite distinct from the reality of actual markets. The issues addressed here help us understand why Adam Smith worried that society might not always secure its "order of nature and reason." Simply put, he believed that human folly would undermine the fluidity that economic incentives and political justice could bring, which would undermine the integrity of markets. To illustrate how these concerns remain as validate today as during Adam Smith's time, I look at several contemporary cases where Smith's "order of nature and reason" are violated.

We learn in this chapter, as noted in Chapter 1, that those who quote Adam Smith cite him in the same way that many people quote from the Bible—imperfectly and selectively. We also learn that it is imperative to take another look at the instrumental role of the state in making market capitalism work (see Chapters 3–12).

Contemporary Views on the State: Anti-Statism Run Amok?

What makes Jeremy Bentham's observations so potent is what they suggest about life outside of civil society. They tell us that living in the "state of nature" does not provide the same opportunities as living in a social setting. The example of Robinson Crusoe is quite useful here. We know that his dwelling provided shelter from the elements, but it had no market value. In an organized society with viable laws, the social order injects economic life into Crusoe's living quarters by turning it into a tangible asset that can be bought and sold. In the process it converts Crusoe's property from "dead capital" into live capital.[7] The utility and convenience of an asset in the state of nature are enhanced by market value and commercial potential in civil society. This allows us to appreciate better how society creates the conditions under which wealth is created.

Still, in some circles there is a general reluctance to acknowledge that— outside of military expenditures, basic provisions of security, and other small institutional arrangements—government is necessary for wealth creation. The state is often viewed as an obstacle to wealth creation and prosperity. This "anti-state" reality has taken many forms and has existed since capitalist societies emerged more than two hundred years ago (beginning with the anti-Federalists). And it resurfaced once again when Margaret Thatcher and Ronald Reagan came to power in the 1970s and 1980s. Buoyed by events that often had little to do with the state, Thatcher's and Reagan's ideologies found traction in societies that were looking for answers (discussed in Chapter 10). Although many argue that "getting the state off our back" is more rhetoric than substance, there's no doubt that the Reagan–Thatcher era saw a marked decline in public support for the state on many fronts. For many, the idea that the privatization of government functions because the state is "inefficient" or "prone to failure" is beyond dispute. This has influenced the public square in ways that allow simplistic sloganeering and misleading political caricatures to dominate debate. Swept aside are discussions of justice and the sustainability of democracy under an economic order hostile to state.[8]

From cries of "no new taxes" to incessant calls for "market deregulation," many policy debates begin in a way that places ideology above results. The fact that two US administrations that embraced the tax-cutting logic of "supply-side" economics, ended up producing record budget deficits illustrates this point. Suggesting that we "get the government out of the market" has turned out to be about as analytically bankrupt as railing against the "death tax" (discussed in Chapter 3). Yet both receive resounding cheers in political forums and have worked their way into serious policy arenas. The danger is these positions has led to increasingly flippant and irresponsible remarks in the public square that fuel the fire. Comments from high-profile legislators—such as "The market is rational and the government is dumb," "Government bureaucracies in general are threats to everyday life," and "Everything the government touches turns to crap"—are just the beginning.[9]

Political commentator James Carville tells us about a former congressman, Dick Armey, inventing a story on the floor of Congress to make a point about government:

> You know who Dick Armey is? Dick Armey [was] the Majority Leader of the House, one of the three or four most powerful Republicans in the country. He started out as an economics professor at a school called North Texas State . . . Armey used to tell people about a mildly retarded janitor there at North Texas State named Charlie. Every day when Armey was coming out of his office he would see Charlie, and Charlie would keep the floors very clean. Armey and Charlie became good friends. One day Charlie disappeared. Armey was worried. What had happened to his friend? The mystery was solved several months later, when Armey was picking up some groceries and ran into Charlie, who was there at the store using food stamps to provide for his wife and infant. It seemed that Charlie had lost his job because of one of those bleeding heart programs, the minimum wage. You see, when Congress increased the minimum wage, North Texas State couldn't afford to employ Charlie anymore and he got thrown out into the streets. And this, Armey explained, is why he became a big opponent of the minimum wage.[10]

After an enterprising reporter went to check the story, it was determined Dick Armey didn't know a Charlie at North Texas State. Armey's university colleagues could not remember seeing Charlie either. Nor could they recall any retarded janitors getting laid off because of the minimum wage.[11] The point is that—even though rhetoric and stories such as these are often viewed as petty grandstanding and lack any real policy analysis—because they are muttered by lawmakers at a national level, they help set the stage for other ill-conceived policy ideas. Dick Armey even went so far as to suggest a flat tax rate of 10 percent. Why? Dick Armey's "biblical tithe" model told him that "if 10 percent is sufficient for God, it ought to be sufficient for government."[12] There are more stories like these. At the end of the day, populist-tinged sound bytes that take gratuitous swipes at the state are no way to develop good public policy.

Another Look at Markets and Wealth in America: Myth and Reality

I spend time discussing the role of the state in setting the conditions for wealth creation in later chapters. Still, it's important to establish that the historical claims of rugged individuals "going it alone" in America's capitalist markets are misguided and wrong. Kevin Phillips tells us that—whether we are talking about the 1790s, the Gilded Age, or the late twentieth century—wage levels and wealth accumulation in the United States have hardly been determined by the market. Writing that the idea of the United States leaving "everything to the marketplace" is historically "misleading" and "a myth," Phillips jumps into twentieth-century America to make his point.[13] Specifically, Phillips argues that wealth accumulation

> required a calculated politics—and effective use of Washington, not marketplace, policy levers. This activism was visible across a wide range of issues, from tax legislation and blueprints for conservatizing the judiciary to economic deregulation, labor policy, trade, and the increasing federal role in bailing out shaky banks, savings and loans, corporations, currencies, and Latin American debtors.[14]

As I show in later chapters, interventions in the form of tariffs, infrastructure subsidies, land grants, legislation to protect producers, import restrictions, and the like have both undermined the logic of free markets and contributed to significant wealth creation. Then we have those who did little to earn their fortunes.

Kevin Phillips reminds us that, at the beginning of the twenty-first century, roughly one-third of America's richest four hundred families did little to create their fortunes. They had the good luck of inheriting it. William H. Gates Sr. and Chuck Collins went a step further and cite studies suggesting that almost 60 percent of America's wealthy "were born well along the base path—meaning they were fortunate enough to inherit a small business, a piece of land with oil under it, or an investment of 'parental equity' on flexible terms."[15] When this isn't the case, it's clear that the contacts that are passed through established family and business networks help others "earn" what they have.[16] Looking at this, Kevin Phillips argues that, rather than try to break the role of the state in the economy, America's economic mandarins use the state to protect and enhance their wealth.[17] This suggests that we need a better way to account for the origins of wealth and success than simple references to the wonders of the market or the "great man" myths that many self-promoting elites embrace.[18]

This is not to suggest that all people who inherit wealth do not work hard or that individual entrepreneurs are unimportant. Whether we look at the nineteenth or twentieth centuries, no one can doubt that Andrew Carnegie and Bill Gates Jr. set new standards for both hard work and business acumen. In the eighteenth and nineteenth centuries many slave-owners worked hard, as did the owners of New York's garment industries. But market opportunities are also formed by an environment that is created by the state and then tweaked and twisted according to legislative pique and social mores.[19] Apart from hard work, wealth and success in markets also depend on legacies, social contacts, and legislated opportunities. How well society receives each market participant makes a difference, too, as the history of women, slaves, and children illustrates (discussed in the next section).

So, although history suggests that the state can not pick individual winners and losers, we need to acknowledge that it at least has a hand in nudging certain players toward the winner's circle. This is important to understand, because we are told that those who dine at the banquet table of capitalism earned their place at the feast. Rarely are those who were born into wealth questioned about its origin. Even though many did work hard to get ahead, many are also economic dilettantes. This is problematic because favorable legislation and family wealth can inflate one's sense of achievement. Nothing illustrates this more in the United States than the fact that "two of every three adults who receive significant cash gifts from their parents view themselves as members of the 'I did it on my own' club."[20] There are several reasons why the mind-set that says "I earned my wealth on my own" serves real national needs, as well as those of the deluded legacy elites.

First, by not challenging the claim that the America's moneyed aristocracy made it on their own, the United States serves its civic interests very well. Over time stories of individual achievement helped create a mountain of disdain for both aristocracy and for entitlement granted by birthright. Fortunately, there are enough "rags to riches" stories to sustain the myth of the "rugged individual." Horatio Alger stories were instrumental in purging aristocratic and royalty myths that were tied to an anachronistic and feudal past.[21] Second, glorifying the rewards of hard work and individual initiative sets the stage for a culture of discipline and a strong work ethic to develop. We know that everything we are told about George Washington is not true. But myths about discipline and never telling a lie serve any culture. Discipline and hard work, in turn, are critical because they tie into a unique set of religious principles—beginning with the Protestant work ethic—and the idea that "my turn will come." The idea that spirituality and hard work lead to providence and prosperity did much to make harsh conditions tolerable.[22] Finally, believing that your turn will come—or that you will be rewarded spiritually in another life—has served society well. Simply put, when others do not question what you have, social stability increases.

Still, we are often led to believe by the Milton Friedmans of the world that everything could be better if only the state would step back and let the market work. The gap between our idealized vision of capitalism and the reality of markets needs to be addressed. But first I illustrate how the moral justification of capitalism—which is capitalism's intellectual lifeblood— has been aided and sustained by the very visible hand of the state.

The Moral Justification of Capitalism: How the State Makes It Work

The moral justification of capitalism in America rests upon one very simple assumption: if you work hard you will get ahead. Remove this promise and work becomes drudgery for the vast majority of us. Idleness and lethargy often follow. Feudal and imperial societies, with subsistence peasant economies and pliant cultures, are examples of social orders that did not always reward hard work. These systems were skewed to reward the noble airs and established positions of monarchs, despots, aristocrats, and sycophantic courtiers. The inability or unwillingness of monarchs, tyrants, and modern governments to correct inequities and imbalances that undermine opportunity and reward in society is important to understand. If you systematically exclude certain groups from participating in the opportunities that markets can offer, you have a society built around the notion that opportunity and reward depend on social position (aristocracies), family networks (elites), or bloodline (monarchies). This undermines the moral justification of capitalism.

The heart and soul of the capitalist revolution was tied to expanding opportunity beyond nobility and privilege. What set the stage for enhancing opportunities was giving life to ideas about human dignity and freedom that came from the Renaissance, the Reformation, and the Enlightenment. What forced the issue were the battles and wars fought in the name of liberty and freedom. Led by the American and French Revolutions, the social contracts that followed these liberal revolutions released individuals from stifling customs and traditions. The result was that talent and innovation, rather than bloodline, became dominant characteristics in helping determine one's station in life. Individual liberty was the key to establishing democracy and capitalism. The idea that you should be free to choose who ruled over you and to choose what you wanted to be "when you grow up" were relatively novel ideas in the human experience at the time (discussed in Chapter 4). Regular elections and the move toward competitive market economies were the result. But, just as democracy had its fits and starts, a funny thing happened on the way to Adam Smith's market society.[23]

On one level, we know that market rewards can be undermined by fraud and schemes that cheat others. Although the penchant to defraud and scheme appears to be a human constant,[24] what worked to undermine the moral justification of capitalism in America were social and personal beliefs, in which women and black Americans were relegated to second-class status.[25] This undermined job prospects and stunted the earning capacity of entire segments of society. And, although it could be argued that the evolution of the slave market in America is evidence of the ability of markets to organize and induce cooperation in diverse settings, it also provides evidence that cooperation in markets can occur with no moral compass (Box 2.1). Under these circumstances, wages and prices are skewed in ways that can shift reward to producers and to those who have the means to consume. For most hardworking women and blacks in

---

Box 2.1 The Swiss and the Laws of Justice

Markets can exist with little or no moral compass. In one of the uglier examples of wealth creation, state policy, and the complete discarding of the principles of Adam Smith's "laws of justice," we can look to the market activities of the Swiss during World War II. In the modern world Switzerland has consistently ranked among the world's richest nations. But it didn't get there simply because of its resorts, sales in clocks, or its chocolates. It is a global leader in finance because, early on, the government made a conscious decision to focus on personal banking. This focus allowed the Swiss to help the Nazis launder the looted treasures that they recovered from occupied territories and from captured Jews before and during World War II. The wealth and contacts gleaned from this era paid significant dividends in the postwar period. After helping finance the Nazi war machine, Swiss bankers switched gears and catered to postwar despots and tyrants. Jean Ziegler writes, "The hubris that gripped Swiss bankers in 1939 has never let go of them. The bank vaults of Zurich, Basel, Bern, and Lugano have become a kind of sewage system into which flow streams of filthy lucre from all over the world . . . No longer called Hitler or Himmler, Göring or Ribentrop, their clients have names like Mobutu, Ceauşescu, Hassan II, Saddam Hussein, Abu Nidal, Duvalier, Noriega, Traore, Suharto, Eyadéma, Campaore, Marcos and Karadžić." Today, in spite of having virtually no natural resources, Switzerland ranks as one of the five richest nations in the world. The point is that states can and do make decisions about industries that lead to vibrant markets. But they also ignore what Adam Smith had to say about the laws of justice.

Source: Jean Ziegler, *The Swiss, The Gold, and the Dead: How Swiss Bankers Helped Finance the Nazi War Machine* (New York: Penguin, 1997), 19.

America 150 years ago, the moral justification of capitalism lacked merit. More than anything else, this helps us understand what Adam Smith was referring to when he wrote about not violating the "laws of justice."[26]

Adding to these dynamics, which distorted the price of labor, was the acceptance of child labor in society. Unable to escape the feudal notion that they had to contribute to the family's well-being (which was an accepted practice, as long as you were talking about herding sheep or caring for a sibling on a farm), the moral questions of child labor were famously raised by Charles Dickens in *Oliver Twist* and later chronicled by E. P. Thompson's *The Making of the English Working Class* (1963). During the initial stages of industrialization, many argued that children were "free agents" who were capable of negotiating on their own behalf. But what chance did a 12-year-old child working in the mines have? Just like the opportunities that existed for women and blacks—who were held to menial and subservient positions—uneducated and frail children had few skills and even fewer options. For these groups, the freedoms glorified during the Enlightenment and fought for during the American and French Revolutions were distant dreams.

For many it's tempting to say, "That's just the way things were. Those who did compete still found an unrelenting system that fostered the 'survival of the fittest' mentality . . . these people were 'survivors' in the Darwinian sense." Even though this may be true, it ignores the logical follow-up: those who participated and prospered in eighteenth and nineteenth century America did so in a system that systematically bottled up the prospects of entire segments of society. This means that we can't attribute great success, wealth levels, and pay disparities to efficient market forces. The analysis is incomplete. And if we did, we would have to conclude that women, for example, simply couldn't cut it then or—if we look at pay disparities today—can't cut it now. We might also have to concur, or at least nod in approval, at those who suggested that 12-year-old children should have done more to prepare themselves for the market place 125 years ago. But we know better. And there are reasons why we know better.[27] The moral justification of capitalism is not simply a function of freedom and open markets. The state has to work to make sure that those who work hard are partnered into the compensation packages that competition can produce. Slaves needed a civil war and a civil rights movement. Women and children needed social justice and protections. There was absolutely nothing "invisible" about these developments.

Today, in spite of the fact that the scourge of child labor, Jim Crow, and gender bias have been dealt with on many levels, there are still other factors that eat away at the moral justification of capitalism. One way to stack the deck for and against certain groups is to use political institutions to secure favors. Favorable legislation that provides government subsidies, market protections, sympathetic regulations, and industry bailouts are all examples. When this occurs, the incentive system may be just as skewed as it was when child labor, Jim Crow, and (extreme) gender bias dominated the day. Perhaps these circumstances aren't as socially demeaning as they were generations ago, but the effect is similar: markets are skewed. This makes it difficult to speak of capitalism in America's history with simple references to the efficiency and the competitive spirit that the invisible hand brought. Market achievements and individual success owed a great deal to state-sanctioned discrimination and state support for injustices that were produced by societal beliefs. Simply put, when states ignore or encourage a way of life that helps determine who emerges at the top of our economic food chain, the moral justification of capitalism is diluted.

We need to acknowledge that what occurs in the market place is influenced by laws and stereotypes—both good and bad—and not just by "hard-nosed" business decisions. The dynamics that create bias and market imbalances must be addressed by the state so that the logic of the market can reward justly all of the factors of production.[28] Still, many politicians and pundits are inclined to downplay the role that the state can play in augmenting the moral justification of capitalism, preferring instead to put their faith in their incomplete understanding of "free trade."[29] Like Galileo's colleagues, who were afraid to look in his telescope for fear of what they might have to acknowledge about their worldview, many *laissez-faire* market proponents do not want to look at or acknowledge the role of the state in making markets work for all of its participants.

This is understandable. Many people are comfortable only in the world that they know. This explains why the beneficiaries of inheritances, family networks, transferred property, and windfalls made possible by favorable legislation would rather believe that what they have is a product of their effort, acumen, or hard work alone. As we will see, these positions are misguided, given what Adam Smith had to say about the laws of justice and natural liberty. He believed that individuals should be free to trade, as long as everyone abided by the laws of justice. If we recognize that we do not always adhere to the laws of justice it is much easier for us to understand the gap that exists between the promise of capitalism and the reality of markets.

Sex and Love Are Like Markets and Capitalism: Really, They Are

At the heart of Arthur Levitt's story presented at this chapter's opening is his point that free markets and the search for profits do not always guarantee "best practices" or professionalism in the market.[30] This violates the order of nature and reason that Adam Smith believed was so critical to the spirit of market capitalism. Part of the reason for this is that our view of capitalism is quite distinct from what actually happens in the market. More simply, people confuse the activities of markets with the theories that surround capitalism and vice versa. This is because we often can't see the forest for the trees and are frequently incapable of distinguishing what we want from what we need. We often don't categorize or think conceptually, and it shows.

Take sex and love, for example. Many confuse the two. Sex, as many realize, involves physical activities, is temporary, and often creates passionate moments that can go in many directions. Love, however, involves very specific ideas about commitment, families, and even religious beliefs. The principles that surround love are tied to moral dynamics that help guide our lives. Although sex might lead to a religious experience for some, most do not allow it to guide their lives. When the two are brought together, you get something called "true love" (or so we hope). And when one exists without the other, you get stalkers or perverts (or both).

Similarly, the market is a physical arena where goods and services are traded. Capitalism is a belief system that involves very specific ideas about the private ownership of the means of production and the existence of free, or wage, labor.[31] Markets are where exchange activities take place. They have probably been around since the first caveman negotiated and then traded a club for food. Capitalism depends on ideas about individual behavior and initiative. Markets involve physical production and trade, often for profit (discussed in Chapter 3). Modern market players are influenced and even guided by the principles of capitalism. And, although some people may reject the long-term utility of capitalism (Marxists for example), they can still operate in competitive markets. When markets and capitalism come together over a broad geographical space and disparate markets are connected under the same ideas and objectives, we can finally speak of market capitalism.[32] More specifically, we can now point to a market economy.

In practical terms, the first market economy experience—in which the price of goods and services is negotiated and profit is considered or encouraged—may have occurred when someone rejected the amount of meat offered for a club. The first widespread market economy, however, may have been launched when land, labor, and capital were traded freely under competitive conditions, without the imposition of the stifling conditions of custom and tradition (discussed in Chapter 4). When no bias or preferences exist in these trading arrangements, "the obvious and simple system of natural liberty establishes itself on its own accord."[33] An advancement from previous market arrangements (mercantilist, feudal, barter, etc.), a key guiding principle of market economies is that they be self-regulating, "open to all potential buyers and sellers," and that they exist under conditions where "no buyer or seller can determine the terms of exchange."[34]

Although this type of market has never existed, it is the model implied in capitalism.[35] The key is recognizing that pure competitive market economies, much like Hollywood's notion of true love, are often idealized or oversimplified caricatures.[36] But because these economies speak to something that we idealize—and play a socially stabilizing role by creating expectations—the Hollywood version of capitalism persists. When we speak of capitalism or free market economies (or true love), we aren't referring to actual conditions as much as we are stressing the common goals and characteristics that we would like to have in a market economy (or a marriage). And this is where we run into problems.

We may want to create free flowing, fluid markets that are free from bias. But even Adam Smith recognized that the "natural liberty" that he wanted for markets could be slowed, or "disturbed and interrupted by innumerable accidents" that are "contrary to the order of nature and of reason."[37] This occurs more often than we care to admit. Three examples of these persistent "accidents" help make this point and illustrate why the state has to be more than a reactive umpire.

Violating the "Order of Nature and Reason" in Real Life

A closer look at how the order of nature and reason in contemporary markets is violated helps us see that our present understanding of Adam Smith's invisible hand needs revision. Rather than drawing from Adam Smith's eighteenth-century examples, I look at how special interests in the contemporary era have approached markets and altered them to their advantage.[38] This explains how the integrity of markets is often affected, if not undermined, by private sector actors and helps us understand why the state is necessary to maintain market integrity.

"Dead Peasant" Insurance[39]

If ever there were "accidents" or market "interests" that act contrary to the order of nature, profiting from your employee's death would have to stand at the top. This is especially so because the number of participants from corporate America who collected on the "Dead Peasant" insurance policies reads like a *Who's Who?* in industry. The insurance program worked like this. We know that firms want to protect themselves against losing key executives. They invest time and resources into their training, so insurance policies allow them to recoup some of their investment in their personnel. That seems fair enough. But, as we shall see, although the incentive was rational from a business perspective (covering a business investment), the outcome ("peasant" death) speaks to a set of broader market goals and instincts (profits and income) that Milton Friedman cannot simply dismiss as a market aberration.

The first twist to reason emerged when, in their rush to cut taxes, the US Congress enacted laws that essentially allowed corporations to use life insurance premiums as a tax shelter. This encouraged companies to purchase life insurance policies for janitors and other low-level employees. By purchasing life insurance policies, companies both reduced their tax bill and started generating income when employees died. Because so many lower-level employees were covered by companies across America, insurance industry analysts began referring to the policies as "Dead Peasant" insurance. So the company won twice—once with the tax break for the premiums and a second time when the "peasant" became a source of cash upon his or her death: the individual didn't have to be employed at the time of death; as long as the policy was in place, the company got paid. These revenue dynamics are a far cry from the revenue-generating activities that Adam Smith argued were the primary objective of political economy.[40] But there's more.

The companies who held policies and found themselves short on cash didn't have to go to money and bond markets to borrow funds. The law allowed them to borrow against the life insurance policies of the "peasants." Like an ATM machine with overdraft protection ("peasant" death), the insurance policies became instruments of credit. How grand was this policy for the industries involved? According to Liz Pulliam-Weston, hundreds of companies, such as Nestlé's, Wal-Mart, Dow Chemical, Procter & Gamble, and Walt Disney, spent more than $8 billion purchasing policies for more than 6 million workers. The program became so big that it amounted to around 20 percent of all of the life insurance policies sold in a single year, and it generated more than $9 billion in tax breaks (known as "tax arbitrage"). On the downside, because companies were spending billions to purchase "Dead Peasant" insurance, they spent less (in the short-term) on productive equipment or other investment instruments.

Even though there is little doubt that corporate-owned life insurance for executives had, and continues to have, a definite business purpose (losing industry knowledge, expertise, and key contacts causes problems), experts agree that the "Dead Peasant" policies for low-level, rank-and-file employees was designed solely to shelter income, generate revenue, and enhance profits. At the beginning of the twenty-first century these policies all but disappeared when the loophole allowing the tax deduction was closed. Still, deliberately purchasing life insurance policies, to increase revenue and decrease tax liabilities, is contrary to the "order of nature and reason" that Adam Smith wrote about.

Bankruptcy Reform or Indentured Servitude in America?

When personal bankruptcies in the United States hit 1.5 million in 2002 and then went to 1.6 million in 2003,[41] one of the goals of the US Congress was to find a way to reduce the number of bankruptcy filings. This led to bankruptcy reform legislation in 2005, the Bankruptcy Abuse Prevention and Consumer Protection Act (BAPCPA). After climbing to 2 million bankruptcies in 2005, filings dropped to 600,000 in 2006.[42] The problem was solved, right? Think again. Bankruptcy filings rose to 822,590 in 2007[43] and were on pace to reach 1 million at the end of 2008.[44] What explains the surge in bankruptcy filings? Several developments are at work here. First, Congress catered to the interests of the financial industry but failed to address the principle causes of bankruptcy. Second, the industry raised fees and reduced grace periods after the BAPCPA was passed. Finally, the credit card companies lent people even more money after 2005 because it became more profitable to do so.

According to noted bankruptcy attorney Leon D. Bayer, in addition to making it more difficult to file for personal bankruptcy, the 2005 legislation didn't wipe out the reasons people file for bankruptcy.[45] More than 90 percent of all personal bankruptcies are filed for three reasons: job loss, divorce, or catastrophic illness.[46] There's little that Congress can do about these life events. Because no provisions were made in the BAPCPA to work with people who are hit by these real-life incidents, debtors soon found that the notion of "broke and in debt" was no longer good enough. The newly divorced, the medically recovering, and the unemployed would have to wait until they hit distressed debtor status to qualify for bankruptcy. Debtors, after all, had to be taught a lesson. This helps explain why military personnel in the National Guard were not given special consideration either. A deadbeat is a deadbeat according to the industry—there are no exceptions. And Congress agreed. So, rather than addressing the underlying causes that lead to bankruptcy in America, the 2005 legislation simply deferred and, more realistically, compounded the situation for those confronting uninvited financial problems.

Now, you're probably scratching your head and asking why legislators didn't anticipate this. It's a good question. To start, we must acknowledge that the biggest supporters of the 2005 legislation were the credit card companies. They aren't run by dummies. Some may get greedy, which compels them to make dumb decisions as a group over time, but the companies are not run by inherently dumb people. The executives in the credit card industry saw that bankruptcy filings were going through the roof in 2005. They also understood that there was an economic bubble waiting to burst. So they moved to protect themselves and their "fee and penalty" gold mine (fee income accounted for 31 percent of industry profits in 2001,[47] whereas total income from late fees jumped from $1.7 billion in 1996 to $7.3 billion in 2003[48]).

To be sure, the industry knew that the vast majority of Americans filing for bankruptcy were placed in their situation by uninvited life circumstances—job loss, divorce, or illness. But the details of their lives were viewed by disengaged industry lobbyists as being as "unfortunate" as they were unimportant. Like the Vegas strip, the goal of "The House" (the credit industry) is to get people in the door, at the table, and to keep them there. If they're not at the table, you can't get debtors, no matter what their circumstances, in the fee and penalty cycle. So the industry went to "their muscle" (i.e., Congress) to make it more difficult for debtors both to qualify for bankruptcy and to discharge their credit card debt. And they got their wish.[49]

Then, in spite of promising that consumers would benefit from the legislation (because fewer losses would accrue to the creditors), the industry immediately reduced grace periods, increased interest rates, and hiked late and over-limit fees (among others). Because the industry already had "universal default" authority, which allows the industry to hike rates on a clients account if the client is late making a payment on a competitor's account, the industry prepared itself for even greater profits. Profits for the industry jumped from about $30 billion per year in 2005 to almost $40 billion in 2007.[50] But the reasons for record profits after 2005 can't be traced simply to increased fees, higher rates, and shorter grace periods.

By helping the credit card industry reduce bankruptcy filings after 2005, Congress ensured that the companies would have fewer losses and more earnings (although I'm not sure whether favorable legislation that generates more income for an industry counts as genuine "earnings"). With more money at hand, the industry, incredibly enough, lent more. You would think that they would have learned a lesson from being just one year removed from record bankruptcies—and the fact that Americans had a savings rate that was effectively zero. Think again. In 2007, according to Laurent Belsie at the National Bureau of Economic Research, the credit card companies did the following:

> [They] started lending more, even to consumers with bad credit. Credit card debt increased more quickly during the past two years [2006–2007] than at any time during the previous five years.[51]

Comfortable in the knowledge that it was more difficult for borrowers to enter into bankruptcy proceedings, the credit industry determined that it was in their financial interest to lend more. Teaser rates, cashable checks, and other industry gimmicks filled our mailboxes. And why not? By raising the bar necessary to file for bankruptcy, the industry knew that fees, penalties, and other charges would add significantly to their client's debt load. According to Robert D. Manning, author of *The Credit Card Nation,* all of this is a good thing for the industry because

> (I)n the old days, the best customer was someone who could pay off their loan. Today the best client of the banking industry is someone who will never pay off their loan.[52]

Keeping distressed debtors in the game longer can make for fatter profits. But there is something else at work here. The industry is increasingly bundling credit card debt into debt contracts. And why not? The credit card companies have hundreds of billions of dollars that are owed to them by consumers. Rather than maintain a debt of, say, $6,000—which most middle-class Americans can't pay off in the immediate term—it's much easier to bundle and sell the debts that are owed to investors who are looking for income streams, with interest. Because the debt is secured by the payments of the credit card holder, the debtor becomes the "collateral" paying the debt—hence, a collateralized debt obligation (CDO) (see Box 2.2). And, with the 2005 BAPCPA to maintain debtor compliance, credit card debtors become government-enforced collateral. The practice of selling credit card CDOs has become so profitable that, by the end of 2007, "one-third of Capital One's $151 billion in managed loans had been sold as securities."[53] This figure is sure to grow. After home equity loans came to a crashing halt in 2007 and 2008, consumers have been forced to rely on their credit cards more and more, often just to pay their mortgages.[54] This helps explain why the credit card industry opposed the 2008 Credit Card Holder's Bill of Rights (HR 5244), which, among other things, imposed industry restrictions on questionable fees, sudden rate hikes, and payment time frames.[55]

Box 2.2 Collateralized Debt Obligations

A collateralized debt obligation, or a CDO, is finance-speak for debt contracts that are bundled up and sold to a buyer. The buyer of the CDO then has the right to the monthly payments made on home loans, student loans, or credit card debt, among others. There are many types of CDO debt instruments, which creates an alphabet soup of debt security categories. CDO became the generic term used for most securitized products, including mortgage debt. With every CDO contract you have hundreds of millions of dollars worth of contract payments shipped around the country. What made mortgage-tied CDOs so valuable early on was how they took a set of high quality mortgages (good debtors) and mixed them in with low quality but high yield mortgages (bad debtors), thus creating a "stable" income producing instrument. The monthly income, as you can imagine, is tied to the underlying debtor's ability to pay the debts. In the housing market this is the individual homeowner. If the debtor can't make the monthly payments, the holder of the mortgage-backed CDO, and those holding other CDO-affiliated products, will find themselves looking at a loss. Because market players always understood this could happen, the CDO market sought insurance, which led to the creation of credit default swaps (discussed in Chapters 10 and 11).

Source: Charles R. Morris, *The Trillion Dollar Meltdown: Easy Money, High Rollers, and the Great Credit Crash* (NY, NY: Public Affairs, 2008), 74–76; Shah Gilani, "How Complex Securities, Wall Street Protectionism, and Myopic Regulation Caused a Near-Meltdown of the U.S. Banking System," *Money Morning*, September 24, 2008, available on line.

These developments explain why the 2005 BAPCPA has become such a moneymaker for the credit card industry. The harder it is for someone to pay off his or her credit card debt, the longer it will be before the debt is paid. And debt that can't be repaid, or repudiated, becomes a continuous source of industry income. Julie L. Williams, chief counsel of the Comptroller of the Currency, explains what's happened: "Today the focus for lenders is not so much on consumer loans being repaid, but on the loan as a perpetual earning asset."[56] Put another way, the bankruptcy bill of 2005 turned personal misfortune and consumer debt into yet another income stream for financiers and Wall Street. Without addressing conditions in the economy, the three primary causes behind bankruptcy, or what the industry has done to entice clients, the BAPCPA does much to violate the integrity of market capitalism while undermining the spirit of Adam Smith's order of nature and reason.

Bubbles and Irrational Exuberance: "But Don't Blame Me"

One of the effects of a market that overreaches and then looks to the federal government for bailouts, subsidies, and favorable legislation is the evolution of a "don't blame me" culture. Here's the mind-set in a nutshell: "How can I be blamed when I was only doing what the market wanted? It's the other people who acted irrationally." At the top of the "don't blame me" crowd is former head of the Federal Reserve, Alan Greenspan. He's also on top of the "free-markets-work-but-let's-prime-the-pump-anyways" crowd. At the beginning of 2008 Greenspan began deflecting criticism of his tenure at the Federal Reserve by pointing to greed and, strangely enough, to the fall of the Berlin Wall.[57] Greenspan even went so far as to suggest that nothing could've been done to prevent the housing market conditions that arrived after he left the Federal Reserve because, even with the "authority to intervene, it's not credible that regulators would have been able to prevent the subprime debacle."[58]

What Alan Greenspan ignores here is that regulators had nothing to do with shoving cheap money into the economy. Also ignored is the fact that the hands of regulators were increasingly tied by deregulation, new and unregulated instruments, and budget cuts that left them understaffed. In order for Greenspan's comments to be credible, one has to suspend the capacity to reason. Think about it. If we let criminals loose from our prisons, stopped pursuing gang-related activities, and cut law enforcement budgets in half, would crime levels remain the same? The analogy might be extreme, but rules matter. Regulations matter too, both in society and in markets. Regardless, according to Greenspan, his policies at the Federal Reserve had little to do with the bubble economy and the rampant speculation in the early 2000s. People are expected to act rationally, even if you hang up a sign that says "For Sale . . . Almost Free Money." Later, Greenspan would say he had made a "mistake" in believing that market players operating in their self-interest would be enough to protect markets, admitting that he had found "a flaw in the model that I perceived is the critical functioning structure that defines how the world works."[59] Incredibly, the former chairman of the Federal Reserve would offer a rather uncreative solution to the disorder that he helped create: he suggested that we let the markets work.[60]

Also at the top of the "don't blame me" crowd is the Chief Executive Officer (CEO) of Bear Stearns, Alan Schwartz. He argued in front of Congress—and presumably with a straight face—that market "rumors" and wild "speculation" drove his company into the ground.[61] What could he do once irrational actors fed themselves on rumors of his company's impending insolvency, right? What he conveniently ignored is that he had allowed his company to build a debt to equity ratio of about 32 to 1[62] at a time when the industry average was on the heavy side of 3 to 1.[63] For many keepers of the market faith, letting Greenspan and Schwartz off the hook because of the "irrational exuberance" of others makes sense.

Company executives and high-level players like Alan Greenspan are smart people. They are rational. It's the borrowers and homeowners who should have known better. They are the irrational ones.

If we listen to Alan Greenspan, Alan Schwartz, and others, the big players can't be blamed for the post-2001 market bubble, deregulation, or rampant speculation—they were simply victims of an irrational herd. Never mind that brokers, underwriters, and financial institutions pushed and sold products with little consideration for the borrower's capacity to pay. What these market players conveniently ignore, as they point fingers at "irresponsible homeowners and borrowers," is that, when things go bad, it's the taxpayer who is expected to pick up the tab. At the time that this work went to print, the federal government had made billions available to the banking sector, put its financial stamp of approval on the takeover of failed financial institutions (such as Bear Stearns, for $39 billion), was on the hook for more than $50 billion in loans to Countrywide Financial, and had made additional billions of dollars available in order to bailout and purchase stock from Freddie Mac and Fannie Mae. And more was to come (see Chapter 10). In sum, the federal government was either offering money or looking into new ways to make money available to irresponsible industry players at the top who bought and sold market garbage and then turned around and said, "Don't blame me. . . ." By continuing to assert "I'm a capitalist and this is how markets works . . ." when profits are good and then asking the wage earner–taxpayer to pick up the tab when things turn sour, America's political and financial mandarins have accomplished several things.

First, downplaying the role of big market players in the 2007–2008 credit crisis (or viewing their failures as aberrations) prevents serious observers from seeing how irrational and criminal deregulated markets can become. As a result, when things began to turn sour, people were blinded to the possibility of criminality in markets. Scant attention was paid to investigations into what the Federal Bureau of Investigation (FBI) called "substantial" mortgage fraud.[64] In fact, nobody really wanted to see it—because of what it would say about the prized market model that they had created. With criminality off the radar screen (for a time) and with others wanting to believe in aberrations, it was much easier for the mortgage industry to convince members of Congress that their companies didn't need others meddling in their affairs (while they had their hands in the government bailout cookie jar). This mind-set helps explain why Congress wrote legislation that would not allow bankruptcy judges to rewrite mortgage loans, no matter how inflated and fraudulent the terms were.[65] The lobbyists of the lending industry argued that allowing bankruptcy judges to modify the terms of loan contracts would force the industry to raise interest rates for borrowers in general (to offset anticipated losses from the modified loans). Incredibly, Congress bought the argument. The reality was that the industry knew that—if a trickle of judges across the country began to independently review and find criminal wrongdoing in mortgage contracts—a flood of class-action lawsuits could follow.

The great imbalance here is that homeowners must pay the costs of predatory lending practices, market deception, and dumb decision making on the part of both parties. Downplaying the taint of criminality and by shielding market players from judicial oversight (once a constitutional guarantee) make it much easier for the big players to get bailed out at the taxpayers' expense. It also buys certain market players the time they need to pull their money out of certain investments. Perhaps more important, they can say with a straight face, "Don't blame me . . . everyone got caught up in market exuberance." Over the long haul these dynamics violate Adam Smith's order of nature and reason on many levels.

Conclusion

When Adam Smith discussed how markets could be disturbed and interrupted in ways that worked contrary to "the order of nature and reason," he was referring to the "interests, prejudices, laws and customs" that unnaturally shift resources and wealth.[66] In the third and fourth books of *The Wealth of Nations*, he argued that activities that create bias and unfairly shift resources distort both reward and initiative. This not only chips away at market efficiency and undermines the integrity of the market, but it alters the "order of reason" and the "order of nature." This begs the question, "What exactly does it mean to act contrary to the 'order of nature' and the 'order of reason'?" Developments such as "Dead Peasant" insurance, the 2005 BAPCPA, and—the bastard stepchild of these distorted policies—the evolution of a "Don't blame me culture" violate not only the spirit of Adam Smith's order of reason and nature but have created imbalances and caused a "disconnect" between ordinary citizens and those in the financial community.[67]

In a perfect world, for Adam Smith's "orders" to work, the following must occur without undue influence or artificial supports. Private investors must figure out on their own what to do with savings. Consumers must figure out when to make purchases and when to save. Production must be left up to merchants and industry. If everything works and undue reward, bias, or egregious errors in behavior (like "Dead Peasant" payoffs) are not introduced, society wins. But we are realistic enough to know that producers, consumers, and investors are always angling for an edge. In the process, individuals don't always respect or pursue Adam Smith's ideals or his laws of justice.

Part of the reason for this, as Milton Friedman pointed out, is that we are not always rational. This virtually guarantees that attempts to cheat or favor one group create inefficiencies in society and markets.[68] In other cases, it pays to be irrational. This occurs when immediate gains can be made (e.g., our excessive trading broker in the Motorola-Telsim example from Chapter 1) and when the long-term looks far away. It also pays when irrational actions have no immediate impact or can be deferred, which can lead to excessive borrowing. When this occurs, or when we begin to relax intellectual and personal standards, it becomes easier to see how society can miss small developments that grow into big market inefficiencies. Subsidies, bailouts, and market protections for certain industries are classic examples.

A tax policy designed to help small businesses purchase a van for deliveries can turn into the loophole big enough to drive a Humvee through. Or policies ostensibly designed to bailout Latin American or Asian states are really little more than undue supports for greed and stupid decisions made in the financial sector.[69] Eliminating a tax to "save the family farm" can turn into a major unearned subsidy for people who did little to earn what birth gave them and what Congress now helps them protect (see the following chapter). Once political campaigns are undertaken to promote these policies, it's difficult to turn the public away from the evolving narrative. The tendency toward uncritical herd behavior makes matters worse and helps explain why societies often make "bad" policy choices—in the political and the economic arenas. Simply possessing the capacity to reason does not mean that we will act reasonably.

Adam Smith, it appears, was quite aware of this. He believed that the decision-making process of investors, consumers, and businessmen would be influenced by special interests, prejudices, unjust laws, and biased customs. The decision-making process of state leaders could be corrupted as well. Smith discussed in the fourth book of *The Wealth of Nations,* for example, how the bountiful commercial rewards granted by import restraints and its colonial possessions worked to Britain's advantage— which was a good thing.[70] What does this say about free and fair trade with Britain in Adam Smith's time? It says that the resources and advantages that Britain used to strengthen its market prospects were hardly the stuff of invisible hands. This helps explain why promoting "freedom of trade" in Great Britain was considered an "absurd" idea by Adam Smith. He understood that "the private interests of many individuals" would "irresistibly oppose" it.[71] Too many private players were getting rich from Britain's state-guided policies. In this instance, nationalism meant so much to Adam Smith that he was willing to turn a blind eye to Britain's violations of the nature and reason. But the very political roots of market capitalism suggest that this has always been the case.

Notes

1. Arthur Levitt (with Paula Dwyer), *Take on the Street: What Wall Street and Corporate America Don't Want You to Know—What You Can Do To Fight Back* (New York: Pantheon, 2002), 22–24.

2. Adam Smith, *An Inquiry into the Nature and Causes of the Wealth of Nations*, The Harvard Classics, Vol. 10, Charles Bullock, ed. (New York: PF Collier & Son Company, 1909), 466.

3. Hernan de Soto, *The Mystery of Capital: Why Capitalism Triumphs in the West and Fails Everywhere Else* (New York: Basic Books, 2002); Paul Starr, *Freedom's Power: The True Force of Liberalism* (New York: Basic Books, 2007).

4. Starr, *Freedom's*, 55. Blog Commentary.

5. Jeremy Bentham, "Bentham on Utilitarianism," Liberal Democrat History Group, available online.

6. Norton Garfinkle, *The American Dream vs. The Gospel of Wealth: The Fight for a Productive Middle Class* (New Haven, CT: Yale University Press, 2006), 14.

7. De Soto, *The Mystery*, 6.

8. Garfinkle, *The American*, 5. Blog Commentary.

9. The first and second quotes are attributed to former representatives Dick Armey and Newt Gingrich; the third is attributed to former Reagan treasury official, Paul Craig Roberts. See James Carville, *We're Right, They're Wrong: A Handbook for Spirited Progressives* (New York: Random House, 1996), 57, 60.

10. Carville, *We're Right*, 34–35.

11. Carville, *We're Right*, 35.

12. Robert D. Atkinson, *Supply-Side Follies: Why Conservative Economics Fails, Liberal Economics Falters, and Innovation Economics Is the Answer* (New York: Rowman Littlefield, 2006), 14, 58. Blog Commentary.

13. Walter La Feber, *The American Age: U.S. Foreign Policy at Home and Abroad, 1750 to the Present* (New York: Norton, 1994), 102. Blog Commentary.

14. Kevin Phillips, *Wealth and Democracy: A Political History of the American Rich* (New York: Random House, 2002), 93.

15. William H. Gates Sr. and Chuck Collins, *Wealth and Our Commonwealth: Why America Should Tax Accumulated Fortunes* (Boston: Beacon Press, 2003), 112.

16. The many works that make it clear that social networks and family contacts—as opposed to hard work alone—are critical to making it in America include Pamela Walker Laird, *Pull: Networking and Success Since Benjamin Franklin* (Boston: Harvard University Press, 2006) and, the 2007 "Economic Mobility Project" put together by the Pew Foundation, available online. One of the most recent works that makes the point that environment and context influence success is Malcolm Gladwell, *Outliers: The Story of Success* (New York: Little, Brown and Company).

17. Phillips, *Wealth,* 117.

18. Gates Sr. and Collins, *Wealth,* 112.

19. Ben S. Bernanke, "The Level and Distribution of Economic Well-Being," Board of Governors of the Federal Reserve System, Speech before the Greater Omaha Chamber of Commerce, February 6, 2007, available online.

20. Gates Sr. and Collins, *Wealth,* 134.

21. An icon of American capitalism, John D. Rockefeller, admiringly noted that Napoleon Bonaparte was "virile because he came direct from the ranks of the people. There was none of the stagnant blood of nobility and royalty in his veins," Gates Sr. and Collins, *Wealth,* 39.

22. Lawrence J. Herson, *Politics of Ideas: Political Theory and American Public Policy* (Chicago: Dorsey Press, 1984), 41.

23. Blog Commentary.

24. Christine Daniels, "Liberty to Complaine: Servant Petitions in Maryland, 1652–1797," in *The Many Legalities of Early America,* ed. Christopher L. Tomlins and Bruce H. Mann (Chapel Hill: University of North Carolina Press, 2001), 219; Edward Chancellor, *Devil Take the Hindmost: A History of Financial Speculation* (New York: Plume, 2000). Blog Commentary.

25. Daniels, "Liberty," 242.

26. Smith, *The Wealth,* 466.

27. Nancy Maclean, *Freedom Is Not Enough: The Opening of the American Workplace* (New York: Russell Sage, 2006). Blog Commentary.

28. Smith, *The Wealth,* 454.

29. David Sirota, "Caught on Tape: Tom Friedman's Shocking Admission," available online.

30. Levitt, *Take,* 24–28.

31. Robert Gilpin, *The Political Economy of International Relations* (Princeton, NJ: Princeton University Press, 1987), 15. Blog Commentary.

32. Duncan K. Foley, *Adam's Fallacy* (Cambridge, MA: Belknap Press, 2006), 8. Blog Commentary.

33. Smith, *The Wealth*, 466.

34. Gilpin, *The Political*, 18–19. Blog Commentary.

35. Gilpin, *The Political*, 18.

36. Blog Commentary.

37. Smith, *The Wealth*, 137.

38. George Soros, *The New Paradigm for Financial Markets: The Credit Crisis of 2008 and What It Means* (New York: Publica Affairs, 2008). Blog Commentary.

39. The information for this section was drawn primarily from Liz Pulliam-Weston, "The Basics: Does Your Boss Want You Dead?" MSN.Money, available online.

40. Smith, *The Wealth*, 25.

41. Administrative Office of the U.S. Courts, "Bankruptcy Filings Continue to Increase, Records Broken for Total Filings and Non-Business Filings," May 15, 2003, available online.

42. National Bureau of Economic Research, "Did Bankruptcy Reform Increase Financial Distress?" November, 2007, available online.

43. UPI.com Business News, "U.S. Personal Bankruptcy Growing," 2008, available online.

44. American Bankruptcy Institute, "Total Bankruptcy Filings Increase to Nearly 27 Percent over First Quarter 2007," press release, June 3, 2008, available online.

45. Leon D. Bayer, "Bankruptcy Quiz: Passing the Means Test," in Newswire.com, October 16, 2006, available online.

46. Demos: A Network for Ideas and Action, "Households at Risk: The Bankruptcy 'Reform' Bill and Its Impact on American Families," press briefing kit, February/March 2005, available online, 4.

47. Lucy Lazarony, "Credit Card Penalties Get More Severe," Bankrate.com, March 7, 2002, available online.

48. Demos, "Households," 14.

49. Bayer, "Bankruptcy."

50. Michael Simkovic, "The Effect of 2005 Bankruptcy Reforms on Credit Card Industry Profits and Prices," July 8, 2008. Available online.

51. National Bureau of Economic Research.

52. William Branigin, "Consumer Debt Grows at Alarming Pace," MSNBC, via the *Washington Post*, January 12, 2004, available online.

53. Gretchen Morgenson, "Given a Shovel, Americans Dig Deeper into Debt," *New York Times*, July 20, available online.

54. Charles R. Morrison, *The Trillion Dollar Meltdown: Easy Money, High Rollers, and the Great Credit Crash* (New York: Public Affairs, 2008), 121–122.

55. David Lazarus, "Bankers Love Bailout, Hate Credit Card Curbs," *Los Angeles Times*, September 28, 2008, available online.

56. Morgenson, "Given."

57. Alan Greenspan, "The Roots of the Mortgage Crisis," *The Wall Street Journal*, December 12, 2007, Opinion, available online.

58. Alan Greenspan, "The Fed Is Blameless on the Property Bubble," *Financial Times*, April 6, 2008, available online.

59. Edmund L. Andrews, "Greenspan Concedes Error on Regulation," *New York Times*. October 23, 2008, available online.

60. Paul Krugman, "Greenspan Lectures Us Again," *New York Times*. March 16, 2008, Opinion, available online.

61. Dana Milbank, "Buddy, Can You Spare a Billion?" The *Washington Post*, April 4, 2008, Washington Sketch, available online.

62. *Money Crashers: The Guide to Financial Fitness*, "What We Can Learn from the Bear Stearns Down Fall," March 26, 2008, available online; Julie Satow, "Ex-SEC Official Blames Agency for Blow-Up of Brokers-Dealers," in the *New York Sun*, September 18, 2008, available online.

63. MSN.Money, "Bear Stearns Cos Fundamentals," available online.

64. Jaymes Song, "FBI Director: Mortgage Fraud Substantial," Federal News Radio, February 1, 2008, available online.

65. Benton Ives, "Senate Reverses on Housing Measure," *Congressional Quarterly Today*, April 1, 2008, available online.

66. Smith, 137.

67. Gretchen Morgenson, "Borrowers and Bankers: A Great Divide," *New York Times*, July 20, 2008.

68. Bryan Caplan, *The Myth of the Rational Voter: Why Democracies Choose Bad Policies* (Princeton, NJ: Princeton University Press, 2007). Blog Commentary.

69. See Robert Reich's Blog, "Moral Hazard," September 7, 2007, available online.

70. Smith, *The Wealth*, 353.

71. Smith, *The Wealth*, 368.

PART II

THE ROLE OF THE STATE IN CREATING MARKET CAPITALISM

CHAPTER 3

THE VERY POLITICAL ROOTS OF CAPITALISM: EMBRACING INDIVIDUAL ACHIEVEMENT AND VANITY

Whatever the roots of his "scathing disdain for the 'waste' of unbridled competition,"[1] John D. Rockefeller's pursuit of monopoly power in the late 1800s helped bring organization and, perhaps more important, steady profits to the oil industry. However, by the early 1930s oil profits were again threatened by too many competitors. By August 1931 producers in Oklahoma and Texas were so plentiful and productive that the price of crude had dropped to thirteen cents a barrel, and, by the spring of 1933, some "hot oil" runners got little more than two cents a barrel.[2] And this occurred after Texas Governor Ross Sterling had, in effect, "declared war" on East Texas—by sending the National Guard and the Texas Rangers to cut off rogue producers—and then "rammed" a bill through the legislature that allowed market prorationing.[3] To stabilize prices, the oil industry turned to the federal government. After initially going after black market producers, Interior Secretary Harold Ickes sought to reduce production by sending production quotas to the governors of each oil state. And why not? According to Ickes, after the Depression many business leaders were shell-shocked and "crawling to Washington on their hands and knees . . . to beg the Government to run their businesses for them."[4]

Unfortunately for Ickes, and Franklin Delano Roosevelt, the US Supreme Court declared much of the National Industrial Recovery Act—which gave the federal government its authority in oil—unconstitutional. However, with memories of oil at ten cents a barrel still fresh, the states decided to follow the federal government-determined quotas on a voluntary basis. To ensure coop-eration, the Interstate Oil Compact was passed in 1935, which provided a "forum for states to exchange information and plans, to standardize legislation, and to coordinate prorationing and conservation in production."[5] To check the flow of foreign oil, which might undermine the "informal" quota system, Congress imposed tariffs on crude, fuel oil and gasoline.[6] This cut in half US oil imports, stabilized sales, and put the US oil industry firmly under a government-escorted quota and tariff system. As was the case during Rockefeller's time, the post-Depression oil industry was able to establish regular profits at "market prices" only after competition had been brought under control. Just as important, the organizational mold that would inspire the creation of the Organization of Petroleum Exporting Countries (OPEC) had been cast.

The key to understanding capitalism is freedom. Simply stated, capitalism cannot exist without liberty, which is critical for the existence of free labor and the private ownership of the means of production.[7] But individual freedom is not enough. Individuals and civilizations have experienced freedom over time but have never duplicated the levels of wealth created in modern Western societies. The difference is that the modern state has created the conditions that are necessary for initiative and talent to prosper by disciplining arbitrary power. To ensure that authorities and rogue groups cannot confiscate the fruits of labor or deny freedom, modern states have turned to institutions and legal infrastructures that are guided by constitutions. Constitutions are every society's social contract and the breastplate of every citizen's independence.

This is important from an economic perspective. If workers suspect that their efforts will not pay off because discriminatory forces threaten to take away what has been fashioned by their hands, production beyond subsistence is unlikely. In a capitalist society the effect is more damaging. If workers and entrepreneurs suspect that working hard will not pay off in the long run—reward being the moral justification of capitalism— initiative is cast aside. Without the promise of improving one's station in life, work, beyond subsistence, becomes drudgery and entrepreneurialism becomes naked avarice and advantage seeking. This is why Adam Smith took care to caution against creating the conditions that favor one group or unduly shifting resources from one party to another. When this occurs, the moral justification of capitalism is compromised and, as Smith argued, the "laws of nature" are violated. Free people, competing with one another in ways that create countervailing power centers, not only enhances personal freedom, which fosters initiative and creativity, but it also works to "discipline" power.[8]

To arrive at the point at which individuals could aspire to great wealth and other vanities beyond subsistence living, changes had to be made in society. Specifically, the state had to work to amend customs and traditions that allowed communities to condemn or expel those accused of making excessive profits and ridicule those demonstrating pride or arrogance in personal achievements. This aided the cause of liberty, but it also led to social changes that brought down the feudal order. But the discarding of antiquated customs and traditions wasn't easily done. The freedom to make decisions about who would rule and what "we want to be when we grow up" was acquired through revolution and has been kept only with great difficulty. Liberty, as we shall see, is a gift of the modern liberal state.

The story behind individual freedom and the right to pursue great wealth takes us from the High Middle Ages, to the Renaissance and the Enlightenment, and through England's Glorious Revolution. What we find is that the ability to pursue riches isn't as simple as saying "Remove the state and I will produce great wealth." Rather, wealth creation at the levels that we see today is intricately tied to the state. More specifically, it is the modern liberal state that creates the conditions for great wealth creation.

Constraints on Individual Liberty Before the "Liberal" Era

Before the rise of capitalism and democracy in the late eighteenth and nineteenth centuries, the search for power and great wealth was considered to be the special province of states, empires, and despots. Because of social and religious beliefs in Europe at the time, in most quarters the deliberate search for handsome profits and great wealth was considered to be an affront to God, and even sinful. The search for wealth and power was viewed as a luxury that belonged mostly to heads of state, the aristocracy, and the clergy (and their sycophants), who often bent rules according to whim and fancy. The pursuit of power and wealth, which ran against moral and spiritual beliefs of the day for commoners, was often justified by notions of a "divine right" to rule, or the idea that God had a hand in directing those who ran affairs of state. For everyone else, acting on personal interests, avarice, and lust was taboo and condemned. Custom and tradition mandated that commoners obey authorities and warned against not accepting your fate in life.

This explains why charging excessive interest (usury) and earning "excessive" profits (avarice) were viewed as ungodly and frowned upon in many places across Europe and early America. Although many people found ways around usury and avarice (cooking the books is an old tradition), getting caught trying to cheat the community could lead to humiliation and even banishment from society. Robert Heilbroner tells us about an incident in Boston in 1639:

> A trial is in progress; one Robert Keayne, "an ancient profes-
> sor of the gospel, a man of eminent parts, wealthy and having
> but one child, and having come over for conscience's sake and
> for the advancement of the gospel," is charged with a heinous
> crime: he has made over sixpence profit on the shilling, an out-
> rageous gain. The court is debating whether to excommunicate
> him for his sin . . . poor Mr. Keayne is so upset that before the
> elders of the Church he does "with tears acknowledge his cov-
> etous and corrupt heart." The minister of Boston cannot resist
> this golden opportunity to profit from the living example of a
> wayward sinner, and he uses the example of Keayne's avarice
> to thunder forth in his Sunday sermon on some of the false
> principles of trade.[9]

Whatever the fate of Mr. Keayne after his "conviction," it's clear that moral conduct and commercial principles were enforced by religious or legal codes or both. These codes worked against what individuals could aspire to, or build for themselves, by sabotaging the system of reward.[10] Although religious and cultural walls were socially stabilizing, they also stifled initiative. Yet, because religious and cultural mores don't change over night, they were still prevalent in many communities well into the nineteenth century. More than two hundred years after Mr. Keayne's ordeal in Boston, English politician and historian Lord Macaulay criti-cized those who doubted the capacity of the human spirit once granted freedom. In 1843 he wrote:

> Many politicians of our time are in the habit of laying it down
> as a self-evident proposition, that no people ought to be free
> till they are fit to use their freedoms. The maxim is worthy of
> the fool in the old story, who resolved not to go into the water
> till he had learnt to swim. If men are to wait for liberty till they
> become wise and good in slavery, they may indeed wait for
> ever.[11]

Before the seventeenth century, arguments for individual liberty were often shot down on the grounds that ordinary men could not be trusted with freedom. It was considered lunacy, or at least pie in the sky thinking, to believe that individuals could survive in a world where ordinary people made decisions for themselves. Led by the American and French revolutions, the struggle for freedom and individual liberty between the eighteenth and nineteenth centuries amended the prospects for individual liberty by freeing nations from the dominion of monarchs, the superstitions of priests, and the traditions of feudalism.

But liberty was not easily won. Liberty was driven—and is still driven—by those who understand that liberty is a messy proposition. Liberty unleashes energy and creativity that transforms passions into novel ideas, which we see in the arts, in our politics, in our inventions, and in the industries around us. But the liberty to create also opens up paths for unrestrained opportunism and vice. French revolutionary, Marie-Jeanne Roland de la Platière (Madame Roland) understood this all too well. As she waited for the guillotine, she cried, "O liberty, O Liberty what crimes are committed in thy name!"[12] Still, cognizant that medieval and feudal traditions condemn humanity to stagnation in perpetuity, early thinkers were adamant about pursuing liberty's cause.

St. Francis, Renaissance, Enlightenment: Challenging the Status Quo

One of the great gifts to come from the Enlightenment was the gradual elimination of entrenched customs, traditions, and beliefs that stifled liberty and held back the human spirit. Specifically, the Enlightenment advocated reason as the primary basis of authority and challenged a feudal way of life that was bathed in religious dogma, tradition, and superstition. Most people never questioned the status quo or tried to improve their lot in life. Why should they? If the Bible, as interpreted by the clergy, said that you should obey and wait for the afterlife, why ask questions? Many of our ancestors were scared into thinking that they only needed to follow, and not act, so they believed that the best they could do was to accept and suffer through a life that was "nasty, brutish, and short." Scholasticism, the dominant intellectual tradition of the time, didn't help matters.

Scholasticism argued that the transfer of learned wisdom and simple explanations of phenomena were the hallmark of a good education. Still, scholasticism piqued the interests of many thinkers and set the stage for active investigation, the hallmark of the Enlightenment. Beginning with St. Francis (c.1181–1226), the intellectual force behind the Franciscans, philosophers and theorists began to challenge the idea that the world was merely a "collection of symbols expressing God's message," waiting to be unraveled by the priests.[13] With the establishment of universities as institutions of higher learning, people in the High Middle Ages (1000–1300 AD), pushed to ask questions by the Franciscans, saw the arrival of a new intellectual era. This brought about the scientific method and the age of discovery. Beginning in the twelfth and thirteenth centuries a combination of reason (employed since the time of Aristotle) and revelation (with a decidedly Christian bias) was the method of choice for passing on information. Initially provided by teachers in informal settings, group lectures by "masters" began in Italy and France[14] and were largely formalized as universities by the fourteenth century. These institutions of higher learning taught medicine, law, mathematics, and religion.

In the area of religion, the transfer of knowledge was expanded to include debates on a variety of topics, like how many angels could dance on the head of a pin. Rather than challenging scripture, the goal of debate was to strengthen Christian theology by clarifying perceived contradictions in the Bible.[15] Although these debates might appear to be intellectually stale by today's standards, they helped set the stage for other questions. This led to active investigations and methods that focused on going to the source, rather than accepting what was explained. By the fourteenth century, study and empirical findings—rather than faith, speculation, and opinion—were embraced as new sources of knowledge.[16] This new "humanist" approach provided the environment for an intellectual rebirth, or Renaissance, in the West.

Because science, investigation, and questioning the status quo undermined conservative beliefs and religious authority, they also elevated the opinions of learned individuals and the activities of adventurers. More important, by consistently creating doubts in what the authorities and the church said about the world, science and investigation initiated a process that brought an end to feudal society. When Martin Luther questioned church practices at Wittenberg, Germany, in 1517 and Galileo (1564–1642) dared to propose that the Earth moved, they raised questions that put the underpinnings of the feudal order in doubt. Put simply, if the Church could be wrong about what it practiced and about its claims regarding the universe, could it also be wrong about original sin, human destiny, and an individual's "divine right" to rule? The new secular approach to studying problems created intellectual holes that neither the Church nor the aristocracy could explain. So the Church turned to threats of excommunication, reactionary claims of blasphemy, or promises of a fiery hell for those who questioned its interpretation of the world. Lies and fear became the ally of the Church and of social conservatives as well.

Although these developments occurred during the period called the Enlightenment, it was the Renaissance and, later, the Reformation that brought real change. By shedding light on the secular world around us, Renaissance- and Reformation-era thinkers moved us beyond the intellectual darkness that compelled individuals to accept explanation and just do what they were told. The ideas of the Renaissance moved human beings beyond what was, for many, a static world and pushed them, at least those in Western Europe, to seek new truths—through the study of politics, literature, science, and the arts (the humanities). Even the events during the period of the Reformation—although the time was wrought with vicious religious battles—helped alter the status quo by forcing society and sovereigns to recognize that there was more than one way to interpret the Bible and to understand spirituality.

The constant warfare during the Reformation also taught sovereigns that it might be best and cheapest to allow other sovereigns to worship as they saw fit and to decide religious questions within their own borders. This fit with the thinking of John Locke (1632–1704). Locke was concerned with freedom of conscience, or religious liberty, because he believed that true faith came from within. This was a powerful insight. If individual notions of spirituality had to be respected, protecting religious freedom would compel respect and cooperation in other areas, which would facilitate political order.[17] This logic helped consolidate the creation of the modern, sovereign, nation-state system, in which freedom to worship also means freedom from imposed beliefs. The impact of the Renaissance and the Reformation cannot be underestimated. They moved Western Europe from the idea that individuals should accept their lot in life and pushed people toward new ideas and an appreciation of what could be accomplished. Individuals pursuing knowledge, investigation, and adventure separated the idea of humanity from the realm of myth and from the outdated teachings of the church.

As secular approaches to knowledge replaced blind faith, humanism nudged aside the stodgy explanations of scholasticism. This enabled intellectuals, philosophers, and other observers to look at the human condition without the blinders of custom or religious dogma. New questions emerged. Could the human condition be improved? Did we have to accept our fate in life simply because we were told that we were condemned by original sin? Could original sin and other passions be subdued or tamed? And, if the answer to these and other questions was yes, could our quality of life perhaps be improved as well? At the end of the day, the great thinkers of the eighteenth and nineteenth centuries did not find it sufficient to use our minds to ponder how many angels could dance on the head of a pin. They questioned a world that was interpreted and explained by narrow-minded priests and clueless monarchs.

The Enlightenment encouraged brilliant minds like Galileo and nurtured the likes of Isaac Newton and Charles Darwin. The era challenged humanity to move beyond accepting what was explained and toward investigating "how" and "why" something happened. This meant allowing individuals to pursue what caught their fancy in politics, in art, and in war. Just as important, it meant allowing them to enjoy their achievements and to exhibit their talents in ways that offended medieval and feudal sensibilities.

The Impact of War on Individualism: Honor and Glory for the Fatherland

The Renaissance and Enlightenment transformed worldviews and provided a critical bridge for embracing individual accomplishment, and even individual vanity, as necessary for human progress. Whether through achievements in research, markets, diplomacy, adventurism, or war, what emerged was a growing awareness that individuals could be inspired by secular pursuits. Included in the mix was the belief that discovery and triumph could lead to individual accomplishments, which were no longer seen in a negative light. This was a fundamental advancement over the earlier Christian motives that had dominated soldiers, dukes, and monarchs. In *The Habsburgs*, Andrew Wheatcroft tells about the *Order of the Golden Fleece*, which was dedicated to protecting and propagating "the Christian Faith" during the time of Philip the Good, Duke of Burgundy (1396–1467):

> Each of the knights wore a heavy scarlet mantle, lined with sable, and embroidered with gold thread; and on their shoulders they bore the heavy golden collar and the ram, emblem of their confraternity. When they met in chapter they sat in silence under their banners and hatchments, listening to the chancellor of the order praise or blame them for their conduct. They were enjoined to be dignified, sober and always zealous for the honour of God and their order.[18]

Because the *Order of the Golden Fleece* sought to bring back chivalry and was driven by religious symbolism, knights were expected to display bravery and to fight until death as a group. They were, after all, fighting the devil and every evil that he would bring forth. Wheatcroft explains:

> The emblem of the Golden Fleece was also a symbolic assimilation. The golden ram stood for the simple ideals of chivalry and presented them as an answer to the manifold exigencies of a chaotic world. The knights, like the Round Table . . . would reverse the spirit of discord, would begin to restore

order to a world where the forces of the Antichrist were about to conquer . . . Eventually the harmony of the order would bring peace to a troubled world.[19]

With moral universalism playing such a critical role in deciding questions of war, it's no wonder that philosophy, science, and discovery raised questions that were perceived as threatening to the established order. The utility of placing humanity's fate in the hands of religious symbols and divine revelations didn't make sense to those who studied the world as it is, rather than as they wanted it to be. The capacity to negotiate, calculate, reason, and plan statecraft free from religious considerations undermined notions of moral universalism. Niccolò Machiavelli (1469–1527) and Cardinal de Richelieu (1585–1642) were particularly important figures.

When making calculations for war, both Machiavelli and Richelieu counseled leaders to replace religious values—which are subjective and not easily shared—with state interests. State survival is easily understood and offers the advantage of bringing disparate groups together for a common interest: security. People united in the pursuit of common survival are less inclined to be divided along lines of faith—both during and after battle. This much was clear to French soldier, writer, and Huguenot statesman, the Duke of Rohan (1579–1638). A contemporary of Cardinal Richelieu, the Duke of Rohan believed that rulers could understand the need to survive and would make rational military calculations toward these ends. He believed that religious questions such as "Who else is worthy to worship my God alongside me?" would bring misguided adventures. Rohan advocated replacing the "disorderly appetites" and "violent passions" driven by subjective religious values with objective state interests guided by reason.[20]

This is critical, because the national interest of state survival put a primacy on individual honor and glory-seeking in the name of the state, rather than leaving allegiances and ferocity in battle to religious belief or the highest bidder (a problem with mercenaries).[21] Glorification of individual accomplishment in the name of the state is a seminal transformation; early writers such as Dante and St. Augustine had viewed glory-seeking as vain and sinful. To be sure, St. Augustine had reluctantly supported a "limited endorsement of glory-seeking" when it was tied to "civil virtue" and to the battlefield (which he admired in the Romans). But St. Augustine's cautious nod of approval for glory-seeking was strongly tempered by his own "guidelines to medieval thinking," which denounced the lust for sex, power, and money or possessions.[22] *Libido dominandi,* or the lust for power, was especially pertinent because of how it corrupted the human condition.

Removing the Taint of Humility

Cardinal Richelieu and the Duke of Rohan lived at a time when it was widely believed that aspirations to power and wealth could only lead to spiritual and moral debasement. One of the accepted arguments for hereditary rights and aristocracy was that those born into power and wealth didn't have to sully themselves with the humiliating indignities of social climbers who aspired to another station in life. Social climbers who have to wait on others and bide their time in lowly positions can never escape the dishonor and shame of having had to serve others. Describing the conditions that Cardinal Richelieu had suffered on his ascent to power, Hilaire Belloc described the mind-set that tainted Cardinal Richelieu's life achievements:

> Those who would attain political position of themselves must—without hope of escape—stoop to baseness in their beginning; and it is the strongest argument for hereditary rule in any aristocracy or crown that it *may* provide the commonwealth with rulers who have not suffered from the taint of intrigue and subservience. Those not acting with hereditary right cannot avoid that taint . . . they will always bear within themselves the reproach and memory of unworthiness in the past.[23]

It was in this environment that the Duke of Rohan and his contemporaries in the seventeenth century began to transform medieval thinking about individual accomplishment and glory-seeking. By wrapping state security around individual honor on the battlefield, the Duke of Rohan and those who shared his intellectual mold helped convert vanity and glory into exalted and respected traditions.

Montesquieu picked up on this line of thinking, to argue that glory-seeking was beneficial for society because "everyone contributes to the general welfare thinking that he works for his own interests," which brings "life to all the parts of the body politic."[24] When Renaissance and early Enlightenment thinkers placed investigation above static explanation, independent thinking and the glorification of personal achievement were elevated. This mind-set was extremely helpful later when economic thinkers began to embrace avarice as crucial for the common good. Specifically, a positive view of individual aspirations and glorifying achievements on the battlefield cleared the path for championing individualism and embracing rational secular approaches to solving political and economic problems.

The pursuit of rationalism and secular accomplishments was not limited to the sciences, political thought, and activities on the battlefield. These qualities were also glorified and grandly portrayed in the arts, which captured a new human spirit. To portray humanity more realistically, artists left behind the abstract and idealized approaches (mostly religious) that marked the Byzantine and Gothic periods. Because Renaissance thinkers looked deeper into the human condition, artists of the day were able to present humanity in ways that glorified individualism and human anatomy. The works of Leonardo da Vinci (the *Mona Lisa*) and Michelangelo (the sculpture of *David*) are both examples of this form.[25] Graphically portraying the human condition in battle, art captured the individual glory in war. Seeking to understand the human condition and individual accomplishment, scientists, thinkers, and artists from the Renaissance and the Enlightenment chipped away at the idea that private aspirations should be curbed. Individuals started to believe that they might be able to control their own destiny.

This contrasted with the medieval order in Europe, which locked most of humanity into rigid belief systems. Supported by subsistence lifestyles and patterns of political subservience, what was produced, learned, and pursued at the time was determined by habit and by the needs of a stagnant aristocracy. This was accepted as the natural order of things. Even though this mind-set began to change with the Renaissance and the glorification of individual accomplishments, William of Orange and the Glorious Revolution (1688) helped cement the role of the state in creating the conditions to produce great wealth for merchants and commoners alike. Increasingly, political change made one thing clear: if Heaven on Earth could not be created, it wasn't God's fault.

The Revenue Imperative[26]

During the medieval period European monarchs found it necessary to extract more payment from their subjects in order to fund wars. The need to borrow and to tax had a profound impact on the relationship between sovereigns and those who were asked to fund the affairs of state—the merchants. Because war consumed up to half of all of the revenue raised in western European states, sovereigns looked for both new sources of tax revenue and new ways to collect taxes more efficiently.[27] To accomplish the first, the state actively courted and encouraged wealth creation by merchants. As well, sovereigns granted monopolies, tax farms, and charters to private parties who promised to generate funds for the state. To become more efficient, as the state grew in size, it required servants who were more than simple court sycophants.[28] State bureaucrats began serving state interests, rather than those of individual monarchs, by carrying out state duties—becoming more professional in the process. This was especially the case as states began recording addresses and keeping more complete records of taxes paid.

With business and tax transactions recorded and documented, merchants began making more political demands. In England, to keep Parliament honest, merchants and commercialized nobles demanded and received political concessions from William of Orange, who became England's monarch after King James was overthrown during England's Glorious Revolution (1688). One critical concession occurred when William of Orange accepted parliamentary control of spending. King William III understood from his experience in the Netherlands that the most effective way to raise revenue and to pay off state loans was to get Parliament to put its stamp of approval on royal spending. If Parliament agreed to foot the bill for expenditures racked up by the Crown, creditors knew that they were more likely to get paid. Legislative control of the purse not only became part of England's Bill of Rights (1689), but it laid the foundation for many of the civil liberties enjoyed by democracies the world over today.[29]

New authority and independence for Parliament were critical because they also gave Parliament greater control over public policy and ensured that Parliament had a say on matters of war. Because greater control over public finances had been granted to Parliament and to the merchants that it represented, creditors understood that Britain's monarchs could no longer arbitrarily break contracts or capriciously and so easily renege on debts owed.[30] Once William of Orange—and, by definition, England—became a more credible debtor, England lowered its cost of borrowing and became an attractive investment destination, which gave merchants even greater influence.

In this manner, the Dutch invasion that brought William of Orange to power during the Glorious Revolution (1688) transformed England's political and economic environment. It established the idea that certain rights claimed by the sovereign who sat on a throne—such as the right to make war—could be reviewed by others. When monarchical absolutism ended in Britain, it became clear that commmoners could make decisions for themselves. More to the point, military demands, followed by political concessions, effectively encouraged, if not begged, merchants and traders to go out and make money for the sake of the state.

The story of William of Orange in England helps us understand how "the creation of liberal political institutions was thus a by-product of the impact of military insecurity upon the need for government revenues."[31]

In many respects, economic organization in post-Renaissance England came to depend on political arrangements produced by war. Other monarchs understood this and, in an effort to enhance their fortunes abroad, made attempts to follow the British example. Britain remained far ahead of others when it came to understanding the intricate relationship between the political and the economic.

Enlightened Thinkers Revise the Passions

When Galileo looked through his telescope and declared that the Earth moved around the Sun, he challenged the standard belief, backed by the Church, that the Earth was the center of the universe. He called his colleagues over so that they could share in his findings and his excitement. His colleagues balked. If Galileo was right—and the Earth really did move around the Sun—the finding would cause profound personal and moral dilemmas. If the universe was not as the Church had described it, what about everything else that the Church said? What about Heaven? What about Hell? Was the end perhaps not so near after all? Galileo's finding would undermine the very foundations of society. Indeed, if the Earth wasn't the center of the universe, could it be that our fate or our station in life was not preordained? Perhaps we could aspire to a better life. And, if this were true, did the idea of a "divine right to rule" have something to do with the misery of the peasantry? For the aristocracy, as you can imagine, this was all blasphemy.

With the genie out of the bottle, the search for new answers and new truths about the world around us led to the scientific method, which undermined even more the beliefs and traditions of the day. This created new fields for thought. If the aristocracy did not have a divine right to rule, Enlightenment thinkers needed to describe how new ways for managing the affairs of state might work. Similarly, they needed to explain how being free from custom and tyranny was a good thing. It was at this point that philosophers and practitioners began to explore how selfish interests could turn individuals into creative and responsible members of society.

Thinkers like Adam Smith looked at personal greed and argued that greed would produce unintended outcomes that were beneficial to the public:

> Every individual necessarily labours to render the annual revenue of society as great as he can. He generally neither intends to promote the public interest, nor know how much he

is promoting it. He intends only his own gain, and he is, in this, as in many other cases, led by an invisible hand to promote an end which was no part of this intention.[32]

Smith was saying that humanity's "destructive energies" could be channeled into constructive ones because people pursuing profit had to provide quality goods to consumers who had other options. The tendency to cheat would be overcome by the need to compete and to make money tomorrow. The immediate passions (cheating) would be overcome by the long-term interests (steady profit). Smith argued that, to achieve this, feudal patterns of control—which rested upon coercive customs and traditions that were largely designed to protect the interests of feudal elites—would have to be challenged and broken down. Freed from both feudal laws and direction from above, Smith argued, our energies could be channeled into mutually beneficial economic patterns:

> [Because the] natural effort of every individual to better his own condition . . . is so powerful, that it is alone, and without any assistance, not only capable of carrying on the society to wealth and prosperity, but of surmounting a hundred impertinent obstructions with which the folly of human laws too often encumbers its operations.[33]

To be sure, this would only come about as long as the modern liberal state removed the threat of arbitrary power. But under a new system, individuals would be disciplined by the prospect of steady profit and by what Sir Thomas More called pride, "which counts it a personal glory to excel."[34] Because discipline (in the pursuit of profit) and ego (pride) were necessary to produce the goods that others wanted, Smith and other Enlightenment thinkers believed that competition would promote both individual restraint and integrity. Little room would be left for depravity. Reason and honor in the pursuit of riches would tame passion and greed.

All of this raises one question. Although avarice might be sufficient, under a new liberal state, to explain new forms of production and cooperation, why would monarchs embrace that other radical new liberal idea, democracy? To do so meant promoting political liberties that undermined a monarch's grip on power. Even though greed, under a nascent liberal regime, might help us understand the capitalist revolution, *raison d'état* also had as much to do with capitalism evolving as any other force in feudal Europe (see Chapter 5). Clearly, without the political and security realities that faced the state, capitalism might never have gotten off the ground.

Liberty and Freedom Take Root in the State: The Emergence of Constitutional Liberalism

The merits of feudalism were put in doubt because of questions raised by the excesses of feudal authority. Discriminatory taxes, arbitrary decrees, unjust excommunications, and church corruption were among the issues raised by the best Enlightenment thinkers. Although great discoveries were made, perhaps the biggest issue centered on how to create a society to replace the economic traditions of feudalism and the political claims of aristocracy. The result was the evolution of two complimentary ideas rooted in freedom. One argued for everyone's liberty to pursue his own path in life. Permission from a lord, or feudal obligations, would no longer dominate society. Rather than being directed by custom and tradition, the material needs of society would be satisfied by merchants and producers who had to please and serve consumers. Greed, hard work, and reward would form the basis of an emerging capitalist system.

The other idea advanced was political freedom. Enlightenment writers argued that, when people had a say in who governed, society would not only be more inclined to respect political outcomes but would also be more willing to participate. A sense of community and civic duty would be the new cornerstones of political society. Both capitalism and democracy were viewed as radical ideas, because the freedoms that they espoused threatened the interests of monarchs, aristocrats, and the Church. The prospect of people making decisions in the political and economic world rang a bell that even the most self-absorbed members of the aristocracy could hear. They knew that doubts about the divine right to rule, backed by new knowledge from Enlightened scholars, had worked to undermine their claim to authority. After the Reformation even the Catholic Church understood that the masses weren't so willing to accept the Church's interpretation of spirituality, faith, and the "natural" order of things. Hypocrisy doesn't play well to a cynical crowd.

Unsure what to do, feudal elites retrenched and became more conservative in their thinking, which produced reactionary solutions. When they weren't busy looking for new ways to undermine liberal ideas and their leaders, in their more contemplative times feudal elites wondered about the folly of it all. How could merchants, the working class, and peasants—their social inferiors—be expected to decide how much to produce and what to do with their lives? This was especially the case considering the level of illiteracy and the long history of conformity in Europe through the seventeenth and eighteenth centuries.[35] For conservative monarchs and an anxious clergy, change meant anarchy rather than stability.

What they didn't, or couldn't, understand was that, after centuries of observation and contemplation, philosophers and other thinkers came to believe that free individuals would act in a manner that produced new energy, a productive order, and a progressive equilibrium in society. This would only occur, they argued, if the social contract agreed to was sufficiently grounded in law that common citizens could leverage it "to resist arbitrary acts of the state" and other tyrants of authority.[36] If this were the case, the state would benefit by applying the law to itself, because transparency and stability would allow the state "to attract investment, obtain credit, and sustain popular loyalty and cooperation" on a new level.[37] But the real benefit to be obtained rested on the intangible benefits that would be derived from a state viewed as an honest broker of law and justice. This occurs when the state embraces the law. As Paul Starr put it, the ruler can do the following:

> reduce power-depleting rivalries among clans and factions by convincing them that the state represents an impartial arbiter of their claims and discouraging those who feel wronged from adopting private alternatives to law, such as by seeking revenge for crimes or personal affronts. Where private vengeance rules, some individuals or groups certainly have more power than others—they can prevail over them. But violent feuds deplete society of the power necessary to achieve collective ends. The rule of law offers an alternative to private justice that instead of consuming power increases it.[38]

Because respect for law channels energy toward positive ends, individuals who have been freed from the need to settle personal scores on their own can dedicate more time to planning and improving their lives. This produces patterns of cooperation that mute the tendency toward anarchy and despotism. Just as conflict depletes the power of states and societies, cooperation and toleration serve "as a paradigm for the state's acceptance of pluralism" and toleration throughout society.[39] This is a significant departure from a past in which elites feared and attempted to repress the "sinful" ideas and interests of commoners. As people became more concerned about improving their lot in life, the emergence of democracy and capitalism would establish dynamic patterns that overshadowed the staid activities of those who simply wanted to protect possessions and positions. Specifically, constitutional liberalism came together in a coherent government philosophy that promoted

> the rule of law, separation of powers, popular consent through representative assemblies, religious toleration and freedom of conscience, protection of the rights of property, and guarantees of freedom of the press and other liberties[40]

To be sure, it was well understood individual "passions" and "vices" might get out of hand and lead people to cheat one another or to elect unqualified leaders.[41] But one of the great things about constitutional liberalism was that both the market under capitalism and the political arena under democracy allowed individuals to get it wrong and try again. From freedom to move about, to bankruptcy laws, to general elections, perhaps the greatest promise of constitutional liberalism was that you were not locked into any particular condition. The system encouraged political and economic redemption.[42]

To control arbitrary power and avoid tyranny, constitutional liberalism grants enough freedom so that "autonomous power centers" are allowed to develop and then set against each other.[43] The interesting point is that competitive markets are only one part of the many autonomous centers that make constitutional liberalism work. In the public square we see public vs. private actors, federal vs. state actors, checks and balances in legislatures, societal pluralism, and contested political elections (among others), all working to guarantee that public and private arenas are never static.[44] Opportunities are always present because of continuous referendums in markets (with consumers) and in politics (with voters).

The key to constitutional liberalism lies not in utopian claims to harmony, as some might preach. Rather, public discord and disagreement are viewed as necessary for both settling disputes and discovering new ideas.[45] Ambition is encouraged to counter ambition at many levels in the public square because it disciplines and enhances competing power centers. Political liberty, public defeats, and the idea that "I can try again" are the necessary foundations of constitutional liberalism and successful capitalist markets.

Conclusion

This chapter makes the case that the state embraced new ideas and worked to amend customs and traditions that at one time encouraged communities to condemn, expel, or punish commoners who were found guilty of pride, excess profits, or both. In the process, the state challenged community mores and religious dogma, while encouraging personal vanity. These efforts were aided and guided by vibrant intellectual environments called the Renaissance and the Enlightenment. This helped propel those capable of great achievements to new levels. During this time liberty unleashed a spirit that led to social change and helped bring down the feudal order. In its place we saw the birth of a modern liberal state that William of Orange understood could create great wealth. He understood that these dynamics would provide the financial resources to turn England into a global power.

The important point is that, even though the gift of the modern liberal state is a new level of human dignity wrapped around individual achievement, William of Orange was arguably the first to see it all in its proper context—as an instrument for creating wealth that the state could tap into. To be sure, the British went through several stages of mercantilism, with colonies, charter corporations, protective tariffs, and the like. But the demand for more money to fund war meant going through the tumultuous process of limiting or abolishing the privileges of Britain's highly polished but increasingly unproductive aristocracy. By the seventeenth century it was well understood in England that, if the state set the conditions for great wealth creation, it could expect more from its elites than simply looking good and commenting (stylishly, of course) on the affairs of day. This is important to understand in contemporary America, where the conditions necessary for creating productive and sustainable wealth are increasingly not understood. Among those who see this are William H. Gates Sr. and Chuck Collins, authors of *Wealth and Our Commonwealth: Why Americans Should Tax Accumulated Fortunes.*[46]

Gates and Collins argue that the fortunes of many wealthy entrepreneurs are the product of hard work. But hard work is nothing new. The builders of the pyramids, the slaves of ancient Rome, the peasants of feudal Europe, and, in the modern era, the citizens of the former Soviet Union can attest to this. Hard work is not sufficient for explaining wealth creation in the modern world in general and in the United States in specific. For Gates and Collins the capacity to create wealth at the levels we see in America is the result of very political decisions that were made by America's Founders. Long ago they determined that educating, protecting, and facilitating the commercial prospects of ordinary Americans were critical for individual success and national prosperity. Specifically, Gates and Collins argue the United States became a success because of "the things we have done to strengthen equality of opportunity."

Although Gates and Collins forcefully argue that one of those "things" that the state did was to put a "brake on the accumulation of hereditary wealth," their point is a simple one: society creates the conditions under which wealth is created. As the intellectual heirs of the Enlightenment, America's Founding Fathers understood from history that individual liberty and individual glory were superior to the stifling "taint of humility" found in the polite societies of Europe. They also understood that entrenched and powerful economic aristocracies would distort democracy while negating equality of opportunity. To avoid the conditions that encouraged inherited power and legacy privileges (the scourge of feudal societies), the Founding Fathers did away with rigid inheritance laws, bankruptcy codes, entail, and a host of other feudal codes and practices that rewarded idleness while stifling talent and initiative.

By weeding out the worst of Europe's feudal past, they prepared a healthy bed for the seeds capitalism to sprout and bear fruit. To ensure that a dynamic market economy would flourish—where ambition and competition crowded out privileged idleness and poorly conceived ideas—investments in public institutions and equitable land distribution policies helped create a land of opportunity in the United States. For creating this environment, Gates and Collins argue that government has a legitimate claim to tax the accumulated fortunes of those who benefited most from the system. This mind-set helps explain why, upon John Jacob Astor's death in 1848, newspaper publisher James Gordon Bennett argued that half of Astor's then-astounding $20 million estate belonged to the city of New York.

According to Bennett, because Astor's wealth "had been augmented and increased in value by the aggregate intelligence, enterprise, and commerce," the city of New York had a legitimate claim to a good portion of his wealth.[47] Taxing wealth was viewed as absolutely necessary if society was to guard against perpetuating a gilded aristocracy in which "the disposition to admire, and almost worship, the rich and powerful" leads to what Adam Smith called "the great and most universal cause of the corruption of our moral sentiments."[48] This explains why a premium was placed on promoting liberty and free enterprise which, contrary to common belief, doesn't simply happen on its own. Creating a system that rewards hard work and talent requires diligence and costs money. As believers in the maxim "To whom much is given, much is expected," Gates and Collins argued that the wealthy must support state institutions that foster great wealth creation. Adam Smith, the intellectual godfather of capitalism, would agree. He even recommended higher road tolls on luxury carriages so that "the indolence and vanity of the rich" could contribute to larger societal goals.[49]

To help sustain the American system—contrary to what anti-tax crusaders might argue—the Framers of the American Constitution made sure that they didn't make the same mistake that was made by the Articles of

Confederation. They created a strong central government. In the Articles of Confederation, for example, the federal government was virtually powerless to tax, whereas individual states had the authority to coin money and to deny the federal government its representatives (by refusing to pay them so they could go to Washington DC). To remedy this, those who attended the Constitutional Convention determined that the federal government would have the means to sustain itself. This brought about Article I, Section 8 of the Constitution (the dynamics behind "The Revenue Imperative" previously discussed).

The freedom to pursue personal wealth and the authority to tax and "regulate commerce" proved to be superior to previous arrangements for generating revenue. Specifically, by creating an environment for opportunities to multiply, individual ambition and talent thrived. The new American state was now able to lean on its entrepreneurs and vice versa. Many people ignore this reciprocal dynamic and argue that taxes on estates, for example, are really some kind of "death tax" that represents an unwarranted government taking—as if the Paris Hiltons of the world deserve all of the money that simply falls into their laps for no other reason than because they came out of the right womb. To make their point, Gates and Collins take on the following "Abolish the Estate Tax" storylines:

- It destroys family farms? When pressed, the American Farm Bureau Federation couldn't produce one example of a family farm that had been lost to the estate tax.
- Family businesses are sold to pay taxes? The vast majority of family businesses fail because of poor management by children who inherit companies but don't understand the industry.
- It unfairly punishes success? Top income earners often pay an effective tax rate that is less than what middle and lower income wage earners pay. The estate tax makes the tax system a fairer code of distributive justice.
- It promotes double taxation? The bulk of assets taxed in an estate represent appreciated property—like real estate, stocks, art, and so on—that weren't properly taxed as their value increased. Also "double-taxation" is a red herring: 98 percent of the population is exempt from capital gains taxes.
- It violates capitalist principles? Nations tax transactions. This allows them to track, understand, and pay for activities that the government is called upon to monitor.

Another area of concern for the authors is how inherited wealth has created a deluded and jaded elite culture. A classic example of this is the astonishing fact that two of every three privileged legacies, who receive significant inheritances, "view themselves as members of the 'I did it on my own' club"—an incredible delusion, given that almost 60 percent of the members of America's moneyed aristocracy were born into money. The authors discuss the corrosive effect that not earning their windfall has had on elites, arguing that most end up "ill-prepared to earn their own way in the world." This helps explain why they become "fearful of losing even part of their inheritance" and either fund think tanks and initiatives that support their individual class cause, or become purveyors of misinformation, or both. These developments work against the entrepreneurial spirit and create a dependent class of people who live "in anticipation of future inheritances."

At the end of the day, Gates and Collins help underscore the primary points of this chapter. Freedom and the ability to be compensated for our efforts at current levels are the products of the state. If the state can create the conditions under which great personal wealth can be created and distributed, it also has a legitimate and moral right to ask those who benefit to help sustain it. Problems emerge when "the state" embarks on activities that undermine societal wealth, like featherbedding and protecting the interests of those who don't earn their riches. I address this topic in the next chapter.

Notes

1. Daniel Yergin, *The Prize: The Epic Quest for Oil, Money, and Power* (New York: Free Press, 1992), 47.

2. Yergin, *The Prize*, 250, 251.

3. Yergin, *The Prize* 250, 251.

4. Yergin, *The Prize* 254.

5. Yergin, *The Prize* 257.

6. Yergin, *The Prize* 258.

7. Robert Gilpin, *The Political Economy of International Relations* (Princeton, NJ: Princeton University Press, 1987), 16.

8. Paul Starr, *Freedom's Power: The True Force of Liberalism* (New York: Basic, 2007), 15.

9. Robert Heilbroner, *The Worldly Philosophers: The Lives, Times and Ideas of the Great Economic Thinkers* (New York: Touchstone, 1986), 23.

10. Larry Kahaner, *AK-47: The Weapon That Changed the World* (New York: Wiley & Sons, 2006); Jared Diamond, *Guns, Germs, and Steel: The Fates of Human Societies* (New York: Norton, 1999). Blog Commentary.

11. Antony Jay, *The Oxford Dictionary of Political Quotations* (New York: Oxford University Press, 2001), 229.

12. Jay, *The Oxford,* 473.

13. Glenn Blackburn, *Western Civilization: A Concise History—From Early Societies to the Present,* combined volume (New York: St. Martin's Press, 1991).

14. These groups of people (mostly men) were known by their Latin name, *universitas,* Blackburn, *Western,* 188.

15. Blackburn, *Western,* 189.

16. Blackburn, *Western,* 189, 191. Blog Commentary.

17. Starr, *Freedom's,* 62.

18. Andrew Wheatcroft, *The Habsburgs: The Embodying Empire* (London, UK: The Folio Society, 2004), 124.

19. Wheatcroft, *The Habsburgs,* 129–130.

20. Albert O. Hirschman, *The Passions and the Interests: Political Arguments for Capitalism before Its Triumph* (Princeton, NJ: Princeton University Press, 1977), 34.

21. Hirschman, *The Passions,* 10, 34.

22. Hirschman, *The Passions,* 9.

23. Hilaire Belloc, *Richelieu* (Norfolk, VA: Gates of Vienna Books, 2006), 72.

24. Hirschman, *The Passions,* 10.

25. Albert M. Craig et. al., *The Heritage of World Civilizations,* 3rd edition (New York: Macmillan, 1994, 501–502). Blog Commentary.

26. Much of this section is drawn from Robert H. Bates, *Prosperity and Violence: The Political Economy of Development* (New York: Norton, 2001), 77–83.

27. Mark A., Kishlansky, Patrick Geary, and Patricia O'Brien, *Civilization in the West: Since 1555,* Vol. II, 4th edition, (New York: Addison-Wesley-Longman), 548.

28. Kishlansky, *Civilization,* 544.

29. Blog Commentary.

30. For a historical review of sovereigns reneging on their debts see Benjamin J. Cohen, *In Whose Interests: International Banking and American Foreign Policy* (New Haven: Yale University Press, 1986), 83–118.

31. Bates, *Prosperity,* 83.

32. Jay, *The Oxford,* 337.

33. Jay, *The Oxford,* 337.

34. Kishlansky, *Civilization,* 234.

35. Fernand Braudel, *The Structures of Everyday Life: Civilization and Capitalism, 15th—18th Century,* Vol. I (New York: Harper & Row Publishers, 1979).

36. Starr, *Freedom's,* 21.

37. Starr, *Freedom's*, 21.

38. Starr, *Freedom's*, 21.

39. Starr, *Freedom's*, 22.

40. Starr, *Freedom's*, 23.

41. Starr, *Freedom's*, 18.

42. David M. Primo and William S. Green, "Bankruptcy Law, Entrepreneurship, and Economic Performance," working paper, University of Rochester and University of Miami, 2008. Blog Commentary.

43. Starr, *Freedom's*, 53.

44. Starr, *Freedom's*, 53.

45. Starr, *Freedom's*, 53–54.

46. Unless otherwise noted, the following is drawn from Mark A. Martinez, review of *Wealth and Our Commonwealth: Why America Should Tax Accumulated Fortunes* by William H. Gates Sr. and Chuck Collins, *Kern Economic Journal*, 9, no. 1 (First Quarter 2007): 19–20.

47. Kevin Phillips, *Wealth and Democracy in America: A Political History of the American Rich* (New York: Random House, 2002), 26.

48. Charles R. Morris, *The Trillion Dollar Meltdown: Easy Money, High Rollers, and the Great Credit Crash* (New York: Public Affairs, 2008), 147.

49. Smith, *The Wealth*, 476.

CHAPTER 4

MANIAS AND THE PHILOSOPHER'S STONE: THE ROAD TO WEALTH AND REGULATED MONEY

In Free to Choose: A Personal Statement, *Milton Friedman took care to review the causes of the Great Depression. With characteristic bravado he declared that "the independent Federal Reserve System was to blame for the mistaken monetary policy that converted a recession into a catastrophic depression." He also claimed, "We now know that the depression was not produced by a failure of private enterprise, but rather by a failure of government." Speaking of failures, Friedman failed to say anything about the well-documented market schemes, market myopia, speculative euphoria, and structural weaknesses in the overall economy at the time. Friedman's greatest failure, however, was to suggest falsely—with his "We now know . . ." claim—that there's scholarly consensus on the causes of the Great Depression. Nothing could be further from the truth.*

Nobel Laureate Paul Samuelson, for example, argues there could be "dozens" of explanations for "cycle theories" that explain business slumps and economic depression. Looking at the claim that the Federal Reserve encouraged speculation early on, John Kenneth Galbraith dismisses the argument as "formidable nonsense."[1] Another Nobel Laureate, Kenneth Arrow, questioned Friedman's focus on monetary policy, warning, "The sole emphasis on incompetent monetary policy as the cause of the Great Depression is disputed by serious scholars." He adds that "really bad turns in monetary policy did not come until the end of 1930" when the recession was already "severe." Friedman also ignores the fact that, before the creation of the Federal Reserve System, capitalist history is rife with market failures on a grand scale, suggesting that "instability" is "endemic in the free enterprise system." Indeed, standard history texts about the American economy point to easy lending by industry (margin purchases, easy credit, shady loans, etc.), structural weaknesses in the banking industry, and slowdowns in the agriculture and housing markets, among other issues. In sum, the causes behind the Great Depression are clearly far from determined, and the manias that lead to destructive herd mentalities in markets may be more common than we want to believe.[2] More important, history tells us that Milton Friedman was prone to making broad statements that aren't supported by the facts.

In *A Short History of Financial Euphoria,* John Kenneth Galbraith discusses the famous case of "Tulipomania" in Amsterdam at the beginning of the seventeenth century. What started as simple prestige for those who possessed novel tulip bulbs turned into wild speculation over successive price increases throughout 1636. Specifically, competition over tulips turned into mania, with single bulbs being traded for new carriages and homes or fetching as much as $25,000 to $50,000 each. Demand reached such heights that the Amsterdam Stock Exchange developed a futures market for the bulb. This market, as well as the dreams of many speculators, collapsed under the weight of its own nonsense and spectacular avarice. As sellers demanded that their tulip contracts be enforced, they were disappointed when their petitions fell on the deaf ears of the courts. Because the market had little to do with the production of actual goods and services, the courts viewed Tulipomania as little more than a gambling operation. As is the case throughout these histories, panic, default, and bankruptcy followed. Galbraith wrote that "no one knows for what reason" the speculation and mania ended.[3] However, there's little doubt that common sense finally prevailed in a market that had spun out of control by deluded buyers and sellers.

Fast forward almost 340 years and we find the creation of another futures market, but this time in US dollars. In *The Vandal's Crown: How Rebel Currency Traders Overthrew the World's Central Banks,* Gregory J. Millman tells the story of how a glut of US dollars (Chapters 10–11) helped turn the world's anchor currency into just another commodity, like corn or beef. Driven by the need to pay for the defense of the West while attempting to solve social problems at home, by the mid-1960s the US government had put too many dollars into circulation. Because too much of anything drives down its value, traders knew that the future price of the dollar would both fluctuate and drop, especially with persistent US budget deficits and growing debt. Like all good entrepreneurs, traders wanted to profit from these dynamics but needed to go beyond what traders in the Euro-currency markets were doing (trading currencies to cover commercial transactions). They wanted to trade dollar futures. By 1970 they were looking to trade and speculate on the dollar, like Chicago Mercantile dealers who bought and sold pork bellies and cattle.[4] To do this they needed to convince the Nixon administration that speculating on the value of the dollar was a good thing. They would say nothing about what made trading on the dollar so profitable: the underlying irresponsibility of bloated budgets, growing debt, and price fixing.

For $5,000 (paid by traders) Milton Friedman was goaded into writing a paper that argued that a futures market was a good idea.[5] Friedman ignored the underlying irresponsibility of bloated budgets and growing debt. Friedman's paper was sent to Nixon's treasury secretary, George Schultz, who bought into the idea, stating, "If it's good enough for Milton [Friedman], it's good enough for me."[6] The result was an explosion in currency trading and other "innovative" financial instruments, the value of which far outpaces the value of goods and services produced around the world. Today, an entire industry of traders, analysts, and lawyers make their living from what Peter F. Drucker called a "symbolic economy" (discussed in Chapter 10).[7] What has been ignored is how little the average person understands this part of the economy and how bloated budgets and growing debt feed it. Also left unaddressed—if not conveniently ignored—is how continued deficit spending and bloated budgets virtually ensure the precipitous decline of the dollar. These dynamics fly in the face of what Adam Smith had to say about the importance of knowledge, transparency, and information in capitalist markets.

Given these two cases (and there are more), do we simply trust market players to do what's right and not succumb to speculation, greed, and the herd mentality that overtook Holland's tulip traders? This is an honest question, because, if history and current events have taught us anything, it is this: the further a generation gets from the great financial disasters of the past, the more their confidence grows in the brilliant and innovative discoveries they've made in the markets of their day. Past experiences and skeptics are "dismissed as the primitive refuge of those who do not have the insight to appreciate" what the new wunderkinds have fashioned.[8]

John Locke and Nicholas Copernicus are among the insightful few who understood these dynamics. They worried about deliberate currency debasement and speculators and about the impact that both had on reward for an honest day's work. Their concern and shock over what transpired in their day—at the hand of rulers, experts, and charlatans alike—led both to advocate for responsible government intervention in monetary matters. Unfortunately for both, when they wrote about the need to keep an eye on financial speculation and fraud, sensible bureaucracies and accountability were not yet part of society's social contract. For Locke the stakes were so high—and the dangers of currency fraud and abuse so great—that he believed stable money was as important a "natural right" as any other of the natural rights that he called for in the social contract. He believed that, without this kind of protection, the economic interests of commoners and small merchants alike would be trampled on. Quality of life and political freedoms would suffer as a result.

This line of thinking has contributed significantly to modern state efforts to protect the integrity of money. This chapter reviews the roots of these concerns by looking at the history of money and by examining the monetary concerns and observations of John Locke and Nicholas Copernicus. The chapter ends with a brief review of what happens when statesmen and speculators alike get drawn into what seems to be a never-ending search for the Philosopher's Stone and the idea that you can—in the words of the music group Dire Straits—"get your money for nothin'."

A Brief History of Barter, Money, and Temple Banks

Money has a long but little understood history. Most people seek it for the everyday purchases and transactions that it allows. Many seek it for the wealth that it creates when accumulated. Others covet it for the status that comes with accumulated wealth. Wealth and status, in turn, are important because of what they can compel others to do, which is the essence of power. Scholars have documented the historical relationship between money and wealth, showing in the process how these two entities can take many forms—land, stones, slaves, precious metals—and be obtained in many ways—war, mining, commerce—with some of these ways—forgeries, fraud, excess printing or minting—being quite damaging to the integrity of monetary systems. What's important here is how money has evolved from a tool that was used initially to facilitate simple transactions into a political instrument that is now used to manipulate markets and to wield power.

Banking and money as we understand the terms today became popular in the region where the Tigris River meets the Euphrates River. This isn't surprising, given how sophisticated markets evolved in the cradle of civilization more than 3,000 years ago. Although societies around the world have used many items as currency—sea shells, fur, beads, and even tobacco—as far back as 2,500 BC societies from the Fertile Crescent to Egypt began producing metal tokens and rings for use as money. This pattern was followed by the Lydians (conquerors of Asia Minor): around 700 BC they began minting coins, which were stamped with figures and facial profiles. In all cases, but especially with the Lydians, trade and coins were used not only to facilitate regional commerce but to expand a vast trading empire. Robert Sobel writes,

> It is very clear that the city-state's great wealth came from trade. It has been estimated that the farmers of Ebla harvested

enough grain to feed 70 times their own population. Add to this the surpluses created in the textile and metal industries and the centrality of trade to Ebla's economy becomes unarguable.[9]

The relationship between economic production and political influence and the role of money becomes clear here. Used in the markets and temples of Sumer, money initially involved the simple exchange of coins for goods. Over time, coins used in exchange for goods were deposited, tracked, and recorded on clay and stone tablets (or, in Egypt, on paper). This enabled money to be used first as a medium of exchange, later as means of storing value, and then as an accounting unit (for record keeping). Money facilitated the expansion of trade because it helped overcome the obstacles of barter. Consider some of the problems associated with barter and how money resolves these challenges.

Imagine that you live in the Fertile Crescent 3,000 years ago and subsist on fish. You grow weary of eating fish every day, but you know bakers and winemakers who like fish. One day you decide to trade fish for bread and wine. However, the winemaker suddenly develops a taste for lamb and the baker moves his bakery next to a lake and, between baking loaves, fishes. Barter becomes problematic because, although you want bread or wine, the producers of bread and wine don't need your fish. You could engage in a series of trades to get something that the baker or winemaker might want for their goods. But it could take days to find a shoemaker, for example, to make the footwear that the baker wants. It could take even longer to locate the services of a shaman whom the winemaker seeks. Apart from this being time–consuming, there remains the possibility that you might not consummate the trade or that the fish you carry might rot. Barter is not very efficient.

The ancients found the solution to this dilemma: use an instrument of exchange that merchants agree carries value across regions. Gold is a good example. This is the genesis of money. Returning to our example, let's say you promise to bring fish to the shoemaker who has no shoes to provide. The shoemaker is hungry, so he provides you with a gold nugget that the fisherman can use to exchange for bread, wine, or other goods. Or, better yet, he scribbles a note promising either gold or a pair of shoes—thus you have the beginning of paper money. Recognized as a promise to present a product (i.e., shoes) or a receipt for gold, the shoemaker's note is acknowledged by the community as a "contract" with value. It becomes an acceptable unit of exchange and a form of money.[10]

In other words, coins or a shoemaker's scribbled contract becomes a money instrument that says you are now entitled to acquire a resource. This contract grants you exchange power in a larger network that goes beyond fish. In this manner a promissory note for a pair of shoes, or a coin whose value is recognized as equal to a pair of shoes, might be traded numerous times between fisherman, baker, winemaker, shepherd, and others before it's finally exchanged for shoes. At the most basic level money is important to an economy because facilitating one-on-one trade enables other transactions to be made, which helps markets broaden and flourish.

Temple Banks

Also contributing to the expansion of trade and the role of money was the power of community and religious temples. Faced with the prospect of being relieved of their goods by thieves and vermin, merchants and producers often looked to temples as warehouses. In addition to being protected by God, most community temples had large, secure doors and were often exempt from taxes. The practice of leaving goods in a temple (for a fee) was not considered unusual. Communities often used temples—or officially sanctioned their use—to house goods harvested from local estates and other local assets, such as mines. Over time temples began operating as a clearing house for payments and settling contracts between merchants and traders, which helped establish many services that resemble those provided by modern banks today. Because early temples didn't often deal with currencies, it is well understood that banking—through the exchange of goods—actually predated money.

Only later, when it came time to pay, did temple authorities begin writing notes authorizing the bearer to take possession of goods that belonged to a temple patron. Merchants who were quick on their feet saw profits that could be made by keeping their goods and providing credit to other merchants. They began striking out on their own. These "merchant bankers" still might trade in commodities, but they found it more profitable to grant credit at a price.[11] As their profits grew, many merchants later branched out and provided loans. In this manner, the rise of temple banks and merchant banking facilitated the creation of money and paved the way for the emergence of modern banks that made loans to individuals and governments alike.[12]

As in the case of all good things, society's increasing dependence on money to facilitate trade—and even to advance its civilization[13]—led many to try to acquire it without actually earning it. Early on, the talent to debase currency by "clipping" the edges of coins or forging notes wasn't very difficult for those with a steady hand. With debasement and forgery many believed that, with enough imagination and patience, money and wealth could be easily secured. The allure of "easy money" was a temptation as great as Eden's apple and it led to more and more creative ways to debase currencies or create forged contracts. Even the mighty Romans couldn't escape the temptation. They authorized the silver-washing of bronze or copper coins, which provided the thinnest of coatings.[14] Over time the ability of merchants and temples to maintain the integrity of money was undermined. This became one of John Locke's great concerns and led him to argue that stable money should be a natural right of humanity.

Prelude to John Locke's Market Views: Understanding the Integrity of Money

To appreciate the importance of Locke's views on stable money, we need to understand the mechanics behind a weakened currency. The best way to do this is to reacquaint ourselves with the logic behind the example of the prisoner of war (POW) camp that is used in many introductory economic courses. Assume that we have a group of POWs who, while locked up, have been stripped of their valuables. In the camp each POW receives regular supplies of chocolate bars, paper, pencils, cigarettes, and other goods from his or her captor every two weeks. Over time the POWs establish a simple monetary system in which cigarettes are used as the common currency, with "dollars" (a pack of cigarettes) and "coins" (individual cigarettes). The system becomes self-regulating and functions well, even when debased currency, in the form of rerolled or trimmed cigarettes, enters the system.

Although rerolled or trimmed cigarettes represent debased currency and are worth less than untouched cigarettes, they often fetch the same amount of goods because POWs know that most smoking prisoners just want a nicotine fix. As long as debasement doesn't get out of hand, history tells us that devalued currencies are accepted at par value. The trading and currency system, however, is prone to break down if everyone starts trimming or when everyone mistakenly receives twenty-five cartons instead of one carton for his or her biweekly ration. The introduction of twenty-four additional cigarette cartons every two weeks quickly undermines the monetary system because, instead of requiring three to five cigarettes for a chocolate bar, POWs now demand, say, two full cartons of cigarettes. In this case the integrity of money is undermined by the "inflationary" pressures caused by introducing too many cartons into the financial system.

What's important to understand is that, on a very general level, debasement can occur when the quality of money is reduced or when the quantity of money is expanded. When this occurs, currencies lose value over time or are devalued. Bankers, traders, and merchants become alarmed and begin dumping or quit using the weakened currency. Drawing from our POW example, the process works like this in the real world today. Rather than accidentally oversupplying cigarettes, individuals or sovereign states might deliberately compromise the integrity of money. As previously noted, the ways to debase a currency include forgeries and the clipping of gold and silver coins. State-sanctioned debasement occurs when states issue substantially more notes than what they produce or when bullion reserves have been depleted (see Chapter 10). Early on, during the days of empire, states debased currencies because the alternative was to pillage and plunder neighbors. In all cases, the integrity of money was undermined.

Perhaps the most important reason for guarding the integrity of money is that no "advanced economy can function without a system for creating credit."[15] Simply put, if your currency is tainted, others are loathe to accept it or reluctant to grant credit. Wealth creation is so dependent on the ability of states to create credit that Susan Strange called it the "lifeblood" of any developed society:

> Credit is literally the lifeblood of a developed economy. Like blood in the human anatomy, money in the predominant form of credit-money has to reach and renew every part of the economy. It has to circulate regularly and reliably. It has to stay healthy and stable or the society suffers, just as the body suffers if there is disorder in the blood or too much or too little of it.[16]

In this respect, a healthy money supply is just as important as the power to provide or deny security and as a state's ability to produce what it needs.[17] The capacity to create or secure credit establishes the power to transfer goods today on the promise of payment tomorrow. With this power come the ability to influence investment outcomes (with loans) and the power to determine the value of money (interest rates charged). Credit allows states to create and manage economic productivity and the wealth of its people. When the money supply is poorly managed, however, the prospects of each citizen are threatened, as John Locke pointed out.

John Locke's View of Money

In practical terms, there is little difference between someone who sticks his hand into your wallet and a state that excessively prints notes, clips coins, or increases its base metal content. The receiver of the notes and coins is robbed of the true value of their "money." One who understood this was John Locke. For Locke the problem was simple. Debasing a currency by shaving, or withholding more and more bullion from coins, or by excessively printing more notes than states could endorse with bullion robbed merchants and workers of their due reward. Locke was such a staunch supporter of maintaining the integrity of money that he believed debasers, clippers, and alchemists should be punished because a crime had been committed.[18] Specifically, Locke wrote:

> This is known to be so in England, and every one may not only refuse any Money bearing the publick Stamp, if it be clip'd, or any ways rob'd of the due weight of its Silver; but he that offers it in payment is liable to Indictment, Fine and Imprisonment.[19]

Encouraged to write to England's Parliament by contemporaries, who believed authorities didn't understand the financial impact of debasement, Locke obliged them. As a way to drive home his point about the dangers of debasement, Locke wrote:

> Suppose then you had lent me last Year 300, or fifteen-score Cacao Nuts, to be repaid this Year: Wou'd you be satisfied and think your self paid your due, if I shou'd tell you, Cacao Nuts were scarce this Year, and that four-score were of as much value this year as an hundred the last; and that therefore you were well and fully paid if I restored to you only 240 for the 300 I borrow'd?[20]

But the impact of debasement went beyond robbing domestic merchants and consumers. Locke was also concerned about the effects of sullied currencies on international trade:

> Clipping by Foreigners is robbing England it self. And thus the Spaniards lately rob'd Portugal of a great part of its Treasure or Commodities (which is the same thing) by importing upon them clip'd Money of the Portugal stamp.[21]

Locke was so concerned about the impact on England of the transfer of debased currencies that he wrote, "Clipping is the great Leak, which for some time past has contributed more to Sink us, than all the Forces of our Enemies could do," adding that "[m]oney is necessary to the carrying on of Trade. For where Money fails, Men cannot buy, and Trade stops."[22]

John Locke's observations are significant for two reasons. First, they underscore the notion that the initial purpose of money was simple: to consummate transactions and facilitate commerce. As a result, anything done to alter the role and value of money must be suspect, according to

Locke. Second, and perhaps more important, because of the dangers posed by debased currencies, Locke helps us understand how money should be part of the larger "social contract" that he discussed with reference to politics.

Specifically, Locke believed that, if a sovereign's position on the content and value of money shifted on a regular basis, that sovereign could not be trusted to protect the value of goods, the sanctity of contracts, or the wages of labor. In this manner, Locke makes it clear that, if societies can demand a new social contract for political mismanagement and ineptitude, they can also demand a new social contract for economic mismanagement and ineptitude. Locke understood that societies that were increasingly consumed by money matters and commerce—as was the case with Britain's growing mercantile empire—had to protect the integrity of money if their economies were to prosper. At a time when the divine right to rule was already in question, Locke makes it clear that "natural rights" also included economic justice, which meant guarding the integrity of money.

According to John Locke, if agreements and contracts denominated in money were to have any meaning for commoners "from year to year" money "should have some stability, some enduring value" that remains consistent and dependable over time.[23] But his position was not the commoner's right at the time, which meant Locke's view was largely unprecedented. To be sure, arguments for stable money had been articulated almost 300 years earlier by Nicholas Copernicus (and others). However, Copernicus was mostly concerned with business affairs and not with larger personal freedoms, which John Locke advocated when he discussed the "rights of man."

In spite of these observations, which established the need for the professional management of money and credit, the demands of war placed great pressures on states to debase money and find new sources of financial support. These pressure convinced heads of state to fund adventurers, several of whom promised to bring back the riches of El Dorado (or to find the Fountain of Youth). These dynamics also convinced normally intelligent men of reason that the Philosopher's Stone was real and a worthwhile pursuit. Although the search for El Dorado led to temporary riches for the Spaniards in Latin America, the search for the Philosopher's Stone made paupers and fools out of others.

The Search for the Philosopher's Stone

Over time the search for "easy money" has come to resemble the ancient search for the Philosopher's Stone. The Philosopher's Stone was a mysterious and unknown substance: alchemists in the premodern period believed that it had the power to turn base metals, or other materials, into gold. Even Sir Isaac Newton is said to have (secretly) dabbled in alchemy in search of the Philosopher's Stone. Sovereigns and alchemists alike believed that, if the Philosophers' Stone could be found or if the right chemical reactions could be produced, their worries about money and finances would be solved. Just like debasement, securing the Philosopher's Stone was viewed as a quick financial fix.

The stories told about the power of the Philosopher's Stone range from the grand fairy tales of Rumplestiltskin (who turned straw into gold) to real-world tales of monarchs who were easily duped by con men and the promise of easy money. In 1716, for example, the desperate king of France tapped Scotsman John Law to be the nation's financial alchemist. Although Law's credentials included escaping from prison for shooting the lover of a British Royal, what caught the king's attention was Law's bragging assertion that he knew the secret behind the Philosopher's Stone. Law said that he could make gold out of paper, and he was right, to a degree. Law proposed little more than turning on the printing presses. Specifically, the regent of France was desperate for funds and bought into Law's plan. He even allowed John Law to put up a bank. Law's bank promised to redeem notes for the value of coins on the day that the notes were issued. In a country where the French kings regularly debased coin, Law's bank inspired confidence and convinced the king to make it the Royal Bank of France in 1716. After bilking thousands from their money on a Mississippi investment scam and issuing legal tender notes beyond the amount of coin that his bank had on stock, Law and his bank went broke. Law's efforts led to financial chaos in France and turned the French off paper money for generations.[24]

But we should not be so quick to condemn the king of France or to judge John Law. It's not entirely clear that printing more notes is immediately bad for an economy. In modern times the United States has experienced phenomenal growth while regularly printing more notes than its economic activity (or its gold supply) suggests is prudent. Other states have enjoyed economic expansion after they debased their currency to promote economic growth. As Robert Gilpin reminds us, "The fundamental fact remains that public consumption in mature empires shows a distinct tendency to rise sharply . . . One of the remarkably common features of empires at the later stage of their development is the growing amount of wealth pumped by the State from the economy . . . In the later Roman Empire, in the late Byzantine Empire, in seventeenth-century Spain, inflation was rampant. Debasing the currency is just another form of taxation."[25] Even Alexander Hamilton chimed in on the matter, asserting that banks should print more money than they could back with assets on reserve.

Part of the reason for accepting a degree of debasement through excess note printing is best explained through the *quantity theory of money*. Although the specifics behind this theory may not be of interest, the mechanics become clear through a return to the writings of stargazer Nicholas Copernicus (1473–1543). Forced to suffer through successive debasements, Copernicus grew concerned over the numerous types of currencies circulating in Poland. He particularly despised debasement for the havoc that it brought into his business dealings. After losing a small fortune to debasement, he turned his great mind to the issue of money. Rather than make shaving or "washing" the cornerstone of all that is evil in his financial world—as John Locke believed was the case—in the *Treatise on Debasement* (1526) Copernicus argued that expanding the *number of coins* in circulation was the real culprit behind stolen wealth. Glyn Davies writes:

> In his treatise, though strongly condemning debasement, he nevertheless argued that it was the total amount of currency, as indicated by the total number of coins in circulation rather than the total weight of metal they contained that really determined the level of prices and the buying power of the currency. [Copernicus] grasped the essential fact that, for the great majority of everyday, internal transactions, coins had already become simply tokens of value.[26]

For Copernicus, quantity rather than quality determined the value of money. This led Copernicus to an observation that preceded John Locke's writings on the topic by almost three hundred years. Copernicus wrote that, in order to avoid instability in both prices and currency exchanges, it was the duty of princes to limit the amount of money in circulation.[27] So, even though Copernicus was concerned about the quantity of money, John Locke was critical of what happened to the integrity of money when currencies were debased. By agreeing that the state should step in to regulate money, both Locke and Copernicus set the stage for what we recognize in the contemporary era as *monetary policy*. But, perhaps more important, both men were adamant about guarding the integrity of money through state policies that were designed to punish those tempted by the prospect of getting "money for nothing."

Still, to put the nonsense of the Philosopher's Stone (and its variant myths) to rest—and to avoid some of the pitfalls that came from debasement—over more than two hundred years societies have sought to educate themselves about money and finance. Through this learning process nation-states have created professional institutions and bureaucracies to monitor the creation and distribution of money. From departments of accounting and economics in universities, to central banks and treasury departments in modern governments, nation-states have worked hard to establish a set of professional institutions that have relegated Rumplestiltskin-like stories to the bedtime books of our children. Removing the allure of the alchemists' promise, however, has proven to be much more difficult.

Proving P. T. Barnum right, stories of investors taken in by frauds who claimed that they had the power to turn base substances into gold are still reported from time to time. The prospect of easy money is a difficult aspiration to break. It's so difficult that modern developed states continue to embrace easy money—by borrowing and printing currencies, which offer expedient solutions to pressing financial problems.[28] But states have also courted restraint, to a degree, by tasking central banks and treasury departments with the objective of monitoring the creation and supply of money. Still, lack of fiscal discipline and the making of war have made printing money a regular feature of modern states. This, in turn, makes debasement and inflation—like death and taxes—realities of the modern world.

Conclusion

For reasons of control, as much as *reason of state,* modern "kingdoms" have slowly come to understand that managing and regulating money and finance are necessary functions of the state. As we have seen, because of political and military considerations, the story of money and credit involves more than facilitating commercial transactions. In spite of the best efforts of modern states to moderate the flow of money and credit, war and free-spending habits suggest that we really haven't advanced much beyond the logic that set people on a search for the Philosopher's Stone. The dynamics behind our Philosopher's Stone may be more sophisticated—central banks, the number and types of credit institutions, megabyte money,[29] the "financial" or "symbolic" economy,[30] and so on— but modern states clearly have not learned any lessons from the vain pursuit of the Philosopher's Stone.

To be sure, rulers of modern states understand the importance of creating money to secure resources and to pursue state goals. This helps explain the very deliberate efforts in the past to manipulate or debase currencies. Debasing currency has enabled both history's tyrants and modern states to fortify their militaries and attack enemies. In this way, money is a useful tool of statecraft and geostrategy. The temptation to debase currency is always present when the *raison d'état* looms large. But facilitating transactions and buying security are only part of money's story in society.

Improperly managed money systems can wreck havoc on societies by undermining the value of a day's work, diminishing the value of a contract, or creating conditions that encourage speculation on debased currencies. Inflation—such as occurred in post-Versailles Germany—is a financial plague for the ages, because it prohibits merchants and laborers alike from reaping the full value of their efforts. Most of us understand intuitively how these dynamics work and see them played out when lottery winners choose to take their winnings all at once instead of having them paid out over time. Without ever having taken a class in economics, people understand that money loses value over time.

This is important because it tells us that money has been transformed—from a simple receipt for goods, to a convenient economic unit used for trade, to an instrument of political and economic development, which means state power. The relationship between money and state power, however, isn't an intuitive undertaking and isn't always accepted (see Chapter 10).[31] Because of its transformation states have come to recognize the necessity of managing and regulating both money and its commercial spin-off, credit. And, although state interference in money flies in the face of what industry and market analysts might want, to do less in times of stress would create an environment for the integrity of money (and credit) to be compromised. This, as we shall see, is a lesson that rulers and states often forget or purposely ignore.

Notes

1. Glyn Davies, *History of Money: From Ancient Times to the Present Day* (Cardiff, UK: University of Wales Press, 2002), 510.

2. The quotes from the first paragraph are from Milton and Rose Friedman, *Free to Choose: A Personal Statement* (New York: Harcourt, Brace, Jovanovich, 1990), 91, 71. The quotes from Paul Samuelson and Kenneth Arrow in the second paragraph are drawn from Elton Rayack, *Not So Free to Choose: The Political Economy of Milton Friedman and Ronald Reagan* (New York: Praeger, 1987), 117–118. The last quotes in the second paragraph are from Gary M. Walton and Ross M. Robertson, *History of the American Economy,* 5th edition (New York: Harcourt Brace Jovanovich, 1983), 510–520.

3. John Kenneth Galbraith, *A Short History of Financial Euphoria* (New York: Viking, 1993), 26–34.

4. Gregory J. Millman, *The Vandals' Crown: How Rebel Currency Traders Overthrew the World's Central Banks* (New York: Free Press, 1995), 101–109. Blog Commentary.

5. Millman, *The Vandals',* 108–110.

6. Millman, *The Vandals'*, 110.

7. Peter F. Drucker, "The Changed World Economy," *Foreign Affairs*, 64, no. 4 (Spring 1986): 768–791.

8. Galbraith, *A Short History*, 13.

9. Robert Sobel, *The Pursuit of Wealth: The Incredible Story of Money Throughout the Ages of Wealth* (New York: McGraw-Hill, 2000), 6. Blog Commentary.

10. Blog Commentary.

11. Joseph Wechsberg, *The Merchant Bankers* (Boston: Little, Brown and Company, 1966), 11.

12. Sobel, *The Pursuit*, 8.

13. Davies, *History*, 25–26.

14. Davies, *History*, 108, 111.

15. Susan Strange, *States and Markets*, 2nd edition (London: Pinter Publishers, 1994), 91.

16. Strange, *States*, 91.

17. Strange, *States*, 90.

18. John Locke, "Further Considerations Concerning Raising the Value of Money, Wherein Mr. Lowndes's Arguments for it in his late Report concerning An Essay for the Amendment of Silver Coins, are particularly Examined," 1824, The Avalon Project at Yale University, Documents in Law, History and Diplomacy, Yale University, available online, 8.

19. Locke, "Further." Whether driven by Locke's concerns or not, a "fine and imprisonment" appears to have been replaced by harsher sentences when more than three hundred people were hanged for counterfeiting Bank of England notes during the "Restriction Period" (1797–1921). The Bank of England, "About Money: Timeline (3)," available online.

20. Locke, "Further," 23.

21. Locke, "Further," 10.

22. Locke, "Further," 46, 11.

23. Millman, *The Vandals' Crown*, 38.

24. Millman, *The Vandals'*, 29–39; Galbraith, *A Short History*, 34–42.

25. Robert Gilpin, *War and Change in World Politics* (Cambridge, MA: Cambridge University Press, 1987), 164–165.

26. Davies, *History*, 231.

27. Davies, *History*, 231.

28. Ha-Joon Chang offers an interesting contrast on the financial solutions practiced between the developed and underdeveloped states: Ha-Joon Chang, *Bad Samaritans: The Myth of Free Trade and the Secret History of Capitalism* (New York: Bloomsbury Press, 2008), 152–154.

29. Joel Kurtzman, *The Death of Money: How the Electronic Economy Has Destabilized the World's Markets and Created Financial Chaos* (New York: Back Bay, 1993).

30. Drucker, "The Changed."

31. Joseph Nye Jr., *Soft Power: The Means to Success in World Politics* (New York: Public Affairs, 2004), 4–5. Blog Commentary.

PART III

MAKING MARKETS WORK IN PRACTICE: THE STATE IN ACTION

CHAPTER 5

WAR MADE THE STATE AND THE STATE MADE WAR

In Sleeping with the Devil: How Washington Sold Our Soul for Saudi Crude, *former CIA operative Robert Baer tells the story of returning from Langley, Virginia. Coming from the direction of the Potomac River was a convoy led by a Chevy Suburban with flashing lights. He suspected it was the President because "he's the only official in Washington who gets that kind of protection." When the convoy turned into an estate, he recognized the enormous iron gates. The next day he learned that the convoy was escorting Prince Bandar, the Saudi Ambassador to the United States— who "alone of all ambassadors got official State Department protection."[1] And why not? Granted the title "Bandar Bush" for his long and cozy relationship with the Bush family, Prince Bandar is dean of the Washington diplomatic corps—its brightest star, with a constellation of resources and political contacts that give him both access and power. But perhaps his greatest trump card is how he uses money and oil to move US-Saudi relations.*

After the oil price hikes of 1973 the United States convinced the Saudis to use their "petrodollars" to help underwrite US budget deficits. Later, a combination of geopolitics and personal greed helped turn a simple funder-borrower relationship into a hydro-headed monster that thrives on national security imbalances and narrow self-interest. Baer writes that things have gotten so cozy between Riyadh and former high-level Washington officials that granting Prince Bandar the same protection afforded the President is only a small part of a larger story.[2] For those fortunate enough to brush shoulders with Prince Bandar and his circle of friends, Saudi Arabia has become "Washington's 401(k) Plan."[3] Former cabinet secretaries, taking advantage of the Saudi Cash Cow, now work with the "good" bin Ladens while the US government works to keep the Saudi regime safe and its oil flowing. The financial cooperation that the

United States received from the Saudis after Saddam Hussein invaded Kuwait at the border is illustrative.

Success in the first Gulf War, in Washington's eyes, guaranteed that a grateful and friendly "House of Sa'ud would remain the world's banker of oil."[4] Perhaps more important, by keeping the Saudis in business, the sources that help fund the American Kingdom would continue.[5] Interestingly, there apparently are historical parallels to this relationship. In many ways the US-Saudi relationship follows a pattern similar to that in the protection racket that existed between prosperous merchants in medieval Europe and their royal protectors. And, just like their aristocratic predecessors, when they're not busy tending to their economic interests or bestowing politically powerful "titles" on their friends, American elites have become consumed with war.[6] Worse, as was the case during the medieval period, when Europe's monarchs tried to keep rogue states and marauding nobles at bay, America's aristocrats have been slow to recognize that the American Kingdom no longer controls its own fate and increasingly depends on the Good Will of others[7]—a point that the well-protected "Bandar Bush" seems to understand quite well.

After the collapse of Rome the Eurasian continent was divided along geographic, linguistic, and cultural lines. Once tied together by Roman conquest, infrastructure, and diplomacy, Europe devolved into a hodgepodge of unconnected regions. While Chinese and Middle Eastern societies made steady advances in the sciences and math, Europe was separated by suspicion, political intrigue, and assorted European claims to Holy Roman Empire status. But the empires claimed were empty shadows compared to Rome at its height. Apart from the challenge of claiming and then maintaining a shadow empire, the efforts of various pretenders to the throne were undermined by other realities. Their empires were really little more than geographic spaces run by ambitious and competing families, which were dominated by strong personalities. The Merovingians during the fifth century and Charlemagne in the late eighth century are classic examples. Making matters more difficult was that, apart from the Catholic Church, coherent and cohesive institutions on the Eurasian continent were largely absent.[8] Simply put, Rome's "successor kingdoms in the west did not learn how priceless" the state institutions that they had destroyed really were, and they were equally ignorant about recognizing how difficult it would be to replace them.[9]

Through the Dark Ages (476–1000 AD) and the High Middle Ages (1000–1300 AD), from the Steppe mountain regions to the Pyrénées of Europe, the Eurasian continent was dominated largely by barbarian clans and feuding nobles. And, although western Europe may not have been, as John Keegan suggested, "a continent without armies," it was probably more realistic to say that Europe was largely a continent without institutions, which are necessary for collecting taxes and building large professional armies. Filling this vacuum were warriors who were "antipathetic to discipline" and committed to "preserving in their hearts a rough Teutonic belief in the freedom of arms bearing warriors."[10] Because competition for land and honor was fierce, simple and petty disputes became prolonged, wide-ranging conflicts. Families, clans, and towns with weak or no allegiances suffered the consequences of what must have seemed to be never-ending conflict and war. During the Dark Ages these conflicts led to regional protection rackets that grew and set the stage for political consolidation. This facilitated the conditions necessary for even larger-scale wars between regional kingdoms, which swelled in size rather quickly.[11]

Grappling with the problem of paying warriors (after a knight's feudal obligations to serve had ended by the 1300s), kings began raising private militias made up of nobles and indentured soldiers. As early as the fourteenth century France's military began operating on a semiprivate cash basis. These arrangements, however, were abandoned because nobles didn't want to serve with common *roturier*—people who were paid with land, viewed as upstarts, and treated with disdain.[12] The private militia system was replaced by professional mercenaries and commissioned officers. These "gentlemen" officers were tasked by the king with raising, equipping, and leading a predetermined number of men, for a set amount of payment. The officers contracted with mercenaries and distributed funds as they saw fit.[13] As war evolved, the arrival of new tactics and technologies—which brought pikemen, artillery, and muskets into warfare—continued to strain state resources. This helped convince Europe's monarchs to pursue administrative competence in the areas of finance and war during the High Middle Ages.

Because of these dynamics, western European states were forced to develop ever-larger political units. Smaller political units, especially those capable of producing regular income, were incorporated or swallowed up in the process. By the fifteenth century, European monarchs looked for ways to manage what had been patched together.[14] These fifteenth-century developments compel us to look at the administrative accomplishments of the Mongol's during the eleventh and twelfth centuries. By constructing a limited but organizationally resourceful empire, the Mongols—whose warriors were famous for their speed and for small supply trains—rediscovered the importance of administrative efficiency in war. And, although there's no doubt that the Mongols didn't have a bureaucracy large enough to compete with fourteenth- and fifteenth-century European bureaucracies, Genghis Kahn showed that the primary function of the state was to organize production and tribute in a way that supported both the conduct of war and the management of empire.

Because the administrative examples of the Mongol Empire weren't well known (let alone understood) at the time, there were limits to what regional warlords could claim territorially. This too helped raise costs. Without the shared experiences that a "national culture" brings, nationalism could not be tapped for war. With weapon innovations proving costlier by the decade, the key problem for monarchs was raising revenue, especially from lesser lords, who often rebelled. To pay for new weapons and to fund military campaigns, Europe's monarchs became creative domestically and more aggressive abroad. The former set the stage for representative government and mercantilism. The latter paved the way for imperialism and colonial wars. Both created the environment for market capitalism. But I'm getting ahead of myself. Let's take a look at how the Mongol Empire reintroduced administrative efficiency, which enhanced the economic well-being of modern states and empires, as well as the art of making war.

1200 AD, Genghis Khan Before the Dawn of the Modern World[15]

Because many factors can turn the narrative of history, it's difficult to point to an individual or an event and say, "This person or that incident made the difference." This is especially so when individual talent's brains are addled by place or circumstance. When he was providing his assessment of Singapore's Lee Kuan Yew, Henry Kissinger admiringly remarked, "One of the asymmetries of history is the lack of correspondence between the abilities of some leaders and the power of their countries."[16] History's account of Lew Kuan Yew's accomplishments, if Dr. Kissinger is correct, is limited by Singapore's small size. Similarly, if a leader's life story is presented in a negative light, his or her achievements are often disparaged or, worse, ignored. When we assess the popular legacy of Genghis Khan and the Mongol Empire—which consists largely of references to uncivilized barbaric practices[17]—it could be argued that one of the great asymmetries of history is the lack of correspondence between the accomplishments of Genghis Khan and the Mongols and the historical legacy that they are granted.

Largely ignored when assessing Genghis Khan's impact is that in "nearly every country touched by the him and the Mongols, the initial destruction and shock of conquest . . . yielded quickly to an unprecedented rise in cultural communication, expanded trade, and improved civilization."[18] If we follow what transpired under Genghis Khan—from the advances in military battle techniques and reforms in weapon technology, to improved communication and legal infrastructures, to new protocols as they applied to looting—we can come to only one conclusion: even if Genghis Khan was a master of intimidation and brutality on the battlefield, he was a genius planner and reformer, with a gift for administration. Although his administrative arrangements for the Mongols weren't large or sophisticated by modern standards—or by those required two hundred years after the Mongol's decline—their ability to manage an empire in post-Roman Eurasia set the bar for future empires.

At the center was Genghis Khan, who demonstrated that he was ahead of his time on many levels when he assigned men to tasks based on talent rather than genealogy. This mind-set was rooted in his disdain for privilege and hierarchy, which dominated the lives of the steppe peoples and pushed their leaders into unrelenting cycles of violent attacks and counterattacks. To disrupt these patterns, after rising to power Khan broke with previous practices and protocols, such as the practice of granting defeated aristocrats special treatment after battle. In one early example Genghis Kahn conducted a public trial after battle and called his council members together. He conducted a public execution of aristocrats who turned down his diplomatic entreaties for peace before the conflict.

The goals behind the public execution of aristocrats were threefold. First, Khan wanted to send a message to future opponents by publicly punishing those who had rebuked prebattle offers of peace. Second, he wanted to send a message to aristocrats far and wide that social standing and rank meant little to the Mongols. Finally, to reduce the administrative costs of empire, he needed to maintain stability in conquered territories. Khan's prospects of doing this were enhanced by offering regional cooperation and alliances to survivors. Acquiescence on the part of the defeated allowed Genghis Khan to establish new patterns of diplomacy, deal-making, and administration that were characterized by skillful negotiation. These practices were lessons in strategic restraint. They also saved troops in the long run and, in many respects, preceded what European nation-states did at Westphalia by four hundred years.

To encourage loyalty Genghis Khan also offered protection and a share of the spoils of war to those who laid down their arms before battle. He also moved to protect and connect trading routes, which expanded both trade and the amount of tribute that the Mongols collected. In a particular stroke of genius, Genghis Khan also encouraged the Mongols to take in the children of defeated armies, making them "adopted" brothers. He even went so far as to have his mother and his family members adopt children from defeated camps.[19] Merit tied to talent, diplomatic rewards for entering into alliances, creation of the conditions for trade to grow, and the establishment of fictive kin relations, all of these brought administrative and tactical dividends. Specifically, they helped slash costs by reducing the size of supply trains that were necessary for war and by cutting the number of men that were necessary for occupation after conquests.

None of Genghis Khan's administrative accomplishments were easily achieved. As noted previously, we often forget or never appreciate how Eurasia was made up of isolated civilizations and warring barbarian kingdoms after the collapse of Rome. The political organization of each regional kingdom was not very complex and generally consisted of the household intrigue of ruling families and clans. Competition for control of land, and over specific regions, was fierce. In Europe before 1400 AD, as noted previously, disputes and conflicts were dominated by prosperous kin groups pursuing expansion in order to secure land for growing families. This forced competing groups into seemingly endless battles, kept rivalries brewing, and helped prevent power and political authority across Europe from consolidating or concentrating in the hands of one family—as was the case with the Steppe region before the arrival of Genghis Khan.[20] To deal with these issues, when they weren't busy raiding or looting neighbors, the Mongols imposed administrative patterns that required tribute, acquiescence, and the support of the leadership from their conquered satellites.

Although the Mongol Empire eventually collapsed (for reasons not yet agreed upon), its administrative performance during its glory years reestablished the standard for the efficient management of an empire. With Europe still dominated by warring clans and "wannabe" kings in the twelfth century, it is clear Europe's regional warlords clearly understood very little about political power beyond using it to avenge perceived wrongs, or to pillage and plunder neighbors. Although it is also clear that Europe didn't take its administrative cue from Genghis Khan, history records the Mongols as the first Eurasian empire after Rome to show that they understood the importance of effective political organization in managing empire and war.

1400 AD, From Street Gangs to Organized Mafia, I: The Arrival of Structured Taxes and the Money Economy

Much like Samuel E. Finer and Charles Tilly, Herman M. Schwartz argues that the roots of modern nation-states can be traced to incessant battles between kings, nobles, and merchants from the Dark Ages (476–1000 AD) through the High Middle Ages (1000–1300 AD). As competing European clans gained control over increasingly more land, they learned that they also needed to defend it. This meant constant preparation for war. Over time the regional kings who emerged from clan warfare understood that, if they wanted to secure the resources necessary to survive, they had to centralize political authority. Even though centralizing authority allowed for greater economies of scale and made the extraction and organization of resources more fluid, something else was at work: from 1000 AD to the latter half of the twentieth century, the dominant activity of European states focused on funding and preparing for war.[21]

War convinced kings—and "wannabe" kings—that they needed to tame and organize those who lived within the geographical boundaries that they claimed. This meant domesticating feudalism's warrior class: the nobles who resided in the countryside. This was a difficult undertaking. Nobles were mavericks, with armor and horses, who possessed a propensity for violence that made them "a kind of dispersed biker gang."[22] Making things especially difficult for monarchs was the fact that, apart from fighting, nobles really did little except extract surplus production from peasant farmers as "rent." In return, the peasants received protection from the nobles and the use of their property. This protection racket created problems for kings because they also wanted to tax the peasantry in order to pay for the defense of their kingdom. What the nobles extracted often left the peasants with little remaining for the kings to squeeze from them. Making financial matters worse for the king was that many, if not most, nobles paid no taxes.

Perhaps the biggest obstacle facing European monarchs was that, even if they wanted to, they couldn't adequately tax the countryside because the rural economy was slow to develop. This was understandable. Economic patterns embraced by most nobles did little to encourage productivity and efficiency. The nobles also did not push the monetization of the economy. Fearful that a money economy would eventually be corrupted by the practice of clipping and debasement—which many monarchs had come to depend on—nobles viewed monetization as a prelude to the theft of their wealth (Chapter 4). These practices brought the nobles into conflict with monarchs who wanted to monetize their economies so that they could assign taxes, which they needed to pay for their growing armies.[23]

With the nobles and the peasantry reluctant or unable to pay taxes, monarchs increasingly looked to town merchants. Since the eleventh century, towns had grown from prosperous villages and had started using money on a regular basis again.[24] For visionary monarchs in western Europe, creating the conditions necessary for enhancing wealth accumulation in their towns became a necessity. This meant finding ways to increase trade. Monarchs worked to increase commercial activity for one simple reason: you can't confiscate or tax what doesn't exist. But this proved costly politically because monarchs were forced to grant, in exchange, increasing amounts of freedom and liberties to merchants and other groups. Just as important, to facilitate their region's commercial prospects, monarchs increasingly turned away from using personal but corrupt courtiers to organize the affairs of state and began creating professional bureaucracies to track and extract resources from their citizens.[25]

A system of taxation already existed in Europe's commercialized cities. But individual sovereigns kept poor records, which explains why fees, tribute, and other sources of income weren't sufficient for the state to prepare and pay for war. Monarchs often had to borrow money to sustain the kingdom. As battles over territory and resources continued, finance ledgers throughout most of the European continent reflected the realities of war. The inability to fund war, in turn, led to more taxes, more debt, more debasement, more defaults, and inflation. Together these dynamics encouraged the monetization of local economies and fundamentally transformed the European state system.

1400 AD, From Street Gangs to Organized Mafia, II: The Roots of the State's Bureaucracies of Violence

As war drove states to develop state budgets, create bureaucracies, monetize their economies, and impose taxes, it also led to the rise of parallel state activities that required professional courts, treasuries, regional administrations, subsystems of taxation, public assemblies, and other state-sanctioned bureaucracies.[26] At this time the "warrior-kings" of Europe's early medieval period were replaced by deskbound bureaucratic kings, who were consumed with documents from rapidly growing state agencies. Because "no state had a national budget in the understood sense of the word" to pay the emerging bureaucracies before 1400,[27] the evolution of the modern state started with individual sovereigns "farming out" the affairs of state—for a price. The selling of official offices led to what, in hindsight, is seen as corrupt routines on the part of the state. The contours of modern state bureaucracies emerged from these practices.

There remained the problem of co-opting the "biker gang" nobles who held regional influence. The monarchs achieved this through intimidation. In mafia-like fashion, monarchs presented the recalcitrant towns and renegade nobles with an offer they couldn't refuse. Charles Tilly explains:

> Over and over, rulers sent troops to enforce the collection of tribute, taxes, and levies of men and materials. But they also allowed localities to buy off the costly imposition of troops by timely payments of their obligations. In this regard, rulers resembled racketeers: at a price, they offered protection against evils that they would otherwise inflict, or at least allow to be inflicted.[28]

When force was insufficient, monarchs across Europe encouraged nobles to come around by bribing them with absolute property rights.[29] By granting and then fixing property rights, monarchs produced another condition that benefited the emerging state. As opposed to the confusion caused by collective land ownership, the state now knew who owned property and could assess taxes with greater confidence and efficiency. Efficiency meant reducing the number of times that citizens were pressed for taxes, which increasingly went over well with merchants and helped create a sense of legitimacy in the system. It also allowed sovereigns to negotiate with nobles over the funding and staffing of national armies. Negotiations were largely amicable because both sides had common fears over common enemies, both internal and external. For example, because nobles feared that kings would use the military against them, they stipulated that any national army raised and called to duty had to be staffed by them. This made it difficult for the king to turn the army against the people and, most important, against the nobles themselves. Over time these agreements were made and legitimized in "people parliaments" that increasingly created the rules detailing the extent and limits of a king's power. This was the genesis of modern democracy and constitutionalism. These parliamentary agreements also achieved something else—they legitimized and made permanent the king's ability to borrow money, raise money, and wage war (see Chapter 3).

By agreeing to help raise money and pay debts, national parliaments removed the burden of debt from individual monarchs and put it on the back of "national" treasuries. Because representative bodies increasingly spoke for the nation and professional bureaucracies were better at securing and keeping track of state resources, medieval biker mercenaries slowly disappeared. They were replaced by an organized state and a disciplined national army that maintained a monopoly over the legitimate use of force. Although war was still a burden to pay for, nationalized debt made expenditures more manageable by spreading the burden of war. Ironically, organizing the state in ways that allowed monarchs to pay for war ultimately ended the monarch's hold on power.

War Forces Consolidation:
Market Towns Join the Nation-State

Noted historian Fernand Braudel tells us that modern states emerged in the fifteenth and sixteenth centuries. As regional leaders were pressed by military demands, they determined that it was in their interest to mix their destinies with increasingly affluent towns and cities. This decision was driven by distinct but mutually supportive needs. For their part, most prosperous towns and cities had grown and mastered the art of security with fortified walls. Politically, astute town leaders figured out that negotiated terms with merchants created political stability, which contributed to economic expansion. They understood that, by granting liberties while offering concessions to merchants and traders, economic activity and taxable wealth would increase. In return for protection and law, merchants were expected to make regular tax payments. In essence merchants and traders funded protection rackets for the sake of new liberties and security.[30] But there were problems with this arrangement.

Economic expansion in many fortified towns and cities ran into natural limits. Walled cities could only grow up, not outward. This stymied economic growth. This was critical, because the size of the security apparatus depended on how much could be extracted from the economy. This problem became especially acute when advances in technology and artillery—especially gun powder—eliminated the advantages of fortified walls in the fifteenth and sixteenth centuries (although earth-filled ramparts reduced some damage). To deal with these and other military developments, changes had to be made. Among the first to adapt was France's Charles VII in 1445. He created the "first standing force of an exclusively 'national' kind, i.e., conceived as owning unique and perpetual allegiance to the nascent state via the person of its ruler(s)."[31] Known as the *Compagnies d'Ordonnance*, Charles' army was joined later by ad hoc *bandes,* who were "used so frequently as to become, in effect, standing forces."[32] The arrival of gunpowder and the advent of standing national armies convinced many towns and cities that absorption into larger political units was a good idea.

From the perspective of the oligarchs, who were now referred to as kings, expansion and consolidation of the state made sense. Small towns and cities, through superior organization and production techniques, were far more efficient than the state in fomenting economic production and securing taxes. Negotiated settlements with cities and towns were more attractive as diplomacy brought native loyalties and allegiances in the outlying areas to the state. Fernand Braudel writes that towns and cities

> had developed as autonomous worlds and according to their own propensities. They had outwitted the territorial state, which was established slowly and then only grew with their interested cooperation—and was moreover only an enlarged and often insipid copy of their development. They ruled their

countrysides [*sic*] autocratically, regarding them exactly as later powers regarded their colonies, and treating them as such.[33]

Absorbing towns and cities proved difficult, because "state" institutions were largely nonexistent or corrupted by privateers, palace courtiers, and political sycophants. State bodies that existed and exhibited a degree of competency couldn't count on other branches within the state to complement their activities. Skilled treasurers, for example, could do little if the money that they carefully cultivated was siphoned off or wasted by greedy generals or incompetent monarchs. There were no checks and balances, no systems of accountability. To be sure, the challenges of incompetence and excess had been addressed, if only temporarily, by leaders as far back as Charlemagne (742–842 AD). He had appointed local administrators and even sent traveling agents and bishops to impose law and legitimize his rule. But this had proved insufficient as the size of Charlemagne's empire and the power of regional warlords overwhelmed the abilities of his mobile representatives.

Still, in spite of administrative and financial challenges, the transformation from relatively weak and small medieval kingdoms to expansive absolutist monarchies and modern nation-states continued apace. Technological and financial changes, driven by the demands of war, forced administrative repair on European states. Samuel E. Finer writes:

> In England, France, and the realms of imperial Spain, a similar development of territorial consolidation and expansion, administrative centralization, and political integration ensued that made the kings a greater power than ever before . . . in all the kingdoms we see rulers and their officials steadily exploiting the older resources and institutions of royal authority and creating new ones . . . In some instances we see them bite deep into their people's purses and acquire armies at their will to chastise refractory subjects and wage foreign war. Their state-building efforts entailed the gradual subjugation of nobilities, the destruction of the independence of the church and clergy, the loss or decay of liberties of many corporate groups, the curbing or disappearance of the autonomy and particularism of provinces and towns.[34]

These advances set the stage for bringing about legal courts, national treasuries, political assemblies, systems of taxation, and other administrative bureaucracies of violence that helped create the modern nation-state.[35] Interestingly, one of the established resources that European monarchs continued to exploit was the medieval claim "to hold their authority immediately from God . . . and to be accountable only to God."[36] Even after England's Henry VIII sent the Catholic Church packing so that he could divorce his first wife and marry Anne Boleyn in 1533, he then created his own church, the Church of England, to help validate his actions.

Although claims of divine guidance and royal prerogative grew with the expanding reach of the state, the reality was that the ability of kings to do as they wished under God's authority was "more often than not greater in theory" than in practice.[37] The growing reach of the state—and the expanded powers of the monarch—was a direct result of war, growing financial demands, and subsequent administrative changes.

1500 AD, Charles Tilly Was Right: "War Made the State"

Negotiations between nobles and monarchs created a series of compromises that brought "biker gangs" of nobles in line by granting them greater liberties and a larger voice in state affairs. In exchange nobles allowed the king's tax farmers to collect duties in areas under their political influence, with some nobles even consenting to paying taxes. This laid the groundwork for representative government, by creating a habit of compromise between kings, nobles, and the money-making merchants of the cities and towns. Even though these compromises were largely self-serving, they were crucial in gradually securing the individual rights that are necessary for establishing representative bodies and professional bureaucracies—all hallmarks of the modern liberal state.

Built on mutual needs tied to money (which the monarchs wanted), protection (which the merchants needed), and land rights (which satisfied the nobles), conflicts and negotiations between these groups have a long history. The foundation of basic civil liberties began with England's Magna Carta in 1215, which required the king to respect basic legal procedures and demanded that the king be bound by law. This established basic governing principles that legitimized constitutions, established legislative bodies, and protected individual rights. Merchants were particularly effective, pushing for these principles because they had what states wanted to tax or needed to borrow. In return for these rights, European Crowns secured agreements from state parliaments—made up of merchants, nobles, and other town elites—to repay the loans that they acquired. In this way, "the intersection between kings and merchants produced the public debt as an institution."[38] This had the parallel effect of elevating the social position of merchants and other creators of wealth in society.[39] This set the stage for the privileges of aristocratic elites to be threatened and later abolished.

As more merchants came to understand the security in lending to the state—even if the lending was tied to war—the size of the state increased. This was followed by increasingly more opportunities for commoners with talent in growing state bureaucracies. Social mobility was no longer confined to merchants, artisans, and military men. As the prospect for improving their position in life improved with state jobs, citizens came to believe that they had a stake in professionalizing the bureaucracy. If they wanted to keep their jobs, they needed to perform. This, in turn, increased demands for greater limits on the king's authority, as accountability and performance became leading topics of discussion. Perhaps just as important, more middle-class players were added to a class that included free nobles and merchants. As the social position of merchants and money-changers improved, by the seventeenth century, the social standing of those who facilitated the work of merchants and traders—that is, public officials and lawyers—was also enhanced.

In spite of these leveling developments, which helped build a viable middle class, social hierarchies remained entrenched. Simply put—and with a nod to Thorstein Veblen—noble rank still retained its allure, especially because acquiring nobility was viewed as "the most desired objective of families on the rise."[40] This happened primarily for two reasons. First, in an era of social change and dynamic political trans-formations, social envy persisted. People felt a need to be accepted by their "social betters," which led them to seek approval by emulating elites. Second, although monarchs acquired new powers that might allow them to squash smaller adversaries, "they did not quarrel with [sharing] social privilege"[41]—in part because they understood that their position was tied to maintaining social mores. They only went after aristocratic rivals who "resisted their authority or claimed immunity from their government."[42] In this manner, political stability owed much to the self-preservation instincts of the monarchy and the coarse aspirations of social climbers.

Still, the mixture of nobles, merchants, bankers, key public officials, lawyers, and other professional groups into a stable middle-class was a dynamic brew. This helped create new pressure groups, who pushed for the consolidation of private property rights (nobles and emerging spec-ulators) and regularized tax patterns (merchants and the state bureau-cracy). But something else happened. With so much money to be made at the feet of the state, compromise and negotiation eventually created "a legal framework in which mercantile activity could flourish."[43] Ambitious citizens understood that, even though individual service in the name of queen and country might bring adventure and fame, investing and trading in the name of queen and country could bring untold riches and profits.

1500 AD, Charles Tilly Was Right, Again: ". . . and the State Made War"

These dynamics not only established a short bridge between mercantilism and modern capitalism, but they help us understand that the evolution of capitalism was dependent on the stability that had been created and the markets that were maintained by the state. Strangely enough, war mandated order—which allowed markets to thrive and wealth to be taxed. From the Early Middle Ages through the Treaty of Westphalia (1648), the state sought to provide protections and guarantees to private property. Growing opportunities for individual wealth and personal fortunes were enhanced, but only for those who agreed to cooperate with the state. In return, the state was able to impose taxes and generate income for waging war and defending its interests. In simpler terms, organized violence brokered by compromise is the genesis of the modern nation-state.[44]

It should come as no surprise that Herman Schwartz made the following observations. First, the modern nation-state and modern capitalist markets "cannot exist without each other." Second, nation-building through the seventeenth century offers a perfect metaphor for understanding the protection rackets of organized crime.[45] What pushed states to support the freedoms and liberties that were necessary for market capitalism to prosper was that they had become financially strapped by the demands of war. Once the road to modern markets had been paved—first by embracing market towns, then mercantilism, and finally by supporting the freedoms necessary for capitalism—it became possible for the state's "bureaucracies of violence" to emerge. This made war, rather than plunder or defeat, possible. States that couldn't generate the funds for state-building, to pay professional armies, or to acquire the technology necessary to fight wars found themselves ever closer to history's ash heap, as the United States learned at the time of its founding.[46] As Charles Tilly pointed out, the "political units" that couldn't fund themselves or pay for war "perished in war."[47]

To obtain funds to fight wars and manage the affairs of state required a highly complex, professional, and centralized administrative body that was capable of collecting taxes and managing money. This, as discussed in Chapter 3, was well understood by William of Orange. William of Orange began the process of granting more rights to citizens in exchange for their acquiescence on taxes. Although he did this to fund a military apparatus that was preparing to expand across the globe, it also laid the groundwork for the principles behind democratic governance. On a broader level, war helped convince states that they needed to centralize authority and establish the institutions necessary for wealth creation—such as capitalism. Charles Tilly described the process:

> Preparation for war, especially on a large scale, involves rulers ineluctably in extraction. It builds up an infrastructure of taxation, supply, and administration that requires maintenance of itself and often grows faster than the armies and navies it serves; those who run the infrastructure acquire power and interests of their own; their interests and power limit significantly the character and intensity of warfare any particular state can carry on. Europe's Mongol and Tatar states resolved the dilemmas by raiding and looting without building much durable administration.[48]

Ironically, just when greater freedoms and liberties were being granted and more wealth than ever imagined was made possible, the modern state that made it all possible also "imposed a heavy burden on the population involved: taxes, conscription, requisitions, and more."[49] Territorial consolidation, centralization, bureaucratic specialization and the monopolization of the means of force freed citizens from the bonds of feudal uncertainty and servitude, only to deliver them into the hands of a state that was organized and built to engage in war. Although keeping and guarding individual property and territory enabled individuals to work hard and get ahead, the tools of the modern state allowed the state bureaucracy to put its citizens consistently in a seemingly never-ending cycle of national debt—all in the name of national security and war.

With few mechanisms to ameliorate the tensions that come from the security dilemma—tied to the constant preparation for war—it's no wonder that the immediate post-Westphalian period saw little improvement in war's prominence. In many respects the evolving nation-state was little more than an innovative but more complex and efficient version of medieval protection rackets. But administrative innovation and technological advances enabled European states to develop ever-more aggressive policies to pursue resources and wealth, at home and abroad. These policies ushered in the era of mercantilism and, more important, opened the door for the various stages of European imperialism. Here, the state's capacity to organize and call on national sentiments meant that modern wars became all-encompassing and more destructive. This is the "total war" scenario that inspired Charles Tilly to write: "War made the state, and the state made war."[50]

Conclusion

When Genghis Khan was born in 1162 AD, Europe and China were largely unknown to each other. After the collapse of the Roman Empire, life in Europe was limited, dangerous, and parochial. Although recent research suggests that life wasn't as bleak as early literature suggests, things were bad enough that much of Europe's peasantry was forced to ally with local lords in exchange for protection from barbarian raids. At the same time, in the perimeters of northern Africa and in the Middle East, advanced Islamic communities were excelling in the fields of mathematics and science (as were the Mayans in the Americas). Still, in Genghis Khan's backyard—which consisted of modern Mongolia, Kazakhstan, Tajikistan, Uzbekistan, and southern China—the Steppe region was dominated by regional clans, who produced little of value and clashed on a regular basis over what little they possessed. Genghis Khan helped change this by waging war.

In a period spanning less than thirty-five years Genghis Khan established commercial connections and political dominance over a swath of Eurasian geography that was unmatched until the United States emerged victorious at the end of World War II. Trade and cultural exchange flourished in every region touched by the Mongols. The Mongol's accomplishments are especially incredible considering that trade and cultural exchanges under the Romans came to a virtual halt and even reversed in some regions of Eurasia. Of Genghis Khan's many accomplishments, several stood out for what he introduced throughout the Eurasian continent. By opening and protecting trade routes, he laid the groundwork for merchants to prosper and allowed the Mongols to increase their resources through tribute-taking. This was a fundamental improvement over simple pillaging. In the areas of communication, by absorbing and spreading ideas and products (including new weapons and gunpowder), the Mongols set the stage for the spread of commerce, scientific knowledge, and diplomatic communication.[51]

Ambitious and curious, the Mongols eventually set their sites on Europe. By surrounding, then cutting off, and finally bombarding city and castle walls, Mongol sieges showed how sedentary, defense-oriented European civilizations could be defeated. Fear of defeat, coupled with the arrival of gunpowder, laid the groundwork for alliances between smaller powers, which was instrumental in the consolidation of modern nation-states. In this manner, the organizational contours of the European nation-state may be linked to the lessons that were first learned at the hands of Genghis Khan's descendants.

Today, the modern nation-state has prevailed as the dominant form of mass political organization that is dedicated to security (over city-states and tribute-taking empires, for example). Its hallmark, although not often recognized or appreciated, is an organized and efficient bureaucracy. In spite of this, the modern nation-state still hasn't demonstrated that it's a superior political form for avoiding conflict and war. On the contrary, the modern state may have simply increased humanity's capacity to marshal resources to fight ever-more devastating wars. To do this, competing monarchs had to get their political houses in order. Unfortunately for European monarchs, once this process began, they were forced to grant greater numbers of political concessions and considerable liberty.

In the immediate post-Westphalian period—1648 to the end of the Napoleonic Wars in 1815—the goals of the state centered around securing territories for colonies and natural resources. The first wave of imperialism (about 1648–1815) laid the groundwork for the classic period of mercantilism, which lasted roughly through the Treaty of Versailles. This sets the stage for the second wave of imperialism. In the second wave of imperialism, the goals of the state focused on national economic development and acquiring markets to sell and dump goods. This period saw the emergence of the United States as the primary supporter of free trade. It also witnessed the arrival of viral economic nationalism, demonstrated by the rise of Nazi Germany, Mussolini's Italy, Japan, and even the Soviet Union and the People's Republic of China. With its zero-sum outlook, post-Westphalian nations continued to prepare for war by looking for new ways to fund it.[52]

The goal here isn't to determine whether mercantilism and imperialism are good or bad or whether they undermine the basic premises of the liberal perspective. Rather the goal is to show that, for well over 450 years, the modern state has actively been engaged in seeking resources and political markets to fund and prepare for war. These dynamics set the stage for bargains that led to the rise of the middle class and paved the way for the emergence of market capitalism.

Notes

1. Robert Baer, *Sleeping with the Devil: How Washington Sold Our Soul for Saudi Crude* (New York: Crown Publishers, 2003), 62.

2. Daniel Yergin, *The Prize: The Epic Quest for Oil, Money, and Power* (New York: Free Press, 1992), 755–758. Blog Commentary.

3. Baer, *Sleeping*, 39–60.

4. Baer, *Sleeping*, 135.

5. Robert Gilpin, *Global Political Economy: Understanding the International Economic Order* (Princeton, NJ: Princeton University Press, 2001), 234, 240; Robert Gilpin, *The Political Economy of International Relations* (Princeton, NJ: Princeton University Press, 1987), 315–316.

6. Chalmers Johnson, *Nemesis: The Last Days of the American Republic* (New York: Metropolitan Books, 2006); David Barstow, "Behind TV Analysts, Pentagon's Hidden Hand," *New York Times,* April 20, 2008, available online; Robert Gilpin's *War and Change in World Politics* (Cambridge, MA: Cambridge University Press, 1987). Blog Commentary.

7. Nicholas Rummell, "Regulators Target Sovereign Wealth Funds: Oil Rich Investors from China to Dubai Suddenly Must Bring an Unknown Factor into Their Deal Math: Washington Politics," *Financial Week,* February 11, 2008, available online; Robert Kimmitt, "Public Footprints in Private Markets," *Foreign Affairs,* 87, no. 1 (January/February 2008): 119–130. Blog Commentary.

8. John Keegan, *A History of Warfare* (New York: Alfred A. Knopf, 1993), 283–284.

9. Keegan, *A History*, 283.

10. Keegan, *A History*, 281–282.

11. Douglass C. North, *Structure and Change in Economic History* (New York: Norton, 1981), 126, 136–137.

12. "Roturier" refers to the land offered to soldiers in lieu of monetary payments. Another problem was that townsmen were averse to increasingly longer military campaigns, according to Samuel E. Finer, "State- and Nation-Building in Europe: The Role of the Military," in *The Formation of National States in Western Europe,* ed. Charles Tilly, (Princeton, NJ: Princeton University Press, 1975), 100.

13. Finer, "State," 100.

14. Perez Zagorin, *Rebels and Rulers, 1500–1660: Society, States, and Early Modern Revolution*, Vol. I (New York: Cambridge University Press, 1982), 89. Blog Commentary.

15. The subtitle and most of the information for this section are drawn from Jack Weatherford, *Genghis Khan and the Making of the Modern World* (New York: Three Rivers Press, 2004). Although I have synopsized Weatherford's review, only quotes and specific points made by Weatherford are cited.

16. Fareed Zakaria, *From Wealth to Power: The Unusual Origins of America's World Role* (Princeton, NJ: Princeton University Press, 1998).

17. Noted war historian Lynn Montross wrote that "the men of Jenghiz [*sic*] Khan appear little better than bandits and slave drivers," Lynn Montross, *War through the Ages,* 3rd edition (New York: Harper & Row, Publishers, 1960), 157.

18. Weatherford, *Genghis Khan,* xxiii.

19. Weatherford, *Genghis Khan,* 44–45.

20. Charles Tilly, 1990. *Coercion, Capital and European States,* AD *990–1990* (Cambridge, MA: Basil Blackwell, 1990), 70–71.

21. Tilly, *Coercion,* 74–75.

22. Herman M. Schwartz, *States Versus Market: The Emergence of a Global Economy* (New York: St. Martin's Press, 2000), 15.

23. Schwartz, *States,* 16.

24. Fernand Braudel, *The Structures of Everyday Life: Civilization and Capitalism, 15th–18th Century,* Vol. I (New York: Harper & Row Publishers, 1979), 510–511. Blog Commentary.

25. Tilly, *Coercion,* 74–75.

26. Tilly, *Coercion,* 75.

27. Tilly, *Coercion,* 74.

28. Tilly, *Coercion,* 75.

29. Braudel, *The Structures,* 510.

30. Schwartz, *States.*

31. Finer, "State," 99.

32. Finer, "State," 99.

33. Braudel, *The Structures,* 510.

34. Zagorin, *Rebels,* 88.

35. Tilly, *Coercion,* 75.

36. Finer, "State," 102.

37. Zagorin, *Rebels,* 92–93.

38. Schwartz, *States,* 21.

39. Zagorin, *Rebels,* 130–134.

40. Zagorin, *Rebels,* 132.

41. Zagorin, *Rebels,* 93.

42. Zagorin, *Rebels,* 93.

43. Schwartz, *States,* 21.

44. Schwartz, *States,* 20.

45. Noting that "state-building was at first a form of organized crime," Schwartz paraphrases Charles Tilly to argue that the state's growing "bureaucracies of violence" owe their life to constitutions driven by lawyers, guns, and money, Schwartz, *States,* 20.

46. Blog Commentary.

47. Charles Tilly, "Reflections on the History of Europeans State-Making" in *The Formation of National States in Western*

Europe, ed., Charles Tilly, (Princeton, NJ: Princeton University Press, 1975), 42.

48. Tilly, *Coercion,* 20–21.
49. Tilly, "Reflections," 42.
50. Tilly, "Reflections," 42.
51. Weatherford, *Genghis Khan,* xix.
52. Gilpin, *The Political,* 1987.

CHAPTER 6

How Medieval Organized Violence Led to Mercantilism, Middle-Class Bargains, and Market Capitalism

Throughout European history no monarch stands as tall as France's King Louis XIV (1638–1715). Forced into the countryside as a young boy by the Wars of the Fronde, the Sun King grew to abhor disorder and uncertainty. Upon consolidating his personal authority at age nineteen—he had been king since age five—he began centralizing state power. But organizing and funding a seventeenth-century state and its military was hampered by the chaos and costs associated with feudal habits, corrupt contractors, and crooked merchants, whose actions limited the king's tax base. Louis XIV understood this and moved to professionalize and modernize France's bureaucracy and economy. This had a ripple effect that transformed European state relations.

To achieve his goals, the Sun King looked to Jean-Baptiste Colbert, who had an instinct for public policy. By subsidizing industries, negotiating treaties, raising tariffs to protect industry, and keeping private contractor corruption to a minimum, Colbert brought prosperity to France. Because of Colbert's policies, France professionalized its military by standardizing uniforms, improving the training protocols, and offering better provisions. Although Colbert's emphasis on negotiation and commercial treaties led many to label him a "Man of Peace," his aggressive trade and tariff policies irked neighbors and competitors alike. In the process—and ironically—Colbert created "more enemies for France" than Louis XIV ever made with the sword.[1] These dynamics, as Charles Tilly noted, created a powerful state that compelled others to pursue trade, adventure, and resources in ways that fostered European mercantilism.

Viewing the world in zero-sum terms—what you gain, I lose—shows that conflict between European states rose to new levels as they competed for territory and markets throughout the seventeenth and eighteenth centuries. As evidence, even though France appeared to be undisturbed by fortresses built in the Spanish Netherlands along its northern borders (part of present-day Belgium and Luxembourg), Colbert became concerned when Dutch and Flemish merchants in the region retaliated against his commercial policies. This convinced Colbert that war was necessary.[2] Although conflict between France and Spain settled little, it raised concerns throughout Europe—and with reason—Louis XIV had his eyes on Holland. In addition to opposing Holland's democratic ideas and its Protestantism, the French king disliked the Dutch because they were prosperous and because they were France's major commercial rivals. To solidify his military position, the Sun King sought out as allies the British, who had their own reasons for fighting. On the eve of the Second Anglo-Dutch War (1665–1667), British Admiral George Monk considered the motives and noted rather bluntly, "What matters 'this' or 'that' reason? What we want is more of the trade which the Dutch now have."[3]

In *States Versus Markets: The Emergence of a Global Economy*, Herman Schwartz explains the rise of the modern state by taking us back to the roots of mercantilism. Rather than focus on the state's need to go abroad in search of trade surpluses and wealth—what most interpretations of mercantilism tell us about—Schwartz points us to domestic dynamics within states. To generate a more efficient tax base to pay for war, the state was compelled to monetize the economy, and it gradually moved toward privatizing property rights. This weakened feudal bonds and fed an era of "organized violence" between kings, nobles, and merchants. Kings wanted order and legitimacy. Nobles were desperate for defined property rights and wanted a voice in state policy. Merchants wanted both protection (to make money) and a say in matters of state. All groups wanted security from outside threats, a concern of sovereigns throughout Europe.

When they weren't busy fighting one another, the negotiations between monarchs, nobles, and merchants were carried out against a backdrop of violence. Over the centuries, negotiation and violence produced compromises that gave birth to greater individual freedoms, liberal constitutions, democratic parliaments, and the gradual elimination of barriers to trade. With regular tax collections, by increasingly professional government agencies, the demands of war forced parliaments to rely on bureaucracies of violence (police and armies) that facilitated economic growth and allowed states to pursue aggressive foreign policies. By establishing monopolies of violence over certain areas, kings became the "Godfathers," conducting affairs as modern-day mob bosses run their business rackets. Consolidating their power over smaller neighborhood gangs—which were lorded over by rogue bands—allowed sovereigns to promise protection and stability (which was delivered sporadically).

Although taxes and kingly discipline were often unwelcome by merchants and nobles, the political payoff came in the form of private property rights, legal infrastructures, professional bureaucracies, and an increasingly larger voice in state policy. All of this improved opportunities for personal wealth and fortune. This helped educate sovereigns, who increasingly understood the value that commerce and trade had for state survival. What emerged was a state built and stabilized by an increasingly independent middle class—made up of nobles, artisans, scholars, and merchants—people who were more interested in money and discovery than in maintaining stifling customs and traditions. These interests drove foreign policy toward mercantilism and the state toward modernity, and initiated a revolution in human thinking.

The revolution embraced radical political and economic ideas that put the aristocrats on notice that they didn't have a monopoly on political power, nor did they possess a divine right to wield it as they saw fit. The revolution in human thinking put a primacy on liberty and the ability of individuals to make choices for themselves.[4] From these dynamics the political conditions for mercantilism and middle-class bargains emerged, which set the stage for the ideas that brought us market capitalism and political democracy. Because capitalism and democracy require that people make decisions about their economic and political world, the feudal customs and the privileges of the Catholic Church came under attack. It shouldn't come as a surprise then that both democracy and capitalism were viewed as radical "liberal" ideas by feudal elites.

Because sovereigns actively pushed for mercantile policies that funded war and made capitalism possible, it is clear that the wonders of the market—that many embrace as the natural order of things—are really not so wondrous. Rather, mercantilism and capitalism are products of state-led initiatives dominated by reason of state. Anthony Smith writes:

> The formation of nations in the nineteenth and twentieth centuries has been profoundly influenced by the examples of England, France, and Spain, and to a lesser extent Holland and Sweden . . . In the case of England and France and to a lesser extent Spain this was hardly accidental. The relatively early development of their nations coincided with successive revolutions in the spheres of administration, the economy and culture. Indeed, many would argue that in these and other cases the state actually "created" the nation.[5]

Contributing to the economic revolution, as Robert Heilbroner tells us, were state-led efforts to commodify land, labor, and capital. When the primary factors of production were freed from the restrictive habits of privilege and tradition, commodification fortified mercantile policies by promoting greater economic efficiency and capital investment. This was followed by state-led efforts to build a middle-class culture, which focused on enhancing opportunity and wealth creation for all levels of society. State efforts to negotiate trade treaties were also instrumental in undermining mercantilism by helping bring the idea of open markets to the rest of the world. These market-supporting efforts were not a product of providence or of a mythical *homo economicus* who suddenly or miraculously broke free from the stifling hand of the state. Rather, the creation of *homo economicus* and the making of free markets required conscientious political decisions that were backed by the power of the state. Nothing that has occurred over the past two centuries has altered this arrangement.

A Few Words on Mercantilism

Mercantilism emerged in a period of social and political transition.[6] After the Reformation and the end of the Thirty Years War (1618–1648), isolated feudal estates were increasingly overrun or replaced by increasingly centralized nation-states. Gun powder helped turn the castle walls of feudal lords into ineffective refuges that were doomed to collapse, while the end of the Thirty Years' War brought the Treaty of Westphalia (1648), which forced national boundaries around reluctant city-states and stubborn rogue nobles. As one account put it, "More than anything else, war propelled the consolidation of the nation-state."[7] The primary problem at this time was paying for war. The nobles were reluctant to provide much beyond their talents in the battlefield (if that). For their part, the peasants lacked both the means (freedom) and resources (money) to produce what the kings needed to confiscate in taxes.

Problems were made worse for sovereigns because they could not turn to domestic agriculture for surpluses. Since the fifteenth century there were natural limits (science, transportation, disease, regional variations, etc.) to what could be extracted from the land. Because "agriculture constituted about 80 percent of economic activity" at the time, it was clear to ambitious sovereigns that they needed to stretch their wings.[8] This forced sovereigns to look for ways to generate wealth abroad, which traditionally meant plunder or trade. Domestically this meant centralizing authority, connecting markets, and homogenizing the economy with similar currencies, weights, and so on. These developments paid dividends in a post-Westphalian world, when an increasingly monetized economy and enforceable property rights encouraged investment and facilated taxation.[9]

Taxes, record keeping, regulations, and the like contributed to the modernization of the state, but were increasingly costly to maintain.[10] But one thing was increasingly clear: security was the primary impetus behind new forms of wealth creation and wealth accumulation.

In its most basic form, mercantilism posits that economic activities are subordinate to the goal of state-building, state security, and military power.[11] One of the key assumptions made by mercantilists is that the amount of wealth in the world is constant so that a nation's share can only increase at the expense of others.[12] Because economic resources are necessary for national power, there is no separation between politics and economics. This explains why mercantilists believe that "every conflict is at once both economic and political."[13] Production and economic activity are important only in that they serve the interests of the state. During the period of adventure and exploration, "enlightened" kings who understood the relationship between wealth accumulation and political power richly rewarded those who could help them raise an army or pay for one. This explains why monarchs took care to protect the urban centers of commerce and embraced those who made the best use of new technologies. But this was only the beginning.

After the discovery of the Americas, the state granted charters of incorporation, promoted adventurism and plunder abroad, granted Letters of Marquee, and protected domestic producers through tariffs. European monarchs competed with one another by sending out adventurers like Magellan and Sir Francis Drake, who promised to bring back riches and glory for the state. Then it finally dawned on mercantilists and others that trading for certain goods was much cheaper than paying for the soldiers of fortune who helped sack and loot neighboring states. It was at this time that trade treaties were taken up in earnest. The state's focus on trade—rather than pillage and plunder—created an environment for the first serious debates on capitalism. Until that happened, however, there was a mad rush for silver and gold (Spain won), efforts to control commercial prospects through various "acts" (especially in England), and the steady creation of charter companies (the predecessor of modern corporations). Under these conditions the state became the linchpin for wealth creation and wealth accumulation.

Beginning with the Netherlands and the British Empire, enlightened leaders demonstrated that they understood the relationship between wealth creation, state capacity, and security. The Dutch actively courted traders and attracted money managers to Amsterdam in the sixteenth and seventeenth centuries, in the process creating perhaps the most dynamic and prosperous city and community in the world at the time. As noted in Chapter 3, the British followed the Dutch example under

William of Orange and were able to attract cheap money to help fund their wars and the industrialization process. The need to compete, and to control assets and resources, led other monarchs to follow suit politically. All of this activity facilitated and speeded up the emergence of national political units elsewhere—although perhaps not as efficiently as in Holland or in England. This set the stage for competitive European imperialism.

Domestically, political centralization, technology, and physical improvements in infrastructures consolidate state authority. Increased taxes to fund centralization at home and adventures abroad also increased merchant demands for more personal liberty and laws to protect assets and to facilitate commerce. Unfortunately for monarchs, granting the liberties necessary for wealth creation at home led to demands for change that undermined both their credibility and their hold on power. Put more bluntly, the need to accommodate those who create wealth meant embracing the rights and liberties that allow ideas to flourish and make democracy possible. In this way, the freedom to choose our leaders politically (democracy) and to do what we want "when we grow up" (capitalism) happened because of very political decisions. The process opened the door for the creation and expansion of the middle class.

Beyond Mercantilism: Transforming the Primary Factors of Production[14]

Before the liberal revolutions of the eighteenth and nineteenth centuries, land, labor, and capital in Britain—the primary factors of production in any capitalist society—were not well understood. They were also largely regulated by societal norms driven by custom and status. For example, throughout Europe, custom dictated that many, if not most, buildings be rented (often for 99-year leases) to the families who lived and worked in them. Thus a landlord renting a shop to a tailor in 1525 could not raise the rent until after 1624. Also, nobles and the aristocracy frequently had the right to purchase basic foodstuffs at a specified price. The system was designed to provide stability, which allowed both lords and peasants to plan ahead. But it also produced a situation in which the king of England in the middle of the seventeenth century "had the right to purchase wheat at prices set 300 years earlier."[15]

These stifling traditions did not end with land ownership. By custom, rural laborers worked the fields of local aristocrats, who agreed to allow peasant farmers to keep a certain amount of what they produced. This arrangement generated resources and income for local aristocrats and met the subsistence needs of local peasants. Depending on the arrangement, excess production went to the peasants or to the owners of the land. This left little incentive to produce beyond what was needed to subsist. And there was no real incentive to change this system. Why would nobles want to change a system that gave them the right to purchase goods at prices determined one hundred years earlier? Bound by feudal obligations, agricultural laborers focused their efforts on producing goods for immediate use rather than for sale or exchange. Even though the peasants might sell or trade some of their goods in a market, what was produced, sold, or traded was exchanged primarily to augment immediate subsistence needs. Outside of guilds, the time and effort that went into the creation of the goods produced were rarely measured or considered (Box 6.1).

Box 6.1 Peasant Societies, Production, and Joseph Stalin

Understanding the logic behind peasant societies is as important today as it was 250 years ago when liberal ideas worked their way into society. Although Imperial Britain, and even Napoleon (in Egypt), ushered in the era of examining "the natives," the study of peasant agriculture economics took off in the twentieth century. In Russia research into peasant societies in the 1920s sought to understand how and why peasants produced goods. This was an important question, because Soviet revolutionaries wanted to use surplus agricultural production to facilitate industrialization. Headed by researchers such as Aleksander Chayanov, institutes throughout Russia learned that subsistence peasants worked until they had enough to feed their families, but not much beyond that point. This meant that peasant households weren't particularly sensitive to prevailing wage or price incentives because they focused primarily on the "use value" of a good in the immediate term rather than its "exchange value" in the market. Producing more than what they needed was viewed as "drudgery." This is important, because it helps us understand the persistence of peasant societies around the world. Profit, greed, and affluence aren't the dominant elements of their social contract. It also helps explain why peasant societies are inclined to sell excess goods and their labor at below-market prices (which subsidizes markets by keeping the cost of goods and wage labor low). Any market society with a large influx of poor peasants understands this. The findings of Chayanov and others, however, didn't sit well with Joseph Stalin. They explained why peasants wouldn't produce the surpluses that the revolutionary Soviet state demanded. Stalin saw these findings as an unwarranted defense of rich kulaks, and he saw traitors in his midst. After Stalin took control of Russian agriculture in 1930, these studies were ignored, and many of the institutes were closed. Subsequent purges, disappearances, and repression of nonrevolutionaries in the 1930s helped stifle the study (and understanding) of peasant economies in Russia for decades.

Source: E. Paul Durrenberger, "Chayanov's Economic Analysis in Anthropology," *Journal of Anthropological Research*, 36, no. 2 (Summer 1980), 133–148, available online; John Adams, Book Review, A. V. Chayanov, *The Theory of Peasant Economy*. Translated by R. E. F. Smith, with introductions by Daniel Thorner and Basile Kerblay (South Holland, IL: Richard D. Irwin, 1966), *Annals of the American Academy of Political and Social Science*, Vol. 374, Combating Crime (November 1967), 217, available online.

Once labor left its feudal obligations, things began to change. Enticed or forced out by industrialization and the enclosure movement, former rural laborers began competing with one another in a growing market of commodified labor.[16] But, by leaving serfdom and feudal subsistence patterns, wage laborers could no longer depend on the land to survive. As wage laborers, workers now had to keep track of how much time they put in and how much money they needed to survive. This was a far cry from tilling fields and counting chickens. On the other side, employers looked for the brightest, most disciplined, and most productive workers. Unable to return to subsistence patterns in the countryside, workers were slowly transformed into a commodity (Box 6.2).

Box 6.2 Workers: Just Another Commodity?

The view that a "worker is just another commodity" has changed significantly. Unlike watermelons and lumber, workers can respond to incentives. As well, simply because you put the same task in front of a group of workers doesn't mean that they will respond in the same way that seeds might when you put them in the same environment. Talent and creative spirit also offer distinct opportunities that enhance or diminish productivity, which you can't see in a seed or in a mountain full of iron. In addition, with more training or new tools, workers can become more efficient. Finally, the revenue that workers receive for their product (labor) can be directed and redirected into an economy in ways that can affect other areas of the economy. There are also the moral issues. Simply put, labor is not just another commodity to be harvested, consumed, and disposed of like an ear of corn.

Directing these developments wasn't, as some Marxists might argue, an industrial conspiracy bent on exploiting workers (not that exploitation doesn't occur). Rather, what helped prop up and drive these dynamics were considerations of state security. The British in particular were focused on creating more wealth to prop up their imperial endeavors. They understood that sheep and the textiles industry made land a more profitable business than simple subsistence agriculture patterns. Textiles could be sold abroad, which generated national income and jobs that contributed to the consumption of other goods, which could be taxed. If the goods came from abroad, a tariff could be applied. If the goods came from domestic producers, a tax could be slapped on them. Either way, as long as growth occurred, the mercantile state prospered. This was especially the case when it came to imports, which brought in all-important customs receipts. As late as 1840, customs receipts amounted to 44.2 percent of the total government revenue in the United Kingdom.[17] This was crucial for state coffers. In this manner, the enclosure movement aided the textile industry, helped subsidize industrialization, and brought in tariff income. This had a significant impact on premodern Britain's primary factors of production.

When Britain's enclosure movement started, "free" labor was largely regulated by custom and guilds. The other factor of production, land, was largely unavailable for trade or development because it was not only a status symbol but largely available only through hereditary rights. People might be inclined to trade or sell their land only if they were willing to trade on their status and the history of their family name. This limited investment and speculation on land because "no self-respecting nobleman would willingly sell his ancestral estates."[18] Similarly, in premodern England, capital wasn't well understood and was more likely to be spent on cathedrals and wars than on productive investments (see Spain). What helped land, labor, and capital become dynamic commodities was that the state made a conscious effort to nudge them into the emerging capitalist market economy as commodities.

Karl Polanyi takes up this theme in *The Great Transformation*. Polanyi argues that the rise of market societies was a result of specific state-building strategies, and he points to the partial repeal of England's Act of Settlement in 1795. Implemented in 1662, the Act of Settlement required paupers to stay and work in their parish districts. The act was even condemned by Adam Smith as another law that was designed to aid business.

> It is every-where much easier for a wealthy merchant to obtain the privilege of trading in a town corporate, than for a poor artificer to obtain that of working in it. The obstruction which

corporation laws give to the free circulation of labour is common, I believe, to every part of Europe . . . It consists in the difficulty which a poor man finds in obtaining a settlement, or
even in being allowed to exercise his industry in any parish but
that to which he belongs.[19]

As a result of the partial repeal of the act, free paupers were effectively
released from "parish serfdom." The partial repeal of the Act of Settlement facilitated labor mobility and was accompanied by the Speenhamland Act, which was also implemented in 1795. Speenhamland provided
"poor relief," which aided industrialists because they didn't have to pay
laborers for the portion that poor relief provided. More damaging was
that labor couldn't find its proper wage level in the early days of industrialization.[20] In this manner, the enclosure movement, the partial repeal of
the Settlement Acts, and the Speenhamland Act were instrumental in helping commodify labor at a pace and price that were favorable to industry.

Polanyi places great emphasis on Speenhamland for two reasons.
First, it demonstrates that the road to market capitalism was paved with
state-led political manipulation. Second, because Speenhamland subsidized the cost of labor, the accomplishments and profits of British merchants and industrialists were artificially inflated from the very beginning.
And we still haven't discussed tariff protections, colonization, charter
corporations, the use of subsidies, monopolies, the Navigation Acts, the
British use of its navy to keep trade routes open, and other such issues.[21]
Contradictions in the rise of capitalist society appear throughout its history, according to Polanyi, as powerful interests sprang up to shield specific groups from competition once "market" societies became entrenched.
In Polanyi's view, because of the state's involvement in facilitating wealth
creation in England, the fundamental assumptions of the liberal creed
and "invisible hands" may have been mistaken from the start.[22] By arguing that Adam Smith's invisible hand was really a very visible hand,
Polanyi demonstrates that political considerations and planning were at
the heart of transforming feudal societies into mercantilist and then capitalist societies.

Finally, according to Karl Polanyi, denying that the state has a role in
organizing and encouraging human behavior while elevating self-interest
as the dominant social principle in society is an "economistic fallacy"—
the willful distortion of thought, which privileges formal economic activities (studied by economists) while excluding equally important factors
that shape human relations, such as religion and government. For this reason, he considers the idea of *homo economicus* to be an artificial creation
of misguided intellectuals. For Polanyi the study of individuals in isolation

from state and society is a utopian pursuit.[23] Put another way, society creates the conditions under which wealth is created. These insights are critical for helping us understand the logic behind the creation and rise of the American middle class.

The Great Transformation, I: Yeoman Farmers Create America's Middle Class[24]

From the very beginning, the specter of European-style feudalism haunted policymakers in colonial and postrevolutionary America. This fear was partially defused when Congress passed the Land Ordinance Act of 1785 and the Land Ordinance Act of 1796. Both guaranteed that land would be broken up into "fee simple" properties, without the multiple ownership claims that flagged England's property rights experience. Disputes, however, emerged over how land would be allocated. The Land Act of 1785 was a concession to conservatives, who argued that land should be a source of revenue for the state and only made available in large lot sizes of 640 acres (at $1.00 per acre). Conservatives also wanted land sold in large lots because of their concern that a labor force that was offered the opportunity to escape to a new life (facilitated by access to land) would lower property values and drive up wages in the East. The Land Ordinance Act of 1796 made permanent the survey patterns that had been established in 1785, but it allowed one-half of the purchase price to be deferred for a year.[25] When multiple ownership was claimed, the courts, local land associations, and the US government regularly ruled in favor of those who worked the land. In spite of conservative fears over falling property values and higher wages in the East, the idea was to encourage settlement, which would occur only as long as those who worked the land believed that they would be rewarded for their efforts. The battles over land drew a line between conservative and liberal groups in America.

Liberals adopted the New England township approach, which called for making small land parcels available at low prices and on easy credit terms. Conservatives wanted to follow the path of the American South, which meant big lots and making land available only to those who could afford to pay, including the following specifics:

> The liberals argued that every person had a right to a piece of land and that the spirit of democracy could best be preserved by affording everyone who wished it an opportunity to own land and to farm for a living. Liberals believed that Americans could never be economically oppressed if the poor could avoid oppression by moving to the West . . . conservatives argued,

not always for publication, that a ragtag population in the West would be a continuing spawning place of political unrest. Furthermore, the values of real property in the East would be weaker if land were readily available . . . and the level of wages in the East would be persistently higher.[26]

There was a good deal of self-interest behind the conservative position, as the Founders of the nation had anticipated (see, especially, *The Federalist Papers*). But liberal forces grew to include new and powerful groups that were focused on making things work to their financial advantage— Western settlers, Eastern laborers, and land speculators, among others.[27] Together they were a dynamic group. The goals of these groups happened to coincide with the larger interests of a growing nation that was bent on expansion. Then-Secretary of State John Quincy Adams built an expansionist foreign policy around the premise that an industrious, adventurous, and multiplying population would push America's interests and eventually suffocate the British on the continent.[28] Geostrategic and national security interests were intricately tied to making sure that ordinary Americans succeeded. But an expansionist policy could only work if settlers and speculators could count on land and the law.

Instead of paying attention to "preserving an old economic order"—as was the case in England and on the European continent—American leaders would use property as "a powerful tool for creating a new one."[29] The idea was that the spirit of democracy only flourished if everyone who wished it was afforded the opportunity to own and farm his own land.[30] For this reason, as Hernan De Soto tells us, the key to building and spreading wealth in the United States during the nineteenth century was getting property rights "right." This helps explain why the US government offered squatters the right to purchase the private or public land that they had worked in the West. The policy of preemption made it clear that the US government would take deliberate steps to stock the country with farmers who were disciplined and productive.[31] For a young Abraham Lincoln, this meant that the purpose of the US government was "to 'clear the path' for the individual to labor and get ahead."[32] This principle found its way into Lincoln's policies and helps explain part of his thinking as he took the nation through civil war.[33]

Because absentee land owner claims to property were ignored and government claims were given up as well, the policy of preemption departed fundamentally from European land practices that had protected the aristocratic elite. This enabled America to do three things that were crucial for building its middle class. First, it made pioneers out of those previously viewed as illegal "squatters" or, worse, labeled as "criminals."[34] Second, instead of supporting a titled or leisure class, preemption encouraged others to go and develop the West—by rewarding hard work and individual initiative.[35] Finally, it helped set the stage for America's yeoman farming middle class to emerge, which became the cornerstone of American democracy.[36]

To facilitate land grabs and economic growth and to deal with periodic economic slumps, the US government promoted settlement through pre-emption and made sure that there would be plenty of land to settle. From 1800 to 1848 a series of treaties, wars, and artful negotiations on the part of the US government (the Louisiana Territory, 1803; Florida, 1819; the Transcontinental Treaty, 1821; the Oregon Territory, 1846; Texas, 1845; the Mexican Cession in 1848) helped the nation acquire more than 2 million square miles of territory. It also turned "Manifest Destiny" into a powerful national movement that promoted economic expansion as much as it inspired a sense that God had chosen America to do His bidding. More specifically, it provided a young nation with the land and resources that mercantilism and colonization had granted to European imperialists. These calculated land acquisitions allowed the United States to promote the "multiplication table" that John Quincy Adams had banked on and enabled the country to side with illegal squatters, because more land was always around the corner. It also bought the government time, which it needed to change conflicting property laws. More succinctly, expansion encouraged America to get land rights "right" for its new middle class—the yeoman farmer.[37]

The Homestead Act of 1862 continued the trend of growing America's middle class by providing 160 acres of free public land to settlers who worked the land for at least five years.[38] Just as important, the Act was accompanied by federally subsidized continent-crossing railroads, the creation of the Army Corps of Engineers (which built much of the country's rural infrastructure), the Morrill Act (1862), US Indian policies that made squatting possible, lenient immigration policies, and other state-sponsored initiatives that worked to encourage, protect, and reward the efforts of individual (white) settlers. To be sure, there were no guarantees of success—as many homesteader families found. Yet there was hardly anything "invisible" about the state policies that had set the stage by offering opportunities to a new middle class that would become the cornerstone of the American experience.

The Great Transformation, II: Blue-Collar Factory Workers Strengthen America's Middle Class

From the time of the Civil War through the Great Depression and the emergence of postindustrial society, America's political and economic landscape was dominated by policies and other agreements between industry and the state. The first of these arrangements, which laid the foundation for America's economic surge and prosperity in the twentieth century, was America's unstated industrial policy. Originally put in place to generate revenue (especially during the Civil War), import tariffs became a useful tool for businesses who wanted or needed protection from competition. Indeed, US custom revenue (as a percentage of total import value) was so high that, with the exception of Russia from 1840 to 1860, the United States ranked well above the industrializing world through 1930.[39] Apart from tariffs, business regularly cajoled and bribed Congress to secure generous subsidies, contracts, and protections to build infrastructures and industry in America. Gary M. Walton and Ross M. Robertson write:

> Tariff protection, especially in textiles before the 1840s, did spur an industrial foothold and generate subsequent cost reductions in textiles through learning-by-doing effects. Moreover, the rate of growth of the manufacturing industry was probably stimulated by tariffs, and in that sense the economic progress of the country was thereby hastened. In addition, tariffs altered the distribution of income in favor of owners of industrial property and to the disfavor of consumption.[40]

Apart from protective tariffs, industrialists in nineteenth-century America counted on a foreign policy driven by Manifest Destiny and by permanent expansion during the 1800s. Unsurprisingly American industry prospered from state-led policies as well as from the US variant of ethnic cleansing (its Native American policies), subsidized railroad expansion, deficit spending (especially during the Civil War), liberal government land policies, favorable court decisions for business, an ideology more favorable to social Darwinism than to *laissez-faire,* loose immigration policies, and the use of state militia and federal troops to break strikes in the nineteenth century (which kept wages low).[41] But the real surge in America's blue-collar industrial workforce did not begin until after the Civil War.

With 50.1 percent of the population employed in agriculture, fisheries, or forestry in 1880, America was still primarily a rural society.[42] As well, apart from Southern plantations and the Springfield Armory (guns for the military), industry of all stripes simply wasn't large enough to generate the economies of scale that were necessary for creating the blue-collar middle class that emerged after the Civil War. This is what made government investment in infrastructure and the financial tailwinds of the Civil War so important. Government deficits, government subsidies, and government financing helped build or subsidize communications and industry of all stripes.[43] Post-Civil War demand and financial forces (tied to debt and currency expansion) created and freed up so much capital that the US railroad, manufacturing, coal, banking, iron, steel, and real estate industries became economic forces to be reckoned with by the 1880s.[44] Many industrialists saw their businesses grow to dominate world markets over the next forty years, with the spillover energizing all segments of the economy.[45] Financier William Dodge acknowledged the conditions created by the Civil War in 1863:

> Things here at the North are in a great state of prosperity. You can have no idea of it. The large amounts of money expended by the government have given activity to everything . . . the railroads and manufacturers of all kinds except cotton were never doing so well.[46]

This was not entirely unexpected. After the Northern Army lost key early battles, one Northern financier predicted a rather long war and wrote in 1861 that a fortune could be made for every person on Wall Street who "is not a natural idiot."[47] Things went so well that wartime profiteer Jim Fisk crowed, "You can sell anything to the government at almost any price you've got the guts to ask."[48] Commerce and financial flows grew to such a degree that, in a span of forty years, the United States catapulted past the rest of the world to become the world's number one manufacturer by 1900, with 23.6 percent of the global share.[49] All of this provided the backdrop for growth in the 1860s, when "capitalists of the decade simply got too much done."[50]

Because favorable legislation and high tariffs for industry were followed by an explosion in factory-related jobs after the Civil War, the American middle class made significant tangible gains during the twentieth century. By using the franchise won for males by the early 1840s, America's new middle class slowly advanced social progress by highlighting social injustices, calling for public education, pushing for improved working conditions, and working to alter America's political and legal systems. All of this worked to energize democracy in America.

Still, after the Civil War, business slumps, depressions, nationalism, and simple greed convinced industrialists that America needed additional markets. To sell more goods abroad and to secure cheap resources, a more aggressive foreign policy was needed.[51] America's post-Civil War foreign policy was shaped by disparate business interests that understood very well that US consumers simply couldn't consume what they produced. Among the many policy initiatives used to find markets and expand political influence were the Monroe Doctrine in Latin America, the Open Door

Policy in Asia, the forced opening of Japan, the Spanish-American War, and Dollar Diplomacy, among others. Of these, perhaps the most profitable was the Spanish-American War of 1898. By freeing the Philippines and Cuba, the Spanish-American War provided the pretext for annexing Hawaii in 1898. Simply put, the war handed President McKinley an empire. Although these efforts helped American businesses gain access to the world, efforts to make American foreign policy more uniform in the name of industry had to wait until after World War II.[52]

What emerged from tariffs, subsidies, deficit spending, liberal land policies, an aggressive Native American policy, industry-friendly legislation, industry-friendly court decisions, industry supporting foreign policies, and other initiatives that fostered industrialization was a net increase in the number of American blue-collar workers. But there were still challenges for labor. In the late nineteenth and early twentieth centuries the physical conditions of many factories and mines were often ghastly. The tedium of work, impersonal discipline, and the imbalance of power that developed over time made the work day "grim and dangerous."[53] As well, workers had to deal with labor organizers being blacklisted, workers discharged for joining unions, the forced signing of "yellow dog" contracts, employer-hired spies, and lockouts, among other anti-labor developments. This was especially the case when mass production, scientific management, and the great trusts were entrenched in the American economy in the last half of the nineteenth century.

It's difficult to discuss "the good times" for labor during this period because "between 1860 and World War I, unions operated in a political and social climate of suspicion and incredible hostility."[54] Even though manufacturing workdays, wages, and the cost of living improved by the 1890s, sudden swings in the economy, unemployment, physical dangers, sexism, Jim Crow (for black Americans), few if any legal protections, and other factors put America's new middle class at a distinct disadvantage. State and federal governments stood so firmly on the side of business that it "was considered a legitimate use of political power to call out troops to break strikes."[55] As Michael Lind put it, although many conservatives today like to attribute economic growth and prosperity to unrelenting market forces, the reality is that the market had been "rigged" for industry from time to time.[56]

Presently, it's easy to wax nostalgic about labor's rising standard of living during this period, as if market forces alone created the conditions for America's blue-collar middle class to emerge and prosper. The reality is that government-sanctioned tariffs, an aggressive foreign policy, and industry-friendly policies helped create the conditions for American industry to prosper and for America's blue-collar middle class to develop and grow in the nineteenth and twentieth centuries. Perks such as overtime pay and the 10-hour workday, for example, had little to do with the collective initiative of industry or with *laissez-faire*. These perks were made possible by an increasingly aggressive middle class that fought its way through legal, political, and cultural battles favoring industry.[57] Adam Smith's invisible hand is largely absent when it comes to explaining the advances made by labor during this time.

The Great Transformation, III: The Social Wage Levels the Playing Field for America's Middle Class

America's second middle class was created in part on a rigged system of tariff protection, state subsidies, industry-friendly courts, and the availability of relatively easy money. These factors allowed industrialization to prosper in ways that it couldn't have in other societies. America's third middle class, however, was made possible by a unique combination of technological, administrative, and government innovations. Specifically, technological advances enabled the "country bumpkin" to become the highly productive and respected American farmer. Technology and administrative advancements urged on by labor law enabled the "greasy mechanic" to become the middle-class assembly line worker. Government policies and other administrative advances turned the American counterpart of the sad and pathetic office worker in Charles Dickens' *A Christmas Carol* into one of the respected accountants and professional bureaucrats seen in government and private offices around the country.[58] But perhaps the greatest change in America's third middle class is how the efforts of America's working class have been augmented by what Michael Lind calls the "social wage."[59]

By putting teeth into labor agreements, promoting worker standards and protections, offering insurance and tax incentives, making cash payments available to those down on their luck, sponsoring regulatory regimes, and other offerings that were advantageous to the middle class, the social wage has helped protect America's middle class, while providing a degree of stability for the economy.[60] Specifically, the social wage has created a second level of "compensation" by softening the effects of cyclical recessions, competition, poor industry decisions, and plain bad luck. Although often referred to degradingly as a "safety net," the social wage—like the corporate executive's social perks, golden handshakes, deferred options, and golden parachutes—recognizes that salaries alone do not fully compensate the "sweat equity" provided by workers on the job.[61] The social wage has helped level the playing field for a majority of America's middle class by providing greater job security, support for unions, better wages, improved benefits, and tax incentives. All of this helped close or compress the wealth and income gaps that have always existed but that had grown significantly just before the Great Depression. As a result of the social wage, between 1947 and 1979, family income and wealth gaps in America dropped to historic lows (see Chapter 1).[62]

These advancements were made possible because of the state-driven accomplishments of the previous two middle-class groups. The yeoman farmer was able to expand the democratic experiment by helping settle issues of land and the law. The blue-collar factory worker used the franchise to call for social progress through improved working conditions and public education. Because these legal and social dragons had been slain (or at least partially slain), the third American middle class looked beyond frontier law and social justice to pursue a standard of living that was advanced by deliberate state policy. Specifically, the social wage helped level the playing field by getting the state to lobby and fight alongside organized labor for middle-class issues that had once been ignored. At the start of the Great Depression, the benefits and protections that many people have come to expect when embarking on a career today were almost entirely absent. Widespread poverty among the elderly, the absence of healthcare for tens of millions of Americans, few collective bargaining arrangements, and other standards that are hallmarks of modern developed nations were not available then.

But these conditions changed when the challenges of the Great Depression deepened in the early 1930s and caused Americans—and others in western Europe—to doubt the viability of free-market capitalism. These apprehensions got worse when Franklin D. Roosevelt's initial programs proved unsuccessful in getting the economy going. Even with creative regional public works programs and production incentive offers, he had little to claim in the mid-1930s other than that he was not Herbert Hoover. Part of the problem was that FDR was locked into the neoclassical economic notion that debt should be avoided at all costs. And he was bent on keeping his campaign promise to balance the budget. Another problem was lagging consumer confidence. Although it took World War II to strip the country of the notion that all debt is bad, FDR embarked on a set of market regulatory efforts that acknowledged the complexities of modern markets but did so in a way that made sure that the market worked for everyone—and not just for the big players.

For example, the Securities and Exchange Commission, the Glass-Steagall Act, and the Federal Deposit Insurance Corporation (FDIC) were created after it was learned that market players had designed, created, and pursued market activities that were secretive, morally bankrupt, and destructive to the integrity of the market. To make sure that the businesses peddled by

Wall Street brokers actually existed (referred to as "due diligence") and that inside deals were kept to a minimum, regulatory agencies were created. These government agencies helped erect firewalls to guard against fraud and unwarranted market exuberance. One of the goals of creating a regulatory framework was to help Americans forget or, at least, ignore that thousands of banks had failed during the Depression.

To rebuild confidence in the market, the federal government also sought to bolster the condition of the middle class in the post-World War II era with progressive tax policies, preemptive regulation for industry, stable money policies, and legislation that was labor-friendly and consumer-friendly. The result was heartening. Real income for families climbed by 30 percent between 1952 and 1960 and jumped by another 30 percent between 1960 and 1968.[63] Growth in family income from 1947 through 1979 grew at roughly the same pace for each quintile group in America (see Figure 1.1 in Chapter 1) at the same time that the share of household wealth for the top 1 percent dropped from 44.2 percent to just over 20 percent by the mid-1970s.[64] While this was occurring, in an effort to assist the chronically poor and impoverished, government-sponsored social programs emerged.

Following in the footsteps of FDR's activist New Deal, state efforts to create a sturdier middle-class foundation were promoted by programs such as Harry Truman's Fair Deal (worker security and consumption) and Lyndon B. Johnson's Great Society (opening opportunities for women and people of color). The GI Bill for higher education—perhaps the greatest affirmative action program in American history—opened the doors to education for millions of middle-class Americans. Without the GI Bill, many postwar American veterans would never have considered going to college.[65] Perhaps more important, the GI Bill demonstrated that government-sponsored programs could open doors. Related to this, state funding for state universities increased. This helped pave the way for other programs, including a bevy of government-sponsored student aid and loan packages in the 1960s and 1970s. By the time President Richard Nixon entered the White House in 1969, there was little doubt that the social wage had paid off handsomely for America's middle class. Ensuing programs for women and people of color, through affirmative action programs, contributed to increased opportunities for more Americans. The logic was simple: why encourage people to get an advanced degree if doors weren't open in other areas of society?

For those on the other end of life's great adventure, reasonable observers recognize that the standard of living for America's elderly improved with the creation of government programs such as Social Security and Medicare. However, what is often misunderstood or ignored is how these programs have directly benefited America's middle class. By freeing families from the financial burden of caring for elderly parents, which could cause financial hardship and lead to bankruptcy, the evolution of social wage programs such as Social Security and Medicare meant that middle-class Americans had more disposable income for themselves. More freedom, larger homes, vacations in Europe, and recreational toys that helped build up the recreational and outdoor industries were the result. Freed from the prospect of having to provide daily support for parents or from having to pay expensive medical bills, the middle class benefited from financial and social wages between 1947 and 1979 that went further than many anticipated.

Although conservative politicians have been able to get political mileage by criticizing government spending and growing national debt (the vast majority created under conservative administrations), the reality is that the success of America's third middle class wasn't made possible by Adam Smith's invisible hand or the magic of the market. State-led initiatives in spending, regulation, and labor made possible what the private sector could not—and would not—have provided on its own. The result of these developments was a precipitous drop in wealth gaps and income inequality in America from the 1930s through the 1970s. The gaps shrank so much that economic historians Claudia Goldin and Robert Margo have labeled the socioeconomic change as the "Great Compression."[66] In this manner, even though the heart of the American middle class may have migrated from yeoman farmers to lunch-bucket laborers to white-collar social wage earners, the creation and maintenance of America's middle class owes much to what Michael Lind called state-sponsored "social engineering on a colossal scale."

Conclusion

When Adam Smith wrote about the laws of justice, he was clear that any system that encourages or restrains capital so that market rewards are not properly earned or distributed "retards" the "progress of society towards real wealth and greatness."[67] For example, when industry organizes and uses its resources to convince governments to disrupt and outlaw labor unions or to support family wage laws (higher pay for men than for women), the prospects for human dignity and better wages are artificially stunted. It's difficult to speak of a harmony of interests when the prospects of labor (one of the primary factors of production) are artificially restrained.

The experiences of coal miners in the mountains of West Virginia help make this point.[68] After several major accidents, numerous violence-studded disruptions, and payroll abuses by mining companies in the state of West Virginia, the state created the West Virginia Department of Mines at the beginning of the twentieth century (1905). Although miners were concerned about many issues, at the heart of miners' concerns was the need to protect themselves from the abuses of working and living in mining towns. Among the many forms of abuse for miners was the requirement to lease or rent company tools and equipment. Being paid in "scrip" was another odious practice that the workers put up with: not only was this token form of currency good only at the company store, but prices there were inflated and the quality of goods was suspect. Worse, debts accumulated at the company store were recorded by less than honest bookkeepers. Among the most important demands made by striking miners—which they placed ahead of a pay increase—were quality of life issues such as sanitation and regular upkeep of homes in the company town. With labor making increasingly more demands, under the guise of protecting property, mining companies had turned to private detectives in 1903. The reality was that the detectives were hired to keep an eye on union leaders and to undermine their organizing activities. After the West Virginia coal fields labor conflicts (1903–1921) began, hired thugs once again were employed to keep an eye on "Negro strikebreakers"—many of whom wanted to leave once they became aware of the working conditions. The presence of the detectives, coupled with the West Virginia governor's use of the National Guard to beat up on strikers—a tactic used as early as 1894—brought real violence to labor disputes. Mining companies even went so far as to erect cement fortifications that resembled the machine-gun bunkers used by the Germans on the hills of Normandy.

The point of outlining the story of West Virginia miners isn't so much to highlight the conditions and demands that existed during this era but rather to demonstrate how the standards and quality of life that have been achieved in the United States in general, and in other Western states, didn't come about because of some mythical invisible hand or because of industry insights into human dignity or the needs of labor. The safety and wage standards that exist today came about because workers in communities across America struggled to change conditions that often pitted a specific industry—which often had interlocking interests with other industries—against American labor.

To be sure, the coal operators in West Virginia argued that they didn't know what all of the fuss was about. How could anyone be against a generous company that provides housing, a place to purchase goods, and a regular job with regular pay? It wasn't until labor rose up and challenged the abusive and monopolistic conditions that actually existed in company towns that others began to see the imbalances between the picture painted by industry and the realities lived by labor.

On many levels, the American miner's story offers us insight into the story of labor's evolution in Europe and America. Like the peasants of medieval Europe, miners needed work and were forced into conditions in which overlords could dominate virtually all aspects of their lives. Rebellion and the introduction of enlightened leaders paved the way for improvements in the miners' standard of living. Subsequent changes and the gains made from these changes were not achieved easily. Just as the progressive ideas of democracy and capitalism were fought by conservative aristocrats in Europe, issues related to social and economic justice in America have always been fought by forces who warn of impending doom if changes are made. But, as noted throughout this work, the successes of labor—as is the case with the successes of industry—did not occur because of some mythical invisible hand.

Notes

1. Lynn Montross, *War through the Ages,* 3rd edition (New York: Harper & Row, Publishers, 1960), 325.

2. Montross, *War,* 326.

3. Montross, *War,* 330.

4. Herman M. Schwartz, *States Versus Market: The Emergence of a Global Economy* (New York: St. Martin's Press, 2000), 11–21.

5. Anthony D. Smith, *National Identity* (Reno, NV: University of Nevada Press, 1991), 59.

6. Robert Gilpin, *The Political Economy of International Relations* (Princeton, NJ: Princeton University Press, 1987), 31. Blog Commentary.

7. Mark A. Kishlansky, Patrick Geary, and Patricia O'Brien, *Civilization in the West: Since 1555*, Vol. II, 4th edition (New York: Addison-Wesley-Longman, 2001), 548.

8. Schwartz, *States,* 12.

9. Schwartz, *States,* 12.

10. Kishlansky et al., *Civilization,* 549. Blog Commentary.

11. Gilpin, *The Political,* 31.

12. Schwartz, *States,* 280.

13. Gilpin, *The Political,* 32.

14. The argument presented here is drawn from Robert Heilbroner, *The Worldly Philosophers: The Lives, Times and Ideas of the Great Economic Thinkers* (New York: Touchstone, 1986).

15. Kishlansky et al., *Civilization,* 512.

16. Glen Blackburn, *Western Civilization: A Concise History—From Early Societies to the Present,* combined volume (New York: St. Martin's Press, 1991), 207–208. Blog Commentary.

17. Arthur A. Stein, "The Hegemon's Dilemma: Great Britain, the United States, and the International Economic Order." In *Theory and Structure in International Political Economy: An International Organization Reader,* ed. Charles Lipson and Benjamin J. Cohen. (Cambridge, MA: MIT Press, 1999), 290.

18. Heilbroner, *The Worldly,* 24.

19. Adam Smith, *The Wealth of Nations,* Complete and Unabridged, Introduction by Robert Reich (New York: Modern Library, 2000), 156.

20. Fred Block and Margaret R. Somers, "Beyond the Economistics Fallacy: The Holistic Social Science of Karl Polanyi," *Vision and Method in Historical Sociology,* ed., Theda Skocpol, (Cambridge, MA: Cambridge University Press, 1991), 54–58.

21. Ha-Joon Chang, *Bad Samaritans: The Myth of Free Trade and the Secret History of Capitalism* (New York: Bloombury Press, 2008), 40.

22. Block and Somers, "Beyond," 54–58.

23. Block and Somers, "Beyond," 63–64.

24. The general outline for the rise of the three middle classes is drawn from Michael Lind, "Are We Still a Middle-Class Nation?" *Atlantic Monthly,* January-February 2004, available online.

25. Lind, "Are We," 2004; Gary M. Walton and Ross M. Robertson, *History of the American Economy,* 5th edition (New York: Harcourt-Brace-Jovanovich, 1983), 187–193.

26. Walton and Robertson, *History,* 187–188.

27. Walton and Robertson, *History,* 187–188.

28. Walter La Feber, *The American Age: U.S. Foreign Policy at Home and Abroad, 1750 to the Present,* 2nd edition (New York: Norton, 1994).

29. Hernando De Soto, *The Mystery of Capital: Why Capitalism Triumphs in the West and Fails Everywhere Else* (New York: Basic Books, 2000), 149.

30. Walton and Robertson, *History,* 187.

31. De Soto, *The Mystery.*

32. Norton Garfinkle, *The American Dream vs. the Gospel of Wealth: The Fight for a Productive Middle Class* (New Haven, CT: Yale University Press, 2006), 28–30.

33. Garfinkle, *The American,* 30. Blog Commentary.

34. De Soto, *The Mystery,* 120.

35. Walton and Robertson, *History,* 187.

36. Lind, "Are We."

37. Douglass C. North, *Structure and Change in Economic History* (New York: Norton, 1981), 24–25. Blog Commentary.

38. Lind, "Are We"; Walton and Robertson, *History,* 436.

39. Stein, "The Hegemon's," 283, 302, Table 3. G. John Ikenberry, *After Victory: Institutions, Strategic Restraint, and the Rebuilding of Order after Major Wars* (Princeton, NJ: Princeton University Press, 2001), 86, Table 4-1. Blog Commentary.

40. Walton and Robertson, *History,* 257

41. Apart from Western Union and retailers such as Montgomery Ward, before 1880 there were no large firms, let alone industrial ones, operating on a national scale in America, Alfred Chandler Jr., *The Visible Hand: The Managerial Revolution in American Business* (Cambridge, MA: Belknap Press, 1977), 64–74, 288.

42. Walton and Robertson, *History,* 436.

43. Arthur M. Schlesinger Jr., *The Age of Jackson* (Old Saybrook, CT: Konecky & Konecky, 1971), 129–130. Blog Commentary.

44. LaFeber, *The American,* 158; Schlesinger Jr., *The Age,* 130; Walton and Robertson, *History,* 321–322, Figure 17-1. Blog Commentary.

45. Kevin Phillips, *Wealth and Democracy: A Political History of the American Rich* (New York: Random House, 2002); La Faber, *The American,* 157–159.

46. Phillips, *Wealth,* 33.

47. LaFeber, *The American,* 157.

48. Phillips, *Wealth,* 39.

49. Ikenberry, *After,* 120, Table 5-1.

50. Phillips, *Wealth,* 39.

51. LaFeber, *The American,* 158–163.

52. Jeff Frieden, "Sectoral Conflict and U.S. Foreign Economic Policy, 1914–1940," in G. John Ikenberry, *American Foreign Policy: Theoretical Essays,* 4th edition (New York: Longman, 2002), 138–167.

53. Robert E. McGinn, *Science, Technology, and Society* (Englewood Cliffs, NJ: Prentice-Hall, 1991), 107–108.

54. Walton and Robertson, *History,* 436.

55. Walton and Robertson, *History,* 436–437.

56. Lind, "Are We."

57. Garfinkle, *The American,* 54–61; Walton and Robertson, *History,* 441. Blog Commentary.

58. McGinn, *Science,* 1991.

59. Lind, "Are We."

60. John D. Nagle, *Introduction to Comparative Politics: Challenges of Conflict and Change in a New Era,* 4th edition (Chicago: Nelson-Hall Publishers, 1996), 50. Blog Commentary.

61. The term "sweat equity" is drawn from Alvin Toffler, *Previews and Premises. A Penetrating Conversation about Jobs, Identity, Sex*

Roles, the New Politics of the Information Age and the Hidden Forces Driving the Economy (Boston: South End Press, 1983).

62. Phillips, Wealth, 123, 137, Tables 3.5 and 3.14.

63. Phillips, Wealth, 78.

64. Phillips, Wealth, 78–79.

65. Ross Douthat, "Does Meritocracy Work? Not If Society and Colleges Keep Failing to Distinguish between Wealth and Merit," Atlantic Monthly, November 2005, available online. Blog Commentary.

66. Phillips, Wealth, 76; Lind, "Are We."

67. Adam Smith, An Inquiry into the Nature and Causes of the Wealth of Nations, The Harvard Classics, vol. 10, ed., Charles Bullock (New York: PF Collier & Son Company, 1909), 466.

68. William C. Blizzard, When Miners March: The Story of Coal Miners in West Virginia (Gay, WV: Appalachian Community Services, 2004). Although the details of the story presented here are drawn from William C. Blizzard's book, additional information can be found at "West Virginia's Mining Wars," state of West Virginia, Archive and History, available online.

CHAPTER 7

TOWARD "FREER" INTERNATIONAL TRADE

Soon after the Japanese attack on Pearl Harbor in 1941, "Argentina blatantly obstructed efforts by the United States to persuade the Latin American nations to break relations with the Axis" powers.[1] Other Argentine activities throughout World War II led many people in the United States to claim that Argentina's wartime neutrality was little more than political cover for deeper pro-Nazi sympathies. In line with these sentiments, statements made by Secretary of State Cordell Hull during World War II suggested that Argentina was hiding German spies and escaping Nazis.[2] Then US-Argentine relations took a turn for the worse after 1946. In an effort to undermine Juan Perón's presidential bid, the State Department issued a "blue book" that detailed collaboration and links between successive Argentine governments, the military, and the Axis powers.

Relations took another turn for the worse after 1948, when the United States declared that Marshall Plan dollars couldn't be used to purchase Argentine goods. The United States was effectively punishing Argentina by authorizing Marshall Plan dollars for farm products produced by the United States and by favored allies. The Agricultural Act of 1948 cemented these policy goals. Specifically, the "federal government would increase grain production by subsidizing American farmers and would finance grain sales in Europe" through the Marshall Plan.[3] The impact was immediate and devastating for Argentina. By 1952 Argentina's share of world wheat markets dropped from 23 percent to 9 percent whereas the United States' share of wheat markets grew from 7 percent to 46.1 percent. By the early 1950s American grain exports to Europe were eight times greater than before the war, and its share of global corn markets jumped from 9 percent to 63.9 percent![4]

Denied access to "Marshall Markets," Argentina sold to smaller markets, which deprived the country of needed dollars.[5] Although Argentina's

*postwar problems were no doubt compounded by Perón's populist poli-
cies, America's decision to shut Argentina out led to lost market share,
compounded its dollar shortage, and helped precipitate a balance of payments crisis. These dynamics undermined Argentine development and
fomented civil unrest. Both helped force Perón from power and brought
about military dictatorship by 1955. Today, many argue that competitiveness and the logic of the market are sufficient to explain America's
postwar agricultural fortunes. The reality is quite different. Expanded
market share after World War II also depended on US military victories
and on the subsequent divvying up of the spoils of war—which speaks as
much to economic nationalism as it does to free market competition.*

Contrary to what many pundits and politicians believe about commerce in general and international trade in specific, free trade and profits
do not just happen if government gets out of the way. Domestic considerations and national security issues have a hand in shifting the commercial
waters, as the Argentine example above illustrates. In the process, specific
economic interests are either promoted or sacrificed, depending on the
economic or security interests involved. This means that, unless ego,
avarice, and fear are either tamed or snuffed out as human emotions, the
fluid economic world envisioned by the followers of Adam Smith isn't
within reach. History shows that even those who push free trade are often
reluctant practitioners.

Many forget that, even though Britain urged other states in the early
nineteenth century to embrace the ideas of Adam Smith and David Ricardo,
the British were hardly free traders. In the immediate post-Napoleonic era,
British artisans weren't allowed to emigrate, and the export of machinery
and gold were restricted. With the Corn Laws and Navigation Acts in place,
protective tariffs jumped from 20 percent of state revenues in 1820 to 44.2
percent in 1840.[6] And there is the matter of Britain's imperial colonies,
which were closed to outsiders and which provided British industry with
cheap resources and captive markets well into the twentieth century. Driven
by very political considerations, these policies were hardly a recipe—or an
indication—of Adam Smith's *laissez-faire* economics.

This suggests that the birth of free trade in the international arena
wasn't governed by Adam Smith's free market principles and that it hardly
comes close to representing the idealized principles that many argue we
need to re-embrace today. Noted economic historian Charles Kindleberger
reminds us that the repeal of Britain's Corn Laws in 1846—which helped
usher in the free trade era—was driven by the desire to stifle competitors
on the European continent and by the need to strengthen the market
prospects of Britain's domestic producers.[7] These realities, combined with

very deliberate and favorable legislation for certain producers, helped generate the wealth that Britain needed in order to maintain Europe's balance of power, defend its far-flung empire, and wage war in the nineteenth century. These dynamics are important to understand, because they illustrate the symbiotic relationship between markets and politics. Montesquieu saw this early on and wrote:

> Peace is the natural effect of trade. Two nations who differ with each other become reciprocally dependent; for if one has an interest in buying, the other has an interest in selling; and thus their union is founded on their mutual necessities.[8]

Montesquieu's statement remains intellectually attractive because it's parsimonious. Unfortunately, its simplicity is also a drawback. It has wrongly suggested to many pundits and politicians that trade is the key variable for bringing peace on Earth. And just as the Beatles's tune "All You Need Is love" is no recipe for making your way through life, neither is the simple embrace of free trade sufficient for bringing harmony and stability to the world. Still, many pundits and politicians remain convinced that free trade is the path to peace. They continue to believe, however naïvely, that, if politics could be removed or if the government could be marginalized in the trading arena, the world would be a better place. But, as James Madison argued in *Federalist #10*, the state has a role in the market place because "the most common and durable source of factions has been the various and unequal distribution of property." Part of the problem can be traced to free market advocates whose statements are often self-serving or blinded by ideology.

Free trade advocates regularly call for getting the government out of the marketplace. They do so not because *laissez-faire* always works (Keynes showed why) but because it paints a self-congratulatory image of the self-made man. Calling attention to subsidies, write-offs, bailouts, and favorable legislation that sustain wealth and the profits of an industry can ruin the false bravado of any self-made man. Others push to keep government out of the marketplace because it serves their economic interests. Effective rules and regulations can both undermine the efforts of the unscrupulous and uncover "creative" bookkeeping. Conveniently ignored is how government efforts have helped maintain the "laws of justice" that Adam Smith said were necessary for fluid markets to function. To demonstrate how prevalent and necessary the state has been to making market forces work historically, this chapter discusses the role of politics in promoting trade between states. To demonstrate how domestic considerations and national security issues have a hand in shifting the commercial waters, I begin by looking at state-led initiatives in the cradle of the capitalism, Britain.

The Political Roots of "Free Trade": Britain Abolishes the Corn Laws

The Corn Laws were first introduced in 1804 when the aristocratic landowners who dominated the British Parliament sought to protect their profits by imposing a duty on imported corn (in Britain "corn" refers to grain, or wheat). After the Napoleonic Wars—during which time imported corn was banned—British landowners succeeded in pressuring the House of Commons in 1815 to pass the Corn Laws, effectively protecting domestic corn producers from competition. It's interesting to note that, when the Corn Laws were implemented, the only real rivals to British goods were, ironically, private British companies that had invested in charter companies and other overseas adventures. So strengthening the market position of British producers wasn't driven by market competition. It was driven by the British government, which catered to the needs of the British aristocracy, even as it was pushing free trade principles.

Eliminating the Corn Laws and other protectionist policies required a good deal of effort on the part of Britain's emerging industrial and middle classes. These efforts paid off, in part, because of two developments. First, Britain's emerging industrial classes complained that the Corn Laws not only favored large landowners but also resulted in a demand for higher wages by workers who were forced to pay higher prices for their food. As well, those living in the country's rapidly expanding towns became increasingly vocal as their numbers increased. Expansion in the towns of England was an interesting development because, in spite of "massive emigration, Britain's population quadrupled from 10.2 million in 1801 to 37 million in 1901."[9] Britain's domestic grain producers simply couldn't accommodate this demographic shift on their own. But, as is the case with many of history's transformations, a bit of dumb luck helped too.

When a trade depression hit in 1839—which was aided by a series of bad harvests—it helped lend credibility to the Anti-Corn League. The Anti-Corn League was becoming a formidable political force, going beyond the Corn Laws to argue that other trade restrictions undermined the commercial prospects of all British producers. Leading the charge against Britain's protectionist policies were machinery manufacturers, who pointed out that competitors couldn't match their quality and that, in any event, the smuggling of machinery undermined restrictions that were in place.[10] Several additional factors contributed to the repeal of the Corn Laws. Specifically, the emergence of the Manchester School and its singular focus on "freedom for industry to buy in the cheapest and sell in the dearest market" appealed to policymakers of the day.[11] Apart from the Enlightenment currents that continued to sweep the intellectual seas, Britain was also the world's dominant manufacturer. Britain produced higher quality goods and it could afford to compete with other producers around the world. In the end, as noted economic historian Charles Kindleberger pointed out, new political pressures, competitiveness, rent seekers, and geostrategic calculations (discussed later) all played a role in aiding the efforts of those who sought to repeal the Corn Laws.[12] Whether we highlight vested interests competing for rents or the efforts of the Anti-Corn League, repealing the Corn Laws was also a product of the work done by one individual—Richard Cobden.

Free trade supporter Richard Cobden (1804–1865) emerged as a dominant political figure in Britain at the same time that the potato famine of 1845 spread over Ireland.[13] The arrival of Richard Cobden is important, because he believed that British policies were often used to pursue ends that benefited its elite class alone. The result was that the people were burdened with self-interested policies, which the middle class paid for by way of excessive taxation and higher prices for food. For Cobden, the Corn Laws represented a clear example of aristocratic selfishness paid for by the masses. When Ireland, a virtual agricultural monoculture society at the time, was hit by the potato blight and resultant famine that left the countryside in a state of starvation, Cobden saw an opportunity. Driven by the disaster in Ireland and by Cobden's unrelenting appeals, Conservative Prime Minister Sir Robert Peel was convinced that he needed to do something. To feed Ireland he had to make bread affordable. This meant importing cheaper American grain and putting an end to the Corn Laws. Interestingly, these developments also help us understand the contours of the modern global trading system.

Up until the early 1830s Britain had imported "negligible quantities of fruit, vegetables, and live animals."[14] But with a growing population, starvation in Ireland, and the natural carrying capacity of Britain (and Europe) at its limits, the growing demands of an industrializing world mandated that Britain look elsewhere for its foodstuffs. This meant that the Corn Laws and the Navigation Acts had to be repealed if Britain wanted access to the world's food. This decision generated significant political and ecological waves around the world. Because of British and European consumer tastes, the geographic areas under the control of the Europeans became populated with the animals and foodstuffs that weren't native to specific regions. As Herman Schwartz put it, the political expansion of Britain and Europe

> caused enormous ecological changes around the globe, for only a few of the foods and raw materials grown for Britain and, later, Europe naturally occurred in the areas Europeans came to control. Even where they occurred naturally, their geographic range was fairly limited. We tend to perceive places like Australia, Malaya, Brazil, or Iowa as having a natural comparative advantage, but the ecology in virtually all of today's agricultural areas with obvious comparative advantages was in fact conquered and transformed by transplanted animals, weeds, pests, predators, and pathogens."[15]

Put together, all of this tells us that state-led British (and European) policies drove markets and globalization early on. More to the point, the factors that led to the repeal of the Corn Laws and the spread of freer trade principles abroad include: (1) domestic political interests competing for rents, (2) the ascent and increasing political influence of Britain's manufacturing sector, (3) changing demographics in Britain, (4) the emergence of the Manchester School's free trade ideology, (5) Ireland's potato famine, and (6) the geostrategic demands of imperialism and empire. Then we have to consider the true governing dynamics of survival in the international arena: funding the security needs of the state. This political and economic mix suggest that free markets and international trade from the past had little to do with Adam Smith's invisible hand. Rather, a very visible, security-oriented, changing hand of the state made freer trade possible in Britain and Europe.[16]

This underscores the point that a magical invisible hand doesn't suddenly emerge domestically or internationally if the state just backs away. It didn't work that way during the nineteenth century, when capitalism first emerged, and it doesn't work that way today at the beginning of the twenty-first century. Highly political interests are also behind the advent of globalization and free trade. Still, because states agreed to cooperate and trade under the guidelines of free trade, it's necessary to ask how states came to accept free trade as a good idea. What we find is that the concessions offered by Britain (and then the United States) induced consent on the part of other states. Put another way, although Charles Kindleberger may be correct in establishing that the ideology and the logic of the market were critical for the emergence of free trade policies in Britain, one of the most powerful market selling points was the "free ride" that Britain offered.

Geostrategy and "Freer" Trade in the Nineteenth Century

Both Britain and the United States benefited from the trading systems forged in the nineteenth and twentieth centuries. Because of negotiations with "followers" and acceptance of asymmetric agreements that discriminated against many of Britain's and America's own goods, both the British and American periods of dominance and free trade deviated greatly from the classic ideals espoused by Adam Smith's disciples. The trading systems created by Britain and the United States may have lowered tariff barriers, but they didn't lead to free trade as much as they led to "freer" trade.[17] The important point isn't that states slowly embraced these wealth-enhancing economic principles. Rather, it's that highly political considerations drove states to embrace commercial cooperation. The following helps us understand the role that politics has played in making market economics attractive.

The Cobden-Chevalier Treaty, I[18]

Although it's easy to point to 1860 and the signing of the Cobden-Chevalier Treaty as the beginning of the freer trade era in Europe, the roots of free trade go back almost twenty years. In the 1840s a report to Britain's parliament pointed out that fewer than twenty goods generated 95 percent of England's custom duties. This was an important revelation, because custom revenues generated 44.2 percent of total government revenue in 1840. British leaders who could read the economic tea leaves saw the report and instantly understood its implications—the income base would remain relatively stable if Britain dropped import tariffs on all but twenty products. Still, many skeptics were wary of losing a source of revenue. They came around only when the British Parliament reinstituted the income tax in 1842. Combined with the repeal of the Corn Laws in 1846 and the abolition of the Navigation Acts in 1849, eliminating tariffs signaled to allies and fence-sitters alike that trade with Britain would bring dividends.[19]

Although Britain began eliminating tariffs unilaterally, it didn't do so simply because it was advantageous commercially or because it mirrored Manchester School ideology. To be sure, agricultural output expanded when tariffs were reduced. But economic historian Charles Kindleberger makes it clear that the expansion of agriculture production wasn't a result of the repeal of the Corn Laws alone. Rather, technical advances and other political factors helped expand Britain's agriculture output in the 1850s.[20] Even though the talking points of Adam Smith and David Ricardo did provide an intellectual framework for eliminating tariffs and promoting freer trade, many visible hands contributed to abolishing the Corn Laws and creating an environment for freer trade. One of these hands was tied to developments in the international political arena and to war.

Specifically, because Britain was so far ahead of the rest of Europe in industrial production, repealing the Corn Laws represented a unique opportunity to deepen the mutually entangling political alliances that had been agreed to at Vienna in 1815.[21] The entangling alliances that each country committed to at Vienna had created the conditions for a world order that "supplemented, and to some extent replaced, balance of power as the core logic of order among the great powers."[22] If the post-Napoleonic European order encouraged cooperation among states (balance of power), almost any excuse to augment would do, such as trade. The complex rearrangement of expectations and norms at the international level is something that Britain's Richard Cobden and France's Michel Chevalier understood and that they worked to take advantage of during their trade negotiations.

Richard Cobden began his career as a commercial traveler and then, with several partners, started his own business, which was a commercial success. This granted Cobden the time and wealth to travel throughout Europe and America. During his travels he collected information that he used to write *England, Ireland and America* (1835). In its pages Cobden was critical of Britain's policies in Ireland and warned that Britain would soon find it difficult to compete with America. As a student of the Manchester School of economics, Cobden argued for policies that facilitated trade—specifically, lower taxes on the middle class, public education, and removal of tariffs, among others. What drove Cobden was his fear that war would come to the continent if Europe didn't find venues for cooperating. Events in Europe in 1848 and the Crimean War (1854–1856) helped convince Cobden that trade could be used as one of those venues.

For his part, Michel Chevalier (1806–1879) was a leader of the French Liberal School. The French Liberal School upheld a strong if not radical *laissez-faire* line. More concretely, it promoted the infallibility of a self-regulating market system.[23] Considered to be the French counterpart to the British Manchester School (but with greater accessibility), the French Liberal School was so optimistic about the purity of market economics that Karl Marx later derisively referred to its proponents as "vulgar" economists. It promoted (more likely, it was founded upon) the teachings of Jean-Baptiste Say's interpretation of *laissez-faire* economics, which worked its way into Chevalier's writings. Chevalier emerged as a leading economist in France and a frequent advisor to the political establishment.

Although Chevalier believed in the power of free markets, what concerned him were the excesses and dangers produced by free markets. This compelled him to accept a limited role for state intervention in the economy. The backgrounds of Richard Cobden and Michel Chevalier are important because, for all of their practical experiences and understanding of market economics, security was their primary inspiration for pursuing freer trade.[24] And the stakes were high.

The Cobden-Chevalier Treaty, II

Britain's deteriorating relationship with Russia helps explain its efforts to expand trade with France. Britain was worried about Russian aspirations in Constantinople, which were driven by Russia's desire to secure access to the straits in Turkey: the Bosporus Straits is located in Turkey and gives Russia access to the Sea of Marmara, which leads to the Dardanelles Strait, the gateway to the Aegean and Mediterranean seas. After the Crimean War (1854–1856), which pitted Britain, France, and the Ottoman Empire against Russia, British concerns over war were especially acute.[25] But what really pushed Britain and France together was the desire to secure an agreement to prevent war between the two over Italy. Strategically, Britain wanted a free and unified Italy, to act as a counterweight to France and Austria. France was concerned that a unified Italy on its southern border would threaten its security. After the 1848 revolutions spilled into Italy, France attacked Rome because of its fear that Italy would unite and become stronger under the newly appointed King Charles Albert. French concerns proved to be well grounded: at the urging of Italian radicals, the new king declared war against Austria in 1849. After invading the peninsula and overthrowing the nascent republic in 1849, the French moved to restore the pope (who fled from Italian nationalists), and they remained in Italy until 1870.

But France was also driven by two pressing realities that were critical to its national security. First, under Napoleon III, the French "wanted to break out of the diplomatic isolation to which the Congress of Vienna had consigned them" to in 1815.[26] With this in mind, Napoleon III "persuaded the Turkish Sultan to grant him the sobriquet of Protector of the Christians . . . a role the Russian Tsar traditionally reserved for himself."[27] Second, because France "could not produce enough iron to supply local demand for rails,"[28] which was crucial for economic expansion, the country needed to embrace free trade with Britain. To be sure, France understood the pitfalls of trading with a superior trading partner. But, like Germany in the twentieth century, France was also seeking redemption for fomenting war through a unified Europe.[29] Free trade served these ends.

Acknowledging these dynamics, Arthur Stein wrote that "political rather than commercial or philosophical considerations motivated Britain's shift in its commercial practices. Both Britain and France looked to a commercial agreement as a basis for improving their relations."[30] The correspondence from Richard Cobden to Michel Chevalier makes this point clear:

> I should be glad to see a removal of the impediments which our foolish legislation interposes to the intercourse between the two countries. I see no other hope but in such policy for any permanent improvements in the *political* relations of France and England. I utterly despair of finding peace and harmony in the efforts of Governments and diplomatists. The people of the two nations must be brought into mutual dependence by the supply of each other's wants. There is no other way of counteracting the antagonism of language and race. It is God's own method of producing an *entente cordiale*, and no other plan is worth a farthing.[31]

There's no doubt that France conceded more to Britain than it gained economically by signing the Cobden-Chevalier Treaty. But by taking care to manage its long-term geostrategic goals, France contributed to a political stability that promoted its long-term security interests. This wouldn't be the last time that political and security considerations would trump economics in the international arena.

Roots of Postwar Cooperation: "If Goods Can't Cross Borders, Soldiers Will"

If we jump forward eighty-five years, we find that among the critical lessons learned after World War II was the importance of political leadership and regulation to markets and global security—both domestically and internationally.[32] Domestically the Great Depression demonstrated that people without jobs and with no hope in the future will question the viability of market capitalism. This occurred as millions of Americans who had worked hard lost everything during the Depression. But losing jobs and material possessions was only a warm-up to losing hope and confidence in the future. This was troubling because, when the moral justification of capitalism—the idea that if you work hard you will get ahead—is in doubt, democratic politics is no longer a celebration of political freedom. It becomes an aimless and desperate search for scapegoats, which often settles for false leadership and empty solutions. Under these conditions, twisted ideas or charismatic megalomaniacs can win the day. From this environment the serpents of fascism and the vermin of radical revolution can emerge, as the 1930s proved.

Internationally, the interwar period made it clear that trade in the twentieth century required guidance and management. Without it, nation-states could be driven into autarky or competitive trading blocs or to invade others, as the interwar period demonstrated. Cordell Hull, FDR's Secretary of State, understood this long before others did. Watching as nation-states became increasingly aggressive and closed themselves off to trade in the mid-1930s, Hull spoke of impending conflict, presciently warning: "If goods can't cross borders, soldiers will." Japan, Italy, and Germany made Hull an unwelcome prophet and had a significant impact on America's postwar trade policies. Specifically, the lessons learned from the Treaty of Versailles and the Great Depression told the post–World War II victors that, if they wanted to avoid the mistakes of the past, they needed to ignore the voices of those who clung to the past—and they were everywhere.

It is often forgotten that, immediately after World War II, there were influential corners who wanted to follow the punitive path of Versailles. Fearful of a resurgent Germany, several proposals were made. One plan called for draining Germany of its economic resources by turning the country into a "pastoral state"—or at least into an industrial lightweight. Led by Secretary of Treasury Henry Morgenthau Jr., a plan was presented that would partition Germany, have its mining centers annexed by its neighbors, and dismantle or destroy its heavy industrial capacity.[33] President Truman was finally convinced to shelve the Morgenthau Plan because of stalled economic development in Europe, malnutrition in Germany, rising communist threats in Europe, and opposition from US allies in the region.

To make sure that markets worked globally and to reduce the tendency toward economic nationalism, the allied powers crafted a liberal but modified arrangement that relied on US leadership. They sought to create the conditions for domestic prosperity and economic interdependence, which would encourage states to see each other as trading partners rather than as trading competitors. To create this world order, postwar leaders followed in the footsteps of the Cobden-Chevalier Treaty. Political leaders worked to enhance a cooperative spirit by making sure that markets worked. Economic interdependence, in turn, facilitated and strengthened political cooperation. In this way the economic agreements signed at Bretton Woods were considered to be as important to the postwar containment strategy as were the security agreements signed at Potsdam (1945), Rio (1947), Brussels (1947), and Washington DC (1949). Security agreements were buttressed by diplomacy and trade. In 1947 President Truman spoke of the need to learn the larger lessons of economic rivalry:

> As each battle of the economic war of the thirties was fought, the inevitable tragic result became more and more apparent. From the tariff policy of Hawley and Smoot [1930], the world went to Ottawa and the system of imperial preferences, from Ottawa to the kind of elaborate and detailed restrictions adopted by Nazi Germany.[34]

President Truman and his advisors understood that, after the Great Depression, each step toward protectionism (Smoot-Hawley), closed borders (the System of Imperial Preferences), and economic nationalism (Japan and Germany) had moved the world closer to war. They also understood that recovery and cooperation had to be achieved, which they didn't trust to the magic of the marketplace.

Trading American Interests, I: The Beginning[35]

By the end of World War II the United States understood that it needed to use its position to do more than dominate selfishly or abandon the world, as many believed it did after the war. The United States used its power to transform the world, by turning allies and former enemies into instruments of order and political stability.[36] To do so, the United States offered economic concessions and granted industrial favors to political allies during the Cold War. By curtailing its own power and tolerating free riders, the United States—like Britain before it—not only demonstrated restraint but also showed that it was going to act "according to a more sophisticated understanding power and order."[37] The result of exercising strategic restraint was increased legitimacy and the gradual acceptance of American political goals by other states after World War II.

To get to this point the United States offered many concessions and, perhaps most important, rewarded allies by literally giving them markets. The flip side of this, however, was that domestic industries were given away as successive postwar presidents sought to buy off cooperating allies. Alfred Eckes writes:

> A succession of presidents, beginning with Harry Truman, have consciously subordinated domestic economic interests to foreign policy objectives. To strengthen free world economies and help contain Soviet expansionism the executive branch has rolled back tariffs and removed trade restrictions, opening the

giant American market to the world's manufactures . . . The record suggests that for diplomatic and national security reasons the US government sacrificed thousands of domestic jobs to create employment and prosperity elsewhere in the noncommunist world . . . [refusing] to grant import relief to trade-sensitive industries in the interests of winning the Cold War.[38]

Borrowing a page from George F. Kennan's containment strategy, America's postwar position toward the Soviet Union went beyond military considerations.[39] It also included the goal of creating stable and prosperous economic partners. The idea was to build partners up economically so that they could stand as a bulwark against communist expansion. America's "liberal grand strategy" included a foreign policy that went beyond military might to also focus on facilitating economic recovery in the West; integrating former enemies, Japan and Germany, into the international economic community; and denying the Eastern bloc access to Western technology.[40] These efforts strengthened America's hand internationally by promoting and strengthening economic interdependence. To do this, the United States had to shelve the notion that an "invisible hand" or the logic of the market created healthy economic partners. Rather, the United States actively pursued the reconstruction of allied infrastructures, encouraged imports from key allies, promoted the exports of Japan, and followed a program of deliberately putting US dollars into other nation's hands by encouraging trade and consumption through domestic legislation. How the United States did this makes for a fascinating historical record.[41]

Building on the Reciprocal Trade Act of 1934, which reduced tariffs on imported goods, the United States lowered tariffs from an average of 40 percent in 1940 to a modest 7 percent by 1980.[42] The downside, according to critics, was that tariffs no longer protected high-wage American workers from low-paid labor abroad. But this was lost on political operatives who were protecting the nation from communism. The State Department regularly used trade concessions as bargaining chips to buy votes in the United Nations or to advance foreign policy negotiations. This fit in with America's increasingly unique worldview. Specifically, because of the "peculiarities of American history," the "United States has tended to favour a plural world political order as opposed to one based on great power divisions."[43] If the United States was going to persuade others to follow its lead, others had to become prosperous and free from the civil strife that led to communist intrigue.

Support for the exports of American allies and for unilaterally opening American markets took root during the 1947 Geneva trade negotiations.

At Geneva the United States initially wanted to create freer trade by getting Britain to abolish its colonial system of preferences (which granted favorable terms of trade to British colonies) but had to settle for an agreement that opened only one market—its own.[44] Although Britain wouldn't relent on its system of preferences, the United States realized that providing a united front against the Soviets and stability was so important that a skewed deal was considered to be better than no deal. This mind-set helped produce the General Agreement on Tariffs and Trade (GATT), which provided a framework for international trade by establishing specific tariff rates, mandating reciprocity, and obligating member states to the principle of most-favored-nation (MFN) status. But concessions to the British were only the beginning.

Trading American Interests, II: The Nuts and Bolts

To drive home the point that economic recovery and growth in Europe and Japan were essential to countering Soviet expansion, the United States sponsored wartime enemies Italy, Germany, and Japan for membership in GATT. This didn't sit well with many, especially those who wanted to punish wartime losers. Sponsorship of former allies was followed by a bilateral trade agreement with Japan in 1955, and, according to critics, stands as perhaps the most egregious example of how the United States sacrificed domestic economic interests to larger international political realities. The National Security Council (NSC) got the ball rolling in 1952 by lobbying the White House and other national-level policymakers to get on Japan's side, by encouraging Japanese exports into the United States. The NSC then convinced the Commerce Department—which stood up for American commercial interests—to drop its opposition to generous policies that supported Japan's economic recovery. With this decision there was little doubt that the State Department would prevail over the Commerce Department throughout the Cold War.

To be sure, authorities understood that domestic industries would complain about the unilateral opening of US markets. President Truman even created the Tariff Commission—forerunner to the International Trade Commission (ITC)—which heard complaints from domestic producers, made recommendations to the president, and then made a "withdraw" or "modify" proposal on specific tariff issues. Yet the Commission was consistently reluctant to find economic injury to domestic producers in the United States. From the manufacture of clothes pins to handblown glassware, fish products, and footwear (among other products), successive presidents ignored the Tariff Commission and ITC recommendations. These tactics didn't go over well with several members in Congress.

Trading away American economic interests so infuriated Senator Russell Long that he regularly criticized the State Department, complaining that to "save the world from a great war" the State Department believed that "it would be worth giving away every industry we have."[45]

During the Eisenhower Administration, Treasury Secretary George Humphrey and Commerce Secretary Sinclair Weeks warned that lowering tariffs would bring increased unemployment, as American workers were forced to compete with cheap labor abroad. But Eisenhower made it clear in 1954 that pressing political demands abroad trumped domestic economic concerns: "Japan cannot live and Japan cannot remain in the free world unless something is done to allow her to make a living."[46] By the mid-1950s, with the Cold War and Soviet domination of Eastern Europe secured, Japan's economic development became a critical national security issue. With the Korean War (1950–1953) weighing on his mind, President Eisenhower concluded that the United States needed a stable anchor in the Far East, and he told Republican congressional leaders in 1955 that "all problems of local industry pale into insignificance in relation to the world crisis."[47]

To further support Japan's economic development, the United States went beyond simple bilateral trade efforts with the Japanese. In 1955 the United States cut tariffs on products of critical interest to Canada, Denmark, Finland, Italy, Norway, and Sweden. In return these countries granted favorable conditions to Japanese exports. These efforts helped Japanese-manufactured imports in the United States double from 1955 to 1960 and saw America's share of manufactured exports to Japan decline from 66.3 percent to 51.7 percent.[48] In this manner, the US balance of trade position with Japan worsened while Japan's export markets grew. While this was occurring, US producers and workers were exposed to cheaper products from other nations that did not grant the United States similar concessions.

Because of similar giveaways during the Kennedy Administration, and because of the State Department's apparent insensitivity to domestic economic interests, Congress retaliated against the executive branch and the State Department by passing the Trade Expansion Act in 1962. The act stripped the State Department of its dominant role in trade policy and established a special representative for trade negotiations.[49] But it had little immediate impact because the Johnson administration, pinned down by Vietnam and an escalating arms race, felt compelled to accept protectionist and discriminatory tariffs from abroad. It also said little about non-tariff barriers imposed on US goods (excise taxes, registration fees, etc.). By 1971 the United States started running regular merchandise trade deficits, which would create serious balance of payment problems—as we see today.

After evaluating this historical record, Alfred Eckes was quite blunt in his assessment. Specifically, he wrote that, by trading away American economic interests, the United States may have compromised "future competitiveness and alienated public support for international coopera-tion in the post-Cold War world."[50] Because we can never be sure about public support for international agreements, Eckes's gloomy view is open to debate. Still, there's no dispute. Political considerations, rather than commercial concerns, had a significant hand in shaping US trade policy and the postwar global economic order.

Conclusion

In this chapter I have looked at the role of the state in making markets and, perhaps more important, national and global economies work. The resulting world order crafted after World War II created a wide range of new institutions that aided in politically uniting those who embraced and traded with the West. These institutions fostered freer trade and economic reciprocity under an American-led liberal world order. The resultant "American Peace" surpassed the achievements of previous empires whose periods of stability we acknowledge today as the eras of *Pax Romana* and *Pax Britannica*. However we want to label the era of *Pax Americana,* there's little doubt that the ideology, the structure, and the process of free trade were all designed to serve larger security and political ends after World War II. In the process it becomes clearer that the economic world painted by Milton Friedman does not quite add up. This is important, because Friedman's disciples continue to make the case that the state is an obstacle to free trade—but history shows otherwise.

Interestingly, noted globalization proponent and free market guru Thomas Friedman has gone to great lengths to promote Milton Friedman's version of trade—without really understanding its history or principles. Through his weekly op-ed articles in the *New York Times* Friedman is one of the most widely read pundits in the United States and something of an icon to free market advocates. This is an interesting development, because it's clear that Friedman—by his own admission— does not delve into the specifics behind the free trade policies that he writes about. David Sirota pointed this out and steered us toward a ques-tion and answer session that Friedman had on trade matters. Sirota observes:

> Friedman now admits his advocacy of "free" trade deals is
> based not on fact or data research, but entirely on faith. In a
> recent interview on CNBC, Friedman told the story of a man

in Minnesota who asked him, "Is there any free-trade agreement you'd oppose?"

"I said, 'No, absolutely not,'" Friedman recounted. "I said, 'You know what, sir? I wrote a column supporting CAFTA. I didn't even know what was in it. I just knew two words: free trade."

Forget about CAFTA's protectionist provisions inflating pharmaceutical prices in Central America. Forget about popular opposition to CAFTA in many of the countries the deal was supposed to "help." Forget about "logical proof or material evidence" to support Friedman's belief that the deal would actually help raise living standards. Friedman didn't know about that. All it took for him to put his pen to paper was the holy incantation of "free trade."[51]

To be sure, one can be forgiven for not diving into the intricacies of the Central American Free Trade Agreement. Official free trade documents are horrendously long technical documents, full of market jargon and industry specific legal terms (which is a bit ironic because, logically, harmonious markets and free trade should occur without government-assisted treaties). For people like Thomas Friedman it's much easier to trust the people he speaks with, labels, and his own gut. Some might be inclined to argue that Thomas Friedman's instincts are guided by his deep understanding of economic history. Think again.

Economist Ha-Joon Chang takes Thomas Friedman to task for ignoring or not understanding the long and storied history of the Japanese auto industry. More specifically Chang points out that Friedman doesn't do his homework and, perhaps more important, doesn't really know what he's talking about. Because Chang's comments support the primary arguments of this chapter, I quote him at length here:

Toyota started out as a manufacturer of textile machinery (Toyota Automatic Loom) and moved into car production in 1933. The Japanese government kicked out General Motors and Ford in 1939 and bailed out Toyota with money from the central bank (Bank of Japan) in 1949. Today, Japanese cars are considered as "natural" as Scottish salmon or French wine, but fewer than 50 years ago, most people, including many Japanese, thought the Japanese car industry simply should not exist.

Half a century after the Toyopet debacle, Toyota's luxury brand Lexus has become something of an icon for globalization, thanks to the American journalist Thomas Friedman's book, *The Lexus and the Olive Tree*. The book owes its title to an epiphany that Friedman had on the Shinkansen bullet train during his trip to Japan in 1992. He had paid a visit to a Lexus factory, which mightily impressed him. On his train back from the car factory in Toyota City to Tokyo, he came across yet another newspaper article about the troubles in the Middle East where he had been a long-time correspondent. Then it hit him. He realized that "half the world seemed to be . . . intent on building a better Lexus, dedicated to modernizing, streamlining, and privatizing their economies in order to thrive in the system of globalization. And half of the world—sometimes half the same country, sometimes half the same person—was still caught up in the fight over who owns which olive tree."

According to Friedman, unless they fit themselves into a particular set of economic policies that he calls the Golden Straitjacket, countries in the olive-tree world will not be able to join the Lexus world. In describing the Golden Straitjacket, he pretty much sums up today's neo-liberal economic orthodoxy: in order to fit into it, a country needs to privatize state-owned enterprises, maintain low inflation, reduce the size of government bureaucracy, balance the budget (if not running a surplus), liberalize trade, deregulate foreign investment, deregulate capital markets, make the currency convertible, reduce corruption, and privatize pensions. According to him, this is the only path to success in the new global economy. His Straitjacket is the only gear suitable for the harsh but exhilarating game of globalization. Friedman is categorical: "Unfortunately, this Golden Straitjacket is pretty much "one-size fits all" . . . It is not always pretty or gentle or comfortable. But it's here and it's the only model on the rack this historical season."

However, the fact is that, had the Japanese government followed the free-trade economists back in the early 1960s, there would have been no Lexus. Toyota today would, at best, be a junior partner to some Western car manufacturer, or worse, have been wiped out. The same would have been true for the entire Japanese economy. Had the country donned Friedman's Golden Straitjacket early on, Japan would have remained the third-rate industrial power that it was in the 1960s, with its income level on a par with Chile, Argentina, and South Africa—it was then a country whose prime minister was insultingly dismissed as "a transistor-radio salesman" by the French president, Charles De Gaulle. In other words, had they followed Friedman's advice, the Japanese would now not be exporting the Lexus but still be fighting over who owns which mulberry tree.[52]

The point here is not to take Thomas Friedman to task for misunderstanding free trade.[53] It's to point out that simply writing well (Thomas Friedman), having beautiful concepts (David Ricardo), or a winning a Nobel Peace Prize (Milton Friedman) is no guarantee that a "free market straitjacket" alone will promote economic growth and development. Perhaps the greatest example of this is how America's deliberate and very political "Grand Liberal Strategy" worked in Europe in the postwar era.

Notes

1. David Rock, *Argentina, 1516–1982* (Berkeley: University of California Press, 1985), 245.

2. Rock, *Argentina,* 258. Blog Commentary.

3. Rock, *Argentina,* 292.

4. Rock, *Argentina,* 292.

5. Rock, *Argentina,* 292–293.

6. Arthur A. Stein, "The Hegemon's Dilemma: Great Britain, the United States, and the International Economic Order," in *Theory and Structure in International Political Economy: An International Organization Reader,* ed. Charles Lipson and Benjamin J. Cohen (Cambridge, MA: MIT Press, 1999), 290, Table 1.

7. Charles P. Kindleberger, "The Rise of Free Trade in Western Europe," in *International Political Economy: Perspectives on Global Power and Wealth,* ed. Jeffrey A. Frieden and David A. Lake (New York: St. Martin's Press, 1995), 78.

8. Baron De Montesquieu, *The Spirit of the Laws,* Vol. 1 (New York: Hafner Press, 1975), 16.

9. Herman M. Schwartz, *States Versus Market: The Emergence of a Global Economy* (New York: St. Martin's Press, 2000), 105.

10. Kindleberger, "The Rise," 77.

11. Kindleberger, "The Rise," 77–79, 81.

12. Kindleberger, "The Rise."

13. This review of Richard Cobden is drawn from "Cobden's Biography," *The London School of Economics and Political Science,* available online.

14. Schwartz, *States,* 105.

15. Schwartz, *States,* 105.

16. Alexander Wendt, "Anarchy Is What States Make of It: The Social Construction of Power Politics," in *Theory and Structure in International Political Economy: An International Organization Reader,* ed. Charles Lipson and Benjamin J. Cohen, 75 (Cambridge, MA: MIT Press, 1999). Blog Commentary.

17. Arthur A. Stein, "The Hegemon's Dilemma: Great Britain, the United States, and the International Economic Order," in *Theory and Structure in International Political Economy: An International Organization Reader,* ed. Charles Lipson and Benjamin J. Cohen, (Cambridge, MA: MIT Press, 1999), 286–287.

18. This section is drawn from Stein, "The Hegemon's."

19. Stein, "The Hegemon's," 291.

20. Kindleberger, "The Rise," 79.

21. G. John Ikenberry, *After Victory: Institutions, Strategic Restraint, and the Rebuilding of Order after Major Wars* (Princeton, NJ: Princeton University Press, 2001), 85. Blog Commentary.

22. Ikenberry, *After,* 82.

23. Joseph T. Salerno, "Comment on the French Liberal School," *Journal of Libertarian Studies,* 2, no. 1 (1978): 65–68, available online.

24. Stein, "The Hegemon's," 292.

25. Henry Kissinger, *Diplomacy* (New York: Simon & Schuster, 1994), 93–95.

26. Stein, "The Hegemon's," 292–293.

27. Kissinger, *Diplomacy,* 93.

28. Schwartz, *States,* 151.

29. Seeking redemption though a unified Europe was used to describe the rationale for Germany's postwar support for the European Union in Zbigniew Brzezinski's *The Grand Chess Board: American Primacy and Its Geostrategic Imperatives* (New York: Basic Books, 1998).

30. Stein, "The Hegemon's," 292.

31. Stein, "The Hegemon's," 293.

32. Philip G. Cerny, "Globalization and the Changing Logic of Collective Action," in *Theory and Structure in International Political Economy: An International Organization Reader,* ed. Charles Lipson and Benjamin J. Cohen (Cambridge, MA: MIT Press, 1999), 111; Robert Gilpin, *The Political Economy of International Relations* (Princeton, NJ: Princeton University Press, 1987); G. John Ikenberry, *After.* Blog Commentary.

33. Initially implemented by President Truman under JCS 1067, the subsequent raiding of German industry by the allies was documented by

C. Lester Walker in "German War Secrets by the Thousands," *Harper's Magazine*, October 1946, 329, available online.

34. Ikenberry, *After*, 171.

35. The outline and general information for the following two sections are drawn from Alfred E. Eckes, "Trading American Interests," *Foreign Affairs*, 71, no. 4 (Fall 1992): 135–154. Only specific quotes and economic data are cited.

36. Ikenberry, *After*, 4–6.

37. Ikenberry, *After*, 12.

38. Eckes, "Trading," 135.

39. For an intriguing argument that highlights pressing security needs, see Melvyn P. Leffler, "The American Conception of National Security and the Beginnings of the Cold War, 1945–1948," in *American Foreign Policy: Theoretical Essays*, 4th edition, ed. G. John Ikenberry (New York: Longman, 2002).

40. For two excellent discussions on the roots and potency of America's "liberal grand strategy" and "national security liberalism," see Tony Smith, "National Security Liberalism and American Foreign Policy," in *American Foreign Policy: Theoretical Essays*, 4th edition, ed. G. John Ikenberry (New York: Longman, 2002).

41. Benjamin J. Cohen, "A Revolution in Atlantic Economic Relations: A Bargain Comes Unstuck," in *Crossing Frontiers: Explorations in International Political Economy* (Boulder, CO: Westview Press, 1991), 94, 101. Blog Commentary.

42. Thomas D. Lairson and David Skidmore, *International Political Economy: The Struggle for Wealth and Power*, 2nd edition (New York: Harcourt Brace, 1997), 66.

43. Smith, "National," 260.

44. Eckes, "Trading," 138

45. Eckes, "Trading," 137.

46. Eckes, "Trading," 140.

47. Eckes, "Trading," 140.

48. Eckes, "Trading," 141.

49. "History of the United States Trade Representative," Office of the United States Trade Representative, available online. Blog Commentary.

50. Eckes, "Trading," 135–136.

51. David Sirota, "Where Economics Meets Religious Fundamentalism," David Sirota Blog, August 11, 2006, available online.

52. Ha-Joon Chang, *Bad Samaritans: The Myth of Free Trade and the Secret History of Capitalism* (New York: Bloombury Press, 2008), 20–21.

53. Blog Commentary.

CHAPTER 8

AMERICA'S POST–WORLD WAR II GRAND LIBERAL STRATEGY

Months before the start of the Second Gulf War in 2003, Secretary of Defense Donald Rumsfeld chided Germany and France for not following the US lead on Iraq—derogatorily referring to their leaders as holdovers from "old Europe." The claim was both misinformed and full of hubris. Since 1945 Europe had embraced democratic and free market principles, was a solid ally during the Cold War, and pursued economic integration as a way to foment cooperation and allay past tensions in the region. Rumsfeld's comments demonstrated a willful ignorance of how "new Europe" fulfilled, if not exceeded, the aspirations of America's postwar architects. Old Europe—if we are to get our history right—would not have waited for the United States to sweep into the Middle East. In the end, Rumsfeld would have done well to have spoken with General Electric's former CEO Jack Welch. He understands "new Europe."

During his tenure as CEO, Welch merged more than nine hundred firms with General Electric. When Honeywell became available in October 2000, Welch went into action. Although Honeywell produced many of the same products as GE—plastics, chemicals, electrical machinery, and aircraft engines—Welch wasn't concerned about anti-trust legislation because he believed that Honeywell's products were "complimentary" rather than competitive. And besides, why should he worry? He was Jack Welch. After getting the green light from the US Justice Department, Welch met with Eurocrat, Mario Monti, the European Union's Director-General for Competition (its "anti-trust" division). In Brussels Welch found the "new Europe." In The United States of Europe, *T. R. Reid described the introduction: "Welch flashed his friendly, casual smile, stuck out a hand, and said, 'Mario—call me Jack' . . . 'Mr. Welch,' [Monti] replied in his accented but precise English, 'we have a regulatory*

proceeding under way. I feel the proper approach would be to keep things on a more formal basis. You can call me Sgr. Monti.'"
Monti's team had done its homework. They secured information from both GE's industry competitors and United Technologies (the firm GE out-bid for Honeywell). At one point, when asked about aircraft electronic parts manufactured by Honeywell, GE's team offered only blank stares. And on it went. When Monti finally called Welch to tell him the "deal is over," he ended the conversation by saying, "Now I can say to you, 'Good-bye, Jack.'"[1] Fifty-five years after the end of World War II Mr. Welch learned the hard way that the system that US postwar architects wanted to build for the world had found a home in Europe. Welch learned something else: by creating the conditions for a prosperous and independent Europe to emerge, America's grand liberal strategy had— apparently without Don-ald Rumsfeld's knowledge—erased "old Europe."[2]

Of the various postwar projects that emerged at the end of World War II, European economic cooperation was perhaps the most watched. And why not? Some of the most vicious battles of World War II were fought in Europe. What separated the postwar European experience of World War II from that of previous wars was how hindsight helped the allies under-stand the relationship between economic failure and war. They under-stood that Adolf Hitler and Benito Mussolini weren't the product of happy and prosperous peoples. Economic collapse created the conditions that allowed Hitler and Mussolini to prey on the sentiments of the unem-ployed. The prospect of economic failure after World War II painted nightmare scenarios for the United States. Today the relatively cooperative spirit and successes of the European Union have converted those prospects and the ugly days of the 1930s into cautionary tales of what not to do.

An interesting if not paradoxical development is that many partici-pants and observers speak of Europe's economic successes in purely mar-ket terms, as if political deliberations had little to do with European recovery and integration. But European economic cooperation in a com-petitive capitalist environment cannot be understood without reference to the very visible hand of the state. The motivation and discipline behind Europe's economic recovery was a product of political rather than eco-nomic dynamics.[3] Diplomacy and political calculation focused primarily on one goal in Europe: eliminating the economic conditions that allowed Nazism to prosper and created an opening for socialist revolution in Russia. To deal with these challenges, postwar leaders fostered European political cooperation by facilitating postwar economic recovery. When it came to economic development, nothing was left to chance—or to the invisible hand.

In addition to guiding economic recovery, postwar leaders also set their sights on two broader postwar priorities that went beyond Europe: promoting sustained economic growth and full employment throughout the West and creating a stable world order internationally.[4] The first meant economic cooperation and the second mandated military alliances.[5] Achieving both helped prevent a return to the destructive days of economic nationalism, which bred contemptuous beggar-thy-neighbor policies.[6] This chapter focuses on these efforts, by highlighting the political realities that drove America and its Cold War partners to embrace market cooperation, mutual aid, and interdependence.

The Grand Liberal Strategy Takes Root

Apart from industrialization and the advent of democracy, the major events of nineteenth- and early twentieth-century Europe were dominated by revolution, depression, and war. Although each of these events was generated by complex dynamics, the unifying element was how each event "demonstrated the colossal costs of failure to achieve cooperation on economic and political matters."[7] Although political and security considerations helped drive the 1860 Cobden-Chevalier free trade pact (Chapter 7), the world stood by and watched as a vengeful and short-sighted mind-set unraveled a flawed treaty penned at Versailles: the Treaty of Versailles set in motion a political chain of events proving that punitive measures, beggar-thy-neighbor policies, and economic failure would pay ugly political dividends in the future. As Treasury Secretary Henry Morgenthau observed after World War II,

> All of us have seen the great economic tragedy of our time. We saw the worldwide depression of the 1930s. We saw currency disorders develop and spread from land to land, destroying the basis for international trade and international investment and even international faith. In their wake, we saw unemployment and wretchedness . . . We saw their victims fall prey . . . to demagogues and dictators. We saw bewilderment and bitterness become the breeders of fascism, and finally, war.[8]

Because of emerging geostrategic pressures, a stable world order and economic recovery were deemed too important to be left in the hands of European leaders alone or to Adam Smith's invisible hand. To secure the future, economic interdependence was pushed, international institutions were built, and a coherent political identity within the West (and Japan) was promoted.[9] The end result was a set of institutions and programs that guided Europe and the West through economic recovery and political cooperation. Perhaps the most significant development was the creation of multilateral institutions to organize commerce and trade: the International Monetary Fund (IMF), the International Bank for Reconstruction and Development (IBRD, or the World Bank), and the General Agreement on Tariffs and Trade (GATT).[10]

Before trade could be facilitated and economic cooperation promoted, the United States had to demonstrate to its wartime allies that it was committed to Europe militarily. This was necessary because, throughout the immediate postwar period, European leaders were more concerned that America would abandon the region—which it had done after World War I—than they were about American domination.[11] Buttressing this concern was the reality that the United States had dropped the ball and then failed to lead when the Federal Reserve deflated the money supply in the late 1920s, which was followed by the incredibly short-sighted Smoot-Hawley Tariff Act.[12] For Europe, America's economic plans had to be backed with a commitment in other areas than trade.

The United States understood that it would have to act and commit itself to helping Europe overcome its fears of renewed German aggression, and it addressed the issue by creating the North Atlantic Treaty Organization (NATO) in 1948. Originally made up of twelve Western states, NATO is a formal military alliance that pledges mutual support against attacks on member states. Its initial goal was to keep "the Russians out, the Germans down, and the Americans in" Europe.[13] By showing that the United States was willing to stand up for Europe's security, NATO helped legitimize US intentions in the eyes of Europeans. With a military commitment and its political leadership guaranteed, the United States could focus on injecting life into what was, until 1948, a rather laggard European recovery.[14]

Still, the problem remained. The best route to European economic recovery meant making sure that Germany's economy was rebuilt. Without it, the United States argued, war would eventually arrive and strangle the Continent's hopes and dreams in the process. Because Germany was at the center of the region's most recent and deadliest wars, rebuilding Germany wasn't a wildly popular idea in Europe. This is where America's grand liberal strategy of inclusion, multilateralism, and restraint proved to be invaluable to economic recovery.

America Takes the Lead in Organizing Financial Leadership

Just as NATO demonstrated the US commitment to managing security, the IMF, IBRD, and GATT confirmed that the United States would facilitate recovery and ensure economic stability. The rationale for creating these international institutions was simple. When countries can't pay the bills, conflict is around the corner. Short-term balance-of-payment issues proved troublesome during the interwar period, when Germany, saddled with a $33 billion reparations bill, couldn't find financial relief. By early 1923 Germany could no longer afford to pay its creditors, which infuriated the French, who, along with Belgium, sent troops into the strategic Ruhr Valley. The Germans responded by calling for a general strike in the region, but they still paid the striking workers. Because the Germans were broke—and couldn't secure loans from outside—Germany simply printed money to pay workers, which fed hyperinflation. This wiped out middle-class savings, with devastating social and political effects.

While this was going on, the United States put pressure on France to pay its bills. Broke and unable to secure payments from the Germans, the French sent a delegation to the United States; the Secretary of State, Charles Evans Hughes, told the French that the US government couldn't help, nor would it eliminate France's debt. The Secretary of State agreed, however, to put together a meeting with US bankers. With the value of the French franc falling fast, the desperate French delegation accepted the offer. The key outcome of the meeting was the Dawes Plan, named after Charles G. Dawes, who pieced the deal together. Apart from reducing the annual payments made by the Germans, the Dawes Plan called for a private-bank-sponsored $200 million loan, with half coming from US banks and the other half from foreign banks.[15] Looking to spread the risk, US banker J. P. Morgan Jr. floated the loan on US capital markets, where it drew more than $1 billion from investors within days.[16]

Although the Dawes Plan helped Germany by providing funds to run day-to-day activities, it also helped players in the postwar period see how an independent international financial institution might operate if it existed. It also helped establish the United States as the world's banking center and gave the United States a whiff of the influence that came with controlling credit. In the immediate term, however, postwar leaders saw how the balance-of-payment problems could be managed with short-term financing. The lesson that many postwar architects drew from this experience was that conflict and war could have been avoided if Germany had had access to financial resources in the short-term (or if the Treaty of Versailles had not been so punitive). The IMF was created in this spirit.

For its part, IBRD or World Bank was designed to help rebuild Europe's infrastructure after World War II. The thinking was that it would be difficult to get goods to market if the goods produced couldn't be transported because of a lack of roads, bridges, or ports. But Europe still needed immediate financing for imports and balance-of-payment support. This helped convince the United States to develop the Marshall Plan. The significance of the Marshall Plan cannot be understated. Former European Community president Roy Jenkins saw the plan as the key to Europe's economic renewal, arguing, "If the Marshall Plan did not prompt the recovery, it served as the crucial underpinnings."[17] Jenkins argues that, to the degree that Europe's economies began to show life before the arrival of Marshall Plan funds, that life was primarily attributable to two factors. First, Europe knew that Marshall Plan money was coming. Second, the promise of funds "provided a critical element without which the continent's rehabilitation would have stalled: relative freedom from balance-of-payments restraints." These two factors allowed "Europe to plan more securely and to embark on an essential program of fixed investment."[18]

After the immediate postwar period, multilateral developing banks (MDB) such as the IBRD and the IMF grew to become the largest official sources of aid and the primary providers of policy advice and technical assistance to developing countries.[19] To be sure, private banks were available, but they were either hesitant to fund infrastructure projects without loan guarantees, weren't up to the task of managing exchange rates, could not facilitate cooperation between states, or were reluctant to get involved in states with balance-of-payment problems.[20] In all cases, through the IMF and the World Bank, the United States took the lead in managing the global economic picture.[21] But managing the global economic system went beyond fiscal authority, creating credit systems, and validating a country's credit worthiness. It also meant making sure that autarky and economic nationalism remained a thing of the past, so market capitalism and an open trading system had to work for everyone (or at least provide the appearance thereof). But there was one last pillar in the economic pantheon created at Bretton Woods.

The Gatt and the Path toward "Freer" Trade (Again)

The General Agreement on Tariffs and Trade (GATT) was patterned after the Reciprocal Trade Act of 1934, which dealt with the challenges brought on by competitive tariff hikes in the 1930s. Originally the United States wanted to push for the creation of an International Trade Organization (ITO) to deal with trade matters that went beyond tariffs, but the US Congress nixed the idea. So GATT was created as a temporary framework until the ITO came into being. Although the US government put its weight and authority behind GATT, it still needed to offer other incentives to convince hesitant states to join. Apart from the concessions previously noted, incentives came by way of guaranteed conferences, or "Rounds," that allowed participating states to air their concerns on trade issues. The primary goal of these Trade Rounds (see Table 8.1) was to turn trading competitors into trading partners.

Tactically, the idea was to avoid the negative trade environment that had been brought on by competitive tariffs that plagued the trading arena throughout the 1930s. The rationale for competitive tariffs is simple. After the Depression spread, state after state sought to protect domestic industries. Protecting domestic industries, it was argued, was necessary to protect jobs. National leaders understood that economic problems in the form of unemployment at home spelled political trouble, especially when a disgruntled and disdainful electorate turned on political parties. This contributed to efforts to protect domestic industries with higher tariffs. The subsequent political environment ensured that the closed borders of colonial holdings remained closed and fed an ugly political beast in the 1930s called economic nationalism.

Although the goals of independence and autonomy are often politically attractive, because they suggest self-sufficiency, in practice they simply aren't feasible in the modern world. Placing higher tariffs on chemicals from Germany, for example, only make economic matters worse in the United States because they beg Germany to counter with higher tariffs of its own. In this instance, when German tariffs take effect, US workers in factories that export their goods find that what they produce costs more in Germany. As sales decline, jobs in the United States are cut back. This, in turn, might lead to another round of competitive tariff hikes. Destructive domestic rhetoric follows and, invariably, focuses on "evil foreigners," who are out to undermine the country's economic vitality. This is what happened in the 1930s. With rampant unemployment in the 1930s, the claims of "evil foreigners"—right or wrong—fell on sympathetic ears.

The primary function of GATT is to facilitate international trade by reducing the proclivity toward competitive tariff hikes, economic nationalism, and other activities that undercut the flow of commerce. To facilitate this, GATT has gone beyond tariffs to include the principle of reciprocity and most-favored nation (MFN) status. After 1960 successive GATT rounds expanded the type of subjects that were covered and embraced other factors that apply to—and might hinder—trade. Nontariff Barriers (NTBs), dumping, quotas, unwarranted regulations, and unrealistic labor or environmental standards, among others, were included. Ultimately the goal was to encourage efficiency and specialization where states had a comparative advantage.

Box 8.1 Desert Islands and Comparative Advantage

To understand the concept of comparative advantage and how it applies to international trade, we can fall back on an old example used in economic lectures around the world. Assume that two people are stranded on a desert island. To survive they must cooperate and focus on a few basic activities, such as carrying water, fishing, security, cooking, and constructing and maintaining shelter, among others. The first person is a young man who is strong, quick, and educated. He has an absolute advantage in all activities. The second person is elderly, a bit weak, and has little training. He has no advantage in any activity. Although the difference between the two men is great in most activities, in others it is small. Because the island is large and has many dangers, it's not in the interest of either person to work in isolation. How should they divide the work? The young man must spend more time on the tasks in which he is much better than the older man (e.g., fishing, carrying water, and construction), whereas the older man must concentrate on the tasks in which he is only a little worse than the younger man (e.g., fishing, maintenance, and cooking). By having the older man work in areas where he is only marginally weaker, the two are following the principle of comparative advantage. The tasks completed are done with the least amount of work and hours expended. Such an arrangement increases total production and or reduces the total amount of labor expired by each person, making both better off.

When reluctant states saw the concessions that the United States had made, and saw that it wouldn't create a fuss over the British colonial system of preferences (which granted favorable terms of trade to British colonies), they understood that there would be flexibility in the system. Coupled with the dangers posed by the Soviet Union, this convinced many states that joining an open global economic system, protected by the US security umbrella, could produce tangible benefits in the long-term. This helped the United States put together a set of institutions and treaties that bound states together in a web of rules that were mutually agreed upon. Convinced of America's commitment to security and trade, country after country agreed to become a member of GATT—because it included "ample escape provisions" and protections, which meant that countries wouldn't have to jeopardize domestic economic objectives or abandon national control.[22] This solidified GATT's place in the Bretton Woods system, created a larger framework for trade, and helped GATT grow beyond its twenty-three founding nations (Table 8.1). In sum, the goals of reciprocity, nondiscrimination, and multilateralism fostered political cooperation and economic growth the world over.

Table 8.1 GATT Negotiations and Subjects

Year	Place/Name	Subjects Covered	Countries
1947	Geneva	Tariffs	23
1949	Annecy	Tariffs	13
1951	Torquay	Tariffs	38
1956	Geneva	Tariffs	26
1960–1961	Geneva Dillon Round	Tariffs	26
1964–1967	Geneva Kennedy Round	Tariffs and anti-dumping measures	62
1973–1979	Geneva Tokyo Round	Tariffs, non-tariff measures, "framework" agreements	102
1986–1994	Geneva Uruguay Round	Tariffs, non-tariff measures, rules, services, intellectual property, dispute settlement, textiles, agriculture, creation of WTO, etc	123

Source: World Trade Organization, "The GATT Years: From Havana to Marrakesh," 2008, available online.

But the Bretton Woods institutions alone didn't create the conditions for prosperity and cooperation. The United States understood early on that creating an international framework for trade wouldn't be enough to generate recovery and growth. There was little investment going on, which convinced the United States that a financial jump start also was necessary to get Europe's economy moving again. This came in the form of the Marshall Plan, which offered Europe roughly 4.5 percent of the US GDP between 1949 and 1952.[23] Although none of it had to be paid back, Marshall Plan aid was made contingent on one condition: Europe had to learn how to cooperate politically.

The Political Roots of European Union and Interdependence

To facilitate recovery and cooperation in Europe, the Organization for European Economic Cooperation (OEEC) was created in 1948. Its first real task was to coordinate Marshall Plan aid. Implied in these and subsequent arrangements were two ideas that undermined the vision for markets and society as held by Adam Smith's disciples. First, the interwar period taught policymakers that desperate people embrace politically popular but economically destructive policies. This reemphasized that people could be persuaded by the irresponsible rants of despots. Second, the challenges that develop when markets collapse and people become unemployed were now viewed as global security issues rather than domestic economic problems. To avoid the competitive consequences that these dynamics brought to the international arena, the OEEC—like the Bretton Woods institutions—was created to provide a set of norms, rules, and procedures that were mutually agreed upon. The difference was that the OEEC focused on European matters.

With these dynamics as a backdrop, a sense of urgency developed when the Soviet Union hot-wired the Cold War by invading Czechoslovakia and blockading Berlin in 1948. The Soviet invasion and the Berlin Blockade occurred at a time when the United States was not only demobilizing troops, but at a time when the Soviets had made it clear that it was going to leave large armies in Eastern Europe. Making matters worse was that Joseph Stalin moved slowly to remove troops from Northern Iran (Russia eventually left, but only under great pressure) and reneged on his promise to allow free elections in Poland. These developments proved that the Soviets weren't going to honor many of the agreements made at Yalta in 1945 and suggested that Soviet expansionism, rather than the cooperative spirit of Yalta, dominated Soviet thinking. It also hinted that the Soviets were prepared to move anywhere that they saw opportunity or weakness. With the Cold War now well underway, the Western world became suspicious of Soviet intrigue and believed that it would find fertile ground in western Europe if those countries didn't recover economically in the immediate term.[24]

Challenges in Europe grew because of several developments. The electoral successes of left-wing parties in postwar European elections (especially in Italy) made it clear that economic depression and the resulting war had discredited not only fascism but *laissez-faire* capitalism in Europe.[25] Making matters worse, until 1947 Europe doubted US motives because of America's moral and crusading diplomacy after World War I, which degenerated into economic nationalism at the first hint of trouble in the 1930s. To overcome these concerns and to make sure that markets worked, political institutions and trust had to be built. Helmut Schmidt, former Chancellor of the Federal Republic of Germany, underscored these points—and echoed the sentiments of Richard Cobden's letter to Michel Chevalier—when he pointed out that economic integration was necessary "less for economic reasons than political reasons" because

> [a]fter the disastrous wars of the past hundred years, in which Germany had played a key role—the Napoleonic Wars, Bismarck's war against France, and the two world wars—I believed it desirable to bind my country into a greater European entity to prevent the recurrence of such conflict."[26]

These security fears—both immediate and historical—helped foster a new intellectual environment that downplayed the theoretical promise of Adam Smith's free markets. It also led a chastened but more politically practical Europe to embrace institutions, economic guidance, and the regional management of markets.[27] In this manner, apart from becoming the principal body responsible for supervising European-wide reconstruction, the OEEC also pushed Europeans toward broader discussions on joint economic management. This paid off big-time, as they learned to accept criticism of internal political discussions, which would have been considered intolerable before the war. On this matter, State Department official (later ambassador to Brazil, 1961–1966) Lincoln Gordon, commented that the OEEC

> instituted one of the major innovations of postwar international cooperation, the systematic country review, in which the responsible national authorities are cross-examined by a group of their peers together with a high-quality international staff. In those reviews, questions are raised which in prewar days would have been considered a gross and unacceptable foreign interference in domestic affairs.[28]

The OEEC—as well as the implementation of the institutional arrangements led by the United States at the international level—helped foster the environment that led to Europe's recovery and the establishment of the European Steel and Coal Community (ECSC) in 1952.[29] The founding member nations of the ECSC—France, West Germany, Italy, Belgium, Netherlands, and Luxembourg—pledged themselves to a unified common market by pooling their coal and steel resources and lifting restrictions on imports and exports in these markets. To deal with labor dislocations posed by shifting production and market shares, the ECSC also created a unified labor market in these industries, which provided funds for training and the development of new industries.

Because the OEEC (later the OECD, 1961) and the ECSC were considered integral to America's "grand design" and to its Atlantic partnership, it was clear from the beginning that the US vision for global order and economic stability did not rest on any assumed notion of *laissez-faire* or on imagined invisible hands.[30] Rather, global economic stability and growth rested upon a web of politically integrated strategic, military, and economic goals. So, although economic integration was viewed as a market objective, the primary goal of market cooperation was to promote political stability in the region. Recovery and growth couldn't occur without stability and security. Referring to NATO and the Marshall Plan as part of a larger institutional package, Lloyd Gardner summed up the importance of the OEEC and the ECSC to European security, stability, and growth:

> Each formed part of a whole. Together they were designed to "mold the military character" of the Atlantic nations, prevent the balkanization of European defense systems, create an internal market large enough to sustain capitalism in Western Europe, and lock in Germany on the Western side of the Iron Curtain.[31]

In a few words, not only did these institutions lay the foundation for European political cooperation but they helped save capitalism in Europe. Later, the successes of the ECSC were followed by the creation of the European Economic Community in 1957 (EEC). Although the EEC was charged with eliminating barriers to trade, its primary US-mandated goal was to promote dialogue and cooperation, to which economic growth and prosperity contributed. In this manner, apart from paving the way for cooperation, recovery, and integration in Europe, the OEEC and the ECSC became the institutional forerunners to the European Community (EC).[32]

Conclusion

Although many people consider US Marshall Plan assistance to Europe as an act of benevolence on the part of the United States, there's another side to the story. Postwar leaders understood that individual investors in Europe were too conservative to go where economies were depressed or where the prospect of conflict remained. Recovery and economic growth remained sluggish throughout Europe, creating the fear that the European economy wouldn't recover on its own in the immediate term. This lack of confidence in the ability of the market to create harmony in the immediate term meant that high point that was produced by ending the war might disappear and that, worse yet, Europe could revert back to its old habits of fear, mistrust, and economic nationalism. These prospects helped European leaders embrace the creation of American-guided multilateral institutions as a way of institutionalizing cooperation that was necessary for regional stability and economic recovery. Security was the key. As David P. Calleo put it,

> A Europe returning to its normalcy [was] not an altogether reassuring prospect. The history is long and bloody, and there is scarcely a tranquil century in it. The first half of the twentieth

century saw the disintegration of the Hapsburg empire; the Soviet, Fascist, and Nazi revolutions; the breakdown of the world economy; and two world wars of astonishing ferocity—an exceptionally violent period, even by Europe's normal standards. If the century's second half was comparatively stable, it is arguably because the Cold War between the superpowers deprived European states of a large measure of their independence.[33]

Although European economic integration and prosperity were the result, as many in the contemporary era have forgotten, viable markets and regional integration were viewed as a means (growth and prosperity) to a highly political end (cooperation and stability). Ironically, Europe's success with state-led economic recovery, regional integration, and global economic cooperation has resulted in pundits and politicians alike ignoring or downplaying the political roots behind Europe's economic successes. Instead, analysts prefer to focus on economic developments that were destined to occur because of "relentless" market forces.

This view of European recovery and integration is misleading and lacks historical perspective. From the very beginning, finding ways to avoid the emergence of future Hitlers and Stalins was the primary goal of the postwar victors. Economic institutions were built to facilitate cooperation, but they had their roots in satisfying political and security needs. As these needs were met, the stable and predictable balance of terror created by the two superpowers eventually became background noise that the market partygoers increasingly ignored as they struck up deals that many claimed were a product of their talent and initiative alone. In this scheme of things Adam Smith reins supreme. Marginalized in this line of thinking are the political agreements and political balancing acts required to create the mutually supportive "three postwar systems" (the Atlantic Alliance, the European Market, and the global economy) that David Calleo argues made postwar Europe a success.[34]

In a few words, the very visible hands of Western governments, but especially that of the United States, were behind both economic integration and sustained prosperity in Europe and around the globe. Losing sight of this reality is disappointing because, apart from mischaracterizing the capabilities of market forces, it has led to "orthodox" economic assumptions taking center stage. And, like an obnoxious party crasher who drinks for free at the bar of success, free market proponents have historically tried to convince others that they alone are the reason for the market party's postwar successes.[35] Ignored in this equation are the efforts of the host, the party planner, and the cooperation of other (more sober) guests. At the end of the day, removing politics and the role of the state from the successes of market capitalism not only flies in the face of what the Founding Fathers of the American Constitution saw in the emerging liberal American republic, but it also ignores what really happened in the twentieth century.

Notes

1. T. R. Reid, *The United States of Europe: The New Superpower and the End of American Supremacy* (New York: Penguin Press, 2004), 94–105.

2. Tony Smith, "National Security Liberalism and American Foreign Policy," in G. John Ikenberry, ed., *American Foreign Policy: Theoretical Essays*, 4th ed. (New York: Longman, 2002), 268–269, 273; G. John Ikenberry, *After Victory: Institutions, Strategic Restraint, and the Rebuilding of Order after Major Wars* (Princeton, NJ: Princeton University Press, 2001), 287. Blog Commentary.

3. Arthur A. Stein, "The Hegemon's Dilemma: Great Britain, the United States, and the International Economic Order," in *Theory and Structure in International Political Economy: An International Organization Reader*, ed. Charles Lipson and Benjamin J. Cohen (Cambridge, MA: MIT Press, 1999). Blog Commentary.

4. David P. Calleo, *Rethinking Europe's Future* (Princeton, NJ: Princeton University Press, 2001). Blog Commentary.

5. For a highly accessible and historical approach to understanding the key players and the framework created on the road to the European Union, see David M. Wood and Birol A. Yesilada, *The Emerging European Union*, 2nd ed. (New York: Longman, 2002). For a review of the North Atlantic Treaty Organization, see Ronald D. Asmus, *Opening NATO's Door: How the Alliance Remade Itself for a New Era* (New York: Columbia University Press, 2002).

6. Robert Gilpin, *The Political Economy of International Relations* (Princeton, NJ: Princeton University Press, 1987), 131.

7. David N. Balaam and David Veseth, *Introduction to International Political Economy*, 4th ed. (New York: Prentice Hall, 2004), 236.

8. Quoted in Ethan Kapstein, "Workers and the World Economy," *Foreign Affairs*, no. 3 (May/June 1996): 20.

9. G. John Ikenberry, "America's Liberal Grand Strategy: Democracy and National Security in the Post-War Era," in *American Foreign Policy: Theoretical Essays*, 4th ed., 274 (New York: Longman Publishers, 2002); Joseph Nye Jr., *Understanding International Conflicts: An Introduction to Theory and History*, 3rd ed. (New York: Longman,

2000), 43; Robert Pastor, *Toward a North American Community: Lessons from the Old World for the New* (Washington DC: Institute for International Economics, 2001), 171. Blog Commentary.

10. Gregory J. Millman, *The Vandals' Crown: How Rebel Currency Traders Overthrew the World's Central Banks* (New York: Free Press, 1996), 73. Blog Commentary.

11. Ikenberry, *After,* 165.

12. Jeff Frieden, "Sectoral Conflict and U.S. Foreign Economic Policy, 1914–1940," in G. John Ikenberry, *American Foreign Policy: Theoretical Essays,* 4th ed. (New York: Longman, 2002), 156–157.

13. Ikenberry, *After,* 166.

14. Gilpin, *The Political Economy of International Relations* (Princeton, NJ: Princeton University Press, 1987), 72–80. Blog Commentary.

15. Walter La Feber, *The American Age: U.S. Foreign Policy at Home and Abroad, 1750 to the Present* (New York: Norton, 1994), 344–345.

16. Frieden, "Sectoral," 155.

17. Roy Jenkins, "Special Relationships: The Postwar Bequest," *Foreign Affairs,* Marshall Plan Commemorative Section, 76, no. 3 (May/June 1997): 201.

18. Jenkins, "Special Relationships," 201.

19. Gilpin, *The Political,* 312.

20. Benjamin J. Cohen and Charles Lipson, "Money and Finance," in *Issues and Agents in International Political Economy: An International Organization Reader,* Benjamin J. Cohen and Charles Lipson, eds. (Cambridge, MA: MIT Press, 1999), 185–186. Blog Commentary.

21. Cohen and Lipson, *Issues,* 185; Ikenberry, *After,* 8–12. Blog Commentary.

22. Gilpin, *The Political,* 191. Blog Commentary.

23. Gilpin, *The Political,* 311.

24. David Reynolds, "The European Response: Primacy of Politics," *Foreign Affairs,* Marshall Plan Commemorative Section, 76, no. 3 (May/June 1997): 171–184.

25. Helmut Schmidt, "Miles to Go: From American Plan to European Union," *Foreign Affairs,* Marshall Plan Commemorative Section, 76, no. 3 (May/June 1997): 216.

26. Schmidt, "Miles," 216.

27. Klaus Stegemann, "Policy Rivalry among Industrial States: What Can We Learn from Models of Strategic Trade Policy?" in *Theory and Structure in International Political Economy: An International Organization Reader,* ed. Charles Lipson and Benjamin J. Cohen (Cambridge, MA: MIT Press, 1999); Judith Goldstein, "International Law and Domestic Institutions: Reconciling North American 'Unfair'

Trade Laws," in *Theory and Structure in International Political Economy: An International Organization Reader,* ed. Charles Lipson and Benjamin J. Cohen (Cambridge, MA: MIT Press, 1999). Blog Commentary.

28. Ikenberry, *After,* 209.
29. Calleo, *Rethinking.*
30. James Lee Ray, *Global Politics,* 6th ed. (Boston: Houghton Mifflin, 1995), 382. Blog Commentary.
31. Ikenberry, *After,* 209.
32. Calleo *Rethinking;* Ray, *Global Politics,* 384.
33. Calleo, *Rethinking,* 4.
34. Calleo, *Rethinking,* Chapter 6.
35. For an interesting take on how World War II and the Cold War created the political conditions for market liberalism to prosper (over authoritarian market systems), see Azar Gat, "The Return of Authoritarian Great Powers," in *Foreign Affairs,* 86, no. 4 (July/August 2007): 59–69; Gilpin, *The Political,* 191.

PART IV

STATES AND MODERN MARKETS: FROM POLITICAL MONEY TO WALL STREET SOCIALISM

CHAPTER 9

FROM KEYNES TO DEREGULATION AND EXPLODING CAPITAL FLOWS

Responding to a stagnating economy and a collapsing housing market, in December of 2007 President Bush remarked that the government "should not bail out lenders, real estate speculators, or those who made the reckless decision to buy a home they knew they could never afford."[1] Speaking as though the American economy operated according to the laissez-faire principles attributed to Adam Smith, the president ignored how (1) the Federal Reserve under Alan Greenspan contributed to a bubble economy with market-defying low interest rates over a six-year span, (2) lax banking rules contributed to asset inflation in the housing and equity markets, and (3) deregulation encouraged an assortment of "liar," "no doc," and "Ninja" (no income, no job, no assets) loans that made "subprime" a talking point the world over.[2] Also ignored was how these developments helped create toxic financial instruments—which generated lucrative loan origination and traders' fees—that passed from one trader to another. But perhaps most disturbing was how President Bush disregarded the bailouts that were presently being orchestrated for the industries that had already feasted at the government-spiked bubble banquet of the early 2000s.[3] Of these bailouts, perhaps the most notorious were government loans to Countrywide Financial.

When the value of Countrywide Financial plummeted from a high of $44 to $5.00 per share (2007–2008), it was discovered that the company had secured more than $50 billion in loans from the federal government.[4] For collateral, Countrywide was allowed to put up its increasingly worthless subprime contracts. Adding salt to the wound of this taxpayer-funded bailout, former Countrywide President Stanford Kurland landed a job where he could use his expertise concerning "which mortgage-backed securities are toxic" to purchase mortgages for his new firm.[5] In this manner, not only did executives like Kurland profit handsomely from the

effervescent and "bubbly" confidence created by industry-friendly govern-
ment policies, but they also were able to keep things moving in their favor—
with federal bailouts that kept their industry afloat and staved off
government investigations. Like all good Ponzi schemes, after the initial
frenzied confidence ran its course, the game continued when a new player
(in this case, the Federal Reserve) was brought in to play the sucker.[6] These
dynamics violate, on many levels, what Adam Smith said about markets
and the "laws of justice" and makes it difficult to understand President
Bush's sanctimonious market hubris toward homeowners. This is especially
the case when we consider that in most instances homeowners simply got
swept up in the same web of euphoria, deception, and fraud that captured
larger market players—a process that the federal government first fed and
then subsidized with bailouts for industry players like Countrywide.

Chapter 8 explained that to speak of Europe's economic recovery and
its subsequent economic interdependence in purely market terms is misleading. The pivotal role played by pressing security needs at the time,
coupled with the political lessons learned from the interwar period, compelled postwar leaders to abandon long-held beliefs about capitalist markets. Specifically, they dispensed with the notion that creating a harmony
of interests was best left to the actions of private players. Postwar leaders
understood that, if Europe and the West were going to reduce the proclivity toward conflict and war, they would have to find common ground.
This meant finding ways to cooperate so that nation-states could prosper
economically without pursuing "beggar-thy-neighbor" policies.

Although the prosperity of the postwar period tells us the path taken
by the victors was the correct one, we often ignore how difficult it was to
craft the postwar order. Specifically, postwar leaders had to deal with the
reality that "opposition to economic liberalism," or resistance to *laissez-
faire* economics, was "nearly universal outside the United States."[7] We
also forget that memories of unfettered markets, greed, and economic
depression during the 1930s were fresh and weighed heavily on the minds
of Europeans and Americans.[8] People remembered how former trading
partners became aggressive trading competitors as economic upheaval
spread across the globe.

Using devalued currencies and competitive tariffs to protect jobs and to
deal with balance-of-trade problems, states soon learned the folly of their
ways: the Depression that began with the Crash of 1929 got broader and
deeper during the 1930s. When this happened, many found it convenient
to blame "internationalists" or specific nation-states for their woes. And
those who couldn't—or didn't want to—piece together the complex
dynamics behind market collapse found it easier to blame specific ethnic or

religious groups for their nation's problems. For added measure, suspicions of foreigners grew as well. All of this contributed to a postwar environment in which trade based on free and open markets became a hard sell.

Renowned British economist John Maynard Keynes understood all of this. He was already at the front of a new intellectual current that reappraised how capitalist markets really worked. Powerful as much for his criticism of neoclassical market assumptions as for what he prescribed, Keynes's observations turned Adam Smith's economic world around. Arguing that market equilibrium could occur when things were bad, Keynes made it clear that depressed economies could remain depressed for long periods of time. To get economies going, Keynes argued, states needed to prime the pump by putting money into the hands of people who would spend it—the workers. On their own, Keynes's ideas might not have gone anywhere, but several factors aided in their acceptance.

First, as noted previously, economic depression was blamed on competitive, unfettered, and impersonal market forces that bred both greed and stupidity. Second, it was well understood that fascism had glorified industrialists and the military goals of the state. This raised serious doubts about giving industrialists and the captains of industry undue influence over economic policy. Those who pushed the view that markets produced efficiency, equilibrium, and harmony were pressed by the hard facts of greed, economic depression, and war. Third, the historical record, the market insights, and the scholarly reputation of John Maynard Keynes were legendary by the 1930s. At a time when "obedience to old poorly understood verities"[9] seemed to paralyze leaders like Herbert Hoover, Keynes offered alternatives. Finally, even though Keynes disagreed with several key neoclassical assumptions, he didn't fundamentally challenge the moral justification of capitalism: if you work hard, you can get ahead. Keynes's genius lay in questioning the conditions under which economic growth and market equilibrium occurred.[10] By leaving the moral justification of capitalism alone, Keynes was able to promote a "genuine Third Way" to prosperity.[11]

The Emergence of John Maynard Keynes[12]

Economists from the time of Adam Smith believed and wrote that markets were self-regulating and could be counted on to work their way out of slumps and even depressions—as long as the state stayed out of the way. The assumption was that the logic of the market, as a self-correcting force, was superior to anything that states could come up with and that markets were efficient over the long term. Writing about these unrelenting dynamics created a sense of confidence within the economics profession and led respected professionals to make assumptions and statements that seem rather silly today. One of the more famous observations about markets was made in 1929 by renowned Yale economist Irving Fisher. Buoyed by the growth of the stock market during the 1920s, Fisher boldly announced that stock prices had reached a "permanently high plateau."[13] This statement was made, to Fisher's ever-lasting regret (if not shame), just one week before the US stock market crashed.

The notion of a plateau, or what economists might call *equilibrium*, was widely accepted in the field of economics. John Maynard Keynes, however, saw a hole in the argument. What Keynes brought to the table was his claim that equilibrium could not only occur when economies were productive and strong but also when markets slumped. There was nothing automatic about recovery, and, worse, depressions could last a long time. In the political world of his time, this meant trouble because, as the interwar period revealed, markets exposed to economic distress for prolonged periods became exposed to the nationalistic rants of megalomaniacs and political despots. Although economists might appeal to the economic ghost of Adam Smith when times got rough, Keynes explained why the political spirits unleashed by unemployment, depression, and despair prevailed: in times of trouble the invisible hand disappeared.

What helped separate Keynes from other economists, however, were the analogies that he used to explain and criticize the field of economics. To those who pointed to market logic, he countered with the "Paradox of Thrift" (if everybody saved, no one would spend). To those who argued that economies would eventually right themselves over the long run, he countered that we couldn't afford to wait because "[i]n the long run we're all dead."[14] The field of economics (and the world) according to Keynes needed to offer more than an authoritative "Let's wait it out" mentality during hard times. Making Keynes's observations more persuasive was that he anticipated much of what occurred in the 1920s and 1930s.

In *The Economic Consequences of the Peace,* Keynes took post-World War I leaders to task for putting together a treaty at Versailles in 1919 that spoke more to vengeance (France's Georges Clemenceau), a "higher calling" (preached by Woodrow Wilson), and political expediency (the United Kingdom's Lloyd George) than to the practical political and economic problems that needed to be addressed.[15] And, as Keynes warned, this came back to haunt Europe—and the world—in the form of political conflict. Keynes wrote,

> The danger confronting us, therefore, is the rapid depression of the standard of life of the European populations to a

point which will mean actual starvation for some (a point already reached in Russia and approximately reached in Austria). Men will not always die quietly. For starvation, which brings to some lethargy and a helpless despair, drives other temperaments to the nervous instability of hysteria and to a mad despair. And these in their distress may overturn the remnants of organization, and submerge civilization itself in their attempts to satisfy desperately the overwhelming needs of the individual. This is the danger against which with all our resources and courage and idealism must now cooperate.[16]

For Keynes, vengeance and despair over the punitive nature of Versailles created the ugly political environment necessary for viral economic nationalism to prosper. This devoured the unrealistic expectations made at Versailles in 1917.

Keynes Saves Capitalism

What Keynes saw in Europe's future after World War I was driven by financial concerns: the need to pay debts and to remain financially solvent. Much of this could be worked out, according to Keynes, if the participants had agreed to cooperate politically on trade and money matters. Although Keynes's prescriptions flew in the face of classic interpretations of economics, his observations proved prescient.[17] Specifically, when the United States decided to work with Europe and developed the Dawes Plan—which sent investment dollars to Germany in 1924—the tendency to embrace aggressive economic policies subsided in Europe (for the time being). Unfortunately, upset with the punitive nature and terms produced by the Treaty of Versailles, the political seeds of betrayal and retribution had already been planted in Germany. The seeds of discontent, as Keynes predicted, blossomed into war when the Depression hit and deepened in the 1930s.

With his prediction that the Treaty of Versailles had doomed Europe to renewed political suspicion and economic aggression, Keynes was in a unique position to dissect the relationship between politics and economics when the Depression hit. But Keynes's focus this time was not on the impact of faulty international treaties. Rather, the depth and breadth of the Depression drove Keynes to look at the factors that promoted economic growth. In particular, at a time when demand was low or stagnant, Keynes took a look at what drove people to save (necessary for banks to lend) and to invest (necessary to create goods and jobs) in society. What he found turned the field of economics inside out and laid out the rationale for a larger state role in the economy.

Keynes argued that a nation's tendency to save and invest would not always be symbiotic, as neoclassical economists argued. Keynes saw that during the Depression "Thrift" and "Enterprise" could act in a seesaw like fashion: if one went up, the other could go down. To explain Keynes pointed out that after prolonged depression and stagnation, the unemployed had nothing to save. Those who had jobs or money despaired for the future and would not spend or invest. Businesses would become cautious too. Neoclassical economists were ill-equipped to solve the challenge of collapsed national savings during an economic slump. Viewed from this perspective, uncertainty rather than assurance lay at the heart of capitalism.[18] Moreover, because the classical interpretation of savings and investment patterns was wrong, the prescription—doing nothing—must be wrong as well. Standing by was no longer a viable option.[19] This insight compelled Keynes to ask questions in a way that "probably saved capitalism from itself and surely kept latter-day Marxists at bay."[20] In the process, Keynes's observations revitalized and remade capitalism for the twentieth century.

Setting the Groundwork for Regulatory Capitalism

These dynamics led Keynes to take another look at the factors that contributed to the "wealth of nations." He looked wide and far. Possession of gold and silver was deemed to be an insufficient explanation for wealth, because many nations—India at the time and Spain historically—had bullion but they weren't commercially competitive. Physical infrastructure also fell short. No bridges or buildings disappeared from 1928 to 1933. Yet national income collapsed in the United States from $77 billion to $39 billion.[21] Intellectual capital wasn't much help either: architects didn't forget how to draw plans, medical doctors still understood medicine, and professors didn't suddenly forget what they knew. For Keynes, wealth creation depended on one simple factor: confidence.

If households and firms were unsure about the future, the factors that create wealth are undermined. In *The General Theory of Employment, Interest, and Money* (or *The General Theory*), Keynes wrote that removing uncertainty and doubt could be done by encouraging governments to put money in people's hands. Keynes's insights rested on two arguments. First, markets weren't always prone to a seesaw-like pattern of boom and bust. Rather, markets acted more like an elevator: they could go up or go down, but they could also stand perfectly still—whether on the ground floor or at the Penthouse Suite.[22] And, just as elevators can get stuck on a floor, so could markets. There was no automatic safety button to take you to the floor that you wanted.[23] So equilibrium could be sustained on the bottom floor (depression) or the top floor (prosperity) for long periods. It's this insight that led Keynes to proclaim that there was nothing automatic about investment or savings.

To explain why economies lacked automaticity, Keynes introduced us to the *Paradox of Thrift*. Keynes explained that, although the field of economics made a virtue of thrift and made it a key component of economic vitality, the possibility remained that everyone might want to save or hoard money at the same time. This included businesses. If this occurred, no one would spend and economies could stagnate. So, even though saving was logical and virtuous and was even encouraged by the classic market model, it didn't always lead to the best outcome. There was nothing automatic about national savings and investment. As Robert Heilbroner put it,

> In 1929 the American private citizenry put aside $3.7 billion out of its income; by 1932 and 1933 it was saving *nothing*— in fact, it was even drawing down its old savings made in the years before. Corporations, which had tucked away $2.6 billion at the top of the boom *after* paying out taxes and dividends, found themselves losing nearly $6 billion three years later. Quite obviously Keynes was right: saving was a kind of luxury that could not withstand hard times.[24]

But there was more to it than that. Not only did savings fail to stand up to economic depression but when people lost confidence in financial institutions—as they did in the 1930s—the entire economy suffered. The primary mechanisms for recycling national income, the banks, became impotent institutional shells. When this type of market failure occurred, the state had to put money in people's hands either by manipulating monetary policy (interest rates) or fiscal policy (legislation designed to influence consumption and investment).

To be sure, after the Depression hit, private efforts—led by Charles Mitchell at National City Bank—were made to build confidence by funneling money into the economy. But these efforts were undermined by the suspicion that profiteering and speculation, rather than consumption and investment, were driving the economy.[25] The motives of private players, whether they're noble or not, always arouse suspicion when panic hits. Because consumers are naturally suspicious of speculators and bankers in hard times, these efforts failed. Making matters worse was that, as people lost faith in America's banking system, they thought it safer to stuff what money they had in shoe boxes and mattresses. This further eroded the funds available from banks.

The financial excesses that were discovered after markets had collapsed created headlines about fraud, shell corporations, and financial pyramids (among others), which only aroused suspicion about bankers. Making matters worse, banks who invested with in-house investors at the time could also borrow from in-house insurance companies. This created conflicts of interest and levels of fraud that startled government inspectors and infuriated small depositors—especially after many prominent financial players began answering subpoenas. These developments helped ensure that government oversight and intervention went beyond fiscal and monetary policies. The result was a bevy of legislation and the creation of the Federal Deposit Insurance Corporation (FDIC), the Securities & Exchange Commission (SEC), and the 1933 Glass-Steagall Act (repealed in 1999), which separated commercial banks from investment houses and the insurance industry. This paved the way for the "regulatory capitalism" that emerged in the latter half of the twentieth century throughout the industrialized world.[26]

Bretton Woods 101

Depression and despair in the 1930s led Keynes to point out that doing nothing enabled the ascent of men of opportunity. He understood that political opportunists could always inflame passions by blaming anyone and everything for the woes of society. As societies in despair demanded action, problems emerged: despots and crackpots always find it easy to oblige a mob. This threat made it incumbent upon government to rally confidence by priming the pump and injecting money into to the economy. Political legitimacy and national security demanded economic stability and growth. For Keynes the threat of political despotism made *laissez-faire* economics, well, *passé*.

On another level, with memories of markets and banking collapses in the 1930s fresh in their minds, members of America's financial community "vowed that never again would they trust their fortunes abroad or respond to the requests of recreant foreign governments."[27] At the same time, unless domestic firms were involved, banks were reticent to engage in banking activities beyond their home markets.[28] And there was still the problem of countries running balance-of-payment deficits. The best way to avoid these and other challenges that plagued the 1930s, Keynes argued, was to manage currencies and to coordinate international payment imbalances.

Before Keynes could see his ideas come to fruition on a global level, he had to collaborate with his chief negotiating partner and rival at Bretton

Woods, Henry Dexter White. As the US Department of Treasury envoy to Bretton Woods, White stood toe-to-toe with Keynes, negotiating the US position for the postwar economic order. Although White was armed with a Ph.D. in economics and had graduated from Stanford and Harvard, he was not Keynes's intellectual match (few were). Still, thanks to the US military and economic position in the postwar order, White had the upper hand. Driven by his disdain for economic nationalism and "beggar-thy-neighbor" policies, White was an avowed internationalist who had opposed the Smoot-Hawley tariff bill. His singular focus on market cooperation resulted in the GATT. His positions contrasted with those of the British, who sought protection from low-wage competitors and a continuation of their imperial preference system.

White also promoted the idea of a global central bank, which he had proposed earlier in Rio de Janeiro as part of an effort to unite North and South America. Keynes had his own ideas. He wanted the United States—which held the vast majority of the world's gold at the time—to provide most of the banks' gold while tolerating balance-of-payment deficits from its allies.[29] The idea was for participating countries to help capitalize the new global bank with gold deposits and to declare a fixed value for its currency. Rights to borrow from this bank would be made available when balance-of-payment problems emerged. What emerged was a hybrid system. To prevent destabilizing patterns in which money easily hopped from one financial center to another, the system allowed countries to impose capital controls (monitored by the IMF). Nation-states were enticed and sometimes coerced into a trading system with low tariff rates (through GATT), which guaranteed them access to the world's biggest markets. The result was a postwar global economy marked by limited capital mobility and international capital markets managed by policymakers in the United States and Europe.[30] The system rested on two premises (as noted previously). The US dollar became the world's anchor currency and the United States provided the capital necessary to jump-start demand internationally.

There were three problems from the very beginning that guaranteed the system would break down. First, as Robert Triffin made clear, the Bretton Woods system was doomed to failure because it rested on one fundamental assumption: the United States had to run continuous balance-of-payment deficits. This eventually flooded global markets with dollars, which undermined the value of the system's anchor currency. So the primary challenge of Bretton Woods was structural, not one of management (discussed in the next section). As well, as Benjamin J. Cohen points out, memories don't last. New generations of self-proclaimed "wonder bankers" will enter the scene. Ignorant of history, they view the firewalls of the system and the caution of others disparagingly. Rather than prudence, they see nervousness and trepidation.[31] Finally, the explosion of global trade and the surfeit of dollars that emerged in the 1960s and 1970s made it increasingly difficult for governments to stabilize or manage currency rates with simple policy coordination. The wonder bankers and their commercial colleagues, confident of the profits to be made in the new environment, made sure of this.

From Triffin's Warning to Exploding Capital Flows: The Collapse of Bretton Woods

Becoming money manager to the world worked out for the United States because as long as others continued to seek and hold US dollars America effectively had a blank check to print and export them. The United States could create and send dollars abroad as though it were writing checks to nice relatives or friendly merchants who had agreed to hold on to them indefinitely. Even when dollar gluts developed, the system continued to work, in part because the postwar system was relatively secure and allowed US allies to grow and prosper at the expense of the United States (see Chapter 8). These dynamics helped convince US allies to continue holding dollars. Still, there were concerns over the value of the dollar as US deficit dollars continued to grow.

Robert Triffin, in *Gold and the Dollar Crisis,* was among the first to point out that if the United States continued to print money, extend credit, and spend freely, there would eventually be so many dollars floating around that the United States would not be able to convert dollars into gold at the rate of $35 dollars per ounce. By the mid-1960s France's Charles de Gaulle understood this and demanded gold instead of dollars from America. By August 15, 1971, there were so many dollars abroad that the United States simply gave up on its twin policy of converting dollars into gold, which meant abandoning all pretenses to managing global currency values—and with reason. Not only did the dollar come under attack (because of US expenditures, budget deficits, and dwindling gold supplies) but the job of supervising exchange rates had become unmanageable.

In spite of these dynamics the "implicit bargain" between the United States and its allies held firm because of two interrelated developments. First, the cooperation planned at Bretton Woods had paid dividends in Europe and Japan.[32] Second, even though cooperation was viewed with suspicion by those partial to the neoclassical economic tradition, habits and results proved that coordination was both a noble and a profitable goal. Cooperation clearly provided a positive-sum and a very profitable environment. But the success of Bretton Woods did not rest simply on creating economic institutions. Rather, the key to the system's success was tied to the ideas and the legitimacy that surrounded the US position from day one.

Grounded in its unique historical experience, the nondiscriminatory and plural world order imagined by American postwar planners was seen as legitimate. It was not lost upon global observers that, as a relative newcomer to world politics, the United States had helped turn the tide in two global conflicts in which imperial "predatory grabs" were beaten back.[33] So, when the United States found itself in a precarious currency position in 1971, its allies were not too keen about abandoning a system that had created prosperity and maintained stability. Nation-states continued to embrace America's "grand liberal strategy." This allowed the United States to continue pushing its grand liberal ideas while exploiting (via deficit spending) its dollar position long after August 15, 1971.[34]

These developments helped expand freer trade and bring about globalization. They also helped ensure that US deficit dollars would continue to find a home in the open arms of global industries and friendly economies around the world.[35] The process of buying and selling dollars (as opposed to just using them for commercial transactions) actually began much earlier, when the British began to solicit US dollars actively in 1957. Driven by their need to restrict the outflow of pounds sterling—and because of the demands of global trading firms—the British began purchasing, loaning, and selling "Eurodollars" throughout Europe.[36] Because global trade was expanding, the British decision helped create a vibrant European commercial market for US dollars, which the Bretton Woods institutions were ill-equipped to track. This was evident as early as 1964, when the Bank for International Settlements was created to help keep track of global capital flows. In the Organization for Economic Cooperation and Development (OECD) states, global trade and international banking increased to such a degree that foreign deposits—which included dollars— as a percentage of all bank deposits grew from 11.3 to 23.4 percent between 1970 and 1981.[37] These amounts continued to grow during the turbulent 1970s.

Specifically, the economic shocks caused by the ascent of the Organization of Petroleum Exporting Countries (OPEC) in 1973 flooded banks with "petrodollar" deposits. Because banks cannot sit on deposits and pay interest without losing money, they went looking for borrowers. New bank lending increased 25 percent per year after the OPEC shocks (most went to the developing world). Earnings from international lending were extraordinary, with profit margins reaching 68 percent.[38] In addition to finding a new and profitable business line, by lending abroad, banks were also freed from domestic reserve requirements, which led several banks to grant more loans than was prudent. This came back to haunt financial institutions in the 1980s when several Latin American states declared they couldn't repay their loans. This led to numerous debt-rescheduling programs and, perhaps not surprisingly, the emergence of new bond and "secondary" markets in which debt contracts could be sold and purchased.

The Continuing Need for Coordination

Because globalization was on the march, continued US budget deficits combined with OPEC petrodollar dynamics, supercharged capital flows to and from the United States in the 1970s and 1980s. New bond and equity markets emerged that both demanded and absorbed even more dollar-denominated instruments. Along the way there was vigorous currency trading, and the creation of numerous and innovative financial instruments in the United States (Chapters 10 and 11). The sheer volume of currency movements alone is telling. Although global capital flows amounted to $12 billion in 1964, by 1972 they had grown by a factor of ten and reached $131 billion (Table 9.1). One year after OPEC's first dramatic price hikes (1973), global capital flows reached $215 billion. Ten years later, they reached $921 billion. Apart from new bank lending and debt rescheduling, what also contributed to these dynamics through the 1980s and 1990s was the rise of secondary and hedge fund markets and the emergence of new debt instruments. Today global capital flows have surpassed $6 trillion.

Because of these financial developments, doomsayers and others were left anticipating a financial day of reckoning, which many believed should have arrived immediately after 1971. But this financial reckoning didn't occur. It didn't happen because, as I have argued, nation-states had learned the benefits of cooperating in an environment that provided both stability and security. Even though the control and management of currencies was no longer possible—in a debt-driven, petrodollar-filled, global economy—the upside was that the benefits of policy coordination had been demonstrated by 1971.[39] So, although the explosion in global capital flows after 1971 might have compelled many to believe that a 1930s-like "free for all" was just around the corner after 1971, something else happened. America's postwar grand liberal strategy of inclusion and transparency was viewed as legitimate and started paying big political and economic dividends.

But, even with these developments, new trends required additional discussions on how to manage the increasingly intertwined and complex global economy. Banks operating in international markets were largely unsupervised and lacked a set of international banking standards.[40] As a result, in an

Table 9.1 U.S. Money Supply/Global Capital Flows (selected years)

Year	U.S. Money Supply, M-1	U.S. Money Supply, M-2	U.S. Money Supply, M-3	Global Capital Flows
1964	$160 billion	$425 billion	$442 billion	$12 billion
1972	$249 billion	$802 billion	$886 billion	$131 billion
1974	$274 billion	$902 billion	$1.070 trillion	$215 billion
1975	$287 billion	$1.017 trillion	$1.170 trillion	$258 billion
1984	$551 billion	$2.312 trillion	$2.991 trillion	$921 billion
1994	$1.150 trillion	$3.498 trillion	$4.370 trillion	$1.4 trillion
2002	$1.219 trillion	$5.801 trillion	$8.568 trillion	$2.4 trillion
2003	$1.306 trillion	$6.062 trillion	$8.872 trillion	$3.0 trillion
2004	$1.376 trillion	$6.422 trillion	$9.433 trillion	$5.0 trillion
2005	$1.375 trillion	$6.692 trillion	$10.154 trillion	$6.0 trillion
2006	$1.367 trillion	$7.036 trillion	$10.299 trillion	N/A
2007	$1.367 trillion	$7.447 trillion	N/A	N/A
2008*	$1.600 trillion	$8.108 trillion	N/A	N/A
2009*	$1.546 trillion	$8.110 trillion	N/A	N/A

Sources: Years 1964–1984: Benjamin J. Cohen, *In Whose Interest? International Banking and American Foreign Policy* (New Haven, CT: Yale University Press, 1986); years 2002–2003: Matthew Higgins and Thomas Klitgaard, "Reserve Accumulation: Implications for Global Capital Flows," Federal Reserve Bank of New York, *Current Issues in Economics and Finance* 10, no. 10 (September/October 2004); years 2004–2005: "Global Capital Flows: Defying Gravity," *Finance & Development: A Quarterly Magazine of the IMF*, 44, no. 1 (March 2007); years 2006–2007: "Money Stock Measures," Federal Reserve Statistical Release, H. 6, Table 1156, Board of Governors of the Federal Reserve System, January 17, 2009, available online.

*2008–2009 figures through January 2009, "Money Stock Measures," Federal Reserve Statistical Release, H. 6, Table 1 (Seasonally Adjusted), Board of Governors of the Federal Reserve System, January 15, 2009, available online.

effort to act preemptively, the heads of the ten major central banks met in Basel, Switzerland, in 1988. Their goal was not to manage currencies or to discuss exchange rate fluctuations. Instead, they met to mandate that banks operating internationally establish a set of global standards, like reserve requirements, equal to 8 percent of total capital assets (although "capital assets" are still ill-defined and not readily agreed upon). In this manner, the global vulnerabilities that emerged after 1971, combined with the successes of postwar institutions, worked to produce an environment that was ripe for a "supervisory regime" to "hold the banks in check."[41] Or, as Michael C. Webb explained, although "the types of policies subject to coordination" had changed, global policy coordination became "at least as extensive in the 1970s and 1980s" as it was during the 1950s and 1960s.[42]

As global capital flows, international trade, and cooperation expanded, several policy areas continued—and continue—to capture the attention of international financiers. Among these are persistent concerns over weak oversight of international lending, currency speculation, structural changes in the global economy, and the increased risk of market failures at a global level (which Keynes identified), among other issue areas. Still, as was the case before 1929, with so many opportunities and new markets available for making money, advocates of free trade market orthodoxy continue to push for policies that either gut or weaken oversight and standards. The irony of their position is that, under the coordinated policies of the Bretton Woods system, global trade and economic growth (and the middle class in the West) have prospered unlike at any other time in human history. Proponents of the neoclassical approach tend to ignore or downplay what was created in a controlled and stable environment. More incredibly, as Nobel laureate Joseph Stiglitz pointed out in 2002, the "Not to worry; markets are self-regulating" mentality appeared to have made a comeback.[43] It's worth noting this was the mind-set before, during, and immediately after the Great Depression.[44]

Keynes's Greatest Insight: Not in Economics?

Milton Friedman and his followers notwithstanding, what precipitated market collapse and deepened economic depression across the globe in the 1930s was the inability of governments to address market failures proactively. Part of the problem rested on the fact that policymakers were wedded to classical theories of economics. Keynes took the neoclassicists to task and helped his contemporaries see that freedom, liberty, and *laissez-faire* meant little without opportunity and stable employment. He tried to demonstrate to policy leaders that, if the moral justification of capitalism disappeared, the entire system would be exposed to social and political calamity.

By demonstrating how an overreliance on *laissez-faire* could undermine the conditions that made liberty and freedom worth the fight, Keynes was able to move Adam Smith's ideas to another level, which offered a "genuine Third Way" for some observers.[45] Although some might see an "either-or" binary option between Smith and Keynes, the reality is that Keynes complimented Adam Smith by demonstrating how to address the more utopian elements of Smith's worldview. In many respects, however, Keynes was not offering anything new. As we saw in Chapter 1, *The Federalist Papers* made it painfully clear that, "if men were angels," we wouldn't have anything to worry about when individuals collectively pursue wealth and prosperity. Unfortunately, as the Founding Fathers of American democracy knew—and as the conditions that led to the Depression illustrate—we are not angels. We don't always do the right thing, and we often violate Adam Smith's laws of justice.

Still, Keynes's less than insightful critics continued to argue that his "collective" action approach was proof that he had socialist tendencies.

Nothing could be further from the truth. Not only did Keynes have little respect for the "dull" logic behind Marxist economics, but he was committed to pointing out that markets could avoid paralyzing collapses—but only if government embraced the tools to correct market failures. He wanted to make sure that markets worked. And, in many ways, he was committed to seeing that the "virtuous citizens" whom James Madison saw corrupted by the prospects of wealth in his day didn't emerge and undermine society in the modern era. These insights point us toward the weaknesses that Keynes perceived in the field of economics.

According to Keynes, the economist's argument that societies needed to be patient because things worked themselves out in the long term might have been true, but it was also vacuous. In his view, the field of economics didn't amount to much if "in tempestuous seasons they can only tell us that when the storm is long past the ocean is flat again."[46] This explains why Keynes embraced cooperation and state intervention. Informed political insights and an understanding of basic economics could offer the necessary tools to ride out the stormy economic seas, if not to avoid them altogether. Like James Madison, Keynes understood that, as long as "the reason of man is fallible, and he is at liberty to exercise it," things can go horribly wrong in markets.

But Keynes wasn't advocating intervention for the sake of intervention (which his critics often get wrong). For example, he believed that priming the pump for the sake of priming the pump (or fiscal stabilization) offered few long-term benefits and might not even stir consumption (a lesson for supply-siders). Similarly, he was also opposed to fiscal "fine-tuning," because he believed that it was necessary to focus on bolstering "permanent income" and other preventative measures.[47]

Contemporaries who call for a return to the free market orthodoxy of the past ignore this aspect of Keynes's wisdom. They also ignore how the institutions and policies that Keynes organized have helped the global economy avoid the pitfalls of the past. On this, Joseph Stiglitz writes,

> Keynes's medicine worked: since World War II, countries like the United States, following Keynesian prescriptions, have had fewer and shorter-lived downturns, and longer expansions than previously.[48]

We need to emphasize that the economic growth of the second half of the twentieth century didn't occur in a vacuum. Economic growth was a direct result of imposed policy coordination. These policies were imposed as a result of very practical, larger geostrategic concerns.

At the most fundamental level, introductory students of international relations can point out that nation-states are inclined to cooperate for one simple reason: they live in the shadow of the future. To ignore the past is to reinvite the debacles of history. Political scientists like Robert O. Keohane, Joseph Nye Jr., G. John Ikenberry, and Tony Smith have gone to great lengths to explain the logic and rationale behind cooperation.[49] Whether we are speaking of America's "Grand Liberal Strategy" or "National Security Liberalism," the end result is a complex global system that is stitched together by diplomats, statesmen, and even a few rogue politicians who are committed to avoiding the sins of the past. Their work, along with the work of others, is what makes the observations of Keynes so important today.

Perhaps Keynes's most profound insight was his ability to illustrate that markets do not operate in isolation from the rest of society. As such, markets cannot always be left to their own devices. Stiglitz offers additional insight:

> [Keynes] showed why there was a need for *global* collective action, because the actions of one country spilled over to others. One country's imports are another country's exports. Cutbacks in imports by one country, for whatever reason, hurt other countries' economies . . . There was another market failure: he worried that in a severe downturn, monetary policy might be ineffective, but that some countries might not be able to borrow to finance the expenditure increases or compensate for tax cuts needed to stimulate the economy. Even if a country was seemingly creditworthy, it might not be able to get money. Keynes not only identified a set of market failures; he explained why an institution like the IMF could improve matters: by putting pressure on countries to maintain their economy at full employment, and by providing liquidity for those countries facing downturns that could not afford an expansionary increase in government expenditures, *global* aggregate demand could be sustained.[50]

Although Keynes made his name in economics, his commentary on the relationship between economics and politics is perhaps his greatest contribution to our understanding of the world. He understood that market competition and market failures could wreck havoc on nation-state relations and bring conflict and war. In this way, Keynes established that an intricate relationship exists between markets and war. If proactive and anticipatory policies were not in place to control rogue market players and stupid decision-making before markets stumbled and then crashed, subsequent events could escape human control. Speculative bubbles, widespread fraud, economic depression, political extremism, and the rise of Nazism in the 1930s are all evidence of this. Clinging to outdated and utopian notions of markets, as Keynes helped illustrate, is hardly helpful. This, as the next three chapters show, appears to be our unfortunate condition today.

Lessons Lost

John Maynard Keynes's greatest contributions may not have been his insights on market failure. Rather, by going beyond the economic, he elevated and reinvigorated our understanding of classical liberalism. Although classical liberalism has always been hopeful about the human condition, as we saw in Chapter 1, classical liberalism has also been realistic about the human condition. Keynes would have been perfectly at home with the Founding Fathers. He understood that capitalism—with its emphasis on wealth and prosperity—and democracy—with its emphasis on rights and justice—both involve freedom of choice and trade-offs. What Keynes helped us see is that market cooperation and management did not undermine the capacity to build wealth and prosperity. He showed us that cooperation could enhance both.

An added benefit, which the fields of political science and sociology help us understand, is how cooperative arrangements advance global security by creating diplomatic protocols and habits of cooperation. In this manner, Keynes helped set the stage for the world to see that the sources of a stable, prosperous, and secure global community rest on creating "complementary agendas" that lead to voluntary cooperation.[51] This requires diplomacy. Perhaps more important, Keynes's insights helped create an intellectual perch for others to see how and why the United States and Britain contributed to a more sophisticated understanding of power—in which cooperation and restraint could actually enhance the legitimacy and authority of leading states.[52]

In spite of these advances in our understanding of the sources of global stability, wealth and security problems loom on the horizon today. Specifically, even though there's little doubt that prosperity and the relatively short-lived economic downturns in the postwar period owe much to following the prescriptions of Keynes and his contemporaries, before the 2008 market collapse a strong current bent on bringing back free market orthodoxy existed.[53] Downplaying advances made in economic theory over the past thirty years,[54] market "fundamentalists" simply ignored how market cooperation has helped bolster political and economic stability at the global level. In the process, they also lost sight of Keynes's lessons on market economies.

Since the 1960s, deficit spending has been used to prime so many pumps in the American economy that politicians on both sides of the isle have become addicted to a continuous flow of state-created or state-sanctioned cash stimulants. What started out as a short-term program to jump-start the economy in the 1930s and 1940s has morphed into a steady stream of "Keynesian" jump-starts, followed by industry bailouts, irresponsible calls for deregulation, and special-interest-driven fiscal policies.[55] Although these demands may have allowed Wall Street and Main Street to prosper together in a seemingly endless pool of money before 2008, very few observers took a step back to ask about fiscal responsibility, business accountability, and the markets impact on democratic patterns in America.

Over the past twenty-five years the end result has been a series of speculative bubbles and near-collapses of the market—only to be alleviated by the concepts and institutions that Keynes promoted. Whether we consider the savings and loan debacle, the Long Term Capital Management bailout, IMF-led loan and bailouts for Latin America and Asia, or other events that have brought America and the world to the brink of economic collapse since then (like the 2008 market meltdown), free-market advocates appear to have little sympathy or understanding of how market "genius" can fail spectacularly in an interdependent world.[56]

Conclusion

By the early 1970s, US budget deficits, globalization, and the sudden slap in the face from OPEC had already sent America's financial and political elites an array of messages: "deficits can't continue," "globalization requires a new approach," "the value of the dollar is collapsing," and "asset inflation matters." Properly warned, but lacking the political will to change course, America not only proceeded to maintain the status quo but began to look for new ways to create wealth from previous patterns. Like a child stacking Lego blocks, one on top of another, the logic of the market said little, because one block of debt added to another looked stable. But as any child knows, there comes a point when the stack of Lego blocks—which appears strong in the core—collapses.

The answer, ironically, was to further embrace deregulation, globalization, and deficit spending. And why not? After the political debacles that surrounded Vietnam, Watergate, inflation, and the nation's seeming impotence in the face of OPEC price hikes, Americans began to question government. Lost in the moment was how unrestrained globalization had damaged labor's bargaining position and how the ascent of OPEC and the increasing market power of the oil industry had violated the laws of justice that Adam Smith spoke about. Increased global competition and market collusion should have sparked a debate about the new direction of global markets. Instead, a sense of desperation—or *malaise*—enveloped America by the late 1970s. Political opportunists, who prospered from postwar stability, but never agreed with Keynes or with FDR's New Deal legacy, saw an opening. They blamed the country's woes on government waste and too much regulation.

This helped spur profound changes in America's economy. Encouraged by favorable legislation domestically and the lack thereof abroad, one industry after another began leaving for cheaper and more profitable shores. This not only pushed globalization, but it helped turn America into a permanent importer of merchandise goods by the 1970s. In the process, more US dollars flowed out. To keep firms at home, developed states began offering concessions, many of which undermined tax revenue streams. In the United States, this came in the form of a Republican-led frenzy of deregulation and tax cuts. An added bonus for industry was an increasing hostile attitude toward labor. But the new policies did little to revive either manufacturing or the salaries of America's middle class. How could they? By the 1980s the heart and soul of the new American economy was its service sector, which was led by finance, insurance, and real estate—or FIRE.[57] Rather than making new refrigerators to sell, the increasingly deregulated FIRE sector manufactured instruments for creative investment and debt that did much for Wall Street's bottom line. But the activity was all tied to a flow of easy money (from home and abroad), favorable legislation (especially deregulation), and debt. This helps explain, in part, the growing earning and wealth gap between America's economic elites and its middle class.[58]

Because the United States couldn't finance its own deficits, it became dependent on others to purchase its debt. But the real and immediate trouble lay in the fact that a new generation of politicians, bankers, economists, and journalists had emerged by the 1980s. Free from the haunting memories of the Depression and largely ignorant of what precedes financial manias and bubbles, they had a collective sense that "We have mastered the universe . . . all shall reap the benefits of our business acumen." As Eric Janszen put it, all "logic and historical precedent were pushed aside."[59] With deregulation leading the way, Wall Street found novel and interesting ways to create wealth. The 1980s, 1990s, and the early 2000s were good times—even if the market breakthroughs were tied to artificially inflated values and debt. The irony is that, in this debt-driven economy, private sector players congratulated themselves for their genius in "democratizing" credit and politicians gloated that "deficits don't matter."

Ignored, however, was the fact that debt-driven bubbles were recreating the conditions that we once saw with Tulips and with South Sea investments—something that Keynes warned against. But with profits growing, market players began to believe that they had once again discovered the key to perpetual wealth and good times. The so-called breakthroughs were based on market players' delusions that they had found the Philosopher's Stone (see Chapter 4). The only difference is that today's financial alchemists were hailed for—and compensated handsomely because of—their creativity in "securitizing" debt, "democratizing" credit, establishing complex debt swaps, and arranging even more complex derivative agreements, among other novel market arrangements.

Notes

1. Office of the Press Secretary, "President Bush Discusses Housing," The White House, December 6, 2007, available online.

2. Charles R. Morris, *The Trillion Dollar Meltdown: Easy Money, High Rollers, and the Great Credit Crash* (New York: Public Affairs, 2008).

3. Greg Ip and Joellen Perry, "Central Banks Launch Effort to Free Up Credit," *The Wall Street Journal* online, Dec. 13, 2007, available online; David Frazier, "Government Bails Out Stock Market . . . For Now," MoneyNews.com, 2008, available online; David Nason, "Subprime Bailout Helps the Greedy," *The Australian*, December 6, 2007, available online.

4. CNBC quotes, Countrywide Financial Corporation, NYSE, available online.

5. "Countrywide Bigs Now Vultures for Your Mortgage," Moneynews.com, March 28, 2008, available online.

6. "Ponzificating: Is the Financial System a Confidence Trick?" *The Economist*, March 20, 2007, available online.

7. John G. Ruggie, "International Regimes, Transactions, and Change: Embedded Liberalism in the Postwar Economic Order," in *Theory and Structure in International Political Economy: An International Organization Reader,* ed. Benjamin J. Cohen and Charles Lipson (Cambridge, MA: MIT Press, 1999), 259.

8. Ethan Kapstein, *Sharing the Wealth: Workers and the World Economy* (New York: Norton, 1999).

9. J. Bradford De Long, review of *John Maynard Keynes: Fighting for Britain,* by Robert Skidelsky. Discussion blog. Available online.

10. De Long, review of Keynes.

11. De Long, review of Keynes. This is significant because, as Douglass C. North points out, to be legitimate all ideologies must explain the rules of the game, account for the past, and be flexible. See Douglass C. North, *Structure and Change in Economic History* (New York: Norton, 1981), 45–53.

12. The general outline for the following two sections is drawn from Chapter 9, "The Heresies of John Maynard Keynes," in Robert L. Heilbroner's *The Worldly Philosophers: The Lives, Times, and Ideas of the Great Economic Thinkers,* 6th edition (New York: Simon & Schuster, 1986). Citations are used where appropriate.

13. John Kenneth Galbraith, *A Short History of Financial Euphoria* (New York: Viking, 1993), 80.

14. John Maynard Keynes, *A Tract on Monetary Reform* (London: Macmillan, 1924).

15. Walter LaFeber, *The American Age: U.S. Foreign Policy at Home and Abroad, 1750 to the Present.* (New York: Norton, 1994), 316. Blog Commentary.

16. Robert Heilbroner, *The Worldly Philosophers: The Lives, Times, and Ideas of the Great Economic Thinkers* (New York: Simon & Schuster, 1986), 260.

17. An interesting critique of Keynes's position on this is offered in Shawn Ritenour, "Keynes the Great?" in *The Free Market,* The Mises Institute monthly, 16, no. 11, (November 1998), available online; Paul Krugman, "Why Aren't We All Keynesians Yet?" 1998, available online; Robert Gilpin, *Global Political Economy: Understanding the International Economic Order* (Princeton, NJ: Princeton University Press, 2001), 311, footnote 13. Blog Commentary.

18. Heilbroner, *The Worldly,* 275.

19. Duncan K. Foley, *Adam's Fallacy: A Guide to Economic Theology* (Cambridge, MA: Belknap Press, 2006), 10–12, 184–188. Blog Commentary.

20. Robert B. Reich, "John Maynard Keynes: His Radical Idea That Governments Should Spend Money They Don't Have May Have Saved Capitalism," *TIME,* March 29, 1999, available online.

21. Heilbroner, *The Worldly,* 249, 253.

22. Heilbroner, *The Worldly,* 271.

23. Heilbroner, *The Worldly,* 271.

24. Heilbroner, *The Worldly,* 272.

25. John Kenneth Galbraith, *A Short History of Financial Euphoria* (New York: Viking, 1993), 75–85.

26. Heilbroner, *The Worldly,* 279. Blog Commentary.

27. Benjamin J. Cohen, *In Whose Interest? International Banking and American Foreign Policy* (New Haven, CT: Yale University Press, 1986), 18.

28. Cohen, *In Whose.*

29. Gregory J. Millman, *The Vandals' Crown: How Rebel Currency Traders Overthrew the World's Central Banks* (New York: Free Press, 1995), 57–58.

30. Michael C. Webb, "International Economic Structures, Government Interests, and International Coordination of Macroeconomic Adjustment Policies," in *Issues and Agents in International Political Economy: An International Organization Reader,* ed. Charles Lipson and Benjamin J. Cohen (Cambridge, MA: MIT Press, 1999).

31. Benjamin J. Cohen refers to this as "disaster myopia," Cohen, *In Whose,* 44.

32. G. John Ikenberry, "America's Liberal Grand Strategy: Democracy and National Security in the Post-War Era," in *American Foreign Policy: Theoretical Essays,* 4th edition, ed. G. John Ikenberry (New York: Longman, 2002), 274–296.

33. Tony Smith, "National Security Liberalism and American Foreign Policy," in *American Foreign Policy: Theoretical Essays,* 4th edition, ed. G. John Ikenberry (New York: Longman, 2002)

34. Ikenberry, "America's Liberal."

35. Much of what is provided in the following three paragraphs was taken from Chapter 3 of "The Incredible Quarter Century," Cohen, *In Whose.*

36. Cohen, *In Whose,* 18–21. Blog Commentary.

37. Cohen, *In Whose,* 25.

38. Cohen, *In Whose.*

39. Webb, "International Economic."

40. Glyn Davies, *History of Money: From Ancient Times to the Present Day* (Cardiff, UK: University of Wales Press, 2002), 425. Blog Commentary.

41. Davies, *History of,* 430.

42. Webb, "International Economics," 217–218.

43. Joseph E. Stiglitz, *Globalization and Its Discontents* (New York: Norton, 2002), 249.

44. Paul Krugman, *The Return of Depression Economics.* (New York: Norton, 2000). Blog Commentary.

45. De Long, "Book Review," 2001.

46. Keynes, *A Tract.*

47. De Long, "Book Review," 3–4.

48. Stiglitz, *Globalization*, 249.
49. See Robert O. Keohane and Joseph Nye Jr., *Transnational Relations and World Politics* (Cambridge, MA: Harvard University Press, 1972); Robert O. Keohane, *After Hegemony* (Princeton, NJ: Princeton University Press, 1990); Smith, "National"; Ikenberry, "America's."
50. Stiglitz, *Globalization*, 196.
51. These insights are the basis for what G. John Ikenberry refers to in his discussion as "liberal internationalism," Ikenberry, "America's," 274–296.
52. Ikenberry, *After*, 12.
53. Stiglitz, *Globalization*, 196.
54. Gilpin, *The Political*, 175–177; Gilpin, *Global*, 206–211; Stigliz, *Globalization*. Blog Commentary.
55. Kevin Phillips, *Wealth and Democracy;* Thomas R. Dye, *Top Down Policymaking* (New York: Chatham House, 2001); William E. Hudson, *American Democracy in Peril: Seven Challenges to America's Future*, 3rd edition (New York: Chatham House, 2001); Robert Reich, *Supercapitalism: The Transformation of Business, Democracy, and Everyday Life* (New York: Knopf, 2007); David Sirota, *Hostile Takeover: How Big Money and Corruption Conquered Our Government—and How We Take It Back* (New York: Crown Publishers, 2006.
56. With apologies to Roger Lowenstein, *When Genius Failed: The Rise and Fall of Long-Term Capital Management* (New York: Random House, 2000). On market "genius" failing, see also Michael Lewis, "The End," Portfolio.com, December, 2008, available online.
57. Eric Janszen, "The Next Bubble: Priming The Markets for Tomorrow's Big Crash." *Harper's Magazine*, February, 2008, available online.
58. Phillips, 2001; William E. Hudson, *American Democracy in Peril: Seven Challenges to America's Future* (New York: Chatham House Publishers, 2001), 202–214.
59. Janszen, "The Next."

CHAPTER 10

AN EMPIRE OF DEBT: VIOLATING ADAM SMITH'S LAWS OF NATURE?

Founded by a group of Wall Street hotshots and leading academics with Nobel prizes on their résumés, Long-Term Capital Management (LTCM) was created in the 1990s to search markets for price anomalies in goods that had shown historical relationships. It didn't matter, for example, why the price of toothpaste was diverging from the price of toothbrushes; the fact that a price divergence existed was all that traders needed to make a move. But LTCM was not trading in toothbrushes and toothpaste. They were trading complex financial instruments that, according to their formulas, had price relationships that rarely diverged. Because the price anomaly in each "product" that they tracked was small, LTCM had to spend big to make money. After securing hundreds of millions from investors, no doubt impressed with their pedigreed analysts, LTCM still had to borrow big to make their wagers pay off. At its height, LTCM was highly leveraged and owed investors and banks billions of dollars.

Recall what happened with Tulipomania (Chapter 4): after the collapse of the tulip market, the players involved argued in court that they had been swindled. The Dutch courts, to the chagrin of those who lost money, disagreed. According to the courts, the purchasers of tulips were not investing—they were gambling. They found no remedy from the courts. In many ways, LTCM had fallen into the same trap as the purchasers of tulips. The company was made up of speculators who wanted to make a quick buck. As Martin Mayer put it:

> *the work done at LTCM, while not illegal or sinful, was totally without redeeming social value. This is not "investing"; it enables the production of no goods or useful services. It is betting.*[1]

LTCM came crashing down in 1998 after Russia defaulted on loans, an event that neither LTCM's computer models nor its Nobel laureates in economics anticipated: LTCM lost billions because they had bet that the value of corporate bonds would increase and that US Treasury notes would decline. When both went in the opposite direction, LTCM was in trouble. The company owed so much money to the banks that the Federal Reserve of New York stepped in and brought the banks to LTCM. The Federal Reserve wanted to make sure that LTCM didn't suddenly dump its assets to pay the banks. The Federal Reserve feared that, if LTCM was forced to sell its assets, it would depress markets by forcing losses on others. The Federal Reserve's then-new chairman, Alan Greenspan, even went so far as to testify that an LTCM "fire sale" could have ended prosperity in our time.[2] The Federal Reserve had to intervene to—by now a standard refrain—"save the system."

Throughout this work I have made the case that trade, national prosperity, and the accumulation of tremendous personal wealth at today's levels don't just happen through hard work alone. The US economy and the global trading system have functioned and prospered, especially in the postwar era, because conscientious efforts were made by the United States (and its trading partners) to go beyond simply providing security and physical infrastructures.[3] Because of state-led initiatives—educating and protecting the dignity of citizens, working to create a viable middle class, and building professional bureaucracies and legal infrastructures dedicated to fomenting commercial prospects—prosperity has become a generational expectation.[4] If history and market developments in 2007–2008 mean anything—and they do—it's clear that the roots of markets and wealth are tied to the capacity of states to maintain viable market infrastructures. In this and the next chapter I demonstrate that, just as states can create the conditions for great wealth creation, they can also create the conditions for its collapse. This helps answer the question presented in Chapter 1: "Is Adam Smith's self-regulating market economy little more than an aspiration, an ideal type?" The short answer is yes.

Rather than offering us a set of economic values or principles, the idea of free markets now speaks more to idealized aspirations for commerce. At the beginning of the twenty-first century, bailouts, favorable legislation, government-brokered assistance, market privileges, and subsidies for industry have turned into entrenched political entitlements. The result of these entitlements is that the laws of justice that Adam Smith wrote about are violated regularly and, apparently, with little concern over how government support undermines the culture of capitalism. Today many Americans who are unfamiliar with the specifics of how modern markets work have come to confuse favorable legislation and making money with capitalism. No matter how you slice it, "Dead Peasant Insurance" and favorable legislation for the credit card industry (Chapter 2) do not reflect free market principles at work. Yet, people in these, and other, industries profited handsomely and were praised for market accomplishments that had been made possible by favorable legislation. Today the notion of free markets has become a caricature, largely a rhetorical device, employed by conservative politicians and media pundits who are unfamiliar with history, blinded by ideology, or both.

This should be unsettling, because Adam Smith, as we saw in Chapter 1, was clear in saying that, when the "laws of justice" or the "order of reason" were violated on behalf of merchants, the wealthy, or the well connected, it was incumbent upon the state to act. Unearned advantage, Adam Smith told us, is the enemy of the market. This lesson, it seems, has been lost on market participants and politicians alike. This is unfortunate, because history shows that intervening on behalf of the well connected and the economically powerful was not supposed to be part of the American story.[5]

Violating the "Laws of Justice" in the Modern World, I: Minsky's Debt, Reagan's Deregulation

In the modern era, firms and industries have been regularly granted access to taxpayer dollars and state assistance on the premise that they are too big to fail. In reality "too big to fail" is little more than a political suppository designed to get taxpayers to absorb the costs of subsidies and bailouts for market players who have run amok. Although this occurs, it's become routine for policymakers to make high-minded speeches about the need to maintain confidence and stability in markets. But this is little more than political theater. We were told about the dangers of allowing market players to write their own tickets long before the market events and bailouts of 2007–2008. Warren Buffett warned the world in 2003 about derivatives and the false sense of security that they provided.[6] Voices of caution were raised, but they were thrown to the wind as debts were bundled and packaged into new instruments called "collateralized debt obligations" (CDOs) that few people understood (see Chapter 2, Box 2.2).[7] And there is the matter of Fannie Mae, an institution that market observers warned would get into trouble if allowed to get bigger and more aggressive, as many free market proponents advocated at the time.[8] None of this mattered, however, as long as people made money.

Apart from making money, the players involved in these markets had one thing in common—a profound belief that their debt-drenched markets were rock solid. They should have read what economist Hyman Minsky said about an economy that becomes dependent on a stream of bad debt and asset inflation. Minsky looked at the investment world and saw three types of investors. First, there are the hedge investors, who go into debt and can meet most of their debt obligations (interest and principal) with cash on hand. Then there are the speculative debtor investors, who may be able to meet regular payment schedules but have to sell assets to pay back the principal. Finally, there are the Ponzi or "pyramid scheme" investors, who must borrow but who can pay neither interest nor principal—they rely on rising asset prices to stay afloat. According to Minsky, when an economy is converted from a predominantly hedge-financed system in which market players can settle accounts at the end of the day (without disturbing their investment portfolios) to a speculative and Ponzi-oriented system, "the greater the likelihood that the economy is a deviation amplifying system."

Minsky's "financial instability hypothesis" makes it clear that market systems can move, often without notice, from a "financing regime" that is patient and stable to one that is anxious and "unstable."[9] This is important, because the American economy became increasingly dependent on a steady stream of debt and asset inflation after the early 1980s. Regulation and oversight, which could have raised a red flag over mounting debt loads and the growing number of market players who couldn't settle accounts at the end of the day, were tossed aside. Deregulation was supposed to be a magic market elixir, but, combined with a market culture of bad debt, it turned out to be economic snake oil. When the September 2008 market meltdown occurred, few if any could say what would happen if the intricate world of debt instruments were allowed to unwind at the feet of a collapsed financial institution.[10]

It would be easy to blame specific incidents of greed or a few bad apples in the market for the 2007–2008 market meltdown, as many tried to do. But policymakers in Washington were complicit in helping create meltdown conditions. Worse, after Ronald Reagan initiated America's deregulated and debt-laden era, policymakers bought into a free market mantra that had little to do with hard work and discipline—and more to do with a pile of debt, favorable legislation, creative financial instruments, and artificially cheap money. Risk and responsibility were downplayed as market players became increasingly reckless in a deregulated environment.

Violating the "Laws of Justice" in the Modern World, II: Market Hubris, Market Bailouts

After 1981, fearful of the financial Medusa that had emerged and ignorant of how to unwind it, government bailouts and deregulation became the signature response to market excess. A short list of a few of the financial market bailouts highlights how prevalent this was: Mexico in

1982; Continental Illinois in 1984; the Discount Window intervention to save floundering banks in the late 1980s; market support after the October 1987 crash; the savings and loan debacle of 1989–1992; intervention to save the Bank of New England and Citibank; the 1994–1995 Mexico rescue; the Asian Currency rescue in the late 1990s; the Federal Reserve-organized LTCM bailout[11]—and the list goes on. In the more immediate period, assistance started with aid to Bear Stearns, Countrywide Financial, Fannie Mae and Freddie Mac, and American Insurance Group (AIG). In all cases, it was clear that the financial sector was not bound by traditional notions of market discipline after 1981. Then came the "mother of all bailouts" on September 19, 2008: the Bush administration's $700 billion bailout proposal for financial markets.

These bailout efforts make it clear that market players have effectively found a license to print money: (1) adopt an aggressive and swashbuckling (read "reckless") attitude and go into debt; (2) threaten bankruptcy when your gamble doesn't pay off; and (3) play up the impact of a market meltdown if nothing is done. A political system that can be held hostage by any industry is an indication that the ghost of John Law (Chapter 4) has returned. But Law did not return uninvited. Law's ghost returned because of specific policies and because of an environment that accommodated America's growing culture of debt.

It's important to keep in mind that, although America's undisciplined spending habits in the postwar era were criticized many times since the late 1950s and 1960s, deficit spending continued in the 1970s and became, quite simply, unhinged under Ronald Reagan (see Figure 10.1 later in the chapter). Record deficit spending, coupled with deregulation, helped jumpstart an era of dollar gluts abroad and a domestic financial scene that was governed by poor oversight, a lack of transparency (especially over complex financial instruments), and misguided incentive schemes, among others.[12] But these policies might have petered out were it not for the system created at Bretton Woods. Specifically, the logic and structure of the system—as we saw in Chapters 8 and 9—encouraged and accommodated America's deficits (both trade and financial); the problem was that the system did so for longer than was economically prudent. This helped convince market players that debts and deficits were fine and that the only things lacking were deregulated markets. As we saw in previous chapters, political demands and national security issues helped feed this mind-set. In the process, the world traded a relatively stable postwar economic regime for one dominated by fast-paced capital movements that were managed by states pursuing increasingly tense (if not antagonistic) policy positions.[13]

This is important, because 1981 marks the period when market players and policymakers began dismissing the role of the state in making markets work. The same attitude was applied to agreements such as those signed at Bretton Woods. Disregarded were the accomplishments that had been made possible by the cooperative efforts of the preceding thirty-five years. In spite of the evidence, the activities of entrepreneurs, the logic of the market, and the practice of deregulation were suddenly elevated as key factors behind globalization and wealth creation. This position was a gross misreading of history. Having lived through the interwar nightmare of depression, conflict, and war, the policymakers who crafted the postwar order were convinced of one thing: glorifying unfettered markets (conservatism), catering to industrialists (fascism), and embracing totalitarianism (ideological extremism) were unreasonable and untenable. With a more sophisticated understanding of human progress, postwar leaders were united in their belief that nations had to work together to foster political stability and economic prosperity.[14] They acted accordingly, which meant cooperating to promote financial stability,[15] security, production, and knowledge on a global level.[16] New forms of political organization were embraced and stable capital markets were pursued—which the cooperative spirit of Bretton Woods helped make possible. Economies and markets grew as in no other time in human history.[17]

The remainder of this chapter illustrates how US policymakers and the events that they helped craft moved the United States—and other nations—away from the spirit of Bretton Woods. For their efforts, after 1981 the policymakers were rewarded with undisciplined deregulation, favorable legislation, record deficits, and the unabashed embrace of market bailouts—which speak more to market socialism than to market capitalism.[18] Several of the following topics have been introduced previously in other contexts but are presented again to demonstrate how commercial actors in the world today—transnational corporations, commercial banks, investment banks, brokerage firms, mutual and hedge funds, extraordinarily wealthy individuals, and private pensions (among others)—have operated and prospered as a result of deliberate actions taken by the state. This chapter ends by showing how warnings of mounting debt loads and increased market instability were first ignored by America's economic and political elites after the 1960s and 1970s and then compounded by policies initiated during the Reagan years.

Charles de Gaulle Confronts America's Exorbitant Privilege and Loses

It was 1967 and Secretary of State Dean Rusk was engaged in yet another round of frustrating talks with the French over defense issues related to NATO and the creation of multilateral forces. The United States was trying to convince the French that its security needs were covered by the US "nuclear umbrella" in Europe. As a way of compromise, Rusk proposed deploying multilateral forces (MLF), made up of mixed national crews, stationed on NATO submarines carrying nuclear weapons. French President Charles de Gaulle's reluctance stemmed from his belief that the US position was a ruse. He believed that the United States wanted to dissuade France from building its own nuclear arsenal because control of NATO enhanced America's status, which enabled the Americans to avoid being held to account in other areas. And de Gaulle's evidence was strong. He had observed America's actions and was not impressed.

As evidence, de Gaulle pointed to the war in Vietnam, which was financed by deficit spending. Coupled with balance-of-payment deficits and the costs of Lyndon Johnson's Great Society programs, the deficit was addressed in the following way: the United States simply printed and issued more money than it could back with gold. Noted historian, Walter La Feber, explained it this way:

> War costs shot upward from $8 billion in 1966 to $21 billion in 1967. Dollars flew out of the United States to pay for both the war and growing American private investments abroad (which rose from $49 billion in 1960 to $101 billion in 1968). The nations export trade could not pull those dollars back.[19]

Charles de Gaulle was particularly miffed that the United States was the only country that could unilaterally print money and issue credit without having to experience the inflationary effects at home. No other country, the analogy goes, had the privilege to write checks that others would hold.[20] According to de Gaulle this was an "exorbitant privilege" that no other nation enjoyed, and he set out to make things right by demanding gold when France's dollar reserves grew.[21] This could have been a significant blow to the US financial leadership position because, by the mid-1960s, "almost two-thirds of America's cumulative deficit was transferred in the form of gold," for which the price was up from 10 percent in 1958.[22] Still, there was no real effort to demand gold collectively as the French did after 1965. The Americans, to de Gaulle's chagrin, could not be disciplined.

There were several reasons for this. First, those who held or traded in US dollars did not believe that it was in their best interests to facilitate a crisis of confidence in the dollar by dumping dollars. Helping America's dollar holders come to this conclusion was the strength of the Eurocurrency market. The Eurocurrency market was a private affair in which private banks openly solicited and kept dollars for use as trade credits and for other forms of international lending. Because banks were making money, it was easy to see that the supply of dollars was far from being overwhelmed by demand. These bankers understood that a concerted effort to "discipline" the United States by sending dollars back *en masse* could harm their long-term interests. Worse, undermining the economy of the world's biggest consumer might even bring down the entire global economic infrastructure.[23] Individual states and key market players had too much to lose by destabilizing the status quo. To be sure, the value of the dollar had dropped. But domestic stability issues and legitimate geostrategic concerns during the Cold War compelled holders of US dollars to ask themselves, "Why ruin a good thing?"

This was the backdrop to de Gaulle's tense meeting with Secretary of State Rusk over NATO in 1967. Events finally came to a head for Charles de Gaulle when he announced that France was pulling its troops out of the military arm of NATO. He went so far as to declare that France's nuclear forces might even be deployed against the West.[24] Making matters worse was the bitter and acrimonious tone surrounding France's break from NATO. When de Gaulle informed Rusk that the French were pulling out of NATO, he bluntly told Rusk that he "wanted every American soldier out of France." Impatient and angry over de Gaulle's lack of decorum, Rusk replied, "Does that include the dead Americans in the military cemeteries as well?"[25] Recognizing his impertinence—and to his credit—de Gaulle fell silent and said nothing more.

Whatever misgivings Charles de Gaulle had, one thing was clear: the military position of the United States and the prosperity generated by the American-led global system meant that the United States could continue spending beyond its means—for the time being at least. As long as the world continued to hold dollars, the United States would be able to avoid financial accountability back home. This privilege did not last. Trouble was around the corner. The collapse of the Bretton Woods currency system and the flood of petrodollars sent around the world after 1973 facilitated the unraveling of America's exorbitant privilege. Ronald Reagan's arrival, as we'll see below, helped accelerate it.

Preparing for an Empire of Debt, I: Breaking Bretton Woods

One of the developments that kept demand for dollars high (and thwarted de Gaulle's efforts to discipline the United States) was the 1957 decision by the British to impose "tight new restrictions on foreign-trade financing denominated in pounds sterling" (Chapter 9).[26] Although it would be easy to suggest that the decision to strengthen the position of the pound was based on financial considerations alone, many people forget that the British were also concerned about reliving nightmare scenarios such as the 1956 Suez Canal debacle, when President Eisenhower threatened to ruin Britain's currency if the British didn't cease hostilities in the Middle East.[27] For the British government, a strong pound sterling was not simply a matter of sound economic principles—it was also a matter of national security.

In response to the restrictions imposed by the British government and in an effort to maintain their global position and business dealings abroad, British banks actively solicited and lent US dollars. Freed from the reserve requirements imposed on domestic banks and liberated from the potential side effects (such as John F. Kennedy's "interest equalization tax"[28]) that came with borrowing from US banks, global borrowers cut a path to London for dollars. The rationale was simple. Why subject yourself to domestic bank requirements when another source could offer capital (in dollars) that was free of prying eyes and other restrictions? The significance of the Eurodollar market cannot be understated. Not only could money move more freely, but new market players emerged to bet on these movements.[29] This new market found a steady stream of willing and creative players.

As well, persistent deficits didn't matter to many companies in the Western world because their growth and prosperity depended on the United States purchasing their goods. By spreading capital around the world (with purchases and debt), the United States helped create a global capitalist system that—as George Soros put it—became like an empire. With its centers in Washington, Frankfurt, and Tokyo, the empire of growing capital markets continuously seeks expansion. Although it has no formal structure, the system rules over people who can't opt out, especially if they hope to achieve a modicum of growth. The brave ones, who seek to work outside of the system, are, according to George Soros, simply labeled "barbarians." Many recognize that they're "subjected to impersonal sometimes disruptive forces . . . [but] they do not understand what those forces are" all about.[30] Soros is clear that, even though he can't pinpoint the exact day when this empire emerged, its livelihood depends on the free movement of capital, which was made possible by the gradual collapse of the Bretton Woods system.

Still, as the United States continued to spend more than it took in, by the mid-1960s, US officials understood that they had to look into mounting deficits—both trade and budget deficits. They understood that America could cover its obligations in three ways. First, it could produce and export more. Second, although it would only exacerbate the "dollar glut" problem, the United States could continue printing and sending out dollars to meet its financial obligations. Finally, the United States could continue exchanging gold for dollars. While meekly pursuing the first option, the United States embraced the last two choices, which contributed to more dollars abroad and less gold in US vaults. Noted historian Walter LaFeber wrote: "the US gold supply, which led the world in 1945 with a total of nearly $25 billion, sank to $19 billion and, by 1968, to $10 billion" so there was not enough gold to "support the dollar bills Americans used everyday, let alone support the dollars moving overseas."[31]

As the United States continued to push deficit dollars out, the value of America's currency continued to fall. These dynamics primed the American economy for inflation and set the stage for Richard Nixon to delink the dollar from gold on August 15, 1971. Because the dollar began to trade like any other commodity and had no fixed or absolute value, merchants, producers, and consumers looked for new ways to protect themselves from speculators and the collapsing value of the dollar. By the mid-1970s America's long-time abuse of its exorbitant privilege eventually turned the world's "anchor currency" into a battering ram, which undermined long-term planning and wreaked havoc on the plans of policymakers. This changed the global economy in ways that few were prepared to deal with (see Figure 9.1).

Because of technological improvements and increased demand for financial services from transnational corporations, the Eurodollar market took off during the 1960s. It really exploded in the 1970s, with the rise of OPEC and the petrodollar recycling process that came after the first oil shock in 1973.[32] A similar explosion in trade and increased speculation for dollars and other financial instruments occurred soon after.[33] According to George Soros, it was at this time that the "real emergence of global capitalism came" about.[34]

Preparing for an Empire of Debt, II: OPEC'S Ascent and Petrodollars[35]

Although a standard line has been to point to the world's growing energy needs as the culprit for OPEC's ascent, this is only half of the story. Overlooked are the political dynamics behind OPEC's rise. In *The Prize: The Epic Quest for Oil, Money, and Power* (1992), Daniel Yergin indicates numerous points at which the United States and private players from the West could have acted with a bit more vision. Numerous ill-advised and arrogant acts by oil firms, by the British, and by the US government helped create the conditions for OPEC's birth. But the situation also helps illustrate that market players don't always make the best decisions, especially when it comes to the public good ("theirs" as well as "ours"). When it comes to winning enemies and alienating societies, the actions of the West in the Middle East in the twentieth century set a standard for arrogance and hubris.[36] The experiences of Abdullah Tariki, Saudi Arabia's directorate of Oil and Mining Affairs in 1950s and 1960s, are illuminating.

Tariki's experiences and views of the United States were shaped while he attended the University of Texas in the 1940s, where he was mistaken for a Mexican and treated as such. After being chosen to head Saudi Arabia's oil and mining agency, the Western-educated Tariki was primarily interested in getting a fair deal for his country. This was his goal when he went to the Arab Oil Congress in 1959. But things didn't go well. As one Aramaco official put it, "when the Western oil men began talking with Tariki along the 'when you have been in the oil business as long as I have, my boy' line," they had done more harm than they could imagine. Tariki's view of Western oil men did not improve when Exxon's CEO, Monroe Rathborne, unilaterally cut the posted price that his company would pay in 1960. Because the posted price was used by oil-producing states to assess taxes, Rathborne's decision effectively reduced their national income. Although Tariki may have been indignant over the way that he was treated in Cairo, he was especially upset with Rathborne's sudden and unilateral actions. Abdullah Tariki called Juan Pablo Pérez Alfonzo, his contemporary from Venezuela.

Juan Pablo Pérez had also lived in the United States (as an exile), but he had lived in Washington DC, where he spent a good deal of time in the Library of Congress. There he studied the agency that regulated oil production in Texas and the nation during the 1930s—the Texas Railroad Commission (TRRC). Upon returning to Venezuela in 1958, Pérez was appointed minister of Mines and Hydrocarbons. After the Eisenhower administration moved to protect domestic oil producers by restricting oil imports, as minister of Mines and Hydrocarbons, Pérez flew to Washington to propose a Western Hemispheric oil system to be operated along the lines of the TRRC (see introduction to Chapter 3). What he was asking for was nothing new, especially given that the American sugar quota system operated similarly. To Pérez's surprise, the offer was ignored. The US oil firms didn't want the competition. Pérez saw in America's attitude an imperial dismissal, which enraged the new Venezuelan government. With no place to turn, the Venezuelans found an open ear and an earnest ally when Tariki called. When OPEC was formed on September 14, 1960, it controlled more than 80 percent of the world's oil exports.[37]

Beyond the painfully arrogant actions of the Western oil industry in 1959 and 1960, what breathed life into OPEC was when the West could no longer meet its own oil needs. In the United States this came to pass in the late 1960s and early 1970s.[38] In addition to the politically charged events of the 1960s and early 1970s, the turbulent 1970s brought changes, on many levels, in the comfortable energy world that the United States had once enjoyed. Politically, although Saudi Arabia's King Faisel had fended off Egypt's Gamal Nasser's efforts to create a united Arab front against Israel (and against the West), he had a change of heart after Anwar Sadat came to power in Egypt in 1970. Buoyed by the fact that Saudi Arabia had become the global "swing producer" in oil (the capacity to increase production when crisis hit), King Faisal was sympathetic to Sadat's efforts to create distance between Egypt and the Soviet Union; Nasser's Soviet-pandering diplomacy had shackled Egypt too. As well, King Faisal didn't see a "radical pan-Arabist" in Sadat, as he had with Nasser. But he was especially concerned about the US position toward Israel, which he went to great lengths to communicate to America—even going on a US media blitz to explain his position in 1973.

When the oil companies met with OPEC leaders in Vienna in September 1973, the idea that OPEC leaders might have a reason to dig in their heels on prices shouldn't have come as a surprise. But it did. Things took a turn for the worse when the Yom Kippur War started on October 6. When the oil companies continued to ignore the demands of the Arabs—seemingly oblivious to the US market position and changing geostrategic considerations—the oil producers prepared to leave Cairo. As the last impromptu session was broken up in the early morning hours of October 12, 1973, a Western oil executive asked what would happen next. The response was ominous: "Listen to the radio." Several days later the posted price of oil was raised by 70 percent, to $5.11 per barrel. This was followed by the announcement of an Arab oil embargo one day later. The Arabs were using petroleum as a weapon to bludgeon the West, and they got rich in the process.

Combined with the Cold War, continuous US budget deficits, and globalization, these oil-related events helped inflate demand for US dollars and sped up their circulation around the globe. Global capital flows jumped, from $131 billion in 1972 to $215 billion in 1974, and reached $1.4 trillion just ten years later (see Table 9.1 in Chapter 9). As persistent US deficits added to inflationary pressures in the 1970s, business planning was disrupted and then undermined. In spite of double-digit inflation and the *malaise* that overtook America in the late 1970s, the federal government did little to rein in spending or to help the American public understand the structural changes that were occurring in the global economy.

These developments provided a political opening for Ronald Reagan and the conservative movement in America. But rather than focus on the problems at hand—persistent budget deficits, an unbridled introduction to globalization, and control of a key resource by a troubled and unfriendly region—policy leaders looked away. And why not? In their scheme of things, a "good ol' shot of capitalism" would set the world right once again. They promised to bring back the glory days of America's pre-Depression era economy. Focusing on deregulation and cutting taxes, to "get government off our back," the end result was a state-led deficit spending orgy, followed by increasingly complex and deregulated financial markets that fewer and fewer people understood.

Reaganomics: State-Led Recovery, Deficit Spending Orgy

When George W. Bush entered the White House in 2001, the centerpiece of his economic program was rooted in Ronald Reagan's supply-side economic policies. He reasoned that, by putting more money in the hands of the nation's wealthy, investments would increase, which would create more jobs and generate more tax revenue.[39] Insisting that the Reagan administration's policies had gotten the economy moving, the Bush administration promised that, just as Reagan had saved the American economy from stagflation and misery, Bush's tax-cutting, favor-the-rich plan would reinvigorate the American economy. Although the rhetoric was strong, a careful examination of the facts illustrates that the Bush administration had misread both Reagan's accomplishments and history.

To understand what President Bush was trying to emulate in 2001, it's necessary to recall the conditions that Ronald Reagan inherited and supposedly tamed while he was in office. With inflation (12–13 percent) and interest rates (20 percent) reaching new heights in the late 1970s and with unemployment on the rise (around 7.5 percent), both confidence and investment were lagging in America. The result was a new term in the field of economics and a fresh challenge in American politics: "stagflation," which meant recession, low productivity, and inflation. By the time that Ronald Reagan left office, inflation and interest rates were back down to single digits and unemployment hovered around a more acceptable 5 percent.

Because of these developments, conservatives and ill-informed talk-show hosts like to claim that a combination of tax cuts, deregulation, bureaucratic reform, and assorted incentives created the environment for investment that energized the economy. According to revisionist historians, the Reagan administration was able to get America moving by reducing the size of government, cutting government spending, and getting "government off our backs." This would be an interesting byline except for one thing—it's not true.

First, it's interesting to note that job creation under Ronald Reagan never matched the levels achieved under Jimmy Carter,[40] even though the size of the federal government's workforce grew from 2.8 million employees to 3.1 million.[41] The number of federally subsidized programs under Ronald Reagan was scaled back only to 1970–1975 levels,[42] which helps explain why the Reagan administration hardly put a dent in the size of government. Acknowledging this, a 1985 *Fortune* magazine article claimed that the "budget is way out of balance because of a little-known fact: real federal spending, adjusted for inflation, has climbed even faster under President Reagan than it did in the Carter years."[43] In the end, in spite of what the supply-side supporters promised, the national debt almost tripled, from approximately $930 billion to $2.7 trillion under Reagan.[44]

So what created the conditions for the American economy to stabilize in the late 1980s and then take off during the 1990s? Primarily there were three factors, all of which undermine the Bush administration's "second coming of Reagan" claim (and pretty much debunk the "first coming of Reagan" claim). On the inflation front, OPEC—an oligopoly that depends on cooperation with imprudent energy policies in the West to sustain itself—found its solidarity undermined by late 1981. With the beginning of the Iran-Iraq War, which Saddam Hussein initiated in part because the ayatollahs were fomenting fanatic revolution in Iraq, black markets in the oil industry grew—as cheating on the part of the two combatants began (to fund their war efforts). In addition, conservation efforts, alternative energy sources, and new oil discoveries, among other developments, helped stabilize oil prices. But these efforts were initiated by President Ford and, to a larger degree, by President Carter.[45] Still, the reality was that OPEC unity—one of the primary catalysts behind price hikes—had unraveled as government-inspired conservation efforts paid off. As the price for oil dropped, so did inflationary pressures.[46]

We also need to recognize a second force on the inflation front. Recall that the strategy employed to control inflation was taken up by Federal Reserve Chairman Paul Volcker. In spite of pressure from the Reagan administration, which initially wanted to expand the money supply, Mr. Volcker, most economists agree, stuck to his guns and maintained a stringent monetary policy, thus helping slay the inflation dragon. Critical here is that Mr. Volcker was appointed by Jimmy Carter, not by Ronald Reagan. Finally, the Reagan administration's deficit spending broke all previous records. The Reagan administration spent twice as much as the previous thirty-nine presidential administrations combined, in the process using taxpayer-funded debt to deposit hundreds of billions of dollars into the national and global economy each year. This government-induced "pump priming" was an artificial stimulus—what economists call a

"Keynesian stimulus" (Chapter 9). It was hardly a vote of confidence for *laissez-faire* economics.[47]

In sum, cracks in OPEC unity, conservation efforts, a tight monetary policy, and a state-led stimulus to our larger economy suggest that the Reagan administration's policies were, at best, supporting rather than leading factors in reversing the dismal economic environment of the 1970s. Perhaps more important, Ronald Reagan used the state to make favorable legislation for industry normal, hostility toward labor a conservative virtue, and debt (of all kinds) an acceptable condition for America. All of this created an economy that was supercharged by deregulation and debt. But it also worked to undermine the laws of justice that Adam Smith argued were necessary for markets to function efficiently and equitably.

Reagan Aftermath: Swamping the American Worker

A casual review of cause and effect factors make it clear that the policy prescriptions of the Reagan administration did not erase inflation, drastically improve the jobs picture, or cut the size of government by any significant level. This is important to understand, because believing otherwise has allowed certain political groups to run with the story that Reagan's tax and deregulation policies were policy silver bullets. That belief also created a sense that expanding credit and undisciplined consumption should continue and could go on indefinitely. Ignored were rising debt loads, record bankruptcies, increasing incidents of corporate bailouts, and a growing sense that simply participating in the market entitled you to riches and wealth, especially if you were big enough. Bailouts for the big players were sold to the public—when people paid attention— as necessary for the public good.

But these erroneous views of Ronald Reagan's legacy could not have survived were it not for a steady stream of studies that extolled the virtues of "supply-side" economics, a discredited theory that argues that tax cuts for the rich are good for the economy. Even N. Gregory Mankiw, a member of President George W. Bush's Council of Economic Advisors, referred to this school of thought as a "crank theory." The theory persisted in political life, however, for two reasons: biased research, funded by conservative family foundations, and fierce political propaganda.[48] Still, deficit spending, coupled with favorable legislation and deregulation, did contribute to an environment that fostered economic expansion. The only problem was that the growth was built on a pile of bad debt, lax oversight, and creative financial instruments.[49] While this was happening, middle-class wages stagnated, deregulation undermined institutions that served the public interest, and American workers were swamped by personal debt and the gradual acceptance of bankruptcy as a sign of the times.[50]

Stagnant Wages and Debt

Among the forces that fed the market exuberance of the late 1990s and the early 2000s were cheap credit and growing debt loads. By feeding consumption, credit and debt fit the goals of both major political parties in America, but for different reasons. Democrats saw the democratization of credit; Republicans saw increased profits. Few thought it was necessary to take a look at collapsed savings rates and soaring debt levels in America (see figures 10.1, 10.2, 10.3, 10.4, and 10.5 later in the chapter). Although credit and debt may have made things easier for US presidents and for the US consumer, billionaire speculator George Soros saw something else—a country living beyond its means.[51] There is little doubt that irresponsible purchases and growing personal debt capture the imagination of critics who want to assign blame for the market conditions of 2007–2008. However, rarely is this question asked: What are the factors that cause many ordinary Americans to borrow beyond their means which leads many into bankruptcy? We know from Chapter 2 that divorce, job loss, and catastrophic illness cause 90 percent of all bankruptcy filings in America.[52] But we need to shift the issue from uninvited life events to specific, policy-driven areas if we want to understand why Americans have been nudged to take on more and more debt. This means looking at wages in America.

In a 2007 speech, Federal Reserve Chairman Ben Bernanke considered incomes and focused on the growing gap between America's middle class and the financial elite. Bernanke reported that, in spite of rising labor productivity and technological advances—which usually find their way into growing wages—income gaps had increased in America since 1979 (see Figure 1.2 and Figure 1.3 in Chapter 1). Bernanke discussed the causes and seemed to make a case for public policies that promoted early childhood education, stronger minimum wage laws, retraining, transitional aid for displaced workers, and the like.[53] But perhaps his most significant observation was what he had to say about the impact that organized labor has on wages. According to Bernanke, unions not only reduce wage inequality, but at least 10 to 20 percent of wage inequality in America can be attributed to the decline of unions.[54]

This is important, because, after Ronald Reagan entered the White House, organized labor was put on the defensive by an alliance of convenience between corporate America and political conservatives. According to *Businessweek,* things worked out so well for industry that as "[c]orporate America has perfected its ability to fend off labor groups"[55] labor union membership dropped from 20.1 percent of the labor force in 1983 to 12 percent by 2006.[56] Although there may be fewer blue-collar jobs in America—jobs that are traditionally union-friendly—corporate America has been hard-pressed to explain why income gaps have widened as union membership has declined. This is especially the case when we consider that rising labor productivity seems to have enabled only America's top wage earners to "strike it richer" (see figures 1.1, 1.2, and 1.3).[57] Economist and Nobel laureate Paul Krugman explains it this way:

> It's often assumed that the U.S. labor movement died a natural death, that it was made obsolete by globalization and techno-logical change. But what really happened is that beginning in the 1970s, corporate America, which had previously had a largely cooperative relationship with unions, in effect declared war on organized labor . . . hardball tactics have been enabled by a political environment that has been deeply hostile to organized labor, both because politicians favored employers' interests and because conservatives sought to weaken the Democratic Party. "We're going to crush labor as a political entity," Grover Norquist, the anti-tax activist, once declared. [58]

The relationship between corporate America and the Republican Party has reaped financial benefits for America's business elites and political payoffs for Republican political candidates. But it has been financially devastating for America's working class. Since the 1970s, inflation, declining or stagnant wages, weakened unions, lax immigration policies, deregulation, and the challenges of having jobs shipped overseas have left ordinary Americans with an increasingly tough financial line to hoe. The arrangement, however, seems to have worked out well for America's CEOs, who have seen their salaries rise in relation to the average worker: from a ratio of about 40:1 in 1980 to 262:1 in 2005 (other reports put the figure around 431:1).[59]

Given that the federal government has been increasingly reluctant to intervene on behalf of labor over the past thirty-five years, ordinary working Americans have had to cope with rising costs and stagnating wages in a number of ways.

- Two-Income Households, 1970s: With the women's movement came the rise of two-income households. Two working parents increased household income significantly.[60]

Figure 10.1 Rising Credit Card Debt in America

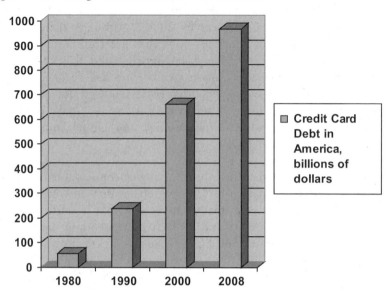

Source: Federal Reserve, "Consumer Credit," Federal Reserve Statistical Release, G. 19, September 8, 2008, available online; U.S. Census Bureau, "Banking Finance, and Insurance," *Statistical Abstract of the U.S., 2001,* available online.

- Credit and Charge It, 1980s: Americans began racking up serious personal debt in the 1980s when, as former Federal Reserve Chairman Alan Greenspan put it, "innovation and deregulation" worked to "expand credit availability to virtually all income classes."[61] At the end of 2008 total credit card debt stood at $969.9 billion (Figure 10.1).[62]
- Decline of Leisure, 1990s: Although divorce and personal debt put a dent in disposable income, Americans began working more hours to make ends meet, even surpassing the Japanese in 1995.[63]
- Household ATMs, 2000: To keep the American Dream alive, many Americans went on a borrowing binge, this time using their homes as ATMs (see Figure 10.2 and Figure 10.3).[64]

With more and more households using their homes as ATMs, we can understand why home-owner equity in America was less in 2007 (at the height of the housing boom) than it had been seven years earlier. At the end of 2008 it was poised to drop below 50 percent for the first time since the government had started keeping track of these data.[65] The end result of stagnant wages, an increasingly hostile environment for labor, and easy credit has been a savings rate in American that effectively stands at zero

Figure 10.2 Personal Savings Rates (as a Percentage of DPI, NIPas), 1952–2006

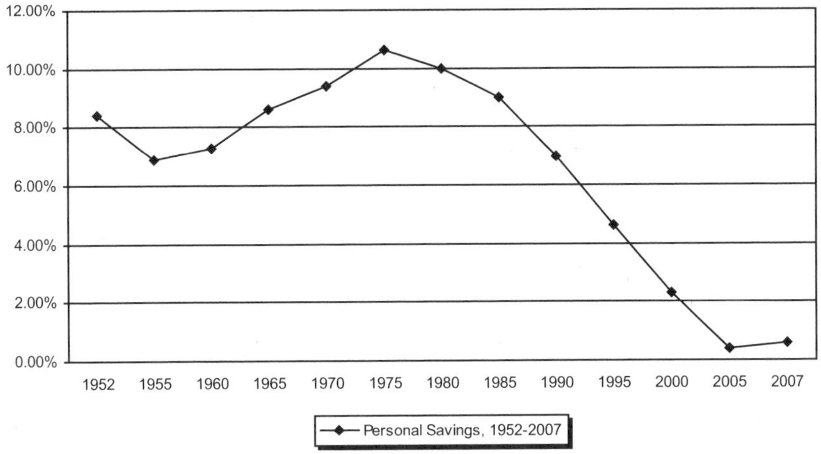

Source: U.S. Department of Commerce, "Comparison of Personal Saving in the National Income and Product Accounts (NIPAs) with Personal Saving in the Flow of Funds Accounts (FFAs)," Bureau of Economic Analysis, National Economic Accounts, available online.

(Figure 10.2).[66] Not surprisingly, when the refinancing boom stalled because of plummeting housing prices and dried up credit markets, more and more Americans found other ways to cope with life's expenditures— they began using "hardship withdrawals" to tap into retirement funds.[67]

"An Environment of Rather Accommodative Financial Conditions" (That Would Swallow Fannie Mae)

In many respects, when market players figured out how to make real money by trading currencies and repackaged debt during the mid-1970s, they became increasingly comfortable gambling on securities of all stripes. Even after Mexico's default scare in 1982, bankers and investors were emboldened. This shouldn't be surprising. Rather than disciplining market players who made dumb decisions and should have known better, the Reagan administration's decision to support a string of bailouts (beginning with Mexico in 1982) effectively guaranteed market payoff. This helped create a state-reliant market culture. This livened up "secondary" markets in which repurchased debt was transformed into a very dependable income stream, which paved the way for the surge of CDOs in the 1990s. Coupled with deregulation, speculation in new debt-tied instruments took off and transformed modern markets. Specifically, by the mid-1990s, money and finance no longer followed trade, they dominated it. In the process, America's market players learned how to use credit and debt not just to invest in the long term, but to bet on markets in the immediate term. It was at this time that entrepreneurialism kicked in, as market players perfected the art of extracting rather than building wealth. The impact of this transformation was made abundantly clear in the 2008 *Bank for International Settlement's (BIS) 78th Annual Report.*

The *BIS Annual Report* looked at the dismal economic picture confronting the United States and the world in 2008 and found its culprit: a chain of events that started with US subprime mortgage contracts that "quickly spread to other markets."[68] Helping spread the problem, according to the BIS, was "an environment of rather accommodative financial conditions" that were tied to complex credit derivatives and new securities. Coupled with lax controls and easy money, appetites were whetted for newer types of risk, which led to "substantial leverage in the financial system as a whole."[69] This eventually created problems when poorly structured and poorly understood products began marbling their way into the American economy at the same time as market players began making bigger and bigger bets.[70] An example of these dynamics at work is the story of LTCM, discussed earlier in this chapter.[71] Although spectacular, LTCM was really only a practice run for bigger problems lurking around the corner.[72] The experience of Fannie Mae and Freddie Mac provides insight into these "rather accommodative financial conditions."

Before discussing the Fannie Mae and Freddie Mac bailout, it's important to understand why Fannie and Freddie were so important to America's economy. We can start by comparing the modern mortgage industry with the pre-Depression industry. Before the arrival of Fannie and Freddie, there were no long-term mortgages. This meant that you borrowed money from a bank and that you could lose your home if you could not pay for it or get the bank to roll over your loan after five years (or so). The bank that made the loan kept the mortgage in-house. This model came tumbling down when the Great Depression hit. Banks that survived the initial wave of bank failures could not find credit and found themselves swamped by loan defaults and home foreclosures. Concerned by the growing number of defaults and foreclosures, Franklin D. Roosevelt recreated the American housing market.

As part of his New Deal programs, FDR created a new housing market model: local savings and loan institutions (S&Ls) provided low-cost (or subprime) loans for home purchases. The S&Ls, or thrift banks, were designed to help build communities, and they focused principally on providing home loans, as mandated by law. After watching Jimmy Stewart's Christmas classic, *It's a Wonderful Life,* most of us came to admire these "thrift" institutions—which brought to mind the biblical story of David, who stood up to the world's Goliath—bravely confronting the big banks. Fannie Mae, the Federal National Mortgage Association (FNMA), began its bureaucratic life in 1938 as one of the New Deal agencies. Fannie

Mae's responsibility was to funnel money back into the banking industry. It did this by purchasing S&L mortgages and other government-approved mortgage debt contracts, such as those from the Veteran's Administration (VA) and the Federal Housing Administration (FHA). Banks and thrifts then lent this money out to other prospective home owners.

Thanks in part to S&Ls, Fannie Mae, and programs such as FHA, home ownership in America went up from less than half (43.6 percent) in 1940 to approximately two out of three households (66.2 percent) by 2000.[73] According to Robert Kuttner, as the biggest buyer of mortgages in the market, Fannie Mae set the guidelines for maintaining industry standards and "worked beautifully until it was privatized." Kuttner writes:

> The system worked like a fine watch. Homeownership rates soared. Loan standards were generous but not stupid. Nobody in the home mortgage business got filthy rich. And mortgage lenders hardly ever went broke. The government's bank insurance funds regularly turned a profit. And here's a quaint, archaic concept: it operated in the public interest.[74]

Things changed in 1968 with increasing concern over budget deficits—Vietnam, the Cold War, and the Great Society were taking their toll. It was decided to get Fannie Mae off the government's books and to "privatize" the agency. Ginnie Mae was also created in 1968 to provide market support (by purchasing a certain class of mortgages). The Federal Home Loan Mortgage Association (FHLMA), or Freddie Mac, was created in 1970 to provide "competition" for Fannie Mae. Although Ginnie Mae's bond issues were federally guaranteed, Fannie Mae and Freddie Mac were on their own—in theory, at least. In reality, because Fannie and Freddie helped guarantee government-sanctioned mortgages, the mortgage debt that they purchased was tacitly backed by the federal government. Some argue that this implied government guarantee helped keep the prices of home loans down.[75] But a report issued by the Federal Reserve suggests that Fannie and Freddie used their privileged positions to "rack up huge profits and squeeze the private sector out" of their market space.[76] Emboldened, Fannie Mae and Freddie Mac "began using their subsidized financing to buy mortgage-backed securities . . . that did not meet their usual standards."[77]

It was at this time that mortgage industry standards and the public good were chipped away in the name of volume and bigger profits. With deregulation and easy money swirling around the economy, the industry of home loans and home refinancing exploded. The results were predictable. Mortgage debt as a percentage of GDP in America jumped from 29.5 percent in 1967 to 47.2 percent in 1997, to an astounding 80.4 percent in 2007 (see Figure 10.3).[78]

Figure 10.3 Mortgage Debt Held as a Percentage of GDP, 1957–2007

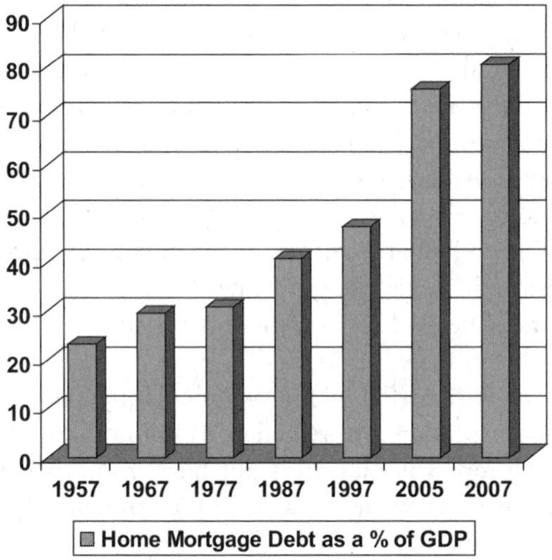

Source: Federal Reserve System, Flow of Funds Accounts of the United States, 2008.

Many of these mortgages were sold and then found their way into government-secured entities (GSEs), specifically Ginnie Mae, Freddie Mac, and Fannie Mae. Problems emerged when Fannie Mae and Freddie Mac, bent on improving profit margins for investors and executives alike, began purchasing mortgage contracts that were based on less than honest accounting and due diligence practices. The goal of advancing home ownership in America was swamped by the need to generate volume and bigger bonuses. Company executives, as Robert Kuttner put it, created "a privatized casino whose big bets enriched a few insiders and then helped crash the entire system." Because of the GSEs' position in the housing market, deregulation and market greed helped drive standards into the ground and turned errors in judgment on the part of Fannie Mae and Freddie Mac into industry routine where Fannie and Freddie were once well-run government agencies that served the public interest, their privatization and subsequent collapse were made possible by "accommodative" conditions that were encouraged by both sides of the political aisle.

Aiding this process was the creation of new financial instruments and an explosion in the amount of "securitized" debt traded in America. The amount of trades using these instruments ushered in an era in which the value of the securities sector overtook the value of bank assets and bank deposits. Patient investment strategies were eventually overtaken by short-term market bets, with many of the wagers made with borrowed money. Kevin Phillips called this development the "financialization" of the American economy.[79] When the bets collapsed or didn't pay off in 2007 and 2008, market players cried foul—as was the case with Tulipomania discussed in Chapter 4—and looked to the government for remedy. While all of this was going on, a mountain of debt was emerging in the background. Federal Reserve Chairman Alan Greenspan seemed unfazed. He even saw new financial and credit opportunities on the horizon, which only exacerbated America's growing empire of debt.

A Symbiosis of Debt and Alan Greenspan's "New Paradigm of Active Credit Management"

Through the last year of President George W. Bush's presidency (2001–2009), increasing consumer reliance on credit and debt—which were once discouraged—became a good thing. And why not? The people who found new ways to package and trade debt were hailed as geniuses for providing new income sources for investors—with a variety of CDOs and related products such as credit default swaps (CDSs) (see Box 10.1).[80] Investors jumped into these largely unregulated markets, in the process providing more capital for booming markets. With oversight largely absent, these securities and derivative markets helped create a symbiosis of debt: consumers wanted it, lenders fed it, and markets clamored for its end product. Because everyone supposedly won, they all found it convenient to ignore red flags that emerged with every trade and every new debt instrument that was created (see Box 10.2). Matters were made worse when Alan Greenspan went beyond providing cheap money: he blessed and supercharged the environment by gushing over a "new paradigm of active credit management" that kept the money flowing while claiming to reduce risk.[81]

Greenspan failed to consider what happens when credit is transformed from a tool of the market into its crutch. Hyman Minsky not only thought about this issue but explained what happened in an economy that became dependent on a steady stream of debt and continuously inflated assets. In Minsky's world, if a "new paradigm of active credit management" only served to feed asset inflation and another cycle of borrowing, Alan Greenspan's new paradigm was bad news. Minsky was on to something. Deregulation and cheap money fed an environment in which incredibly complex financial instruments were created and stacked upon one another, while new models of risk calculation were developed. By 2001 Hyman Minsky's "financial instability hypothesis" had begun to rear its ugly head and which helps explain how the fundamental characteristics of the American economy had been altered.

In just one example, the size of the CDS insurance portfolios grew from a "modest" $1 trillion in 2001 to an astounding $54.6 trillion by 2008—which was more than double the size of the US stock market, and far

---

Box 10.1 Understanding Credit Default Swaps

Credit default swaps (CDS) are insurance-like contracts that promise to cover losses on certain securities in the event of a default. They typically apply to municipal bonds, corporate debt, and mortgage securities. They are sold by banks, hedge funds, and other market players. Like anyone who purchases car insurance, those who purchase a CDS contract make payments on a regular basis. In return they get peace of mind, knowing that losses on their securities are covered if a default happens. The process is supposed to work similarly to someone taking out car or home insurance to protect against losses from fire and theft. Except that it doesn't. Banks and insurance companies are regulated; the CDS market is not. This explains why CDS contracts were traded, or swapped, from market player to market player without any oversight. Most market players simply wanted the income stream from the "premiums" paid. Not surprisingly, many buyers did not have the resources to cover losses if the securities that they had insured failed. This is what happened in 2007 and 2008. Like small insurance companies that never want to face claims from a regional earthquake or a Katrina-like event, market players who provided insurance for CDS portfolios weren't properly capitalized and could not pay out claims when the securities market (CDOs) collapsed.

Source: Janet Morrisey, "Credit Default Swaps, The Next Crisis?" *Time.com*, Business & Tech, March 17, 2008, available online.

exceeds the $7.1 trillion mortgage and $4.4 trillion US treasuries market.[82] The CDS market grew when reputable firms, such as insurance giant AIG, decided that they could cover the complex and murky world of CDOs just as they insured lives, homes, and cars.[83] In reality they were covering poorly researched and improperly constructed CDO mortgage contracts (see Chapter 11). The market became increasingly cloudy when investors started looking at the CDS market as a source of income (from premiums paid) rather than as a potential obligation (insurance that has to be paid out). As CDS and CDO instruments grew in popularity, few could see how the markets that these instruments insured and modeled had changed with every new loan, debt contract, and transaction made. George Soros, who spent the last twenty years of the twentieth-century discussing how analyst assumptions about markets are quickly out of date, describes what happened:

They [market players] took past experience as their starting point, with suitable allowances for deviation and emerging new

---

Box 10.2 The Logic Behind the 2008 Market Collapse (as an Analogy)

Imagine taking out a loan against your home to help out Deadbeat Relative #1. Then, imagine that you're talking with a cynical cousin and he says, "You know, you're never going to get the money back." You respond, "I bet you I do." You make the bet. The silliness continues, and other cousins take you up on your bet. Rather than starting a bakery, Deadbeat Relative #1 took the money and foolishly "lent" it to other relatives. Some repaid Deadbeat Relative #1, but most did not. As your cousin expected, Deadbeat Relative #1 doesn't pay. You not only lose the money that you lent to Deadbeat Relative #1 but you lose your house as well. Because you have such a dysfunctional family, you're now faced with the prospect of having to pay off your cynical relatives. You don't have the money. They could care less. They panic because they have already purchased goods on credit, believing that you would pay them in your proceeds from the bet. Others partied with the money and now have bar tabs to pay. They don't care that you've lost your house. They're now camping out at the doorstep of your new apartment. They want you to go to your parents for a loan. They are already overextended. You pray for a miracle.

---

trends, but they failed to recognize the impact that they themselves made. Households became increasingly dependent on the double-digit appreciation in house prices. The savings rate dropped to below zero, and households withdrew equity by refinancing their mortgages at an ever increasing rate. Mortgage equity withdrawals reached nearly a trillion dollars in 2006. . . . When house prices stopped rising these trends had to moderate and eventually reverse. Households found themselves overexposed and overindebted. Eventually consumption had to fall.[84]

What Soros describes isn't new. Deregulated markets that build wealth on a pile of debt can lead to unsustainable bubbles, which undermine market performance and expectations. Put another way, "Minsky's Law" supercedes "Greenspan's Paradigm."

In this instance, although the underlying contracts and transactions may model well in a computer, like a child stacking Lego blocks, the integrity of the market structure changes with every debt-laden block that is added. Unfortunately, because they're busy making money, few market participants take the time to recognize how markets change and alter previous assumptions. Believing in the strength of their models—and with money so easily accessible—market players ignored how much total

Figure 10.4 US Credit Market Debt as a Percentage of GDP, 1957–2007

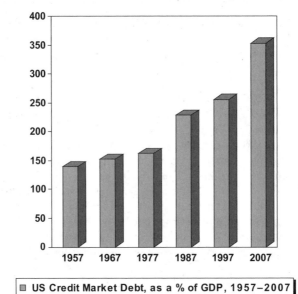

US Credit Market Debt, as a % of GDP, 1957–2007

Source: Federal Reserve System, Flow of Funds Accounts of the United States, 2008.

credit and debt levels in the United States had grown. They jumped from 162.1 percent of the GDP in 1977 to 255.3 percent of GDP ten years later and then to a whopping 352.6 percent by 2007 (see Figure 10.3).[85] With history as a backdrop, these numbers do not bode well for America, as Figure 10.4 and Figure 10.5 make clear.

These figures help us understand why the 2007–2008 market meltdown compelled the Federal Reserve and other government institutions to intervene. They wanted to prevent what they believed could turn into a 1929-style system collapse. Still, even with the government-orchestrated rescues, fears over "price deterioration," margin calls, and "deleveraging" remained.[86] These concerns were so real that, during summer 2008, a frustrated President Bush not only heaped scorn on the "fancy financial instruments" that made government bailouts necessary but blamed the economy's problems on the fact that "Wall Street got drunk."[87] Insightful observers, however, understood what had really happened. After focusing primarily on feeding consumer consumption (with low interest rates and easy money) and encouraging the short-term extraction of wealth (with new and largely unregulated financial instruments), America's political and economic elites had simply ignored how securitized debts piled on top of one another could change market dynamics.

Figure 10.5 US Credit Market Debt as a Percentage of GDP, 1916–2006

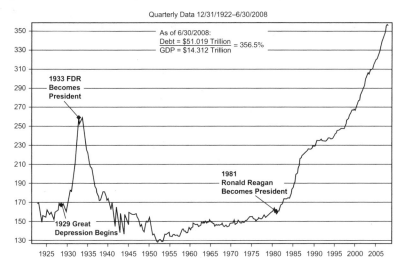

Quarterly Data 12/31/1922–6/30/2008

As of 6/30/2008:
$\dfrac{\text{Debt} = \$51.019\ \text{Trillion}}{\text{GDP} = \$14.312\ \text{Trillion}} = 356.5\%$

1933 FDR Becomes President

1929 Great Depression Begins

1981 Ronald Reagan Becomes President

Annual interpolated GDP (including estimates prior to 1929) used prior to 1946. Domestic Nonfinancial Debt used prior to 1946. As of December, 1946 Domestic Nonfinancial Debt represented 99.4% of Total Credit Market Debt.

Source: Ned Davis Research, Inc.

At the end of 2008, with exploding debt loads, a credit meltdown, bank failures, and a record bailout package in the works, Alan Greenspan's declaration of a "new paradigm of active credit management" looks more like a twisted echo of economist Irving Fisher's assertion in the autumn of 1929 that "stock prices have reached what looks like a permanently high plateau."[88]

Conclusion

In this chapter I have looked at how capital movements reached new levels by showing how the actions of the US government and market players worked to facilitate the creation and distribution of tremendous amounts of capital. Specifically, we saw how politically driven budget deficits in the United States were accepted and encouraged, which, as Peter F. Drucker showed, helped spike capital markets.[89] But these dynamics also weakened postwar Bretton Woods institutions, allowed the United States to ignore the concerns of its allies (especially France) in the 1960s, contributed to a symbiosis of debt, and facilitated the emergence of an economy that encouraged market players to focus on the short-term extraction of wealth through the creation of novel debt instruments.

These and other developments helped create an environment in which global GDP "increased spectacularly over the past twenty-five years" but was dwarfed by financial credit claims that were about 3.7 times as high as global GDP by 2008.[90] One way of thinking about this is to consider how tenable it would be if your home were worth only $100,000 but the bank decided to give you a $370,000 line of credit. If you have the home paid off and are a good credit risk, this might make sense for some (I'm not sure for whom it would make sense, but play along here). Now consider what would happen if the bank did this in most of the neighborhoods in your city—because you had proven to be such a good client and because they were therefore able to "model" your experience. When this is done throughout an entire economy . . . well, you see where this is going. Even well-financed borrowers can be dragged down by debt-laden financial millstones in another corner of the economy.

Peter F. Drucker saw this happening as far back as 1986 and described a new "symbolic" economy in which capital and wealth creation are separated from the real economy.[91] Rather than look toward history for clues as to what happens when market players focus on wealth extraction and creating paper empires tied to debt, policymakers and market players largely ignored Drucker's observations because of the new wealth that was created. This allowed financial instruments and financial assets around the world to become increasingly separated from the production of real goods and services. This explains why the US government was reluctant to allow financial institutions that were deemed "too big to fail" to collapse. There was simply too much nervousness about what would happen if the opaque world of debt-laden financial instruments began to unravel.

In just one example, by the end of 2007 it was revealed that Countrywide, the largest mortgage company in the United States, had gone to the federal government for a series of loans that totaled more than $50 billion. At the time that the company secured the loans, Countrywide's stock price was in a free fall. At the end of 2007 Senator Charles Schumer (D-NY) sent a letter questioning how and why Countrywide was able to secure more than $50 billion in taxpayer-backed loans, especially when the company put its increasingly toxic subprime loan contracts up as collateral. At the same time this was occurring, the Federal Reserve began a series of interest rate cuts that defied logic, given that the value of the US dollar had fallen in previous years as a result of bloated US budget deficits. The goal behind the loans was help to keep Countrywide afloat and American home owners in their homes. This helped maintain the façade that things were okay in the American economy, even as the value of the dollar continues to slide. Perhaps more important, apart from keeping companies like Countrywide from being disciplined by common sense market players, interest rate cuts, bailouts, and loans continued to mask genuine problems in the American economy.

I want to be clear here: the stated goal of federal officials to inject money and credit into the economy is laudable. Money and credit are absolutely necessary for capitalist markets to prosper (as is market speculation[92]). As Susan Strange noted some time ago, money and credit creation go hand in hand and are the lifeblood of any market economy. For capitalist markets to function, both money and credit have to circulate regularly and reliably.[93] However, when money and credit are used to bail out failed institutions, while investments in debt instruments of dubious structure and weak vetting are protected, things can get out of hand. Hyman Minsky understood this. Even Herbert Hoover (albeit, after 1929) pointed out:

> Money is apt to be like a cannon aboard an old-fashioned sailing ship: it is a source of strength and power when kept under control but lethally destructive when it breaks loose.[94]

Hoover is telling us that money and credit must be properly managed if they are to serve markets and society. But this has not been happening since the early 1980s. This raises another issue addressed earlier. If financial institutions can dominate markets and states to a point at which they are too big or too important to fail, they can always call on the government to rescue them when their executives make poor decisions. At this point they have the power to "raise revenue" by imposing on the state, taxing its resources through credit extensions, bailouts, transfer payments, and favorable legislation, among other methods. This type of control and influence over the state, according to Susan Strange, is akin to the systematic poaching of state prerogatives.[95] History and common sense tell us this should not happen in viable democratic societies. Recent developments, however, tell us that it is now an accepted practice that raises few eyebrows. What follows in the next chapter is a discussion of how contemporary markets—which have not followed the market principles discussed by Adam Smith—may have moved beyond the control of the modern nation-state.

Notes

1. Martin Mayer, "Bailing Out Billion-Bettors," *Los Angeles Times,* October 5, 1998, A15.

2. Mayer, "Bailing Out."

3. Hernando De Soto, *The Mystery of Capital: Why Capitalism Triumphs in the West and Fails Everywhere Else* (New York: Basic Books, 2000).

4. To arrive at this point, as we saw in Chapter 1, the US Constitution filled political gaps that the Articles of Confederation had demonstrated needed filling. By protecting liberty and freedom, over time the Constitution made it possible for opportunity and creativity to flourish. As Paul Starr put it, public policy in the United States "did not merely support the rights of individual property owners; it supported the rights of a particular kind" that allowed property and initiative to prosper. Paul Starr, *Freedom's Power: The True Force of Liberalism* (New York: Basic Books, 1997), 71.

5. In the process, the Framers empowered Congress to encourage commerce and competition by promoting the sciences, regulating the value of money, and giving it control over piracy and counterfeiting, among other powers. Implied in Article I, Section 8 of the Constitution was that individual effort paid off if the state were vigilant in opening opportunities and keeping a level playing field, Lawrence Herson, *The Politics of Ideas: Political Theory and American Public Policy* (Chicago: Dorsey Press, 1984).

6. Helen Simon, "Are Derivatives Financial 'Weapons of Mass Destruction'?" Investopedia.com, available online.

7. David Leonhardt, "Can't Grasp Credit Crisis? Join the Club," *New York Times,* March 19, 2008, available online.

8. Robert Kuttner, "Little Orphan Fannie," *The Huffington Post,* September 11, 2008, available online.

9. "Ponzificating: Is the Financial System a Confidence Trick?" *The Economist,* March 20, 2007. Available on the CFO.com Web site. Hyman Minsky, "The Financial Instability Hypothesis," The Jerome Levy Economics Institute of Bard College, Working Paper No. 74, May 1992, available online.

10. Worse, presidential candidate John McCain claimed that market fundamentals were sound.

11. Kevin Phillips, *Wealth and Democracy: A Political History of the American Rich* (New York: Broadway Books, 2002), 105–106.

12. For a quick overview of the financial conditions that enveloped the globe by late 2008, see Nouriel Roubini, "The Coming Financial Pandemic," *Foreign Policy,* no. 165 (March/April 2008): 44–48.

13. The dynamics described here refer to the classic concern and battle that states have over maintaining currency stability (necessary for confidence), capital flows (for investment and growth), and monetary policy autonomy (to manage jobs, inflation, and debt). On this see Benjamin J. Cohen, "The Triad and the Unholy Trinity: Problems of International Monetary Cooperation," in *International Political Economy: Perspectives on Global Power and Wealth,* ed. Jeffry A. Frieden and David A. Lake (New York: St. Martin's Press, 1995), 255.

14. Dean Acheson, *Present at the Creation: My Years in the State Department* (New York: Norton, 1987).

15. George Soros, *The Crisis of Global Capitalism: Open Society Endangered* (New York: Public Affairs, 1998), 106. Blog Commentary.

16. Susan Strange, *States and Market,* 2nd edition (London, UK: Pinter Publishers, 1994); James Fallows, "How the World Really Works," *Atlantic Monthly,* December 1993, available online. Blog Commentary.

17. To be sure, all types of economic activities are not necessarily good for society. On this see Clifford Cobb, Ted Halstead, and Jonathan Rowe, "If GDP Is Up, Why Is America Down?" in *The Atlantic Monthly,* October 1995, available online.

18. Kevin Phillips, "Why Wall Street Socialism Will Fail," *Huffington Post,* April 15, 2008, available online.

19. Walter La Feber, *The American Age: U.S. Foreign Policy at Home and Abroad, 1750 to the Present* (New York: Norton, 1994), 615.

20. La Feber, *The American,* 644. Blog Commentary.

21. Benjamin J. Cohen, *In Whose Interest? International Banking and American Foreign Policy* (New Haven, CT: Yale University Press, 1986), 227.

22. Cohen, *In Whose,* 224.

23. Cohen, *In Whose,* 227.

24. Thomas J. Schoenbaum, *Waging Peace and War: Dean Rusk in the Truman, Kennedy and Johnson Years* (New York: Simon & Schuster, 1988), 420–421.

25. Schoenbaum, *Waging,* 421.

26. Cohen, *In Whose,* 19.

27. Harold Macmillan, *Riding the Storm, 1956–1959* (New York: Harper & Row, 1971), 164–165; Peter Clarke, *Hope and Glory: Britain, 1900–1990,* (London, UK: Allen Lane, 1996), 261.

28. Gregory J. Millman, *The Vandals' Crown: How Rebel Currency Traders Overthrew the World's Central Banks* (New York: Free Press, 1995), 83–86. Blog Commentary.

29. Henry Kissinger, *Diplomacy* (New York: Simon & Schuster, 1994), 547. Blog Commentary.

30. Soros, *The Crisis,* 103–104.

31. La Feber, *The American,* 561.

32. Cohen, *In Whose.*

33. Phillips, *Wealth,* 138–147.

34. Soros, *The Crisis,* 108.

35. Daniel Yergin, *The Prize: The Epic Quest for Oil, Money and Power* (New York: Free Press, 1992), 508–523. Unless otherwise noted, this section is drawn from Yergin's book.

36. See Blog Commentary.

37. Yergin, *The Prize,* 523.

38. Yergin, *The Prize,* 567.

39. Robert D. Atkinson, *Supply-Side Follies: Why Conservative Economics Fails, Liberal Economics Falters, and Innovation Economics Is the Answer* (New York: Rowman Littlefield, 2006).

40. "Rating Bush's Jobs Record," *The Wall Street Journal,* 2005, available online.

41. *The Fact Book, 1997 Edition: Federal Civilian Workforce Statistics.* United States Office of Personnel Management. Washington DC, 9, available online.

42. *Tax and Budget Bulletin.* "Number of Federal Subsidy Programs Is Soaring," Cato Institute, no. 41, October 2006, available online.

43. *Fortune,* "How To Cut the Budget," in *Fortune,* CNNMoney.com, (March 4, 1985), available online.

44. U.S. Census Bureau, "Federal Budget Debt: 1960–2007," in *The 2008 Statistical Abstract: The National Data Book,* Table 456, available online.

45. Daniel Yergin, *The Prize: The Epic Quest for Oil, Money and Power* (New York: Free Press, 1992), 659–664.

46. Frederick S. Weaver, *Economic Literacy: Basic Economics with an Attitude,* 2nd edition (New York: Rowman & Littlefield, 2007), 160–161; Thomas Sowell, *Basic Economics: A Common Sense Guide to the Economy,* 3rd edition (New York: Basic Books, 2007), 283–286. Blog Commentary.

47. The price drop acted like an "OPEC tax cut" that resulted in billions of dollars transferred back to American consumers through the mid-1980s. Yergin, *The Prize,* 764.

48. Phillips, 336–337; Thomas R. Dye, *Top-Down Policymaking* (New York: Chatham House, 2001), 52–57; Elton Rayack, *Not So Free To Choose: The Political Economy of Milton Friedman and Ronald Reagan* (New York: Praeger, 1987); William H. Gates Sr. and Chuck Collins, *Wealth and Our Commonwealth: Why America Should Tax Accumulated Fortunes* (Boston: Beacon Press, 2003); Blog Commentary.

49. See, for example, Hayne E. Leland and Mark Rubenstein, "The Evolution of Portfolio Insurance," available online. Blog Commentary.

50. George Soros, *The New Paradigm for Financial Markets: The Credit Crisis of 2008 and What It Means* (New York: Public Affairs, 2008), 106–110.

51. Soros, *The New,* 96–97.

52. Federal Reserve, "Report to the Congress on Practices of the Consumer Credit Card Industry in Soliciting and Extending Credit and

Their Effects on Consumer Debt and Insolvency," *The Federal Reserve Board,* June 2006, available online.

53. Ben S. Bernanke, "The Level and Distribution of Economic Well-Being." Speech given before the Greater Omaha Chamber of Commerce, Omaha, Nebraska, February 6, 2007, available online.

54. Bernanke, "The Level," 4.

55. *Businessweek,* "How Wal-Mart Keeps Unions at Bay," Businessweek.com, October 28, 2002, available online.

56. U.S. Census, "Labor Union Membership by Sector: 1983–2006," Table 642, available online, http://www.census.gov/compendia/statab/tables/08s0642.pdf.

57. Emmanuel Saez, "Striking It Richer: The Evolution of Top Incomes in the United States," University of California, March 15, 2008, available online.

58. Paul Krugman, "State of the Unions," *New York Times,* December 24, 2007, available online.

59. Jeanne Sahadi, "CEO Pay: Sky High Gets Even Higher," CNNmoney.com, *Jobs and Economy,* August 30, 2005, available online; Lawrence Michel, "CEO-to-Worker Pay Imbalance Grows," Economic Policy Institute, *Economic Snapshots,* June 21, 2006, available online.

60. John McNeil, "Changes in Median Household Income: 1969 to 1996," U.S. Department of Commerce, Economics and Statistics Administration, Bureau of the Census, Current Population Reports, P23-196, July 1998, available online.

61. Bob Davis, "Lagging Behind the Wealthy, Many Use Debt To Catch Up," *The Wall Street Journal,* May 17, 2005, available online.

62. Federal Reserve, "Consumer Credit," in *Federal Reserve Statistical Release,* G. 19, September 8, 2008, available online.

63. Porter Anderson, "Study: U.S. Employees Put in Most Hours," CNN.com/Career, August 31, 2001, available online.

64. Davis, "Lagging."

65. Louis Uchitelle, "A False Sense of Security? You Must Own a Home," *New York Times,* July 1, 2007, available online.

66. *Bureau of Economic Analysis,* "Personal Income and Outlays," U.S. Department of Commerce, National Economic Accounts, July 2008, available online.

67. Mara Der Hovanesian, Christopher Palmeri, Nanette Byrnes, and Jessica Silver-Greenberg, "Over the Limit," *BusinessWeek,* February 7, 2008, available online.

68. Bank for International Settlements, *78th Annual Report 2007/2008* (Basel: Bank for International Settlements, 2008), 88, available online.

69. Bank for International Settlements, *Annual Report,* 88.

70. See "The LTCM Bailout" on Blog Commentary.

71. Roger Lowenstein, *When Genius Failed: The Rise and Fall of Long-Term Capital Management* (New York: Random House, 2000).

72. Charles R. Morris, *The Trillion Dollar Meltdown: Easy Money, High Rollers, and the Great Credit Crash* (New York: Public Affairs, 2008), 37–58.

73. U.S. Census Bureau, "Historical Census of Housing Tables: Homeownership," *Housing and Household Economic Statistics Division*, Historical Census of Housing Tables, available online.

74. Robert Kuttner, "Little Orphan Fannie," in "The American Prospect, Tapped," The Group Blog of the American Prospect, September 8, 2008, available online.

75. Morris, *The Trillion*, 40–41.

76. Steven D. Levitt, "Diamond and Kashyap on the Recent Financial Upheavals," *The New York Times*, September 18, 2008, available online.

77. Levitt, "Diamond."

78. Federal Reserve System, *Flow of Funds Accounts of the United States*, "U.S. Credit Market Debt as a Percentage of GDP," March 2008, available online.

79. Phillips, *Wealth*, 138–147.

80. Soros, *The New*, 97. Blog Commentary.

81. Morris, *The Trillion*, 61.

82. Morris, *The Trillion*, 75; Karen Freifield and Shannon D. Harrington, "Cuomo Investigates Credit-Default Swaps along with Short Sales," Bloomberg.com, News, September 27, 2008, available online.

83. Boyd Erman, "Counterparty Risk and Credit Default Swaps," ReportonBusiness.com, September 17, 2008, available online. Blog Commentary.

84. Soros, *The New*, 98.

85. Federal Reserve System, *Flow of Funds Accounts of the United States*, "U.S. Credit Market Debt as a Percentage of GDP," March 2008, available online.

86. Bank for International Settlements, *Annual Report*, 92, 95.

87. Sheryl Gay Stolber, "A Private, Blunter Bush Declares, 'Wall Street Got Drunk'," *New York Times*, July 23, 2008, available online.

88. John Kenneth Galbraith, *A Short History of Financial Euphoria* (New York: Viking, 1993), 79–80.

89. Peter F. Drucker, "The Changed World Economy," *Foreign Affairs*, 64, no. 4 (Spring 1986): 768–791.

90. Morris, *The Trillion*.

91. Drucker, "The Changed," 781–783.

92. Sowell, *Basic Economics,* 261–266. Thomas Sowell provides perhaps the simplest and best argument for the role of speculators in an economy. His examples, however, focus on speculation in the real economy.

93. Strange, *States,* 91.

94. Strange, *States,* 92–93.

95. Strange, *States,* 86.

CHAPTER 11

THE DEREGULATION GAME

After conquering the gold-laden Aztec and Incan empires, the Spaniards went on a spending binge. What they didn't do was develop the capacity to produce goods that would make them competitive during the commercial and industrial revolutions of the eighteenth and nineteenth centuries. Why should they? With an "unlimited" source of gold and silver in the mines of Guanajuato, Potosi, and Zacatecas, they had found El Dorado. This enabled Spain to purchase what it needed and to conduct affairs as if tomorrow would never arrive. Rather than turning to commerce and industry, as bullion-deprived North American colonialists did, the Spaniards focused on extracting resources, purchasing useless titles, and acquiring assets of questionable commercial utility.

By the end of the seventeenth century, after recklessly spreading its wealth across Europe, Spain retained perhaps 5 percent of the bullion that the conquistadors had extracted from the Americas.[1] Like Don Quixote, the mythical character created by Cervantes, the Spaniards finally came to their senses but only after it was too late. Inflation arrived in Europe, making the goods that Spain sought more expensive. Worse, Spain faced the prospect of competing commercially with its more industrious neighbors—specifically England and France. No amount of commercial treaties, taxes, or other gimmicks could make up for generations of ignoring industry and squandering Spain's economic trump card on castles, monasteries, and global adventures. Like Don Quixote, the Spanish Empire tilted at the "windmills" of war and debt—finally collapsing at the feet of America in the Spanish-American War in 1898.

Fast forward one hundred years and another empire is in trouble. Believing that the sun would never set on its capacity to spread gold-backed dollars across the globe, successive American administrations spread credit and deficit dollars around the world. And why not? After World War II the dollar was considered to be "as good as gold" and was actively sought by allies

*and traders alike in an American-led trading regime. No longer were the
sketchy claims and promises of a John Law, or the convoluted sorcery of
scheming alchemists, necessary to create wealth through paper. As long as
America paid for the defense of the West and no viable currency alternatives
emerged, dollars were accepted on demand. This was an arrangement that
the Spaniards, with all of their bullion, could not match. But, then again,
the Spaniards had never leveraged their gold in an effort to build an international trading regime that others sought to join.*

*Perhaps more important, Spain never built a credit superstructure that
allowed it to borrow so liberally from its neighbors. These arrangements
worked so well that Vice President Dick Cheney dismissed the idea of
paying down deficits (to help support the value of the dollar), claiming
that "deficits don't matter." By ignoring how its wealth was dissipated at
the beginning of the twenty-first century—via borrowing and commercial
deficits—America now finds itself tilting at the same economic windmills
that confronted Spain at the end of the nineteenth century.*

Adam Smith's spirit of *laissez-faire* has been replaced in present-day
America by a world of very visible hands. When the size of an industry's profits (or losses) and an economy's survival depend on government support for market players who are deemed "too big to fail,"
something is amiss. Market subsidies, favorable legislation, and regular
bailouts all point to a market that not only violates Adam Smith's laws
of nature but is a far cry from the market vision that the private sector
claims to follow. But this is just the beginning. By pushing for and
accepting government favors while speaking admiringly of the wonders
of the market, America's market fundamentalists expose themselves to
a new reality. In many respects, they are on no firmer intellectual
ground than Vladimir Lenin and Joseph Stalin. Both Lenin and Stalin
spoke enthusiastically about the virtues of socialism while using the
state to reach production goals, discredit political enemies, and impose
ideas that did not work. The increasing use of the state to achieve or
maintain goals, whether in capitalist market societies or in a worker's
paradise, says much about the chasm between theory and reality for
America's free market proponents.

This is important. As noted previously, perhaps the key element that
made the liberal revolutions of the twentieth and nineteenth centuries
successful was how the ideas of John Locke and Adam Smith had pushed
humanity to restrict and tame the arbitrary use of state power. The fact
that America's merchants, entrepreneurs, and workers didn't have to
worry about some tyrant's agent arriving to confiscate arbitrarily what
had been created, accumulated, or produced was a good thing. But an

arbitrary taking doesn't occur only when private goods are confiscated. There are few events that represent an arbitrary taking better than when the state takes taxpayer money and props up a company or an industry because it's deemed "too big to fail." It's made worse when the state forces standards and conditions on society in general while offering relief and state resources to specific industries.

An arbitrary taking occurs when state institutions like the Federal Reserve or the Treasury Department are forced to intervene in the economy because market players have concocted such a toxic brew of financial agreements and credit instruments that the state is fearful that their unwinding will lead to a market crash. To be sure, maintaining stability in the name of the public good is a laudable goal, as John Maynard Keynes pointed out. But providing money and political cover to collapsing industries that operate in the name of *laissez-faire*—while continuing to push the myth of "free markets"—imposes an *Alice in Wonderland* character on modern markets in America. You can't say a "market" is whatever you want it to be simply because it fits what you believe. Even though we may not be on the path toward Marxist-style socialism in America, as some might claim, there are elements of market socialism on the horizon. But these elements have always been there. Steady bailouts, government debt, favorable legislation, and subsidies for teetering or failing industries put off what could actually correct the problem—a day of financial reckoning that forces citizens and market participants alike to reevaluate unrealistic world views.

The Gifts of Liberal Revolution Threatened?

Among the cornerstones of the American Revolution has been the removal of the scourge of tyranny so that freedom and liberty can prosper. The taming of arbitrary power, coupled with the elimination of liberty-denying feudal customs, is the continuing gift handed down by the liberal revolutions of the eighteenth and nineteenth centuries.[2] Constitutional stability and political control over the use of arbitrary power have been maintained because of continuous refinements via court decisions, combative legislation, impeachment threats, political movements, legal restraints, partisan gamesmanship, and even a civil war. Liberty is not automatic. It requires work. It requires democracy. Constitutional stability and political control are threatened by a state that abdicates its oversight responsibilities and permits any sector of the economy to call on the resources of the state on a regular basis. When the state permits the creation of complex investment instruments and reckless speculation, and then consents to the use of state resources to stave off bankruptcy (or to guarantee payoff), serious questions are raised. As Kevin Phillips put it:

> If the important mega-banks are too big or too interconnected to fail, then why are they allowed to indulge in every form of speculation and anti-social behavior, from counseling Enron on tax evasion to gouging on credit-card interest and fees? Martin Wolf, chief commentator of the *Financial Times*, has contended that "what we have [in banking] is a risk-loving industry guaranteed as a public utility." If banks are to be rescued because they are too big to fail, they should also become, in the manner of a public utility, too well-behaved and too responsible to fail.[3]

There's no doubt that society has evolved or that complex market settings in the twenty-first century require complex arrangements. But there's also no doubt that, if the state is to be used as the babysitter for the market's largest players, the state needs to have the resources to do more than simply stand by and hope that floundering private actors don't call on it after they've made a mess of things. The state can't create the conditions under which wealth is created if its resources are consistently hijacked by market players who overplay their hands. When the state allows the private sector to draw on the public treasury when markets break down, it also allows the private sector to act like history's tyrants, who placed their needs above those of the public. The gifts of the liberal revolution are threatened when the public interest is absorbed by careless and destructive market forces. Taming or controlling these forces not only requires organization and resources that should be used for building opportunities, but it also suggests that Milton Friedman's "umpire" model of government (see Chapter 1) is woefully inadequate for understanding modern markets.

The point is not to deny the logic behind Adam Smith's "invisible hand" when the state gets it right. The success of Bill Gates, Steven Jobs, and Google's founders illustrate that the logic is alive and well. The prospect of profit and wealth are great motivators. But let's be clear. The genius of Bill Gates and Steven Jobs did not hinge on tax cuts. Nor was their success inspired by the prospect of deregulated financial markets. Everything that they required was already in place when they began their entrepreneurial journeys. We also want to keep in mind that everyone who participates in markets is not creative nor deserves to get rich. Creating the conditions for market players to secure wealth, or to stay in business after they've made a mess of things, works against this logic. But what do we have today? After working diligently to create opportunities, while removing the scourge of tyranny and arbitrary power from society, the United States is inviting tyranny and arbitrary power to come back—because of the actions of market players who once denounced the poor judgment and plodding inefficiency of government.[4]

What many in the private sector have ignored is how individual liberty and the rule of law blossomed in America. They flourished because the liberal state wiped away the whims of despots while removing the stifling demands of custom and tradition.[5] Ponder for a moment what it means that you and I aren't subjected to the whims of a tyrannical ruler or obligated to till the land and work for someone 90–120 days a year. Although media pundits and politicians may score points by cynically asserting "We work the first 3–4 months of the year to pay the tax man," they miss the larger issue. There is a payoff in the modern liberal state. It's called opportunity. Unlike peasants and the politically oppressed merchants from the past, modern people can work hard and get ahead. This is the moral justification of capitalism.

Creating opportunities for all members of society, however, is not free. Nor is opportunity for all created overnight. It took modern liberal states a hundred years or more to create broad-based opportunities and options, but those efforts have borne fruits that our ancestors could only dream about. The "true force of liberalism" lies in its ability to discipline and tame agents who can extort state resources, in the process denying the state what it needs to open doors.[6] Since the early 1980s state power has been increasingly used to prop up and stabilize market outcomes for market players who have run amok. Whether orchestrating a bailout or simply providing investors with enough time to flee, the state has stepped in, on numerous occasions, in order to maintain confidence, ensure payoff, and guarantee market results. This is an ironic state of affairs, given that Milton Friedman forcefully criticized attempts to promote "equality of opportunity" in society because he believed that those efforts had morphed into a quest to ensure "equality of results."

Making matters more challenging at the beginning of the twenty-first century is the fact that very few understand the relationship between deregulation, complex investment instruments, and the speculative investments schemes that have forced the state's hand. From the broad strokes of Enron's collapse to the intricate debt instruments that led to the financial meltdown of 2008, it is clear that market players and government leaders know very little about—or choose to ignore—the cause and effects of deregulation in modern markets. This explains why intervention and government efforts to support markets have become commonplace—market players who do understand these dynamics have learned to stay quiet and profit from a pattern of US government bailouts. The remainder of this chapter presents a discussion of deregulatory developments and investment patterns that have occurred in the American economy from the 1970s through 2008. I start by looking at developments that initially compelled market players to protect themselves with creative financial instruments but then morphed into a quest to turn protective instruments into financial jackpots. I end with a discussion of the market bailout proposals that took place at the end of 2008.

Enron: The Canary in the Mine

The collapse of energy giant Enron drew a great deal of attention from the US Congress and the world's press. In a rush to "guard the public interest," politicians and media hounds stumbled over themselves to understand the problem and establish blame for Enron's demise. Scapegoats were found; some even went to jail. These triumphs, however, were short-lived and largely hollow. Politicians and pundits continued to embrace the policies that contributed to Enron's collapse because, in part, they never understood what happened.

Part of the Enron mess can be tied to firms and transnational corporations of all stripes having to operate in increasingly unstable financial waters. These conditions can be traced in part to 1971, when the United States pulled the plug on the gold standard. As we saw earlier, the dollar went from stable financial anchor to fluctuating commodity in the international financial system. Part of the blame can also be placed on the rise and growth of largely unregulated capital and Eurocurrency markets, in which currencies and other products are bought and sold as investment, speculative, and insurance products. With the collapse of the Bretton Woods system and the forces of globalization, these transactions increased exponentially, which explains why money and capital flows exploded worldwide to the tune of $3.4 trillion every day by 2007—more than double what it was in 2001 (see Table 11.1). What does this have to do with Enron? Everything.

Table 11.1 Global Foreign Exchange Market Turnover (in Billions of Dollars)

	1992	1995	1998	2001	2004	2007
Daily Average	880	1,150	1,750	1,510	2,110	3,475

Source: Bank for International Settlement, *78th Annual Report,* April 1, 2007–March 31, 2008, Basel, June 2008, available online.

Companies like Enron need stable financial horizons to plan and invest. The explosion of capital flows—in part a product of US budget deficits and of the Nixon administration's decision to allow speculation on dollar futures (Chapter 4)—disrupted currency price stability. This meant that US companies doing business abroad could no longer simply invest or set prices as they did in the past. To do so invited unanticipated losses or profits, depending on the direction that the dollar went. To combat this, transnational corporations looking for money went abroad to borrow. They could either go to the Eurodollar market or issue corporate bonds (another form of borrowing). In the process, they found creative ways to guard against currency market spikes with short-term swap purchases (different from CDSs) or by acquiring other financial products (such as CDSs). These tactics became part of the corporate world's "insurance" strategy against financial uncertainty.

To appreciate better why these insurance activities are necessary, imagine that your paycheck depends on your company's monthly sales and profits. The amount that you see in your check might go up, but it might go down. Although the law of averages suggests that things will even out, most workers would have to borrow or cut back at some time, given that monthly debt obligations remain the same. Transnational corporations experienced the same dilemmas, albeit on a much larger scale. The point is that, if you do not know your balance sheet or what price your wares will fetch from month to month (because of currency shifts), things can get unpredictable and downright ugly. The people at Enron understood this and entered financial markets with the idea of stabilizing the books—at least initially.

These dynamics help explain why US corporations took a competitive beating in the 1970s and the 1980s. Simply put, many companies didn't anticipate or fully appreciate the dynamics of currency prices. For example, Kodak lost global sales to Fuji as the dollar became relatively expensive in the 1980s. This meant that anything originally priced in dollars—such as Kodak film—became more expensive because other currencies could no longer purchase as many dollars (or as many goods). Retailers who wanted to buy Fuji could purchase Fuji film (and Japanese yen) at a lower cost and then pass the savings on to US consumers. Conversely, goods made and priced in another currency, such as the yen, found markets as they became cheaper vis-à-vis dollar-denominated goods. This was good for US consumers who purchased imported goods but bad for US exporters. One estimate suggests that Kodak lost more than $3.5 billion in earnings during the 1980s. This didn't happen because Fuji had a superior strategy or a superior product (not that they didn't). Currency price dynamics in the 1980s had played a significant role.

What was happening in currency markets in the 1980s was intricately tied to the US economy. To help curb inflation, the Federal Reserve, under Paul Volcker, pushed commercial bank prime rates above 20 percent. With interest rates high and with the full faith and credit of the US government behind treasury bonds, which were paying nearly 15 percent in 1982, foreigners sent their investment funds to the United States. To purchase US bonds, investors had to get their hands on dollars. This pushed the price of the dollar up. The strong dollar wreaked havoc on America's export-oriented manufacturers while helping European and Japanese manufacturers sell their goods in America. After making appeals to Washington to do something about high interest rates—and being rebuffed—US firms began looking for others ways to protect themselves. Cumulatively, their efforts energized the financial sector.

To combat the uncertainty of fluctuating currency markets and high interest rates at home, corporations went beyond borrowing abroad (or issuing bonds) and employed strategies designed to level out the roller-coaster ride of currency markets. Specifically, firms added hedging (purchasing money) and swaps (trading blocks of money) to their insurance repertoire (Box 11.1). By purchasing currency and other financial contracts, to be cashed out at a later date, companies had a better idea of their financial horizons. Although they might not get the best currency price when they cashed out (then again, they might do even better), at least they had an idea what their accounts might look like in the future. Borrowing abroad and purchasing novel contracts provided US corporations with financial insurance policies that allowed them to plan and invest with greater confidence.

Box 11.1 Explaining Currency Swaps

One of the unanticipated developments of globalization has been how transnational firms and other market participants found they could make money by "swapping" currencies that they might be holding but didn't need at the moment. Gregory Millman tells the story of the World Bank, which wanted to loan money to developing countries in 1981. The World Bank didn't want to go to the United States and borrow money and then have to lend at the rates of 17 percent and more that were demanded by US institutions. By coincidence, IBM needed dollars but was sitting on Swiss Francs and Deutsche Marks. These currencies cost 8 percent and 12 percent each. Because of capital controls that had been put in place by the German and Swiss governments, the World Bank couldn't borrow the francs and marks that they needed to lend. The solution? The World Bank borrowed dollars and then, after working out the interest rate disparities, "swapped" what they borrowed with IBM. And, just like that, IBM made money off their currency holdings and the World Bank was able to lend currencies to the developing world at rates that were lower than what was being charged for US dollars.

Source: Gregory J. Millman, *The Vandals' Crown: How Rebel Currency Traders Overthrew the World's Central Banks* (New York: Free Press, 1995).

Enron's problems began when it went from purchasing products to stabilize its financial horizons to making big bets to bolster its bottom line. Its position collapsed when the executives got greedy, overplayed their hands, tried to speculate their losses away, and then hid and lied about what they were doing. Investors in Enron (like their employees) lost out—because rules kept them from selling off their Enron shares, while company executives dumped theirs. The media and the general public are still largely baffled by the fact that the collapse of Enron was tied to financial markets and not to developments in the energy industry. More interesting is that, even though what Enron's executives did was over the top, it was an indicator of systemwide problems with speculation, wealth extraction, and accounting gimmicks. America's financial problems were just beginning (or getting deeper).[7] In hindsight Enron may have been the miner's canary.

Preparing for Deregulation

We know from the previous chapter that deficit spending, a culture of debt, and deregulation helped elevate finance above banking and manufacturing in the American economy. The purchase of complex financial instruments is no longer done simply to diversify or protect investment portfolios. The Enron case makes it clear that money and finance no longer follow trade in goods and services but now lead it. At the beginning of the twenty-first century, complex financial instruments have been used increasingly to fill immediate needs and make quick returns. Like the praetorian guards of ancient Rome, instruments that were once used to protect the empire have morphed into kingmakers and destroyers of kingdoms. How has this played out in the modern world? Let's take a closer look at the mechanics behind the CDO market.

As explained in Chapter 2, CDOs are debt contracts that have been bundled together and sold to investors. In return for their money, investors receive a steady income stream produced by monthly payments that people make on their homes, student loans, or credit card debts, for example. The primary benefit of CDOs is that they're designed to provide a steady source of income for the purchaser who puts cash back into the market. Ultimately, CDOs serve the interests of consumers by injecting cash into the mortgage, car, and credit markets, among others. These are the broad contours of the mortgage and CDO instruments that were bought and sold by Fannie Mae and Freddie Mac, among other large financial institutions. The emergence of the CDO (and other asset-backed security markets) is important for several reasons.

First, it shakes money loose that might not otherwise be available. We often forget that, during the 1960s and even the early 1970s, private market players did not think too much about buying and selling mortgage contracts. Home mortgages weren't attractive to investors because incomes (or yields) were paltry and not always dependable. More specifically, there was always the concern that a default, payoff, or refinance might occur. On another level, mortgages were usually held by local banks or S&Ls, which depended on regular mortgage payments for their income. Federal regulations designed to keep home ownership stable and local discouraged the buying and selling of home mortgages to investors and, more important, to speculators. This helps explain why the amount of mortgage-related debt contracts held by Fannie Mae and other GSEs equaled only 2.2 percent of America's GDP in 1967 (see Figure 11.1).

By 1970, however, Fannie Mae had been "privatized" (in 1968) and replaced by Ginnie Mae. This paved the way for the arrival of Freddie Mac,

Figure 11.1 Government Secured Enterprise Debt Held as a Percentage of GDP (Includes Federally Related Mortgage Pools)

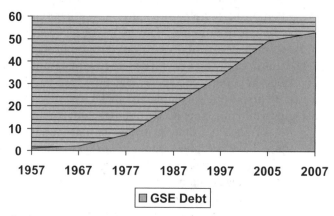

Source: Federal Reserve System, Flow of Funds Accounts of the United States, 2008.

which was created in 1970 to provide "competition" for Fannie Mae. Together they purchased mortgages, which they eventually turned around and sold to investors as mortgage-backed securities (another type of CDO). Bank of America followed suit, packaging and selling a limited number of home loan contracts in the early 1970s. Although the market for mortgage debt tripled (it was a paltry amount to begin with), GSE debt as a percentage of GDP reached only 7.2 percent in 1977 (see Figure 11.1). There were several reasons that the "mortgage bond" market remained relatively small at this time.

The primary reason that buying and selling mortgages did not take off as a market was that, state and federal laws frowned on investing and speculating in mortgages. Home ownership was too close to the American Dream. Government policy focused on stabilizing that dream, at least until the late 1970s. As a result, mortgage-related security bonds were legal in only three states. Here we have the state working to stabilize home ownership in America by creating laws that put some distance between homeownership and the investment industry. On another level, potential investors in the mortgage market were discouraged by how quickly mortgages might mature. The primary drawback was that those who purchased mortgage-tied instruments ran the risk of having mortgages refinanced or paid off early. If interest rates fell and home owners refinanced their mortgages, the mortgage "bondholder" would be sitting on a pile of cash. Why take the risk? These and other limitations convinced market players to pursue wealth the old fashioned way—by getting the government to change the rules.

The Deregulation Game Is On: Salomon Brothers Goes to Washington for a Favor and Gets Three Wishes[8]

In *Liar's Poker,* Michael Lewis takes us through the history and challenges that surround "structured finance" and explains the rise of the mortgage CDO market. To do this, he introduces us to one-time Salomon Brothers trader Lewis Ranieri. He paints a picture of an extremely talented, smart, and eccentric man. Lewis also makes it clear that Ranieri knew that Bank of America and Fannie Mae were on to something in the mortgage market. Regulations had kept this market clear for Ranieri. Where others saw a wall, he saw opportunity. At the time, Ranieri saw that Fannie Mae was buying and selling a limited class of government-backed mortgages across the country. They had the authority to do so. Bank of America originated and sold a small number of mortgages, but only in a handful of states. The challenge was to get the federal government to permit an expanded class of home mortgages (like the ones handled by Bank of America) to be packaged and sold across the nation (which Fannie Mae had a hand in). So, in the late 1970s, Ranieri "hired a phalanx of lawyers and lobbyists in Washington to work on legislation to increase the number of potential buyers of mortgage securities."[9] Although he acknowledged the role of others in creating the home mortgage security market, Ranieri was not shy about discussing his contribution:

> I had a team of lawyers trying to change the law on a state-by-state basis. It would have taken two thousand years. That's why I went to Washington. To go over the heads of the states.[10]

Still, getting Congress to sign off on home mortgages as an income-producing investment for market players beyond the banking community wasn't enough. Very few investors wanted to touch the interest-rate sensitive mortgage securities market in the late 1970s, especially after Federal Reserve Chairman Paul Volcker raised interest rates in 1979.

By 1980 the industry was losing money in a big way. The math was simple. Although the S&L industry borrowed at 10 percent, for example, it was legally obligated to lend at 7 percent. New home loans from S&Ls hit a wall. The S&Ls were also losing long-time clients. As inflation took off, S&Ls lost deposits to higher-yielding money-market funds, most of them uninsured and unregulated. Making matters worse, the S&Ls were sitting on millions of home loan contracts that had been written up in more stable times which paid 5 percent or lower. Almost one-quarter (962 S&Ls) of America's 4,002 S&Ls collapsed between 1980 and 1982.[11] With the industry losing money, S&Ls were desperate to dump their home loan contracts. With the exception of Lewis Ranieri and Salomon Brothers, there were few to no buyers for these contracts, even at a discount price. And Salomon drove a hard bargain, demanding that contracts be sold for 70–80 cents on the dollar or less. Then the Gates of Heaven opened for the S&L industry and Salomon Brothers.

At the beginning of the 1980s, with S&Ls across the country closing their doors, Congress passed several pieces of legislation designed to address the issue of S&L insolvency (see Box 11.2). Because the industry got what amounted to three wishes the legislation might as well have been called the "Genie Acts." The Acts allowed the S&Ls to sell the money-losing mortgages that they had on the books and then to use the proceeds for investments outside of home loans, even if they were unsecured investments. The industry was now unshackled from regulations that for decades had moored the S&L industry to investing primarily in home loans. Many in the industry went wild, investing in speculative and tax-driven projects such as high rises and ostrich farms.[12] Confident that the money they lent was FDIC–guaranteed, S&L loans in the 1980s were often granted with little or no concern for the borrower's ability to pay.[13] The environment was enhanced by budget constraints (caused by record deficits) and political ideology ("get government off our back"), which combined to reduce the relative size of regulators' staffs. But this was only the primer.

Box 11.2 Deregulating the Savings and Loan Industry

Because of inflation, interest rates started to rise in the 1970s. This put S&Ls in a bind: they were borrowing money from the Federal Reserve at high interest rates but did not have the income to pay higher interest rates to their customers. The market for their primary earning asset, homes, had stalled while the home loans they had on their books were locked into long-term and low-interest contracts that didn't produce enough cash to pay rising costs. This resulted in catastrophic losses for S&Ls in 1981 and 1982. Congress was inundated by requests and demands to do something. In its first legislative effort, Congress responded with the Depository Institutions Deregulation and Monetary Control Act (effective March 31, 1980). This allowed thrifts to make investments beyond the housing market. Specifically, thrifts were allowed to invest up to 20 percent of their assets in a combination of corporate and consumer loans. Later, the Depository Institutions Act, a bipartisan bill sponsored by Congressmen Fernand St. Germain (D-RI) and Jake Garn (R-UT), was passed on October 15, 1982. It permitted even greater diversification and allowed S&Ls to invest in commercial, corporate, business, agricultural, consumer loan (40 percent), other nonresidential real estate (40 percent), and personal property (10 percent) assets. Although diversification allowed S&Ls to increase their earnings by investing in assets beyond traditional home and consumer loans, they also exposed the S&Ls to greater market risk. This was the genesis of the S&L debacle that hit markets in the late 1980s.

Source: Ahmad W. Salam, "Congress, Regulators, RAP, and the Savings and Loan Debacle," *The CPA Journal,* January 1994, available online.

New accounting rules granted the S&L industry a second gift. According to Michael Lewis, author of *Liar's Poker,* thrifts were allowed to take a tax deduction from selling their loans at a loss. The deal got even better with wish number three. The S&Ls were permitted to apply losses incurred from selling mortgages at a loss to taxes paid over the previous ten years. Put another way, if you had an S&L that lost money in previous years and was also losing money presently, you didn't have to worry. The American taxpayer would pick up the tab.[14] According to Lewis, for the thrifts, "the name of the game was to generate lots of losses to show to the IRS," which they did after 1982.[15] Like a piñata that had just been split open by a more than generous government genie, mortgages were dumped on the market, where both buyers and sellers made money instantly. The American taxpayer, however, did not fare too well.

With deregulation and favorable legislation allowing market players to simultaneously dump mortgages at a loss and a profit, a new earnings machine had been created in the 1980s—albeit at taxpayers' expense. The market was now ready to consume virtually anything related to mortgages. Debt obligations were especially attractive: not only were they backed by hard collateral (the actual homes) but, when the brokers got the federal government involved, they had the full faith and credit of the United States on their side. To be sure, securities from Fannie Mae and Freddie Mac weren't explicitly backed by the federal government. But this didn't matter. Serious market players had always understood that the federal government would not let these markets collapse if things went south—as we saw with the GSE bailout in 2008. During the 1980s, with federal legislation subsidizing mortgage market losses, the value of mortgages held by GSEs almost tripled from 1977 to 1987. With more players in the game, the value of GSE-held mortgages jumped from 7.2 percent to 20.6 percent of GDP (see Figure 11.1).

More Deregulatory Fun: The Fed's 1987 Decision and a Surge of Collateralized Debt Obligations

Properly primed, the mortgage market took off for GSEs after 1982. Even though the S&L crisis of the late 1980s and early 1990s had provided a sober moment, the government-led bailout of the S&Ls (and other institutions) served to reopen the industry's Happy Hour bar. It also reaffirmed the mind-set that, if the problem was big enough, the federal government would bail out an industry to keep the market's party going. Perhaps more important, by assuming that their market conditions "starting point" never changed—even when their actions altered market stability—market players proved that George Soros's assertions about markets were correct. Both market and government players could fail (spectacularly) to either monitor or recognize the impact that their collective actions had on markets and on society. The gradual entrance of commercial banks into the underwriting (of securities) business is an example of how this happened.

In 1987 the Federal Reserve Board voted 3–2 to allow banks to handle a limited amount of underwriting for financial instruments such as municipal bonds and mortgage-backed securities. By allowing banking institutions to take on the risk of distributing these types of securities, the Federal Reserve was effectively undermining one of the principal firewalls of the 1933 Glass-Steagall Act. Specifically, one of the Act's goals was to keep commercial banks away from selling (underwriting) securities or getting involved in investment banking. The thinking was that banks might get reckless and, because of their FDIC guarantee, force the federal government into a bailout situation. Before the collapse of 1929, commercial banks had done this by pushing faulty investment products, but with little concern for their clients' interests. Investors and bank depositors lost millions because, ultimately, the banks' "overriding interest was promoting stocks of interest and benefit to the banks."[16] The voting members of the Federal Reserve in 1987, however, had been convinced that this could not happen in the modern era.

Then Citicorp vice-chairman, Thomas Theobald, argued that corporate misbehavior couldn't occur like it did before 1933 because the economy had seen the emergence of (1) a "very effective" SEC, (2) knowledgeable investors, and (3) "very sophisticated" rating agencies. Three members were convinced. Two were not. One of the "nay" votes from the Federal Reserve Board came from Chairman Paul Volcker. He believed that if commercial banks were allowed to get back into underwriting securities (such as mortgage-backed securities), they would lower lending standards in an effort to gain lucrative fees from underwriting bonds, which would strengthen their securities market position and generate more profits.[17] Still, without veto power, Volcker's nay vote didn't matter. His argument lost the day.

Paul Volcker notwithstanding, the Federal Reserve Board members who voted to allow commercial banks to underwrite securities failed to recognize the weakness in Theobald's argument. The SEC could always be converted into a toothless tiger if its chair and staff were governed by ideology rather than by the public interest. Greed can get the best of investors in an increasingly deregulated environment. Ratings agencies could be co-opted and even consumed by market euphoria. A mentality of "running with the market herd" could quickly swamp market players who, as John Kenneth Galbraith pointed out in *A Short History of Financial Euphoria*, are filled with fast profits and a sense of their own genius because of what they see as their "novel" wealth-generating skills.[18] With the walls between S&Ls, commercial banks, and investment banks crumbling in the 1980s, US banks dove into lucrative mortgage and security instruments. Rather than learning from the intoxicating effects of previous periods of deregulation, speculation, and debt-driven growth, they threw caution to the wind. The commercial banking sector slowly came to depend on mortgage-backed assets as their primary earnings tool, which jumped from about 28 percent of bank earnings in 1985 to more than 60 percent in 2005.[19]

Box 11.3 From Glass-Steagall to Gramm-Leach-Bliley

The Glass-Steagall Act of 1933 created a legal wall between commercial banks (where most people keep their checking and savings accounts) and investment banks (where people go to find start-up capital for a business). The Glass-Steagall Act was deemed necessary after it was discovered that banks had used depositors' money to purchase investment products and then turned around and sold the same products to their customers before the 1929 market crash. Apart from establishing the FDIC, Glass-Steagall also prohibited commercial banks from using the deposits of customers to speculate or invest in financial markets. Glass-Steagall was repealed in 1999 by the Gramm-Leach-Bliley Act (GLB), also known as the Financial Services Modernization Act. Before the GLB, commercial banks were not allowed to participate in the securities market beyond government-issued securities. This changed with the GLB. Because the mortgage industry was already packaging and repackaging home loan contracts as mortgage-backed securities (another CDO form), the volume of trade in the securities and affiliated markets took off after the GLB. As traders exchanged securities, sought insurance for them, and chopped off principal and interest rates into earning "tranches" (sold to a specific class of market players), the securities market was flooded with investment cash at the beginning of the twentieth century. This cash was then funneled right back into markets, which helped keep a steady flow of credit available to consumers and other market players.

Source: Mark W. Olson, "Implementing the Gramm-Leach-Bliley Act: Two Years Later," The Federal Reserve Board, Remarks before the American Law Institute and the American Bar Association, Washington DC, February 8, 2002, available online.

As the federal government continued to follow the deregulation path in the 1980s and 1990s, market protections, bailouts, and subsidies continued apace, and the eventual elimination of the historic Glass-Steagall Act took place in 1999 (see Box 11.3). These deregulatory dynamics inspired confidence about the direction of the US economy in the 1980s, which helped funnel even more money (from abroad) into financial and other US markets. Domestically, deficit dollars helped provide a Keynesian stimulus to the economy but masked another emerging reality. The country was becoming increasingly dependent on debt and deregulation for its prosperity. As well, what started as a tax revolt in California with Proposition 13 in 1978 turned into a full-fledged "tax cut" party platform for Ronald Reagan.

But cutting taxes meant that state and local governments also had to begin cutting services, borrowing more to pay for them, or both. With stagnant wages (Chapters 2 and 10), both ordinary Americans and local governments were forced to borrow to meet expenses (see Chapter 10). Relatively cheap money fed the process. In addition to serving the interests of the financial sector, these debt-driven dynamics provided the products necessary for many of the CDO instruments that came to dominate markets at the beginning of the twenty-first century.

Although debt and favorable legislation helped prop up the economy during the Reagan and Bush I years, lax oversight and poor judgment in the mortgage industry inspired investors in the late 1990s and early 2000s. Specifically, driven by fees and bonuses that came with selling in volume, both the mortgage industry and its profits grew as brokers and agents offered loans with interest-only terms, no documentation provisions, higher loan-to-value ration, and greater use of "automated" appraisal evaluations, among other enticements. These poorly structured and poorly vetted products became part of the industry routine. These risky products were quickly sold off, only to become the gruel for securities that helped create the subprime mess of 2007–2008. Securitized debt instruments became so profitable that even the loans that banks were making to hedge-fund managers and others were quickly bundled together, securitized and sold off as collateralized loan obligations (CLOs).[20] Making things even more exciting and profitable was the emergence of the CDO^2—a CDO of a CDO—and other "synthetic" investment instruments.[21]

Still More Deregulation: The Financial Services Modernization Act, 1999

Accompanying the emergence of the CDO^2 and other "derivative" market instruments was the rise of credit default swaps (CDSs), which, although technically incomprehensible to many, are essentially insurance for those who have CDOs and other debt instruments. For a functional analogy of this arrangement, think about being invited to a party and sitting at the bar drinking the night away with your buddies, only to find that the host (the provider of insurance) never had the money to pay the bar bill. You (the CDO holder) thought you were covered for your good time. But everyone had been invited only to provide a room full of circulating guests and a friendly environment that the "host" needed to accomplish other goals. What you thought was a free stream of drinks must now be paid for in full. Worse, you've now got a hangover. This was the flip side of the CDS market. Many of those who sold CDS "insurance" (the host) for

CDO-like products (you and your buddies) created an environment (free drinks and "friends") that they benefited from but ultimately could not pay for at the end of the night (a failed CDO claim). Now imagine this happening with market players across the country. Now imagine this happening for years. This helps explain why, as we saw in Chapter 10, the size of the CDS insurance market grew from a "modest" $1 trillion in 2001 to an astounding $54.6 trillion by 2008.

Still, the CDS market was viewed by many observers as a positive development because of how the CDS market helped spread debt across the country, rather than concentrating it in the hands of a few firms. If we stick with our bar-party analogy, this is akin to the bar owner breathing a sigh of relief because he sees that there are more than enough party-goers to pay the tab—only to find out that the guests can't pay, or have left. In the real world, the owner would stop serving drinks. This didn't happen on Wall Street. In spite of the fact that many issuers of CDS products did not have the capacity to pay "insurance claims," CDS contracts continued to be traded with few to no impediments. Put another way, rather than looking into whether the party goers could pay or not, Wall Street allowed the financial drinking binge to continue. The bar owner, host, and party-goers, in this analogy, have many faces.

Not surprisingly, the wide availability of insurance for bundled mortgage contracts encouraged traders to seek even more CDO instruments to insure, regardless of their quality. Cheap money fed the cycle. As CDOs were stacked on top of one another and built into CDO² instruments, and then insured by CDSs, the complex world of security markets became increasingly "disconnected from reality."[22] The binge was on. Incredibly, rather than raise questions about the health of the underlying mortgage products or look into the solvency of debt-laden CDS market players, Alan Greenspan sang their praises. He marveled over how the CDO and CDS markets helped provide more liquidity while dispersing debt across the economy. He seemed almost oblivious to the fact that the money running through the American economy was a product of foreign funds (in part caused by dollar gluts), deregulation, and his cheap-money policies. In effect, Greenspan had decided to ignore the "credit-market Chernobyl" lurking around the corner.[23] By the beginning of the twenty-first century, Adam Smith's invisible hand had little to do with what was going on in America's financial markets.

When markets stumbled at the turn of the new century (tied to the tech-boom collapse and the events of September 11, 2001), the economy and the mortgage industry received another shot in the arm when Alan Greenspan lowered interest rates. As interest rates dropped, a flood of new borrowers entered the market who might not have been able to qualify for home loans before 9/11. But it wasn't just low interest rates pulling them into the market. Lax oversight and deregulation also had a hand in qualifying borrowers. Virtually every level of the mortgage industry got creative and greedy. The industry offered teaser rates, adjustable-rate mortgages (ARMs), No Doc loans (no documentation), and NINJA loans (No Income, No Job, No Assets required). These new loans seemed a perfect fit for new low- to middle-income borrowers, who were the target of the Community Reinvestment Act (CRA).

The CRA was part of the deal offered by Congress to get President Clinton to sign off on the Financial Services Modernization Act (1999), which removed restrictions for commercial banks seeking to enter the lucrative securities and insurance markets. These restrictions, as we saw above, were put in place in 1933 with the Glass-Steagall Act, which removed commercial banks from the risky business of investment banking. The name of the game—as Paul Volcker feared—was to create more mortgage contracts that could now be wrapped up into CDO contracts, which could then be converted into other "synthetic" instruments, which were then "insured" by yet another layer of "investors." If this proves difficult to follow, go back to our party analogy above and think about the host leaving and the bartender responding by putting up a sign that says "Open Bar."

In effect, the Financial Services Modernization Act had removed the practical barriers that existed between commercial banks, insurance companies, and commercial banks. Everyone was competing for everyone else's business with a reckless disregard for one's ability to pay. In many cases in the housing market it really didn't matter what the borrowers said they did or how much they earned as long as they had a pulse and signed on the dotted line. Driven by growing commissions and a seemingly endless stream of new fees and bonuses, real estate agents, lenders, underwriters, and other industry participants reveled in the euphoria that came with cheap money and deregulation.

The story of securitized CDO contracts offers lessons into what happens when poorly structured instruments, put together by poorly regulated market players, are piled on one another and then insured by poorly vetted "investors." When they are sold to other market players, who have no interest in keeping the product over the long term, standards and due diligence are compromised. Worse, keeping these market arrangements going proved tricky because they depended on a steady stream of money, driven by both good and bad debt. The investor who purchased any one of the long line of products had to come up with cash if loans couldn't be rolled over, or because investors get spooked and quit lending money.[24] Even market players who have money are affected by markets that are laced with bad debt.

All of this underscores what Hyman Minsky (Chapter 10) had to say about an economy that suddenly finds itself dependent on a continuous stream of bad debt for its growth: an economy that increasingly depends on investors who are not well hedged, and who depend on speculation and Ponzi-like conditions, can bring down everyone around them. In varying degrees, this is what happened to the auction-rate securities (ARS) market during the 2007–2008 meltdown.

Anatomy of a Meltdown (Ignored): From Auction Rate Securities to "Ghost Assets"

Although much has been written about mortgage products in 2008, it's important to understand there was much more to the 2008 market meltdown than Countrywide, Fannie Mae, and CDOs. One of the more interesting but ignored stories of 2008 was the collapse of the ARS market. The ARS market worked much like a regular bond market. Those who bought an ARS were lending money to corporations and municipal governments, which allowed governments to build bridges and schools, enabled corporations to make investments, and allowed investors to get higher than generic bank returns for their money. Properly managed and in the right environment, the ARS market created a win-win situation for all involved. Although the ARS instrument is a knockoff of the bond market, it had a different structure.

Generally government or corporate bonds are written as long-term securities, with relatively high interest rates (say, 12%). Companies and municipal governments don't like the idea of paying higher interest rates, but they are willing to pay (say, 8%) higher than bank interest rates under the right conditions. This worked well because, unlike long-term investors, many market players—who don't want to have their money wrapped up for long periods of time—still wanted higher than bank rate returns. The ARS market helped match these two needs. In the ARS market, investors didn't enter the market with the idea of holding onto a bond over a long time period: they entered with the idea of making a little more money than they would get from a bank, but also with the notion that they could sell their bond at one of the regularly scheduled auctions put on by the bond brokers. Auctions were put on and managed by some of the biggest financial players in the game (at the time): Citigroup, UBS, Morgan Stanley, Goldman Sachs, JP Morgan, Bear Stearns, Merrill Lynch, and others. The bond brokers got a great deal too because they received a percentage for every sale, and sales were held at regular intervals.

Problems emerged for the ARS market, however, when brokers began marketing the ARS as profitable investment instruments that could be accessed quickly. In some cases they made investors feel like they could dump the bond and access their money as if it were in a local bank. But there was no guarantee that investors could access their money as suggested. Everything hinged on what markets have always depended on since the days of medieval fairs, a steady flow of customers. That flow could be disrupted by the weakest link in the chain—in this case, poorly capitalized borrowers. If this happened, the ARS market would dry up. The brokers knew this too. But they camouflaged this fact in a number of ways. They had to. If they didn't, how else could they convince municipal governments and corporations to buy into their ARS market? Telling the primary issuers that they would always have investors' money in their bonds was a marketing pitch, not a statement of fact. But it worked.

When the credit crunch hit, the links that provided a steady stream of ARS investors dried up. Many investors who had put money into the ARS market, with the idea of opting out on a certain day or month, found that they had to wait to withdraw their money from the ARS market. They also found that the ARS market relied more on the very visible hand of the Federal Reserve and the policy deregulation gods of the preceding twenty years than it did on *laissez-faire* principles. Once doubt and panic set in, investors were no longer interested in securing a short-term tax break or squeezing a few more points of interest in the immediate term. They wanted their money.[25] What they ended up with were what one source called "ghost assets."[26] The ARS markets collapsed in 2008 under a barrage of lawsuits.

This is truly unfortunate because the concept behind the ARS market is sound. Unfortunately, the fundamentals behind the economy that helped sustain the ARS market were not. The integrity of the market had always been compromised by lax oversight, a steady stream of artificially cheap money, and increasingly risky debtors. The ARS market collapse offers a number of insights into larger market dynamics.

First, the ARS market collapse was not an aberration. It was a manifestation of larger developments that go back many years and can be traced to a culture of debt that Charles de Gaulle called attention to—but he was ignored. This culture of debt was compounded by the emergence of unstable markets in the 1970s that forced market players to look for creative ways to defend themselves, as we saw with the Enron example. With dollar gluts abroad (from budget and trade deficits), foreigners found it easier to reinvest in US markets, which made money accessible (and cheaper) in the 1980s. These dynamics encouraged market players to borrow and bet on a wide array of products in the short term throughout the 1980s and 1990s. Many bets worked out well and paid off. Others, as the S&L and LTCM events demonstrated, did not. In the meantime, many market players who speculated and bet on continuously rising asset prices convinced themselves that their short-term bets made them serious investors. They were deluding themselves. They were gambling. In many respects they are in the same class as the aforementioned Tulipomania and LTCM players. This became clear when the ARS market collapsed and the players sought justice from a market that many claimed had duped them.

There's little doubt that the growing and cumulative effort to extract wealth in the shortest term possible has become something of a parlor game. But, unlike the games played by elites during the Victorian era, what occurred at the beginning of the twenty-first century was a different type of parlor game. The game came to resemble a giant casino. As is the case in Las Vegas, the players wanted the tables open all of the time. But market players wanted a better deal than Vegas. They wanted to keep the bets safe and the earnings stable. Both Democratic and Republican politicians in Washington obliged the needs of the players through deregulation, favorable legislation, market protection, easy money, and bailouts. Then Congress went beyond the call of duty, as the 2008 market intervention and bailout makes clear.[27]

Conclusion

In the modern era it is clear that, thanks to deregulation, market players have been able to borrow aggressively and speculate their way to wealth. As investor George Soros points out, this is a far cry from the conservative, stable, and patient market activities that dominated the early postwar years.[28] What has also been created is a complex market system, in which poor decisions and failure have been followed by bailouts and other market supports. An unintended product of these developments has been a market subculture of unrealistic expectations and declining standards. One of the more interesting, if not bizarre, developments of 2008 was when Washington Mutual announced its decision to disregard market performance when evaluating executive bonuses.[29] They explained that a "challenging business environment and the need to evaluate performance across a wide range of factors" needed to be taken into consideration when considering bonuses. In effect, Washington Mutual essentially said mediocrity and poor performance were okay and would be rewarded. Washington Mutual declared bankruptcy September 2008.[30] This "don't blame me" mind-set (see Chapter 2), along with a string of bailouts and favorable legislation, has created a sense of market entitlement that Kevin Phillips has labeled "Wall Street socialism."[31] These dynamics constitute a genuine threat to the gifts that were gained from the American Revolution. How we got to this point is important to understand.

In his book *Wealth and Democracy in America* (2002), Kevin Phillips points out that the world of stable financial institutions created in the immediate postwar era was nudged aside by an increasingly deregulated world that was governed by less than transparent financial markets. Specifically, Phillips points to the rise of the securities market, which has had fewer restrictions (because of deregulation) and the capacity to take and recycle money through the system quickly. By the mid-1990s the securities market blew past both manufacturing and banking sectors in terms of wealth managed and market value.[32] In the process, the American economy was effectively "recapitalized" so that banks and the manufacturing sectors now played second fiddle to financial players in the securities market.[33] At this point some may be inclined to ask, what's the big deal? As long as money is available and circulated, everyone wins, right? But this misses the point.

Because of deregulation and lax oversight, market players have become increasingly loose with standards and with the amount of wealth that they are playing with. In effect they have created more financial instruments and are making bigger bets with borrowed money. Buying and selling debt and other novel financial contracts, however, is not a new phenomenon. At the global level, as far back as the early 1980s, Susan Strange saw a world in which "recondite financial inventions" created a speculative environment that contributed to what she called "casino capitalism."[34] Subsequent challenges and bailouts in the 1980s and the 1990s showed how dangerous these types of transactions could be.[35] However we label these dynamics in America or describe their impact, one thing is certain. They draw their life blood from a culture of debt, deregulation, lax oversight, and favorable legislation. Easy money, asset inflation and, ironically, a politically born-again faith in market "fundamentalism" all helped to square the circle. Although debt and asset inflation are hardly part of a recipe for sustained and healthy growth, they are integral for featherbedding speculative profits and creating market bubbles.[36]

These dynamics have occurred because the apostles of the born-again capitalist movement—primarily politicians, conservative media pundits, and industry executives—didn't quite understand the relationship between easy money, deregulation, favorable legislation, and debt. And they certainly didn't understand how market environments and structures would change as all four of these were sprinkled on society over a twenty-five-year period. They operated as though Vice President Dick Cheney's proclamation that "deficits don't matter"[37] was somehow an authoritative "Financial Sermon from the Mount." But buying into this mentality requires a rather thick set of ideological blinders, especially when easy money and debt have created record debt loads across all sectors of the

Figure 11.2 America's National Debt, in Trillions of Dollars, 1970–2008

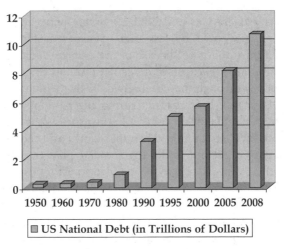

US National Debt (in Trillions of Dollars)

Source: US Department of Treasury, "Debt to the Penny and Who Holds It," available online; "Historical Debt Outstanding—Annual 1950–1999," available online; "Historical Debt Outstanding—Annual 2000–2007," available online.

American economy, for all to see. And, in spite of the fact that national debt as a percentage of GDP did not climb at the same rate as personal or corporate debt (for example), there is no escaping the conclusion that America's deficit spending (see Chapter 10), growing national debt (Figure 11.2) and poor regulatory performance at the beginning of the twenty-first century have the world's attention. This is important because, Dick Cheney's pronouncement notwithstanding, debt matters. Although foreigners hold about 26 percent of all US Treasury Securities today,[38] there will come a day when they stop buying America's debt or when they start to demand higher interest payments.

If national deficits and personal debt patterns continue apace and the circular flow of money dries up, the trading value of the dollar will collapse. This observation isn't simply a mechanical embrace of some arcane economic theory. The practice of creating more of anything because you can has a long history of catastrophe. The more debt and legislatively driven paper wealth that the American government creates, the sharper the collapse of both the dollar and the economy will be. Perhaps more important, the US stock market will take a devastating hit as firms are forced to liquidate assets, while US banks will lose accounts, value, or both. Bond markets in the United States will hardly fare better. When this time arrives, if it hasn't already, Charles de Gaulle's intuitive sense about the impact of a looming debt monster will be nothing compared to the financial Frankenstein that emerges from the debt-ridden towers that have held up and bailed out the American economy since the early 1980s. The spate of politically driven but debt-laden bailout proposals that were drawn up for markets at the end of 2008 could help make this scenario a reality.

Notes

1. John Charles Chasteen, *Born in Blood and Fire: A Concise History of Latin America* (New York: Norton, 2001).

2. Paul Starr, *Freedom's Power: The True Force of Liberalism* (New York: Basic Books, 2007).

3. Kevin Phillips, "Bubble and Bail," *The American Prospect,* May 2008, 29.

4. Starr, *Freedom's.*

5. Starr, *Freedom's,* 15–16.

6. Starr, *Freedom's.*

7. As Ronald Suskind points out, the Bush administration failed to do anything of substance about Enron because ideology and Republican donor threats had won the day. Ronald Suskind, "The Crisis Last Time," *New York Times,* September 25, 2008, available online.

8. Except where specifically referenced, this section is drawn primarily from Michael Lewis's *Liar's Poker* (New York: Penguin Books, 1990), 87–122, 136–139.

9. Lewis, *Liar's,* 100–101.

10. Lewis, *Liar's,* 101.

11. Lewis, *Liar's,* 100.

12. Amy Waldman, "Move over Charles Keating—Causes of the Savings and Loan Scandal," *Washington Monthly,* May 1995, available online.

13. Waldman, "Move."

14. Blog Commentary.

15. Lewis, *Liar's,* 103–104f.

16. Frontline, "The Long Demise of Glass-Steagall," Public Broadcasting Service, available online.

17. Frontline, "The Long."

18. John Kenneth Galbraith, *A Short History of Financial Euphoria* (New York: Viking, 1993), 12–17.

19. Paul Kasriel, "Regulatory Suasion—An Attempt at Deflating the Housing Bubble," Northern Trust Company Research Department, May 26, 2005, available online.

20. Morris, *The Trillion,* 60, 74.

21. Morris, *The Trillion,* 75.

22. Ari J. Officer and Lawrence H. Officer, "Let Risk-Taking Financial Institutions Fail," in Time.com, September 29, 2008, available online.

23. Morris, *The Trillion*, 121.

24. Morris, *The Trillion*, Chapter 4, 59–85.

25. The Associated Press, "UBS to Buy Back $20 Billion in Securities," *New York Times*, August 10, 2008. Blog Commentary.

26. Global Europe Anticipation Bulletin, "Global Systemic Crisis: Four Big Trends over the 2008–2013 Period," LEAP/Europe 2020, Public Announcement GEAB, no. 24, available online.

27. Lisa Lerer, "Fannie, Freddie Spent $200 Million To Buy Influence," Politico.com, July 16, 2008, available online; Mother Jones, "McCain's Fannie and Freddie Connections," *MojoBlog*, September 10, 2008; Jackie Calmes, "'08 Rivals Have Ties to Loan Giants," *New York Times*, September 9, 2008, available online.

28. George Soros, *The New Paradigm for Financial Markets: The Credit Crisis of 2008 and What It Means* (New York: Public Affairs, 2008), 105–113.

29. Stephen Taub, "Washington Mutual Moves to Insulate Bonuses from Loan Crisis," CFO.com, March 6, 2008, available online.

30. Jeff Feeley and Steven Church, "Washington Mutual Lists $8 Billion Debt in Bankruptcy," *Bloomberg.com*, September 27, 2008.

31. Phillips, "Bubble."

32. Kevin Phillips, *Wealth and Democracy: A Political History of the American Rich* (New York: Random House, 2002), 138–140.

33. Phillips, *Wealth*, 138–140.

34. Susan Strange, *Casino Capitalism* (Oxford, UK: Blackwell Publishers, 1983).

35. Paul Krugman, *The Return of Depression Economics* (New York: Norton, 1999).

36. John Kenneth Galbraith, *A Short History of Financial Euphoria* (New York: Viking, 1993); Eric Janszen, "The Next Bubble: Priming the Markets for Tomorrow's Big Crash." *Harper's Magazine*, February, 2008, available online.

37. Ronald Suskind, *The Price of Loyalty: George W. Bush, The White House, and the Education of Paul O'Neill* (New York: Simon & Schuster, 2004), 291.

38. U.S. Department of Treasury, "Major Foreign Holders of Treasury Securities," 2008, available online. Sovereign Wealth Funds may also be helpful here, but concerns over national security and nativism pose a problem to SWF as a potential source of capital.

CHAPTER 12

FROM DEREGULATION TO
THE MOTHER OF ALL BAILOUTS

In 1998 the FDIC issued a set of guidelines for member banks that managed transactions involving collateralized securities.[1] Concerned that deposit-taking institutions had not exercised sufficient risk management, the FDIC distributed a "Statements of Policy" (SOP) document at the beginning of 1998, making it clear that collateralized security transactions were on its radar screen. Although it set out to reacquaint institutions with basic due-diligence procedures, it also listed ways that private firms could defraud FDIC-backed institutions. The SOP guidelines said that private financial institutions weren't always playing fair with FDIC-backed institutions, especially when it came to complex financial instruments.

Included among the embarrassingly basic rules of caution covered were "know your counterparty," credit analysis, and credit-limit reviews. The guidelines were so simple that it was difficult to tell whether they were issued for seasoned FDIC-affiliated banking institutions or were really geared to the new finance guy at the local car dealership. Still, one thing stood out: in the wake of the 2008 market collapse, the 1998 SOP offered a crow's nest view of what went wrong. Pointing to the tactics of subsidiaries belonging to "financially stronger and better-known firms," the SOP warns that larger corporations "may not be legally obligated to stand behind the transactions of related companies," so the subsidiary may not be credit worthy. What is the FDIC's advice? Don't trust the other guy's "character" or "integrity" until you get "the stronger firm's" signature. That this needed to be said should have raised red flags back in 1998. Incredibly, the guidelines get even more basic.

We all know when we purchase a new car that we have to deal with the sales staff, and then with the finance and credit team, who also want to sell us stuff. There's a reason why the owners of car dealerships keep these two positions separate. Apparently these auto dealer concerns were

267

not always prevalent within the FDIC. Burned by too many conflict-of-interest transactions involving sales and finance pulling double duty, the FDIC found it necessary to remind banking institutions that credit evaluations for CDO-affiliated purchases, for example, should be done by "individuals who routinely make credit decisions" and not by those involved in sales. Incredibly, the SOP then advised institutions to be on the lookout for buyers who were already overextended.

Perhaps the greatest words of caution are saved for institutions that are inclined to believe that CDO instruments could be used as market collateral. The FDIC guidelines make it clear that because a bank has a CDO-affiliated instrument it doesn't mean that it's sitting on an asset for which the book value is equal to the market value.[2] The 1998 guidelines suggest, for example, that, if a $100 million CDO transaction has occurred, "experience has shown" that the underlying product or contract "will not serve as protection" if the subsidiary fails or if the firm does not have control over the security. Put more simply, the tone of the 1998 SOP guidelines tells us that market players and the federal government had an idea that the US financial system was sitting on a financial powder keg at least ten years before the 2008 market meltdown began.

The 1998 SOP document from the FDIC is important to our understanding of the 2007–2008 meltdown of the financial markets for several reasons. First, it illustrates that the FDIC understood—long before 2007–2008—that the collateralized securities market was wrought with real concerns over creditworthiness, transparency, and deception among financial institutions. Second, the SOP helps us understand that Wall Street's financial players were creating financial instruments that may have added assets and receipts to an institution's books but that did little to build real capital and sustainable wealth in the overall economy. Finally, because the number of liabilities and receipts claimed between financial institutions was allowed to grow with little concern for the demands that those liabilities placed on the supply of money, the gap between what Main Street did and what Wall Street took away almost doubled in a span of fourteen years. But rather than trigger change, patterns of deception, weak or nonexistent collateral, and asset inflation only led to more calls for more deregulation (to keep the bubble going), which, ultimately, set the stage for market collapse and market bailout.

The more that we dig into the 1998 SOP, the clearer it becomes that the concerns the FDIC had about collateralized securities were genuine. In the SOP we find a sense of anxiety over repricing issues, contract responsibilities, default obligations, interest and principal payment rights, and questions about how securities were "segregated." This can be attributed, in part, to complex financial instruments becoming so difficult to track and monitor that few market players understood how to value the instruments on the books, let alone establish who was legally liable for the various instruments that had been sliced off (or "segregated") and packaged into other instruments. As a result, claims on security contracts between financial institutions grew to such a degree that overlapping claims, ownership, and legal obligations were not always transparent, nor understood by market players. With debt, deregulation, and a financial culture of moral hazard leading the way, this proved to be disastrous.

Keeping Score: The Toxic Brew of "Free Money" and Debt

In the aftermath of the 2007–2008 market meltdown it became increasingly clear that greed and a lack of oversight not only undermined the integrity of the market but that many financial players and rating agencies were working together to "feed the enthusiasm" that attacked market integrity. This environment helped subprime mortgage foreclosures climb to around 9 percent from mid-2000 through mid-2002 and pushed default rates for high-yield corporate bonds to an average of 8 percent from 2000 through 2003.[3] One would think that these default rates might have sounded an alarm or put a damper on the securities market. Think again. It was at this time that Alan Greenspan's "free-money" policies began to kick into gear. Investors who found themselves in trouble simply borrowed their way out of a financial corner. This helped high-yield bond markets recover by 2006, and gave the impression that everything was sound.[4] Worse, it allowed market players to ignore both the anomaly of immediate history and their better judgment. Charles R. Morris, author of *The Trillion Dollar Meltdown*, writes:

> When markets are rising and money is free, it's easy to borrow your way out of a crunch.[5] But it is obviously irresponsible to treat a couple of years of unusual performance as the new norm. The ratings agencies doled out all those investment-grade ratings, in short, not because their models were hostage to recent history, but because they strenuously ignored it.[6]

Market players became so confident during the easy-money days of 2005 and 2006 (the boom years for securities) that they began creating and trading "some of the most egregiously irresponsible loans in history."[7] As trading in collateralized securities and derivatives swelled, partly as a result of poorly vetted loans, record receipts and growing claims on money between financial institutions climbed as well.[8] The dreams and transactions created on Wall Street, no matter how dubious, were only matched by what seemed like an endless supply of money in America (Figure 12.1).

For pundits, market players, and national politicians, there seemed to be little to worry about—because the GNP, consumption, and America's

Figure 12.1 U.S. Money Supply, 1964–2006 (Trillions of Dollars)

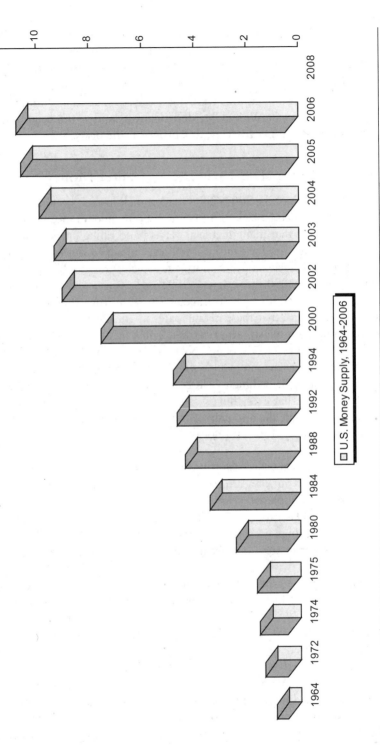

U.S. Money Supply, 1964-2006

standard of living all looked solid and appeared to serve everyone's interests. But there was trouble on the horizon. With easy money ruling the day, the financial scorecard between Main Street and Wall Street—which had a gap that lurched between 3.5 to 5 times between 1972 and 1994—embarked on a growing but increasingly divergent path after 1994.[9] Specifically, by 2006 the amount of money spent by Main Street ($1.367 trillion) was swamped by new debt and new claims on the money supply from Wall Street ($10.299 trillion), and reached a factor of 7.5 times (Figure 12.2).[10] This is significant because, as late as 1994, the Main Street vs. Wall Street claim to money had diverged by as little as a factor of 3.79.

Although we can point to the growing and hardening gaps between Main Street's purchasing power and the claims on money made by America's financial institutions, there was another set of factors at work. In addition to free money feeding asset inflation and debt, deregulation and lax oversight were working their way through the system. This—as the FDIC memo above suggested was happening in 1998—fed a market environment that focused on quick hits and wealth extraction. This would all work to undermine the integrity of markets (Chapters 1 and 2).

Keeping Score II: Easy Money And Wealth Extraction

Although the FDIC did not predict a market collapse, when it issued its 1998 SOP, the FDIC correctly pointed to the conditions that led to asset inflation and, ultimately, to disappearing assets in 2008: easy money, a lack of oversight, and less than transparent transactions in complex financial instruments. At the time, however, few seemed interested in tying increasingly complex financial instruments to debt, growth in the supply of money and inflated asset values. This shouldn't come as a surprise. Creating money and credit for commercial transactions and then tracking their impact on the value of money has always been a tricky affair. Knowing when to stop creating money and credit is still not an exact science. Regulators who ignore or sign off on complex instruments of shifting value, and dubious utility, only make the task more difficult. Then we have the problem of politicians who don't care to put a stop to market feasts that artificially inflate values because the frenzy serves their political interests. Ancient Rome's days of "Bread and Circus" have nothing over the American era of "Easy Money and Deregulation."

The problem is that fiat money and inflation have always ended up causing considerable pain and suffering for unwitting and innocent players down the road. We saw this in our discussion of Nicholas Copernicus and John Locke in Chapter 4. Both men were consumed with how currency debasement and inflation took a slice out of their lives, and they both chose to make their concerns over the issue public. What I noted in Chapter 4 bears repeating:

Figure 12.2 U.S. Money Supply: Main Street *vs.* Wall Street, 1964–2008 (Trillions of Dollars)

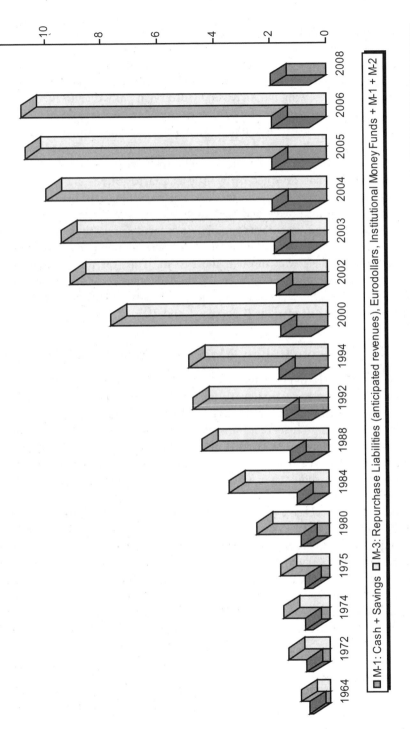

□ M-1: Cash + Savings □ M-3: Repurchase Liabilities (anticipated revenues), Eurodollars, Institutional Money Funds + M-1 + M-2

For Locke the stakes were so high—and the dangers of currency fraud and abuse so great—that he believed stable money was as important a "natural right" as any other of the natural rights that he called for in the social contract. He believed that, without this kind of protection, the economic interests of commoners and small merchants alike would be trampled on.

In spite of having history as our guide, what do we have today? A situation in which financial players have been allowed to borrow money and trade toxic financial instruments that created receipts and claims for money that often didn't exist—except in the formulas and models of America's largest financial institutions. How else can we explain the sudden percentage spike in the total money supply in the United States after 1994, without a parallel rise in the amount used by Main Street?

One person who saw what was happening to the money supply was Tim McMahon, editor of *Financial Trend Forecaster*. He watched the money supply climb in America through 2006. After looking for data that might explain the growth, specifically for the amounts being pushed around by Wall Street, he saw no viable justification and he predicted inflation. But this wasn't the real gem of McMahon's analysis. At the time, his real concerns were the motives behind the Bush administration's 2006 decision to quit tracking America's total money supply (Box 12.1).[11] McMahon concluded that, because it wasn't convenient to have such startling inflationary figures staring Americans in the face, the best thing was simply to stop publishing the figures in 2006.

Unfortunately, policymakers did nothing to slow the amount of trading done in credit, debt, and futures contracts (among others), which allowed demand for money to accelerate after 2006. These policy approaches rewarded market players and speculators who pursued wealth by focusing on the exchange of money, debt contracts, and rights over production.[12] In the process, market activities were redirected "from the efficient production of wealth to the extraction and concentration of wealth."[13] To paraphrase Joseph Schumpeter, the goal wasn't to build monopolies, but to play monopoly. This helps explain the growing income disparities in America that were noted in Chapter 10.

We shouldn't be surprised by this new focus on wealth extraction and wealth concentration. As noted in Chapters 4 and 10, since the beginning of the 1970s, financial innovations in the United States have accelerated, as mutual funds, hedge funds, private pensions, insurance companies, transnational corporations, wealthy individuals, and other financial actors looked for insurance—and sought profits—through novel financial instruments (as the Enron case showed). With lax controls internationally (expected to change with Basel II agreements), relatively easy money, and

---

Box 12.1 Explaining the Money Supply and How Institutions Help Create It

Most Americans have little beyond what's in their checking accounts or wallets when it comes to their purchasing power. Economists have a name for this supply of money, M-1. Those who are better off also have access to M-1, but they also have access to personal time deposits under $100,000 (the FDIC limit until 2008), relatively large personal savings, and what they have stuffed away in mutual funds. Economists call this money category M-2. Finally, there are the real big players. They count M-1 and M-2 as part of their money base as well, but they can also look to what they have in Eurodollar accounts, institutional money funds, and collateralized instruments (or repurchase liabilities) that they trade among one another. Economists call this M-3. As more and more complex financial instruments were produced, the number of "repurchase agreements" logged into the books of the world's financial institutions grew. This means that M-3 grew as well. As financial institutions continued to trade security instruments, every repurchase agreement translated into more receipts and assets on the books. The institutions were literally creating money off each security traded. Soon the amount of money that Americans had in their wallets and checking accounts was left in the dust by the amount of new money that had been created by financial institutions that were trading security obligations among one another. Since the early 1960s through 1994 the total amount of receipts (or M-3) logged into the books of large financial institutions did not grow much beyond 2.5 to 4 times the total amount of money used by ordinary citizens using checks or cash on hand to complete a transaction (M-1). So, for example, while ordinary Americans wrote a check or used cash in a way that pushed $1.150 trillion (of M-1) around the nation's economy in 1994, financial institutions logged about $4.369 trillion in (M-3) transactions (3.79 times M-1). This disparity more than doubled after 1994, when we began to see a real disconnect between what Main Street citizens had in their wallets and what Wall Street players claimed on their books.

---

favorable legislation, the worst elements of a financial bubble economy were nurtured. In addition to these developments, a key contributing factor to the market meltdown of 2007–2008 was the financial systems increasing dependence on deregulation.

Keeping Score III: Drinking The Deregulation Kool-Aid

Apart from cheap money and the ability to extract wealth from the system, market players who understood what was happening, and said nothing, had a couple of aces up their sleeves to keep their game going. They came in the form of favorable agency rulings and more deregulation. Savvy industry players always understood that they could count on timely deregulation when they ran into market cul de sacs. In 2004, for example, the SEC met to consider a request from the five largest investment banks in America at the time: Bear Stearns, Lehman Brothers, Merrill Lynch, Goldman Sachs, and Morgan Stanley.[14]

Leader of the industry pack was Goldman Sachs' then-CEO Hank Paulson. The group wanted an exemption to industry debt limits and asked for approval to more than double the amount of debt that they could keep on the books. Until 2004 the industry's "net capital rule" had confined brokerage firms to a maximum debt to equity ratio of 12 to 1. After the exemption was granted in 2004, debt to equity ratios jumped to around 33 to 1 for Bear Stearns and 40 to 1 for Merrill Lynch.[15] This means that, for every dollar-based asset Bear Stearns and Merrill Lynch had, they had $33 and $40 of debt.[16] The 2004 decision by the SEC allowed the financial sector to take money that had been put aside for a rainy day (its reserves) so that it could continue betting that complex financial instruments—such as mortgage-backed securities and derivatives—would pay off.

At the same time that Henry Paulson and his industry colleagues were able to convince the SEC to allow their industry to increase its debt to equity ratios, the SEC caved in to another industry request: they agreed to allow SEC regulators to use the computers of the companies that they were inspecting. In essence, the SEC was not only outsourcing its job (in part because it didn't have the staff) but it was allowing the industry to police itself.[17] As a result, when regulators did uncover risky debt loads and other "signs of trouble," the findings "were all but ignored."[18]

When the wheels of the market started to fall off, in 2007 and early 2008, more than $600–800 billion in emergency loans and credits was made available by the Federal Reserve and other central banks from around the world.[19] This amount proved to be little more than a speed bump on the road to market collapse. The US Congress was forced to make an additional $810 billion available to the market in October 2008. While market players wanted to call this bailout a "market rescue" these dynamics already had a name, and some good analysis too: "moral hazard" induced by "disaster myopia."

Keeping Score IV: Looking for Answers in a World of "Moral Hazard"

One of the dirty little secrets of the financial sector has been an underlying—and unspoken—assumption that the government would bail out their industry if things got out of hand. This mind-set encourages executives to discount long-term future risks, and reward short-term "performance." In 1986 Benjamin J. Cohen described how this process contributed to "disaster myopia"—a distorted decision-making culture that undermines long-term planning by the financial sector.[20] Later the mind-set surrounding disaster myopia would morph into the "Greenspan Put": "No matter what goes wrong, the Fed will rescue you by creating enough cheap money to buy you out of your troubles."[21] Today the frame of mind that ultimately leads industry to socialize the losses while privatizing the profits is simply called "moral hazard." A broader if not better term for this safety net mentality might be "corporate welfare."

Regardless of how we describe or dress up these dynamics, bailouts and government-orchestrated rescue programs from the 1980s and 1990s made it clear that, if things get bad enough, the state will step in to help the financial sector. This is hardly the hallmark of the brand of rugged capitalist individualism that market fundamentalists have promoted since the early 1980s. Many holders of CDOs, CDSs, and ARS (among others)—who often liked to portray themselves as risk takers and entrepreneurial investors—are at the center of this "moral hazard" universe. After 2008 many sought bailouts because they believed they were cheated by others. In reality, apart from their poor judgment, what they failed to do was take into consideration one simple fact: the market that they bought into was only as good as the rules they played by and the underlying products that they purchased. Because of their short-term horizons they failed to understand that the favorable legislation that helped make their new "investments" possible could also be swamped by a constantly moving financial field that pushed for more deregulation and less oversight. The poetry of disaster myopia is really quite simple, and can be understood by using the following analogy.

Imagine that you buy or rent a car but find that the agent, dealer, or manufacturer failed to do quality checks. Their decisions were tied to short-term considerations, like immediate costs. Because they failed to do quality control you may well find yourself sitting on the side of the road. If everyone else in the industry is doing the same thing, you will have company. To be sure, cars and people will still be moving about, but people will always be worried about whether their car will break down. People will eventually be forced to seek other modes of transportation, while traffic will slow because of the stalled cars on the roads. The towing industry (initially) will find its resources taxed by constantly coming to the rescue of our bewildered auto enthusiasts. This, in essence, explains the market collapse in 2007–2008. In this example, however, the state doesn't pay for the tow trucks, or to get the cars repaired. If the state did pay for the tow trucks and repairs—and the auto industry knew it would—we would then have moral hazard.

Right before the 2007–2008 market collapse, the holders of complex financial instruments were initially unconcerned about the quality of their products. They assumed that the legal and financial train had been transparent and thorough. They trusted that the "due diligence" had been done by the financial players involved, and that the market analysts had been placated. That's the way that free markets are supposed to work, right? And besides, trusted brokers wouldn't sell shoddy products—would they? Forgotten is the fact that due diligence is not always mandatory or useful when the goal is simply to produce and sell a product. People will often do what's in their short-term economic interests, and even try to cheat one another. The FDIC's SOP example at the opening of this chapter makes this clear (as do chapters 1 and 2).

A byproduct of the financial sector's myopic and carefree approach to the market is the buck-passing attitude that escorts the industry's frame of mind. For example, knowing that mortgage contracts—and the prospect of having to perform customer service—are virtually guaranteed to pass out of their hands soon after the transaction is completed, did much to feed a business environment that thrived on quick fees and bonuses. If things did go wrong the market players involved did not have to worry. Mortgage brokers and others in their financial train were able to pass the buck, with plausible deniability as their fallback. They could claim, with a degree of truth, that "Borrowers overextended themselves and should have known better." Others in the financial train could always blame "unforeseen market forces" or scapegoat the always dependable "excessive government regulations" meme. Those so inclined find enough evidence to scapegoat government agencies lending to African Americans and Latinos who "never should have qualified"—with all its racial overtones.[22] Then we have those who point at deregulated private market players who created a less than transparent "shadow banking system"[23] that encouraged even more lending. With disaster myopia and moral hazard as their backdrop, it really should come as no surprise that the "Don't Blame Me" culture I discussed in Chapter 2 became such an integral part of America's capitalist culture by 2008.

"... Ashes, Ashes, We All Fall Down"

Apart from the myopic and carefree approach in the financial sector during the 1980s and 1990s, few paid any attention to how lightly regulated financial instruments (which transferred risk and acted as liquidity pumps) could create a "wall of money" and have an impact on markets.[24] Worse, policymakers and analysts wrongly believed that the "tsunami of dollars" that had landed in America was a sign that a new era of free markets had arrived, one which would help organize the global and American economies.[25] Many no longer believed that the stodgy institutions and rules of a crumbling Bretton

Woods system were necessary. A continuous flow of money from abroad— from individual investors and sovereign wealth funds—allowed policymakers to believe in the magic of free markets once again. Money flooding into America effectively "let policymakers off the hook" because, according to the emerging worldview, market forces were now "shaping events toward a high-efficiency outcome."[26] If Ronald Reagan started the party, George W. Bush and his privatization and deregulation initiatives would ensure it had a continuous merry-go-round.

While politicians and pundits, like Thomas L. Friedman, started passing around the "deregulation Kool-Aid" that this wall of money inspired at the beginning of the the twenty-first century,[27] something important had been ignored. Forgotten were the reasons why Congress had put up regulatory walls around markets and industry in the first place. In the housing market, the goal was to prevent investors and speculators from entering under the guise of providing liquidity and then creating havoc by lending and speculating their way through the market. The idea for this position was very simple. Home ownership lies at the heart of the American Dream. That dream should not be tossed to the winds of speculation and market bubbles—especially since the middle-class homeowner is the heart and soul of American democracy. But none of this mattered at the beginning of the twenty-first century. In an era of cheap money and deregulation, market players got what they wanted, and the financial sector threw a party.

But once the cheap money dried up and the subprime mess deepened, the partygoers had to face a party without a fresh punch bowl. As things began to unravel, the Federal Reserve (and other central banks from around the world) stepped in to provide fresh cash in 2007 and 2008. The Federal Reserve's public rationale for intervention was that it wanted banks to inject a new stream of money into the economy. But, like addicted junkies, the financial institutions didn't want to share. The financial institutions, who were offered more than generous terms, no longer wanted to lend—especially to each other. In late 2007 the *Wall Street Journal* explained:

> It is now clear that a lack of cheap funding is only one reason banks and investors are so reluctant to lend. Financial institutions remain suspicious of each other after multiple rounds of announcements of mortgage-linked losses, and are anticipating more. They also are eager to hold onto cash to shore up their troubled balance sheets.[28]

Worried about their own exposure to crumbling markets, banks really wanted a bailout in order to dump their now-toxic instruments on others (the US taxpayer) while keeping what money they had (or had access to) in reserve for themselves. When banks did offer to lend money, which had been made available to them by the Federal Reserve, several banks did so on the condition that the borrowers use the loans to purchase the increasingly toxic debt obligations of the lending banks.[29] If we go back to the prior analogy of our cars breaking down on the side of the road, this is akin to having the federal government agreeing to pay for a tow truck. Only, when the tow truck driver arrives, he offers to tow your car on the condition that you get out and push.

Strangely, in what can only be called an ironic twist of fate, not even the king of mortgage securities escaped the financial firestorm of defaults on the securitized CDOs that he helped create. By May 2008 the one-time king of the risk management community, Lewis Ranieri, found that he could not stave off the collapse of the financial institution that he founded. This is interesting because Ranieri had warned market players that most of the consumers who bought the security instruments that he helped make popular didn't know what they were buying. Nor did they understand how these instruments could have an impact on markets. Apparently neither did Ranieri. He was swamped by debt by the end of May 2008: the share price of his bank had fallen from $20 a share to 96 cents.[30]

The Mother of All Bailouts: Some Thoughts

After the market collapsed in September 2008, it was clear that the "Mother of All Bailouts" was required to help rebuild confidence in American and global markets. Four bailout proposals were floated around the halls of Congress. The initial Bush-Paulson proposal (three pages) asked for a blank check and effectively said, "Trust us." Then there was the "market" model, which demanded government insurance (or security) for markets and said, rather ironically, "Let the market fix the problem."[31] The House of Representatives version (109 pages) promised bailout money for the financial industry and said, "This should work, for now." Ultimately, the US Congress adopted a larger Senate version (431 pages), which was riddled with congressional pork and said, "Happy Birthday, Wall Street." What ties all of these versions together is one common theme: there was absolutely no confidence in the idea that the market could fix the financial market mess on its own. Even the market model proposal acknowledged this. This proposal—which promised "to have Wall Street fund the recovery, not taxpayers"[32]—depended on government insurance, more deregulation, and more government tax credits to industry. This is hardly a model of *laissez-faire*. But there was something else that held these proposals together—the primary assumptions behind the plans.

Economist Joseph E. Stiglitz looked at the House of Representatives' plan and saw three flaws that could easily be applied to all three proposals.[33] First, all of the plans relied on a "trickle down" mentality. Simply put, they were organized around the assumption that, if we throw enough money at the problem, it will eventually trickle down to Main Street. Second, all of the plans viewed the collapse of markets as a "crisis of confidence"—when deregulation, bad loans, and the creation of even worse toxic financial instruments were to blame. The problems were structural and real, not the product of an unreasonable imagination. Finally, Stiglitz pointed to the "contradictory dynamics already in play," which none of the proposals addressed with any seriousness. He was looking at local and state governments and at American households, which became financially strapped as they sustained their activities through debt. As I have pointed out in this work, America's state and local governments, its households, and its businesses have seen their combined debt loads climb from a ratio of 127.7 percent of GDP in 1977 to 200.7 percent of GDP in 1997, to an incredible 302.3 percent by 2007 (see Figure 10.4 in Chapter 10). Still, Congress pushed through an ill-conceived and pork-laden piece of legislation because they bought into Federal Reserve Chairman Ben Bernanke's threat that "jobs will be lost, the unemployment rate will rise, more houses will be foreclosed upon, GDP will contract . . . the economy will just not be able to recover."[34]

Not surprisingly we ended up with a bailout proposal that amounted to little more than Congress rearranging deck chairs on the Titanic, with President Bush playing the role of Titanic Captain Edward John Smith. This was made evident by the fact that the bailout said little to nothing about the useless and redundant financial instruments that were largely "disconnected from reality."[35] Only a handful of congressional representatives demanded a discussion of the economic culture and the deregulatory mind-set that had brought the financial crisis upon America. Further debate would have allowed America to see how debt, deregulation, and wealth extraction had become the economic pillars of the American economy for the better part of thirty years. As well, little was said about working with homeowners who were upside down on their home loans because of collapsing market prices, or about the millions of homeowners facing adjustments on their mortgage loans. Fixing these loans would have gone a long way in shoring up the housing market. But it would have also meant having a discussion on what to do with the bundled loans that would have to be written off, or discounted. In this case, the needs of Wall Street clearly trumped those of Main Street. Nothing could demonstrate this more clearly than the fact that after committing more than a trillion taxpayer dollars to America's financial sector, Congress stalled and made stern demands—while wagging its finger—after Detroit's automakers asked for a $34 billion rescue package. If the American Congress had had a sincere discussion on the challenges facing America (as opposed to simply passing bailout legislation), it would have become clearer that credit and derivative instruments had gotten out of hand because of deregulation.

Also ignored was any real discussion of the numerous bailouts and market interventions during the 1980s and 1990s, as previously noted. This moment of collective ignorance was made possible because most Americans, who don't normally follow economic issues beyond their household bills, didn't understand the problem. How could they be expected to understand the issues behind the 2007–2008 bailout when Congress and the president had failed to educate America about what was happening? A simple statement repeated over and over would have initiated this education process, and it could have started with something like this: "Wall Street was betting on things they never should have, and were using borrowed money to do so . . . then they tried to insure their bets with money they didn't have." Unfortunately, even the 2008 presidential candidates—in the heat of battle over the White House—chose not to focus on the bailout issues for electoral reasons. This helps explain why the bailout proposal that passed effectively rewarded the very market players who had turned the American economy into a multitiered debt-infested casino. Specific provisions of the 2008 bailout bill offer ample evidence of this.

Specifically, in Section 132 of the 2008 bailout provision, the Treasury Secretary is given the authority to revalue or fix the price of assets whose value had collapsed.

Gaming the System (Again): More Personal Thoughts

When credit started drying up in 2007, market players in the United States and from around the world didn't want to step forward to keep the game going—in spite of the fact that the federal government had provided US financial institutions with hundreds of billions of dollars in emergency credits and loans in 2007 and in the early part of 2008.[36] This credit problem was compounded by the fact that market players from around the world did not want to touch the now toxic market instruments that were coming out of the United States.[37] With so many market players staying or running away from America's financial markets, the Federal Reserve and the Secretary of the US Treasury Department entered the scene. Ben Bernanke and Henry Paulson argued that, in order to maintain price stability and stave off a market depression, they needed the authority to adjust the price of products that had hit bottom. What they were really asking for was the authority to suspend "mark-to-market" practices, which forced companies to tell the world what their goods were worth at the end of the business day. Section 132 of the 2008 bailout (the Troubled Assets Relief Program, or TARP) gave them the authority to suspend the mark-to-market accounting method.

To help suspend mark-to-market valuations, at the height of the bailout discussions, former Speaker of the House of Representatives Newt Gingrich put forward a proposal in *Forbes* magazine calling for changing the accounting rules so that the Treasury Secretary could revalue financial instruments that had collapsed.[38] According to Gingrich,

> Because existing rules requiring mark-to-market accounting are causing such turmoil on Wall Street, mark-to-market accounting should be suspended immediately so as to relieve the stress on banks and corporations. In the interim, we can use the economic value approach based on a discounted cash flow analysis of anticipated-income streams, as we did for decades before the new mark-to-market began to take hold. We can take the time to evaluate mark-to-market all over again. Perhaps a three-year rolling average to determine mark-to-market prices would be a workable permanent system . . . It is not widely understood that the adoption of mark-to-market accounting rules is a major factor in the liquidity crisis which is leading companies to go bankrupt. But it is destructive to have artificial accounting rules ruin companies that would have otherwise survived under previous rules.[39]

Here it's clear that Newt Gingrich is setting a storyline suggesting that the market meltdown was the result of faulty regulations, not underlying structural problems. He's effectively saying "don't look at the collapsed prices; think about what you could get for the product if the markets were fine." Gingrich had many allies on his side. To fix the problem, Gingrich called upon Congress to allow for another set of accounting standards that would permit the Treasury Secretary to revalue financial instruments along a three-year average. This would make it so that the toxic financial instruments and the financial institutions holding them would not have to suffer the financial consequences of "impaired" values. Ultimately what Paulson, Bernanke, and Gingrich were asking for was the authority to ignore market prices, all in the name of "price stability" (Box 12.2).

Box 12.2 Mark-to-Market Logic in Your World

If you're having trouble understanding how Newt Gingrich's proposal to do away with "mark-to-market" accounting would work in the real world, let's try this. Assume that you own a home with an average value of $500,000 over the past three years. At the end of 2008 the home is worth $325,000. According to Newt Gingrich's argument, you should be able to value your home according to its three-year average, even though you can only get $325,000 for it today. Think about the benefits that this accounting trick could bring you. Can you imagine going to your bank and saying, "How about an equity loan? My house is worth $325,000 on the market, but the average value has been $500,000. So give me $100,000 even though I owe $400,000." Or can you imagine turning over your $325,000 house to the bank and telling them, "It's worth $500,000, so pay me the difference"? Better yet . . . well, you get the picture. You can imagine how an accounting arrangement like this would be beneficial for you, especially in a collapsed housing market. But Newt Gingrich wasn't talking about your situation or your home. He was talking about revaluing the toxic market instruments that financial institutions held.

Also ignored by Gingrich and his supporters were very real problems associated with debt, poor oversight, greed, and simple stupidity. Worse, there seemed to be little appreciation for the role that present "mark-to-market" accounting had played in exposing the conditions that led to the meltdown of financial markets. As one market observer put it,

> The truth that needs to be front-page news [is] that if there wasn't Fair-Value, mark-to-market accounting we would never have seen this crisis coming. Doing away with mark-to-market accounting does not change the value of problem securities. Period. Doing away with mark-to-market will only bury the bodies under the rubble. The stench will eventually suffocate us all . . . to death.[40]

In spite of the fact that suspending the "mark-to-market" accounting method would do nothing to advance free market principles, Gingrich and his congressional supporters had enough clout in Congress to get their way. In essence by getting Section 132 into the bailout bill they created the tools for "deregulating" market-price forces out of the market. Those who had foolishly traded and held toxic market instruments could gain billions in the process—all at the expense of the American taxpayer. Making this episode more incredible is that Congress ignored the experts, with many of the nation's chief financial officers speaking out against the ideas that Newt Gingrich put forward. They not only thought that a few small adjustments were more responsible but they were also concerned that changing accounting standards would ratchet prices upward. They feared that this would force the federal government—and the American taxpayer—to pay more than was necessary for toxic garbage.[41]

Conclusion

In this review of the trends that led to market euphoria and market collapse at the beginning of the twenty-first century, I have left much out. I make no apologies. To do otherwise would have made this work more technically challenging and much longer. The goal of this chapter is to help the reader conceptualize and understand what has been happening in society and the economy over the past fifty years. I have sought to present a reasonable overview of how we have arrived at the point that we are at today: where debt, market collapse, "Depression-era actions," and market bailouts dominate national discussion. What should be clear—if I have gotten things right—is that the conditions that set the tone for economic growth, economic well-being, profit levels, and market euphoria are tied to the policies that are adopted and pursued by the state. But this is not a startling revelation.

In a paper delivered before the Greater Omaha Chamber of Commerce, Federal Reserve Chairman Paul S. Bernanke made it clear that the policies that states make in creating opportunities and providing social insurance—issues that are tied to ethics and values—are as important to developing the talents and skills of ordinary Americans as any other factor in America.[42] Put another way, both opportunity and wealth distribution in America depend on the state getting policies right. This is an important revelation, because it also acknowledges that states can get things wrong, as we have seen when the state accommodated the needs of the financial sector with deregulation and easy-money programs. Simply put, when the state—whether it is a liberal republic or a socialist state—overdoes it, things can go horribly wrong. Echoing the tone that I have tried to set throughout this work, Ben S. Bernanke's Omaha presentation suggests that he understands that society creates the conditions under which wealth is created and that state policies are instrumental in getting things right.[43]

But what do we have today? A mind-set carved out by aggressive conservative politicians and less-than-informed media pundits who push the misguided notion that markets operate best when the government takes a step back and allows market players to regulate themselves or write their own legislation. What happened in the real estate market, the CDO market, and with securitized lending (among other sectors) demonstrates this. These stories help explain the financial challenges that America and the world confront at the beginning of the twenty-first century. Blind faith in market fundamentalism has given the world a debt-laden mess on a scale that is still to be determined. This shouldn't be a surprise to anyone (but I'm sure it is).

If we take this a step further, we need to recognize that notions of a harmony of market interests that create fluid "invisible hands" is backed neither by history nor by contemporary reality. As I pointed out in chapters 1 and 2, Adam Smith, if we are to get our history right, did not argue for removing the state from the market. He understood how industry could manipulate the state to do its bidding. Like all good liberal thinkers of his day—and being the philosopher that he was—Smith feared what would happen if industry were allowed to violate the laws of justice or the order of nature and reason. The job of commerce and industry, according to Adam Smith, was to serve the interests of both the state and the consumer.[44] On this, Duncan K. Foley tells us that

> Smith's vision of *laissez-faire* is not a one-sided encouragement of private enterprise and the market to the neglect of political and government institutions, but a balanced understanding of the interplay between market and state institutions in allowing the virtuous circle of economic development to proceed.[45]

On this, Foley makes it clear that it would be wonderful if "the ruthless pursuit of self-interest, which can lead people to do bad things to other people" did not occur.[46] But people do bad things to another. We need to recognize that—as the Framers told us in *The Federalist Papers*—the human condition is not dominated by angelic spirits. We might wish for it to be otherwise, but this isn't the case. In the real world Bambi's mother dies. Love often stinks and doesn't really conquer much. Good and innocent people end up in prison. And crime often pays (especially "white-collar" crime). To believe that it could be any other way in a market arena driven by profit and greed suggests a level of naïve utopianism, which should be embarrassing for people who like to claim a ruthless sense of individualism in markets. Locking families into perennial credit card debt (Chapter 2) or creating toxic goods and dumping them on others simply because "it's legal" (Chapter 11) doesn't contribute to the market society that Adam Smith spoke about.

To be sure, we would all like it if the pursuit of profit in capitalist societies produced a harmony of interests. In spite of the doubts that I have laid out here, I would like this to be so. As Foley points out, "how much simpler the history of capitalism would have turned out to be" if this were the case.[47] But it is not the case. And herein lies the problem. Do we continue trying to force Adam Smith's square peg into a round hole, when bailouts, favorable legislation, subsidies, government loans, and other market supports are regularly made available to the nation's biggest industries when they get into trouble? Or do we recognize, as John Maynard Keynes clearly did, that our capitalist system consists of many holes, made up of different shapes and sizes? If we see the world as John Maynard Keynes did, instead of embracing the utopian views of those who claim to be Adam Smith's disciples, we would do two things.

First, we would quit looking at the writings of Adam Smith and John Maynard Keynes as if they are contrasting poles in our intellectual universe. Why are regulation and state intervention cursed when Adam Smith argued that state intervention could help create balance in society by advancing the laws of justice? Adam Smith was quite clear that banking systems on their own might encourage the multiplication of credit but that they could also trigger a chain of events leading to crises. He even cautioned against overtrading "bills of exchange," by having banks follow a strict policy of lending only in "real bills"—or bills of exchange backed by actual goods sold, and in transit to their purchasers.[48] Although Smith's rationale might be a bit extreme for some of his disciples today, there's little doubt that Smith is advocating a policy position that, if pursued, would enhance the integrity of the market on many levels.

Second, embracing the writings of both John Maynard Keynes and Adam Smith as intellectual contributors to a larger project would make it much easier to see the human condition as the Founding Fathers saw it: full of fallen "angels" who need to be watched and checked in virtually every social setting. This would take us away from naïve and utopian notions of markets that compel politicians and pundits to embellish the virtuous nature of merchants in the pursuit of profit. This would also allow citizens to see the contributions that America's liberal republic has made in their lives. They could see that there are no education fairies, no just wage fairies, no infrastructure fairies, and no security fairies. The roots of markets and wealth depend on an active and vigilant state. Freedom and the laws of justice are expensive and require maintenance. Understanding this simple point would help dispense with discredited policy positions and wishful thinking about the human spirit, which speak more to chimera and fantasy. Opportunities don't magically appear. Like wealth, they are created when the state gets markets right.

Finally, as noted earlier, nothing that I've presented here is new. As we saw in the introductory chapters, favorable legislation, a lack of transparency, con artists, and misguided incentive schemes are old hat. The "brilliant" financial schemes and the new instruments that seem to be hailed by successive generations as novel developments— stripped of their modern sheen and the enormous government-escorted profits that they generate— aren't really much more advanced than what the alchemists of the sixteenth century and John Law in the eighteenth century attempted to create. Subprime CDOs bought on credit are little more than Tulipomania run amok. The desire to create money and wealth out of thin air (through cheap money, deregulated markets, no oversight) is conceptually on par with diluting the silver content of coins and issuing bills beyond actual inventories. The tendency to cheat one another or to hide behind the notion that "it was legal" does not disappear simply because we want to believe that people are honorable in a commercial setting. We have to come to terms with the fact that the advances in the human condition over the past two hundred years are the product of collective vigilance, not individual greed and unbridled competition. The myth of the free market needs to end.

Notes

1. The FDIC information for this section is drawn from the February 20, 1998 *Federal Register*, "FFIEC Supervisory Policy— Repurchase Agreements of Depository Institutions with Securities Dealers and Others," *FDIC Law, Regulations, and Related Acts,* 5000-FDIC Statements of Policy, 5265–5271, available online.

2. There are many reasons for this. For example, although mark-to-market accounting was developed to bring book value (or market value) to the price of assets, the balance sheets of banks are interest-rate sensitive. As interest rates change, so do asset values (often faster than liabilities) as a result of longer maturities. To manage bank balance sheets, bankers are expected to manage assets, liabilities, or both at the same time. If the market asset value drops, the equity drops as well.

3. Charles R. Morris, *The Trillion Dollar Meltdown: Easy Money, High Rollers, and the Great Credit Crash* (New York: Public Affairs, 2008), 78–79.

4. Morris, *The Trillion*, 78.

5. One of my colleagues, Ken Shakoori, pointed out that this would not be true if basic credit standards were applied to every loan. But this wasn't always the case. Forecasts of future economic activity were rosy and viewed as never-ending.

6. Morris, *The Trillion*, 78.

7. Morris, *The Trillion*, 78.

8. I want to thank my colleague Ken Shakoori for pointing out that collateralization was not the driving force behind record receipts and growing claims between institutions. Poor lending practices were.

9. See Blog Commentary.

10. On this, see Tim McMahon, "Goodbye M–3—What Is the Government Hiding?" Inflation Data.com, March 16, 2006, available online. See Blog Commentary.

11. McMahon, "Goodbye."

12. On this, see Peter F. Drucker, "The Changed World Economy," *Foreign Affairs*, 64, no. 4 (Spring 1986): 768–791. See Blog Commentary.

13. David C. Korten, *When Corporations Rule the World* (West Hartford, CT: Kumarian Press, 1996), 186.

14. Stephen Labaton, "Agency's '04 Rule Let Banks Pile up New Debt," *New York Times*, October 3, 2008, available online.

15. Julie Satow, "Ex–SEC Official Blames Agency for Blow–Up of Brokers–Dealers," *New York Sun*, September 18, 2008, available online; Labaton, "Agency."

16. Labaton, "Agency."

17. Labaton, "Agency."

18. Labaton, "Agency."

19. Greg Ip and Joellen Perry, "Central Banks Launch Effort to Free Credit," *Wall Street Journal*, December 14, 2007, available online; CNN.com, "Uncle Sam Taps Piggy Bank, Borrows to Aid Market: Uncle Sam's Financial Promises—More Than $600 Billion in All—Requires Tapping Reserves, Borrowing," CNN.com, September 17, 2008, available online; Harold Brubaker, "Taxpayers Have $800 Billion at Risk So Far," *Philadelphia Inquirer*, September 17, 2008, available online.

20. Benjamin J. Cohen, *In Whose Interest? International Banking and American Foreign Policy* (New Haven, CT: Yale University Press, 1986), 44–46.

21. Morris, *The Trillion*, 65.

22. David Goldstein and Kevin G. Hall show that this characterization is false. On this, see David Goldstein and Kevin G. Hall, "Private Sector

Loans, Not Fannie or Freddie, Triggered Crisis," *McClatchy News,* Washington Bureau, October 12, 2008.

23. Mort Zuckerman, "The Anatomy of the Financial Crisis and Why We Must Get It Right, " Huffingtonpost.com, October 22, 2008, available online.

24. Morris, *The Trillion,* Chapter 4, 59–85.

25. Morris, *The Trillion,* Chapter 5, 87–105, 121.

26. Morris, *The Trillion,* 93.

27. Apart from his columns in the *New York Times,* see Thomas L. Friedman, *The Lexus and the Olive Tree* (New York: Anchor Books, 2000).

28. Ip and Perry.

29. Morris, *The Trillion,* 120.

30. Rachel Beck, "Loan Crisis Even Blinded King of Mortgage Securities," *The Record* (online edition), available online.

31. Tami Luhby, "Bailout Talks in Disarray," CNNMoney.com, September 25, 2008; See also "A Common Sense Plan to Have Wall Street Fund the Recovery, Not Taxpayers" Economic Rescue Principles, available online.

32. Luhby.

33. Joseph Stiglitz, "We Aren't Done Yet: Comments on the Financial Crisis and Bailout," *The Economists' Voice,* 5, no. 5, Article 11 (2008). *Berkeley Electronic Press,* available online.

34. Scott Lanman and Craig Torres, "Bernanke Says Normal Markets Needed or Growth to Halt" (Update 3), Bloomberg.com, September 23, 2008, available online.

35. Ari J. Officer and Lawrence H. Officer, "Let Risk-Taking Financial Institutions Fail," Time.com, September 29, 2008, available online.

36. This was made possible by the Federal Reserve, which had grafted three additional tools onto its mandate to create money: the Term Securities Lending Facility (TSLF), the Primary Dealer Credit Facility (PDCF), and the Term Auction Facility (TAF). See David Frazier, "Government Bails Out Stock Market . . . For Now," MoneyNews.com, April 1, 2008, available online.

37. Alistair Barr, "Toxic Export: How America's Risky Subprime Mortgages Fouled the World's Markets," *Wall Street Journal,* Market Watch, November 15, 2007, available online; Heather Steward, "Markets' Week of Living Dangerously," *The Observer,* Business news and features, August 19, 2007, available online.

38. Newt Gingrich, "Suspend Market To Market Now!" Forbes.com, Commentary, September 29, 2008, available online.

39. Gingrich.

40. Shah Gilani, "Heads I Win, Tails You Lose: Why the Senate Bailout Will Fail Taxpayers," *Money Morning,* October 2, 2008 (updated October 7, 2008), available online.

41. Marie Leone, "Fair Value: Now a Little Easier To Swallow?" CFO.com, September 30, 2008, available online; Alan Rappeport, "Investment Pros Like Bailout, Fair Value," CFO.com, September 26, 2008, available online.

42. Ben S. Bernanke, "The Level and Distribution of Economic Well-Being." The Federal Reserve, Speech given before the Greater Omaha Chamber of Commerce. Omaha, Nebraska, February 6, 2007, available online.

43. Bernanke, "The Level."

44. Starr, *Freedom's,* 67, 68–69.

45. Duncan K. Foley, *Adam's Fallacy: A Guide to Economic Theology* (Cambridge, MA: Belknap Press, 2006), 39–40.

46. Foley, *Adam's,* 43.

47. Foley, *Adam's,* 43.

48. Foley, *Adam's,* 41.

BIBLIOGRAPHY

Every effort has been made to ensure that the URLs and Internet sources cited in this book are accurate and up to date. However, with the rapid changes that occur in the World Wide Web, it is inevitable that some pages or other resources will have been discontinued or moved, and some content modified or reorganized. The publisher recommends that readers who cannot find the sources or information they seek with the URLs in this book use one of the numerous search engines available on the Internet.

Acheson, Dean. *Present at the Creation: My Years in the State Department.* New York: Norton, 1987.

Almond, Gabriel A. "The Return of the State." In *A Discipline Divided: Schools and Sects in Political Science,* 189–219. Newbury Park, CA: SAGE Publications, 1990.

Anonymous (Michael Scheuer). *Imperial Hubris: Why the West Is Losing the War on Terror.* Dulles, VA: Brassey's, 2004.

Asmus, Ronald D. *Opening NATO's Door: How the Alliance Remade Itself for a New Era.* New York: Columbia University Press, 2002.

Atkinson, Robert D. *Supply Side Follies: Why Conservative Economics Fails, Liberal Economics Falters, and Innovation Economics Is the Answer.* New York: Rowman Littlefield, 2006.

Baer, Robert. *Sleeping With the Devil: How Washington Sold Our Soul for Saudi Crude.* New York: Crown Publishers, 2003.

Balaam, David N., and Michael Veseth. *Introduction to International Political Economy.* 4th ed. New York: Prentice Hall, 2004.

Bates, Robert H. *Prosperity and Violence: The Political Economy of Development.* New York: Norton, 2001.

Belloc, Hilaire. *Richelieu.* Norfolk, VA: Gates of Vienna Books, 2006.

Blackburn, Glenn. *Western Civilization: A Concise History—From Early Societies to the Present.* New York: St. Martin's Press, 1991.

Blazer, Dan G. *The Age of Melancholy: Major Depression and Its Social Origins.* Sussex, UK: Routledge, 2005.

Blizzard, William C. *When Miners March: The Story of Coal Miners in West Virginia.* Gay, WV: Appalachian Community Services, 2004.

Block, Fred, and Margaret R. Somers. "Beyond the Economistic Fallacy: The Holistic Social Science of Karl Polanyi." In *Vision and Method in Historical Sociology,* edited by Theda Skocpol. Cambridge, MA: Cambridge University Press, 1991.

Braudel, Fernand. *The Structures of Everyday Life.* Vol. I. *Civilization and Capitalism, 15th–18th Century.* New York: Harper & Row Publishers, 1979.

Bruce Bueno de Mesquita. "Game Theory, Political Economy, and the Evolving Study of War and Peace." *American Political Science Review* 100 (2006): 637–642.

Calleo, David P. *Rethinking Europe's Future.* Princeton, NJ: Princeton University Press, 2001.

Carville, James. *We're Right, They're Wrong: A Handbook for Spirited Progressives.* New York: Random House, 1996.

Cerny, Philip G. "Globalization and the Changing Logic of Collective Action." *Theory and Structure in International Political Economy: An International Organization Reader,* edited by Charles Lipson and Benjamin J. Cohen, 111–146. Cambridge, MA: MIT Press, 1999.

Chancellor, Edward. *Devil Take the Hindmost: A History of Financial Speculation.* New York: Plume, 2000.

Chandler, Alfred Jr. *The Visible Hand: The Managerial Revolution in American Business.* Cambridge, MA: Belknap Press, 1977.

Chang, Ha-Joon. *Bad Samaritans: The Myth of Free Trade and the Secret History of Capitalism.* New York: Bloombury Press, 2008.

Chasteen, John Charles. *Born in Blood and Fire: A Concise History of Latin America.* New York: Norton, 2001.

Clarke, Peter. *Hope and Glory: Britain, 1900–1990.* London, UK: Allen Lane, 1996.

Cohen, Benjamin J. *In Whose Interest? International Banking and American Foreign Policy.* New Haven, CT: Yale University Press, 1986.

————. "A Revolution in Atlantic Economic Relations: A Bargain Comes Unstuck." In *Crossing Frontiers: Explorations in International Political Economy*, 94–124. Boulder, CO: Westview Press, 1991.

Craig, Albert M., William A. Graham, Donald Kagan, Steven Ozment, and Frank M. Turner. *The Heritage of World Civilizations*. 3rd ed. New York: Macmillan, 1994.

Crane, Edward H. *Cato Handbook Policy*. 6th ed. Washington, DC: Cato Institute, 2005.

Daniels, Christine. "Liberty to Complaine: Servant Petitions in Maryland, 1652–1797." In *The Many Legalities of Early America*, edited by Christopher L. Tomlins and Bruce H. Mann. Chapel Hill: University of North Carolina Press, 2001.

Davies, Glyn. *History of Money: From Ancient Times to the Present Day*. Cardiff, UK: University of Wales Press, 2001.

De Long, J. Bradford. Review of *John Maynard Keynes: Fighting for Britain*, by Robert Skidelsky. Discussion blog. Available online.

De Soto, Hernando. *The Mystery of Capital: Why Capitalism Triumphs in the West and Fails Everywhere Else*. New York: Basic Books, 2000.

Diamond, Jared. *Guns, Germs, and Steel: The Fates of Human Societies*. New York: Norton, 1999.

Douthat, Ross. "Does Meritocracy Work? Not If Society and Colleges Keep Failing to Distinguish Between Wealth and Merit." *Atlantic Monthly*, November 2005.

Drucker, Peter F. "The Changed World Economy." *Foreign Affairs* 4 (1986): 768–791.

Dye, Thomas R. *Top Down Policymaking*. New York: Chatham House, 2001.

Eckes, Alfred E. "Trading American Interests." *Foreign Affairs* 4 (1992): 135–154.

The Economist. "Ponzificating: Is the Financial System a Confidence Trick?" March 20, 2007. Available on the CFO.com Web site.

Ellis, Diane. "The Effect of Consumer Interest Rate Deregulation on Credit Card Volumes, Charge-Offs, and the Personal Bankruptcy Rate." *Bank Trends*, no. 98-05 (March 1998), available online.

Fallows, James. "How the World Works." *Atlantic Monthly*, December 1993, 61–87.

Finer, Samuel E. "State- and Nation-Building in Europe: The Role of the Military." In *The Formation of National States in Western Europe*, edited by Charles Tilly. Princeton, NJ: Princeton University Press, 1975.

Foley, Duncan K. *Adam's Fallacy: A Guide to Economic Theology*. Cambridge, MA: Belknap Press, 2006.

Frank, Ellen. "The Great Stock Illusion: The Enormous Paper Wealth 'Created' by the Stock Market Was Bound to Dissolve, Because It Never Existed, Save as a Kind of Mass Delusion." *Dollars & Sense*, November/December 2002, available online.

Frieden, Jeff. "Sectoral Conflict and U.S. Foreign Economic Policy, 1914–1940." In *American Foreign Policy: Theoretical Essays*, 4th ed., edited by G. John Ikenberry, 138–167. New York: Longman, 2002.

Friedman, Milton, and Rose Friedman. *Free to Choose: A Personal Statement*. New York: Harcourt, Brace, Jovanovich, 1990.

Friedman, Thomas L. 2003. "The Long Bomb." *New York Times*, March 2, 2003, available online.

Galbraith, John Kenneth. *A Short History of Financial Euphoria*. New York: Viking, 1993.

Garfinkle, Norton. *The American Dream vs. The Gospel of Wealth: The Fight for a Productive Middle Class*. New Haven, CT: Yale University Press, 2006.

Gat, Azar. "The Return of Authoritarian Great Powers." *Foreign Affairs* 4 (July/August 2007): 59–69.

Gates, William H. Sr., and Chuck Collins. *Wealth and Our Commonwealth: Why America Should Tax Accumulated Fortunes*. Boston: Beacon Press, 2002.

Gibbons, Edward. *History of the Decline and Fall of the Roman Empire*. Vol. I, *The Turn of the Tide*. London, UK: Folio Society, 1983 (1776).

Gilpin, Robert. *War and Change in World Politics*. New York: Cambridge University Press, 1981.

———. *The Political Economy of International Relations*. Princeton, NJ: Princeton University Press, 1987.

———. *Global Political Economy: Understanding the International Economic Order*. Princeton, NJ: Princeton University Press, 2001.

Gregory, Paul R., and Robert C. Stuart. *Soviet Economic Structure and Performance*. 2nd ed. New York: Harper & Row, 1981.

Hayek, Friedrich A. *The Road to Serfdom,* with an Introduction by Milton Friedman. Chicago: University of Chicago Press, 1994.

Helibroner, Robert L. *The Worldly Philosophers: The Lives, Times and Ideas of the Great Economic Thinkers.* New York: Simon & Schuster, 1986.

Herson, Lawrence. *Politics of Ideas: Political Theory and American Public Policy.* Chicago: Dorsey Press, 1984.

Hirschman, Albert O. *The Passions and the Interests: Political Arguments for Capitalism before Its Triumph.* Princeton, NJ: Princeton University Press, 1977.

Hodgson, Godfrey. *The World Turned Right Side Up: A History of the Conservative Ascendancy in America.* New York: Houghton Mifflin, 1996.

Holmes, Stephen, and Cass R. Sunstein. *The Cost of Rights: Why Liberty Depends on Taxes.* New York: Norton, 1999.

Hudson, William E. *American Democracy in Peril: Seven Challenges to America's Future.* New York: Chatham House Publishers, 2001.

Ikenberry, John G. *After Victory: Institutions, Strategic Restraint, and the Rebuilding of Order After Major Wars.* Princeton, NJ: Princeton University Press, 2001.

———. "America's Liberal Grand Strategy: Democracy and National Security in the Post-War Era." In *American Foreign Policy: Theoretical Essays,* 4th ed., edited by G. John Ikenberry. New York: Longman, 2002.

Janszen, Eric. "The Next Bubble: Priming the Markets for Tomorrow's Big Crash." *Harper's Magazine,* February 2008, available online.

Jay, Antony. *The Oxford Dictionary of Political Quotations.* New York: Oxford University Press, 2001.

Jenkins, Roy. "The Postwar Bequest." Marshall Plan Commemorative Section: Special Relationships, *Foreign Affairs* 3 (May/June 1997), available online.

Johnson, Chalmers. *Nemesis: The Last Days of the American Republic.* New York: Metropolitan Books, 2006.

———. *The Sorrows of Empire: Militarism, Secrecy, and the End of the Republic.* New York: Metropolitan Books, 2004.

———. *Blowback: The Costs and Consequences of American Empire.* New York: Owl Books, 2000.

Kahaner, Larry. *AK-47: The Weapon That Changed the World*. New York: Wiley & Sons, 2006.

Kaplan, Fred. *The Wizards of Armageddon*. New York: Simon & Schuster, 1983.

Kapstein, Ethan. *Sharing the Wealth: Workers and the World Economy*. New York: Norton, 1999.

————. 1996. "Workers and the World Economy." *Foreign Affairs* 3 (May/June 1996): 16–37.

Keegan, John. *A History of Warfare*. New York: Alfred A. Knopf, 1993.

Keohane, Robert O. *After Hegemony*. Princeton, NJ: Princeton University Press, 1990.

Keohane, Robert O., and Joseph Nye Jr., *Transnational Relations and World Politics*. Cambridge, MA: Harvard University Press, 1972.

Keynes, John Maynard. *A Tract on Monetary Reform*. London: Macmillan, 1924.

Kindleberger, Charles P. "The Rise of Free Trade in Western Europe." In *International Political Economy: Perspectives on Global Power and Wealth*, edited by Jeffrey A. Frieden and David A. Lake. New York: St. Martin's Press, 1995.

Kishlansky, Mark A., Patrick Geary, and Patricia O'Brien. *Civilization in the West*. Vol. II, *Since 1555*. 4th ed. New York: Addison-Wesley-Longman, 2001.

Kishlansky, Mark A., ed. *Sources of the West: Readings in Western Civilization*. Vol. I, *From the Beginning to 1715*. 4th ed. New York: Longman Publishers, 2001.

Kissinger, Henry A. *Diplomacy*. New York: Simon & Schuster, 1994.

Korten, David C. *When Corporations Rule the World*. West Hartford, CT: Kumarian Press, 1996.

Krugman, Paul. *The Return of Depression Economics*. New York: Norton, 2000.

Kurtzman, Joel. *The Death of Money: How the Electronic Economy Has Destabilized the World's Markets and Created Financial Chaos*. New York: Back Bay, 1993.

La Feber, Walter. *The American Age: U.S. Foreign Policy at Home and Abroad, 1750 to the Present*. New York: Norton, 1994.

Leffler, Melvyn P. "The American Conception of National Security and the Beginnings of the Cold War, 1945–1948." In *American Foreign*

Policy: Theoretical Essays, 4th ed., edited by G. John Ikenberry. New York: Longman, 2002.

Levitt, Arthur (with Paula Dwyer). *Take on the Street: What Wall Street and Corporate American Don't Want You to Know*. New York: Pantheon Books, 2002.

Lewis, Michael. *Liar's Poker*. New York: Penguin Books, 1990.

Lind, Michael. "Are We Still a Middle-Class Nation?" *Atlantic Monthly*, January/February 2004.

Lowenstein, Roger. *When Genius Failed: The Rise and Fall of Long-Term Capital Management*. New York: Random House, 2000.

Maclean, Nancy. *Freedom Is Not Enough: The Opening of the American Workplace*. New York: Russell Sage Foundation Books, 2006.

Macmillan, Harold. *Riding the Storm, 1956–1959*. New York: Harper & Row, 1971.

Mansfield, Edward D., and Jack Snyder. "Democratization and War." *Foreign Affairs* 3 (May/June 1995): 79–97.

Martinez, Mark A. Review of *Wealth and Our Commonwealth: Why America Should Tax Accumulated Fortunes*, by William H. Gates and Chuck Collins. *Kern Economic Journal*, 1 (First Quarter 2007): 19–20.

McGinn, Robert E. *Science, Technology, and Society*. Englewood Cliffs, NJ: Prentice-Hall, 1991.

Mearsheimer, John J. *The Tragedy of Great Power Politics*. New York: Norton, 2001.

Millman, Gregory J. *The Vandals' Crown: How Rebel Currency Traders Overthrew the World's Central Banks*. New York: Free Press, 1995.

Montesquieu, Baron de. *The Spirit of the Laws*. Vol. 1. New York: Hafner Press, 1975.

Montross, Lynn. *War Through the Ages*. 3rd ed. New York: Harper & Row, Publishers, 1960.

Morris, Charles R. *The Trillion Dollar Meltdown: Easy Money, High Rollers, and the Great Credit Crash*. New York: Public Affairs, 2008.

Nagle, John D. *Introduction to Comparative Politics: Challenges of Conflict and Change in a New Era*. 4th ed. Chicago: Nelson-Hall Publishers, 1996.

Naylor, R.T. *Hot Money and the Politics of Debt*. New York: Black Rose Books, 1994.

North, Douglass C. *Structure and Change in Economic History*. New York: Norton, 1981.

Nye, Jr., Joseph. *Soft Power: The Means to Success in World Politics*. New York: Public Affairs, 2004.

———. *Understanding International Conflicts: An Introduction to Theory and History*. 3rd ed. New York: Longman, 2000.

Phillips, Kevin. *American Dynasty: Aristocracy, Fortune and the Politics of Deceit in the House of Bush*. New York: Viking, 2004.

———. *Wealth and Democracy: A Political History of the American Rich*. New York: Random House, 2002.

Primo, David M., and William Scott Green. "Bankruptcy Law, Entrepreneurship, and Economic Performance." Working paper, University of Rochester and University of Miami, September, 2008.

Putnam, Robert. *Bowling Alone: The Collapse and Revival of American Community*. New York: Simon & Schuster, 2001.

Rand, Ayn. *Atlas Shrugged*. New York: Plume, 1999.

Ray, James Lee. *Global Politics*. 6th ed. Boston: Houghton Mifflin, 1995.

Rayack, Elton. *Not So Free to Choose: The Political Economy of Milton Friedman and Ronald Reagan*. New York: Praeger, 1987.

Reich, Robert B. *Supercapitalism: The Transformation of Business, Democracy, and Everyday Life*. New York: Knopf, 2007.

———. "John Maynard Keynes: His Radical Idea That Governments Should Spend Money They Don't Have May Have Saved Capitalism." *Time*, March 29, 1999.

Reid, T.R. *The United States of Europe: The New Superpower and the End of American Supremacy*. New York: Penguin Press, 2004.

Rock, David. *Argentina, 1516–1982*. Berkeley: University of California Press, 1985.

Rostker, Bernard. *I Want You! The Evolution of the All-Volunteer Force*. Santa Monica, CA: RAND Corporation, 2006.

Ruggie, John G. "International Regimes, Transactions, and Change: Embedded Liberalism in the Postwar Economic Order." In *Theory and Structure in International Political Economy: An International Organization Reader*, edited by Benjamin J. Cohen and Charles Lipson, 245–282. Cambridge, MA: MIT Press, 1999.

Ruttan, Vernon W. *Is War Necessary for Economic Growth? Military Procurement and Technology Development*. New York: Oxford University Press, 2006.

Salvatore, Dominick. *International Economics.* 5th ed. Englewood Cliffs, NJ: Prentice Hall, 1995.

Schattschneider, E.E. *The Semisovereign People: A Realist's View of Democracy in America,* with an Introduction by David Adamany. Hinsdale, Ill.: Dryden Press, 1975.

Schlesinger, Arthur M. Jr. *The Age of Jackson.* Old Saybrook, CT: Konecky & Konecky, 1971.

Schmidt, Helmut. "From American Plan to European Union." Marshall Plan Commemorative Section: Special Relationships, *Foreign Affairs* 3 (May/June 1997).

Schoenbaum, Thomas J. *Waging Peace and War: Dean Rusk in the Truman, Kennedy and Johnson Years.* New York: Simon & Schuster, 1988.

Schwartz, Herman M. *States Versus Market: The Emergence of a Global Economy.* New York: St. Martin's Press, 2000.

Sherman, Dennis, and Joyce Salisbury. *The West in the World.* Vol. I, *To 1715.* New York: McGraw-Hill, 2001.

Sirota, David. *Hostile Takeover: How Big Money and Corruption Conquered Our Government—and How We Take It Back.* New York: Crown Publishers, 2006.

Smith, Adam. *An Inquiry into the Nature and Causes of the Wealth of Nations.* The Harvard Classics, vol. 10, edited by Charles Bullock. New York: PF Collier & Son Company, 1909 (1776).

————. *The Wealth of Nations: Complete and Unabridged,* with an Introduction by Robert Reich. New York: The Modern Library, 2000 (1776).

Smith, Anthony D. *National Identity.* Reno: University of Nevada Press, 1991.

Smith, Tony. "National Security Liberalism and American Foreign Policy." In *American Foreign Policy: Theoretical Essays,* 4th ed., edited by G. John Ikenberry. New York: Longman, 2002.

Sobel, Robert. *The Pursuit of Wealth: The Incredible Story of Money Throughout the Ages of Wealth.* New York: McGraw-Hill, 2000.

Soros, George. *The New Paradigm for Financial Markets: The Credit Crisis of 2008 and What It Means.* New York: Public Affairs, 2008.

————. *Open Society: Reforming Global Capitalism.* New York: Public Affairs, 2000.

————. *The Crisis of Global Capitalism: Open Society Endangered.* New York: Public Affairs, 1998.

Sowell, Thomas. *Basic Economics: A Common Sense Guide to the Economy.* 4th ed. New York: Basic Books, 2007.

Starr, Paul. *Freedom's Power: The True Force of Liberalism.* New York: Basic Books, 2007.

Stegemann, Klaus. "Policy Rivalry Among Industrial States: What Can We Learn from Models of Strategic Trade Policy?" In *Issues and Agents in International Political Economy: An International Organization Reader,* edited by Charles Lipson and Benjamin J. Cohen, 35–62. Cambridge, MA: MIT Press, 1999.

Stein, Arthur A. "The Hegemon's Dilemma: Great Britain, the United States, and the International Economic Order." In *Theory and Structure in International Political Economy: An International Organization Reader,* edited by Charles Lipson and Benjamin J. Cohen, 283–314. Cambridge, MA: MIT Press, 1999.

Stiglitz, Joseph E. *Globalization and Its Discontents.* New York: Norton, 2002.

Strange, Susan. *States and Markets.* 2nd ed. London: Pinter Publishers, 1994.

Suskind, Ronald. *The Price of Loyalty: George W. Bush, The White House, and the Education of Paul O'Neill.* New York: Simon & Schuster, 2004.

Tilly, Charles. *Coercion, Capital and European States, AD 990–1990.* Cambridge: Basil Blackwell, 1990.

Toffler, Alvin. *Previews and Premises. A Penetrating Conversation About Jobs, Identity, Sex Roles, the New Politics of the Information Age and the Hidden Forces Driving the Economy.* Boston: South End Press, 1983.

Tomlins, Christopher L., and Bruce H. Mann, eds. *The Many Legalities of Early America.* Chapel Hill: University of North Carolina Press, 2001.

Tzu, Sun. *The Art of War.* Edited by James Clavell. New York: Delta, 1983.

Walker Laird, Pamela. *Pull: Networking and Success since Benjamin Franklin.* Boston: Harvard University Press, 2006.

Walker, Lester C. "German War Secrets by the Thousands." *Harper's Magazine,* October 1946.

Walton, Gary M., and Ross M. Robertson. *History of the American Economy.* 5th ed. New York: Harcourt-Brace- Jovanovich, 1983.

Weatherford, Jack. *Genghis Kahn and the Making of the Modern World.* New York: Three Rivers Press, 2004.

Weaver, Frederick S. *Economic Literacy: Basic Economics With an Attitude.* 2nd ed. New York: Rowman & Littlefield, 2007.

Webb, Michael C. "International Economic Structures, Government Interests, and International Coordination of Macroeconomic Adjustment Policies." In *Issues and Agents in International Political Economy: An International Organization Reader,* edited by Charles Lipson and Benjamin J. Cohen, 217–240. Cambridge, MA: MIT Press, 1999.

Wechsberg, Joseph. *The Merchant Bankers.* Boston: Little, Brown and Company, 1966.

Wendt, Alexander. "Anarchy Is What States Make of It: The Social Construction of Power Politics." In *Theory and Structure in International Political Economy: An International Organization Reader,* edited by Charles Lipson and Benjamin J. Cohen, 75–110. Cambridge, MA: MIT Press, 1999.

Wheatcroft, Andrew. *The Habsburgs: The Embodying Empire.* London, UK: Folio Society, 2004.

Wolin, Sheldon S. *Politics and Vision: Continuity and Innovation in Western Political Thought.* Boston: Little, Brown and Company, 1960.

Wood, David M., and Birol A.Yesilada. *The Emerging European Union.* 2nd ed. New York: Longman, 2002.

Woolrych, Austin. *Commonwealth to Protectorate.* New York: Oxford University Press, 1982.

Yergin, Daniel. *The Prize: The Epic Quest for Oil, Money and Power.* New York. Free Press, 1992.

Zagorin, Perez. *Rebels and Rulers, 1500–1660: Society, States, and Early Modern Revolution.* Vol. I. New York: Cambridge University Press, 1982.

Zakaria, Fareed. *From Wealth to Power: The Unusual Origins of America's World Role.* Princeton, NJ: Princeton University Press, 1998.

Ziegler, Jean. *The Swiss, the Gold, and the Dead: How Swiss Bankers Helped Finance the Nazi War Machine.* New York: Penguin, 1997.

INDEX

About the Author

Mark A. Martinez is Department Chair and Professor of Political Science at California State University, Bakersfield. He earned his B.A. in political science from California State University, Chico and his Ph.D. from the University of California, Santa Barbara. Dr. Martinez has taught and lived in Mexico, is a current Research Associate at the *Universidad Autonoma de Queretaro*, and has published articles and book chapters on political and economic development. Dr. Martinez hosts and produces his own radio program in Bakersfield, *The Mark Martinez Show: Talk Radio for Liberals and Real Conservatives*. He is also blessed with two wonderful children, Monica and Sebastian.

Also From Kumarian Press . . .

International Economics:

The World Bank and the Gods of Lending
Steve Berkman

Capitalism and Justice: Envisioning Social and Economic Fairness
John Isbister

Running Out of Control: Dilemmas of Globalization
R. Alan Hedley

New and Forthcoming:

How the Aid Industry Works: An Introduction to Development Studies
Arjan de Haan

Freedom from Want: The Remarkable Success Story of BRAC, the Global
Grassroots Organization that's Winning the Fight Against Poverty
Ian Smillie

Strategic Moral Diplomacy: Understanding the Enemy's Moral Universe
Lyn Boyd-Judson

Visit Kumarian Press at **www.kpbooks.com** or
call **toll-free 800.232.0223** for a complete catalog.